THE OFFICIAL ARSENAL FACTFILE

Compiled by Kevin Connolly

THE OFFICIAL ARSENAL FACTFILE

Compiled by Kevin Connolly

hamlyn

CONTENTS

ARSENAL CONTACT DETAILS

Arsenal Stadium
Avenell Road,
Highbury,
London N5 1BU

Telephone (Club)
020 7704 4000

Box Office
020 7704 4040

Recorded Ticket information
020 7704 4242

Commercial Department
020 7704 4100

Web Site
http://www.arsenal.com

Information
email: Info@arsenal.co.uk

Chairman
Peter Hill-Wood

Vice Chairman
David Dein

Directors
Sir Roger Gibbs, Richard Carr,
Daniel Fiszman, Ken Friar OBE

Managing Director
Keith Edelman

Secretary
David Miles

Manager
Arsène Wenger

Assistant Manager
Pat Rice

First Team Coach
Boro Primorac

Head of Youth Coaching
Don Howe

Head of Youth Development
Liam Brady

Physiotherapist
Gary Lewin MCSP, SRP

ARSENAL HONOURS

Champions:
1931, 1933, 1934, 1935, 1938, 1948, 1953, 1971, 1989, 1991, 1998, 2002

F.A. Cup winners:
1930

Arsenal 2	Huddersfield T 0
James 17	
Lambert 83	

1936

| Arsenal 1 | Sheffield U 0 |
| Drake 74 | |

1950

| Arsenal 2 | Liverpool 0 |
| Lewis 17, 63 | |

1971 (a.e.t.)

Arsenal 2	Liverpool 1
Kelly 101	Heighway 92
George 111	

1979

Arsenal 3	Manchester U 2
Talbot 13	McQueen 87
Stapleton 44	McIlroy 89
Sunderland 89	

1993 (a.e.t.)

Arsenal 2	Sheffield Wed 1
Wright 33	Waddle 66
Linighan 119	

(replay after Arsenal 1 (Wright 23) Sheffield Wednesday 1 (Hirst 68)

1998

Arsenal 2	Newcastle U 0
Overmars 23	
Anelka 69	

2002

Arsenal 2	Chelsea 0
Parlour 70	
Ljungberg 80	

League Cup winners:
1987

| Arsenal 2 | Liverpool 1 |
| C. Nicholas 44, 83 | Rush 23 |

1993

Arsenal 2	Sheffield Wed 1
Merson 20	Harkes 8
Morrow 68	

Fairs Cup winners:
1970

1st leg

Anderlecht 3	Arsenal 1
Devrindt 25	Kennedy 82
Muller 30, 76	

2nd leg

Arsenal 3	Anderlecht 0
Kelley 26	
Radford 71	
Sammels 73	

European Cup Winners' Cup winners:
1994

| Arsenal 1 | Parma 0 |
| Smith 19 | |

History:
Formed: 1886
Turned Professional: 1891
Grounds: 1886, Plumstead Common; 1887, Sportsman Ground; 1888, Manor Ground; 1890 Invicta Ground; 1893, Manor Ground; 1913, Highbury

CLUB RECORDS:
Biggest league win: 12-0 v Loughborough T, Division 2, March 12, 1900
Biggest league defeat: 8-0 v Loughborough T, Division 2, December 12, 1896

Record points total (2 pts for a win): 66 from 42 matches, Division 1, 1931

Record points total (3 pts for a win): 87 from 38 matches, Premiership, 2002

Most goals scored: 127 in 42 matches, Division 1, 1931

Least goals conceded: 17 in 38 matches, Premiership, 1999

Most appearances (League, FA Cup, League Cup, Europe and Charity Shield): 722 by David O'Leary, 1975-93

Most goals: 185 by Ian Wright, 1991-8

Most League goals: 150 by Cliff Bastin, 1929-39

Most League goals in a season: 42 by Ted Drake, 1935

Most League goals in a match: 7 by Ted Drake, v Aston Villa (away) on December 14, 1935

Most European goals: 19 by Thierry Henry, 1999-

Most international appearances: 77 by Kenny Sansom for England (from a total of 86 from 1979-88), 1980-8

Record attendance (at Highbury): 73,295 v Sunderland, League, March 9, 1935

Record attendance (at Wembley): 73,455 v Panathinaikos, Champions League, September 30, 1998

(League, FA Cup, League Cup, Europe and Charity Shield)

TOP SCORERS

Ian Wright	185
Cliff Bastin	178
John Radford	149
Jimmy Brain	139
Ted Drake	139
Doug Lishman	137
Joe Hulme	125
David Jack	124
Reg Lewis	116
Alan Smith	115
Jack Lambert	109
Frank Stapleton	108
David Herd	107
Joe Baker	100

ARSENAL MANAGERS

WOOLWICH ARSENAL

1897-8:   **Thomas Brown Mitchell**
Previous club: Blackburn Rovers
Left in March 1898

League record (Division Two):

Season	Pld	W	D	L	F	A	Pts	Position
1897-8	30	16	5	9	69	49	37	5th

1898-9   **George Elcoat**
From: Stockton-on-Tees
Left in May 1899

League record (Division Two)

Season	Pld	W	D	L	F	A	Pts	Position
1898-9	34	18	5	11	72	41	41	7th

1899-1904:   **Harry Bradshaw**
Previous club: Burnley
Achievements: Promotion to the First Division in 1904
Left in the summer of 1904 to become Fulham manager

League record (Division Two):

Season	Pld	W	D	L	F	A	Pts	Position
1899-1900	34	16	4	14	61	43	36	8th
1900-1	34	15	6	13	39	35	36	7th
1901-2	34	18	6	10	50	26	42	4th
1902-3	34	20	8	6	66	30	48	3rd
1903-4	34	21	7	6	91	22	49	2nd
Total	170	90	31	49	307	156	211	

1904-8:   **Phil Kelso**
Previous club: Hibernian
Achievements: Took Woolwich Arsenal to their first FA Cup semi-final in 1906
and another semi-final appearance the following year. Woolwich Arsenal's
seventh place in 1907 was their best in the Football League to date
Left in February 1908 to run a hotel in Largs, Scotland

League record (Division One):

Season	Pld	W	D	L	F	A	Pts	Position
1904-5	34	12	9	13	36	40	33	10th
1905-6	38	15	7	16	62	64	37	12th
1906-7	38	20	4	14	66	59	44	7th
1908-9	38	12	12	14	51	63	36	14th
Total	148	59	32	57	215	226	150	

1908-15:   **George Morrell**
Previous clubs: Glasgow Rangers, Greenock Morton
In charge when Woolwich Arsenal were relegated in 1912-13 with the worst
record in the club's history. Also in charge for Arsenal's first season at
Highbury in 1913-14
Resigned in 1915 when the club shut down because of the First World War

League record (Division One):

Season	Pld	W	D	L	F	A	Pts	Position
1908-9	38	14	10	14	52	49	38	6th
1909-10	38	11	9	18	37	67	31	18th
1910-1	38	13	12	13	41	49	38	10th
1911-2	38	15	8	15	55	59	38	10th
1912-3	38	3	12	23	26	74	18	20th (relegated)

League record (Division Two):

Season	Pld	W	D	L	F	A	Pts	Position
1913-4	38	20	9	9	54	38	49	3rd
1914-5	38	19	5	14	69	41	43	5th
Total	266	95	65	106	334	377	255	

ARSENAL

1919-25: Leslie Knighton

Previous clubs: Huddersfield Town, Manchester City

Joined Arsenal in May 1919 and was manager when Arsenal were elected to the enlarged First Division in 1919

Left in June 1925. Later managed Bournemouth, Birmingham and Chelsea

League record (Division One):

Season	Pld	W	D	L	F	A	Pts	Position
1919-20	42	15	12	15	56	58	42	10th
1920-1	42	15	14	13	59	63	44	9th
1921-2	42	15	7	20	47	56	37	17th
1922-3	42	16	10	16	61	62	42	11th
1923-4	42	12	9	21	40	63	33	19th
1924-5	42	14	5	23	46	58	33	20th
Total	252	87	57	108	309	360	231	

1925-34: Herbert Chapman

Joined Arsenal in 1925 after building Huddersfield Town's triple championship team, having previously managed Northampton Town and Leeds City.

Visionary manager who made Arsenal into the world's most famous club. Introduced latest medical facilities for players, had Gillespie Road tube station re-named Arsenal. Advocated floodlights and numbering of players long before they became fashionable.

Achievements:

League champions 1931, 1933

FA Cup winners 1930

League runners-up: 1926, 1932

FA Cup runners-up: 1927, 1932

Died on January 6, 1934 with Arsenal on the way to the second of their three successive Championships. Memorial bust stands in Highbury entrance hall

League record (Division One):

Season	Pld	W	D	L	F	A	Pts	Position
1925-6	42	22	8	12	87	63	52	2nd
1926-7	42	17	9	16	77	86	43	11th
1927-8	42	13	15	14	82	86	41	10th
1928-9	42	16	13	13	77	72	45	9th
1929-30	42	14	11	17	78	66	39	14th
1930-1	42	28	10	4	127	59	66	Champions
1931-2	42	22	10	10	90	48	54	2nd
1932-3	42	25	8	.9	118	61	58	Champions
1933-4	42	25	9	8	75	47	59	Champions

(Arsenal's record when Chapman died: Pld 23, W14, D6, L3, F41, A20, Pts 34)

Total	359	171	90	98	777	561	432	

1934-47: George Allison

Arsenal director – joined board in 1926 – who took charge after Chapman's death. Ably assisted by Joe Shaw and Tom Whittaker (see below). Kept Arsenal going during the Second World War then retired in May 1947.

Achievements:

League champions 1934, 1935, 1938

FA Cup winners: 1936

Died in 1957, aged 73

League record (Division One):
(Arsenal's record in 1933-4 after Chapman died: Pld 19, W 11, D 3, L 5, F 34, A 27, Pts 25)

Season	Pld	W	D	L	F	A	Pts	Position
1934-5	42	23	12	7	115	46	58	Champions
1935-6	42	15	15	12	78	48	45	6th
1936-7	42	18	16	8	80	49	52	3rd
1937-8	42	21	10	11	77	44	52	Champions
1938-9	42	19	9	14	55	41	47	5th
1946-7	42	16	9	17	72	70	41	13th
Total	271	123	74	74	511	325	320	

1947-56: **Tom Whittaker**
Former Arsenal player and trainer. Appointed assistant to Allison in 1946 and manager on his departure.
Achievements:
League champions: 1948, 1953
FA Cup winners: 1950
FA Cup runners-up 1952
Died in October 1956 from a heart attack

League record (Division One):

Season	Pld	W	D	L	F	A	Pts	Position
1947-8	42	23	13	6	81	32	59	Champions
1948-9	42	18	13	11	74	44	49	5th
1949-50	42	19	11	12	79	55	49	6th
1950-1	42	19	9	14	73	56	47	5th
1951-2	42	21	11	10	80	61	53	3rd
1952-3	42	21	12	9	97	64	54	Champions
1953-4	42	15	13	14	75	73	43	12th
1954-5	42	17	9	16	69	63	43	9th
1955-6	42	18	10	14	60	61	46	5th
1956-7	14	7	1	6	31	25	15	
Total	392	178	102	112	719	534	458	

1956-8: **Jack Crayston**
Former Arsenal great who was appointed to the coaching staff in 1946. Became Whittaker's assistant and was promoted to manager in October 1956. Left in May 1958 after disagreement with the board over money for new players. Later managed Doncaster Rovers.

League record (Division One):
(Arsenal's record when Whittaker died: Pld 14, W7, D1, L6, F31, A25, Pts 15)

Season	Pld	W	D	L	F	A	Pts	Position
1956-7	28	14	7	7	54	44	50	5th
1957-8	42	16	7	19	73	85	39	12th
Total	70	30	14	26	127	129	89	

1958-62: **George Swindin**
Former Arsenal goalkeeper. Took over from Crayston after successful spell in charge of (then) non-league Peterborough
Left in May 1962. He later managed Norwich City before retiring to the Canary Islands.

League record (Division One):

Season	Pld	W	D	L	F	A	Pts	Position
1958-9	42	21	8	13	88	68	50	3rd
1959-60	42	15	9	18	68	80	39	13th
1960-1	42	15	11	16	77	85	41	11th
1961-2	42	16	11	15	71	72	43	10th
Total	168	67	39	62	304	305	173	

1962-66: **Billy Wright**

Appointed to succeed Swindin after a glittering playing career with Wolverhampton Wanderers and England, although he had no managerial experience and no previous links with Arsenal

Achievements: In charge when Arsenal won the FA Youth Cup for the first time in 1966

Left in June 1966. Later became head of ATV sport. He died in September 1944.

League record (Division One):

Season	Pld	W	D	L	F	A	Pts	Position
1962-3	42	18	10	14	86	77	46	7th
1963-4	42	17	11	14	90	82	45	8th
1964-5	42	17	7	18	69	75	41	13th
1965-6	42	12	13	17	62	75	37	14th
Total	168	64	41	63	307	309	169	

1966-76: **Bertie Mee**

Arsenal physiotherapist, appointed to succeed Wright in the summer of 1966. Had a proviso in his contract that he could return to being physiotherapist if he was unsuccessful.

Achievements:

Football League Cup runners-up 1968

Football League Cup runners-up 1969

Fairs Cup winners 1970

League champions and FA Cup winners – The 'Double' 1971

FA Youth Cup winners 1971

Manager of the Year 1971

Paid British record transfer fee for England midfielder Alan Ball from Everton in 1971.

FA Cup runners-up 1972

League runners-up 1973

Left in May 1976. Later became general manager and then a director at Watford. Died in October 2001, aged 82.

League record (Division One):

Season	Pld	W	D	L	F	A	Pts	Position
1966-7	42	16	14	12	58	47	46	7th
1967-8	42	17	10	15	60	56	44	9th
1968-9	42	22	12	8	56	27	56	4th
1969-70	42	12	18	12	51	49	42	12th
1970-1	42	29	7	.6	71	29	65	Champions
1971-2	42	22	8	12	58	40	52	5th
1972-3	42	23	11	.8	57	43	57	2nd
1973-4	42	14	14	14	49	51	42	10th
1974-5	42	13	11	18	47	49	37	16th
1975-6	42	13	10	19	47	53	36	17th
Total	420	181	115	124	554	444	477	

1976-83: **Terry Neill**

Ex-Arsenal player, who began in management with Hull City and Tottenham. Hotspur.

Appointed in July 1976.

Made immediate impression by signing striker Malcolm Macdonald from Newcastle – a record fee for Arsenal

Achievements:

FA Cup winners 1979

FA Cup runners-up 1978, 1980

European Cup Winners' Cup runners-up 1980

Left in December 1983. Became media pundit and restaurant owner.

League record (Division One):

Season	Pld	W	D	L	F	A	Pts	Position
1976-7	42	16	11	15	64	59	43	8th
1977-8	42	21	10	11	60	37	52	5th
1978-9	42	17	14	11	61	48	48	7th
1979-80	42	18	16	.8	52	36	52	4th
1980-1	42	19	15	.8	61	45	53	3rd
1981-2	42	20	11	11	48	37	71	5th. (3pts awarded for win)
1982-3	42	16	10	16	58	56	58	10th
1983-4	17	7	.0	10	27	25	21	-
Total	311	134	87	90	431	343	398	

1983-6: Don Howe

Ex-Arsenal player, coach to the Fairs Cup and 'Double' winners. Left to manage West Bromwich Albion.

Coached in Turkey, then at Leeds United before returning in in 1977 as assistant to Neill. Initially appointed as caretaker after Neill's departure. Confirmed as manager in April 1984.

Left in March 1986. Later coached Wimbledon and managed Queens Park Rangers. Now backat Highbury as head youth coach.

League record (Division One):

Season	Pld	W	D	L	F	A	Pts	Position
(Arsenal's record when Neill left: Pld 17, W7, D0, L10, F27, A25, Pts 21)								
1983-4	25	11	9	5	47	35	42	6th
1984-5	42	19	9	14	61	49	66	7th
1985-6	31	17	7	7	42	32	58	7th
Total	98	47	25	26	150	116	166	

(Arsenal's record when Howe left: P31, W17, D7, L7, F42, A32, Pts 58. Steve Burtenshaw was caretaker until the end of the season with a record of P11, W3, D2, L6, F7, A15, Pts 15.)

1986-95: George Graham

Ex-Arsenal player and Millwall manager, appointed Arsenal boss in 1986.
Achievements:
League champions 1989, 1991
European Cup Winners' Cup winners 1994
FA Cup winners 1993
League Cup winners 1987, 1993
League Cup runners-up 1988
Manager of the Year 1989, 1991

Left in February 1995. Later managed Leeds United and Tottenham Hotspur.

League record (Division One/Premiership):

Season	Pld	W	D	L	F	A	Pts	Position
1986-7	42	20	10	12	58	35	70	4th
1987-8	40	18	12	10	58	39	66	6th
1988-9	38	22	10	6	73	36	76	Champions
1989-90	38	18	8	12	54	38	62	4th
1990-1	38	24	13	1	74	18	85	Champions
1991-2	42	19	15	8	81	46	72	4th
Premiership:								
1992-3	42	15	11	16	40	38	56	10th
1993-4	42	18	17	7	53	28	71	4th
1994-5	42	13	12	17	52	49	51	12th
(Arsenal's record when Graham left: Pld 28, W8, D10, L10, F31, A32, Pts 34)								
Total	350	162	106	82	522	310	592	

1995 and **Stewart Houston**
1996: Assistant to Graham. Named as caretaker after his departure. Also stood in for a short while after Bruce Rioch (see below) left in 1996.
Achievements:
European Cup Winners' Cup runners-up 1995
Left in September 1996 to become Queens Park Rangers' manager. Now on the coaching staff at Ipswich Town.

League record (Premiership):

Season	Pld	W	D	L	F	A	Pts	Position
1994-5	14	5	2	7	21	17	17	-

1995-6: **Bruce Rioch**
Appointed after taking Bolton Wanderers into the Premiership and the League Cup final. In charge when Arsenal signed Dennis Bergkamp and David Platt Took Arsenal to a UEFA Cup place and the League Cup semi-final.
Left in August 1996

League record (Premiership):

Season	Pld	W	D	L	F	A	Pts	Position
1995-6	38	17	12	9	49	32	63	5th

1996-: **Arsène Wenger**
Former coach of Monaco and Japanese side Nagoya Grampus Eight. Joined Arsenal from Nagoya at the end of September 1996
Achievements:
League champions and FA Cup winners – The 'Double' 1998, 2002
League runners-up 1999, 2000, 2001
FA Cup runners-up: 2001
UEFA Cup runners-up: 2000
Manager of the Year 1998, 2002

League record (Premiership)

Season	Pld	W	D	L	F	A	Pts	Position
1996-7	38	19	11	8	62	32	68	3rd
(Arsenal's record under Houston before Wenger arrived: Pld 7 W4 D2 L1. F15 A8 Pts 14)								
1997-8	38	23	9	6	68	33	78	Champions
1998-9	38	22	12	4	59	17	78	2nd
1999-2000	38	22	7	9	73	43	73	2nd
2000-1	38	20	10	8	70	38	70	2nd
2001-2	38	26	9	3	79	36	87	Champions
Total	221	128	56	37	396	191	440	

PLAYER APPEARANCES FOR THOSE WHO PLAYED FOR ARSENAL AFTER 1970

Season	League	FA Cup	League Cup	Europe
TONY ADAMS (CENTRE BACK)				
Born: Romford, October 10, 1966				
1983-4	3	-	-	-
1984-5	15+1	1	-+1	-
1985-6	10	-	-	-
1986-7	42(6)	4	9	-
1987-8	39(2)	4	8	-
1988-9	36(4)	2	4	-
1989-90	38(5)	3	4	-
1990-1	30(1)	3(1)	4(2)	-
1991-2	35(2)	1	3	4
1992-3	33+2	8(2)	9	-
1993-4	35	3(2)	2	8(2)
1994-5	27(3)	-+1	4(1)	10
1995-6	21(1)	2	5(2)	-
1996-7	27+1(3)	3	3	1
1997-8	26(3)	6	2	2
1998-9	26(1)	5	-	4(1)
1999-2000	21	1(1)	-	11
2000-1	26(1)	4(1)	-	8
2001-2	11	3(1)	-	-
Totals	501+4(32)	53+1(8)	57+1(5)	38(3)
Grand total	655 apps, 48 goals	England caps: 66, 5 goals		
JEREMIE ALIADERE (STRIKER)				
Born: Rambouillet, France, March 30, 1983				
2001-2	-+1	-	-+2	-
IAN ALLINSON (STRIKER)				
Born: Stevenage, October 1, 1957				
1983-4	7+2	-	1	-
1984-5	20+7(10)	-+2	1(1)	-
1985-6	28+5(6)	5(3)	5+1(1)	-
1986-7	5+9	2(1)	1+4(1)	-
Total:	60+23(16)	7+2(4)	8+5(3)	-
Grand Total:	105 apps, 23 goals			
KWAME AMPADU (STRIKER)				
Born: Bradford, December 20, 1970				
1989-90	-+2	-	-	-
VIV ANDERSON (RIGHT BACK)				
Born: Nottingham, July 29, 1956				
1984-5	41(3)	3(1)	3(1)	-
1985-6	39(2)	5	7(1)	-
1986-7	40(4)	4(2)	8(1)	-
Total:	120(9)	12(3)	18(3)	-
Grand total:	150 apps, 15 goals			
England caps:	30			

NICOLAS ANELKA (STRIKER)
Born: Versailles, France, March 24, 1979

1996-7	-+4	-	-	-
1997-8	16+10(6)	8+1(3)	3	1+1
1998-9	34+1(17)	5	-	5(1)
Total:	50+15(23)	13+1(3)	3	6+1(1)
Grand total:	89 apps, 28 goals			
France caps: 27, 5 goals				

GEORGE ARMSTRONG (WINGER, 1944-2000)
Born: Hebburn, Durham, August 9, 1944, died October 31, 2000

1961-2	4(1)	-	-	-
1962-3	16(2)	-	-	-
1963-4	28(3)	4(2)	-	3
1964-5	40(4)	2(1)	-	-
1965-6	39(6)	1	-	-
1966-7	40(7)	4(1)	3	-
1967-8	42(5)	5	8	-
1968-9	26+3(5)	2+1(1)	6(2)	-
1969-70	17(3)	2	1	8+2
1970-1	41+2(2)	2	3	5(1)
1971-2	41+1(2)	9(2)	3	5(1)
1972-3	29+1(2)	7(1)	-	-
1973-4	40+1	3	1	-
1974-5	21+3	7+1(2)	2	-
1975-6	28+1(4)	1	-	-
1976-7	37(2)	2	6(1)	-
Total:	490+10(53)	58+2(10)	35(3)	24+2(2)
Grand total:	621 apps, 68 goals			

ALAN BALL (MIDFIELD)
Born: Farnworth, Lancashire, May 12, 1945

1971-2	18(3)	9(2)	-	-
1972-3	40(10)	7(4)	3	-
1973-4	36(13)	3	1	-
1974-5	30(9)	8(1)	-	-
1975-6	39(9)	1	2	-
1976-7	14(1)	-	6	-
Total:	177(45)	28(7)	12	-
Grand total:	217 apps, 52 goals			
England caps:	72, 8 goals			

GEOFF BARNETT (GOALKEEPER)
Born: Northwich, November 16, 1946

1969-70	11	-	-	2
1970-1	-	-	-	-
1971-2	5	2	1	-
1972-3	20	1	4	-
1973-4	-	-	-	-
1974-5	2	-	-	-
1975-6	1	-	-	-
Total:	39	3	5	2
Grand total:	49 apps			

GRAHAM BARRETT (WINGER)
Born: Dublin, October 6, 1981

Season				
1999-2000	-+2	-	-	-
2000-1	-	-	1	-
Total:	-+2	-	1	-

PAUL BARRON (GOALKEEPER)
Born: London, July 16, 1953

Season				
1978-9	3	-	-	-
1979-80	5	-	-	-
Total:	8	-	-	-

VINCE BARTRAM (GOALKEEPER)
Born: Birmingham, August 7, 1968

Season				
1994-5	11	-	-+1	-

BRENDON BATSON (DEFENDER)
Born: Trinidad, February 6, 1953

Season				
1971-2	-+2	-	-	-
1972-3	3	-	-	-
1973-4	3+2	-	-	-
Total:	6+4	-	-	-

Grand total:10 apps

DENNIS BERGKAMP (STRIKER)
Born: Amsterdam, May 18, 1969

Season				
1995-6	33(11)	1	7(5)	-
1996-7	28+1(12)	2(1)	2(1)	1
1997-8	28(16)	7(3)	4(2)	1(1)
1998-9	28+1(12)	6(3)	1	3(1)
1999-2000	23+5(6)	-	-	11(4)
2000-1	19+6(3)	4+1(1)	-	3+2(1)
2001-2	22+11(9)	4+2(3)	1	3+3(2)
Totals	171+24(69)	24+3(11)	15(8)	22+5(9)

Grand total: 325 apps, 97 goals
Holland caps: 79, 37 goals

MICHAEL BLACK (WINGER)
Born: Chigwell, October 6, 1976

Season				
1998-9	-	-	-	-+1

TOMMY BLACK (WINGER)
Born: Chigwell, July 3, 1979

Season				
1999-2000	-+1	-	1	-

JEFF BLOCKLEY (CENTRE BACK)
Born: Leicester, September 12, 1949

Season				
1972-3	20	4	-	-
1973-4	26(1)	3	1	-
1974-5	6	-	2	-
Total:	52(1)	7	3	-

Grand total: 62 apps, 1 goal
England caps: 1

LUIS BOA MORTE (WINGER)
Born: Lisbon, August 4, 1978

Season				
1997-8	4+11	1+3	1(2)	-+1
1998-9	2+6	1(1)	2	2+1(1)

1999-2000	+2	-	-	-
Total:	6+19	2+3(1)	3(2)	2+2(1)
Grand total:	37 apps, 4 goals			
Portugal caps: 4, 1 goal				

STEVE BOULD (CENTRE BACK)
Born: Stoke, November 16, 1972

1988-9	26+4(2)	2	5	-
1989-90	19	3	-	-
1990-1	38	8	4	-
1991-2	24+1(1)	-	-	-+1
1992-3	24(1)	1	5	-
1993-4	23+2(1)	3	3	5+1
1994-5	30+1	1	5	7+1(2)
1995-6	19	-	5(1)	-
1996-7	33	3	3	1+1
1997-8	21+3	4+1	3	2
1998-9	14+5	3+1	-	2+1
Total:	271+16(5)	27+2	33(1)	17+5(2)
Grand total: 371 apps, 8 goals				
England caps: 2				

LIAM BRADY (MIDFIELD)
Born: Dublin, February 13, 1956

1973-4	9+4(1)	-+1	-	-
1974-5	30+2(3)	2+3	2(1)	-
1975-6	41+1(5)	1	1	-
1976-7	37+1(5)	3	6	-
1977-8	39(9)	6	7(4)	-
1978-9	37(13)	10(2)	1	4(2)
1979-80	34(7)	9	6(5)	9(2)
Total:	227+8(43)	31+4(2)	23(10)	13(4)
Grand total: 306 apps, 59 goals				
Ireland caps: 72, 9 goals				

STEVE BRIGNALL (MIDFIELD)
Born: Tenterden, Kent, June 12, 1960

1978-9	-+1	-	-	-

FABIAN CABALLERO (STRIKER)
Born: Misiones, Argentina, January 31, 1978

1998-9	-+1	-+1	-+1	-

GUS CAESAR (DEFENDER)
Born: Tottenham, March 5, 1966

1985-6	2	-	-	-
1986-7	6+9	-+1	1	-
1987-8	17+5	-	2+1	-
1988-9	2	-	-	-
1989-90	-+3	-	-+1	-
Total:	27+17	-+1	3+2	-
Grand total: 50 apps				

KEVIN CAMPBELL (STRIKER)
Born: Lambeth, February 4, 1970

1987-8	-+1	-	-	-
1988-9	-	-	-	-
1989-90	8+7(2)	-	-	-

1990-1	15+7(9)	4+2(1)	-+4	-
1991-2	22+9(13)	1	2	4(1)
1992-3	32+5(4)	4+3(1)	5+4(4)	-
1993-4	28+9(14)	3	2+2(1)	6+2(4)
1994-5	19+4(4)	1+1	5(1)	3+2
Total:	124+42(46)	13+6(2)	14+10(6)	13+4(5)
Grand total:	226 apps, 59 goals			

SOL CAMPBELL (CENTRE BACK)
Born: Newham, September 18, 1974

2001-2002	29+2(2)	7(1)	-	10

England caps: 51, 1 goal

LEE CANOVILLE (CENTRE BACK)
Born: Ealing, March 14, 1981

2000-1	-	-	-+1	-

JIMMY CARTER (WINGER)
Born: Hammersmith, November 9, 1965

1991-2	5+1	1	-	-
1992-3	11+5(2)	1+1	1	-
1994-5	2+1	-	-	-
Total:	18+7(2)	2+1	1	-

Grand total: 29 apps, 2 goals

TOMMY CATON (CENTRE BACK, 1962-1993)
Born: Kirkby, October 6, 1962, died April 30, 1993

1983-4	26	1	-	-
1984-5	35(1)	3	3(1)	-
1985-6	20(1)	-	7	-
Total:	81(2)	4	10(1)	-

Grand total: 95 apps, 3 goals

BRIAN CHAMBERS (MIDFIELD)
Born: Newcastle, October 31, 1949

1973-4	1	-	-+1	-

LEE CHAPMAN (STRIKER)
Born: Lincoln, December 5, 1959

1982-3	12+7(3)	-+1	-+2	2(2)
1983-4	3+1(1)	-	-	-
Total:	15+8(4)	-+1	-+2	2(2)

ADRIAN CLARKE (WINGER)
Born: Haverhill, Suffolk, September 28, 1974

1994-5	-+1	-	-	-
1995-6	4+2	1+1	-	-
Total:	4+3	1+1	-	-

ANDY COLE (STRIKER)
Born: Nottingham, October 15, 1971

1990-1	-+1	-	-	-

England caps: 15, 1 goal

ASHLEY COLE (LEFT BACK)
Born: Stepney, December 20, 1980

1999-2000	1	-	-+1	-
2000-1	15+2(3)	5+1	1	8+1

2001-2	29(2)	4	-	6+1.
Total:	45+2(5)	9+1	1+1	14+2

Grand total: 75 apps, 5 goals
England caps: 13

DAVID CORK (MIDFIELD)
Born: Doncaster, October 28, 1962

1983-4	5+2(1)	1	-	-

ALEX CROPLEY (MIDFIELD)
Born: Aldershot, January 16, 1951

1974-5	7(1)	2	-	-
1975-6	20(4)	-	2(1)	-
1976-7	2+1	-	-	-
Total:	29+1(5)	2	2(1)	-

Grand total: 34 apps, 6 goals
Scotland caps: 2

JASON CROWE (DEFENDER)
Born: Sidcup, September 30, 1978

1997-8	-	-+1	-+1	-
1998-9	-	-	-+1	-
Total:	-	-+1	-+2	-

TOMAS DANILIEVICIUS (STRIKER)
Born: Moscow, Russia, July 15, 1978

2000-1	-+2	-+1	-	-

Lithuania caps 7

PAUL DAVIES (STRIKER)
Born: St Asaph, Wales, October 10, 1952

1971-2	-+1	-	-	-

PAUL DAVIS (MIDFIELD)
Born: Dulwich, December 9, 1961

1979-80	1+1	-	-	-
1980-1	9+1(1)	-	-	-
1981-2	37+1(4)	1	4	1+1
1982-3	40+1(4)	5+1(2)	6+2(2_	2
1983-4	31+4(1)	1	4	-
1984-5	21+3(1)	-	-	-
1985-6	28+1(4)	1	5	-
1986-7	39(4)	3(1)	9(2)	-
1987-8	28+1(5)	-+1	5+1	-
1988-9	11+1(1)	-+2	2	-
1989-90	8+3(1)	2	-	-
1990-1	36+1(3)	6+1	4	-
1991-2	12	-	2	3
1992-3	6	3	2	-
1993-4	21+1	-	1+2	9
1994-5	3+1(1)	-	2	-
Total:	331+20(30)	22+5(3)	46+5(4)	15+1

Grand total: 445 apps, 37 goals

JOHN DEVINE (RIGHT BACK)
Born: Dublin, November 11, 1958

1977-8	3	-	-	-
1978-9	7	-	-	1

1979-80	20	5	3	5
1980-1	38+1	1	4	-
1981-2	10+1	-	1	2
1982-3	8+1	-	-	-
Total:	86+3	6	8	8

Grand total: 111 apps
Ireland caps: 13

KABA DIAWARA (STRIKER)
Born: Toulon, France, December 16, 1975

| 1998-9 | 2+10 | 1+2 | - | - |

PAUL DICKOV (STRIKER)
Born: Glasgow, November 1, 1972)

1992-3	1+2(2)	-	-	-
1993-4	-+1	-	-	-
1994-	54+5	-	2+2(3)	-
1995-6	1+6(1)	-	-	-
1996-7	-+1	-	-	-
Total:	6+15(3)	-	2+2(3)	-

Grand total: 25 apps, 6 goals

LEE DIXON (RIGHT BACK)
Born: Manchester, March 17, 1964

1987-8	6	-	-	-
1988-9	31+2(1)	1	5	-
1989-90	38(5)	3	4	-
1990-1	38(5)	8(1)	4	-
1991-2	38(4)	1	3	4
1992-3	29	8	7	-
1993-4	32+1	3	4	8
1994-5	39(1)	2	5	11
1995-6	38(2)	2	7	-
1996-7	31+1(2)	1	3	1
1997-8	26+2	7	3	2
1998-9	36	5	-	5
1999-2000	28(3)	3	-	13(1)
2000-1	26+3(1)	6	-	11(1)
2001-2	3+10	2+2	-	2
Total:	439+19(25)	52+2(1)	45	57(2)

Grand total: 614, 28 goals
England caps: 22, 1 goal

JUAN MALDONADO DUARTE (LEFT BACKMIDFIELD)
Born: Sao Paulo, Brazil, February 6, 1982

| 2001-2002 | 1 | 1 | - |

EDU (MIDFIELD)
Born: Sao Paulo, Brazil, May 16, 1978

2000-1	2+3	-	-	-
2001-2	8+6(1)	-+1	-	-
Total:	10+9(1)	-+1	-	-

MARK FLATTS (MIDFIELD)
Born: Islington, October 14, 1972

1992-3	6+4	-	1	-
1993-4	2+1	-	-	-
1994-5	1+2	-+1	-	-

Total: 9+7 -+1 1 -
Grand total: 18 apps

REMI GARDE (MIDFIELD)
Born: L'Arbresle, France, April 3, 1966

Season				
1996-7	7+4	-	-	-
1997-8	6+4	1	-	-
1998-9	6+4	2+2	2	3+2
Total:	19+12	3+2	2	3+2

Grand total: 43 apps
France caps: 6

STEVE GATTING (MIDFIELD)
Born: Park Royal, May 29, 1959

Season				
1978-9	19+2(1)	6(1)	-	2+1
1979-80	9+5(1)	2+1	1+1	1
1980-1	22+1(3)	1	2	-
Total:	50+8(5)	9+1(1)	3+1	3+1

Grand total: 76 apps, 6 goals

CHARLIE GEORGE (MIDFIELD/STRIKER)
Born: Islington, October 10, 1950

Season				
1969-70	21+7(6)	1	2	8(4)
1970-1	17(5)	7+1(5)	-	2+1
1971-2	20+3(7)	8(3)	2	5(1)
1972-3	18+9(6)	4(3)	3(2)	-
1973-4	28(5)	-	-	-
1974-5	9+1(2)	1	1	-
Total:	113+20(31)	21+1(11)	8(2)	15+1(5)

Grand total: 179 apps, 49 goals
England caps: 1

PAUL GORMAN (MIDFIELD)
Born: Dublin, August 6, 1963

Season				
1981-2	4	-	-	-
1982-3	1+1	-	-	-
Total:	5+1	-	-	-

BOBBY GOULD (STRIKER)
Born: Coventry, June 12, 1946

Season				
1967-8	15+1(6)	3(2)	-	-
1968-9	33+5(10)	4(1)	5+2(3)	-
1969-70	9+2	-	1+1	2(1)
Total:	57+8(16)	7(3)	6+3(3)	2(1)

Grand total: 83 apps, 23 goals

GEORGE GRAHAM (STRIKER/MIDFIELD)
Born: Bargeddie, Lanarkshire, November 30, 1944

Season				
1966-7	33(11)	4(1)	-	-
1967-8	38(16)	5	8(5)	-
1968-9	23+3(4)	1	3+2	-
1969-70	36(7)	2	4(2)	10+1(5)
1970-1	36+2(11)	6(1)	5(1)	7+1(1)
1971-2	39+1(8)	9	4(1)	6(1)
1972-3	14+2(2)	-	3	-
Total:	219+8(59)	27(2)	27+2(9)	23+2(7)

Grand total: 308 apps, 77 goals
Scotland caps: 12, 3 goals

JULIAN GRAY (MIDFIELD)
Born: Lewisham, September 21, 1979

Season				
1999-2000	-+1	-	-	

GILLES GRIMANDI (DEFENDER/MIDFIELD)
Born: Gap, France, November 11, 1970

Season				
1997-8	16+6(1)	3+2	4	-
1998-9	3+5	1+1	2	1+1
1999-2000	27+1(2)	3(1)	1	9+1(1)
2000-1	28+2(1)	2+1	-	8
2001-2	11+15	1+3	2	5+3
Total:	85+29(4)	10+7(1)	9	23+5(1)

Grand total: 168 apps, 6 goals

PERRY GROVES (STRIKER/WINGER)
Born: Bow, April 19, 1965

Season				
1986-7	19+6(3)	2+1	4+2	-
1987-8	28+6(6)	3+1(1)	7+1(2)	-
1988-9	6+15(4)	-+2	1+1	-
1989-90	20+10(4)	3	1+2(1)	-
1990-1	13+19(3)	3+1	4(3)	-
1991-2	5+8(1)	-+1	1+2	-+4
1992-3	-+1	-	-	-
Total:	91+65(21)	11+6(1)	18+8(6)	-+4

Grand total: 203 apps, 28 goals

JOHN HALLS (CENTRE BACK/RIGHT BACK)
Born: Islington, February 14, 1982

Season				
2001-2	-	-	-+3	-

RAY HANKIN (STRIKER)
Born: Wallsend, February 21, 1956

Season				
1981-2	-	-	-+2	-

LEE HARPER (GOALKEEPER)
Born: Chelsea, October 30, 1971

Season				
1996-7	1	-	-	-

JOHN HARTSON (STRIKER)
Born: Swansea, April 5, 1975

Season				
1994-5	14+1(7)	-	-	6+1(1)
1995-6	15+4(4)	1	1+2(1)	-
1996-7	14+5(3)	1+1(1)	1+2	2
Total:	43+10(14)	2+1(1)	2+4(1)	8+1(1)

Grand total: 71 apps, 17 goals
Wales caps: 29, 5 goals

JIMMY HARVEY (MIDFIELD)
Born: Lurgan, N.Ireland, May 2, 1958

Season				
1977-8	1	-	-	-
1978-9	1+1	-	-	1
Total	2+1	-	-	1

JOHN HAWLEY (STRIKER)
Born: Patrington, Yorkshire, May 8, 1954

Season				
1981-2	12+2(3)	-	1	-
1982-3	2+4	-	-	-
Total:	14+6(3)	-	1	-

MARTIN HAYES (STRIKER)
Born: Walthamstow, March 21, 1966

Season				
1985-6	11(2)	1	2(1)	-
1986-7	31+4(19)	4(2)	7+1(3)	-
1987-8	17+10(1)	3+1(1)	3+2(1)	-
1988-9	3+14(1)	-	-+4	-
1989-90	8+4(3)	-	2	-
Total:	70+32(26)	8+1(3)	14+7(5)	-

Grand total: 122 apps, 34 goals

NEIL HEANEY (WINGER)
Born: Middlesbrough, November 3, 1971

Season				
1991-2	-+1	-	-	-
1992-3	3+2	-	-	-
1993-4	1	-	-+1	-
Total:	4+3	-	-+1	-

Grand total: 8 apps

MARK HEELEY (WINGER)
Born: Peterborough, September 8, 1959

Season				
1977-8	3+2	-	-	-
1978-9	6+4(1)	-	-	4+1
Total:	9+6(1)	-	-	4+1

THIERRY HENRY (STRIKER)
Born: Paris, August 17, 1977

Season				
1999-2000	26+5(17)	3	2(1)	7+5(8)
2000-1	27+8(17)	3+1(1)	-	14(4)
2001-2	31+2(24)	4+1(1)	-	11(7)
Total:	84+15(12)	10+2(2)	2(1)	32+5(19)
Grand total:	150 apps, 44 goals			

France caps: 37, 12 goals

COLIN HILL (DEFENDER)
Born: Uxbridge, November 12, 1963

Season				
1982-3	7	-	-	-
1983-4	37(1)	1	4	-
1984-5	2	-	-	-
Total:	46(1)	1	4	-

Grand total: 51 apps, 1 goal
Northern Ireland caps: 27, 1 goal

DAVID HILLIER (MIDFIELD)
Born: Blackheath, December 19, 1969

Season				
1990-1	9+7	3+1	2	-
1991-2	27(1)	1	-	-
1992-3	27+3(1)	4+1	7+1	-
1993-4	11+4	3	-+1	2+1
1994-5	5+4	2	2	2+3
1995-6	3+2	-	-	-
1996-7	-+2	-	-	-
Total:	82+22(2)	13+2	13+2	4+4

Grand total: 142 apps, 2 goals

JOHN HOLLINS (MIDFIELD)
Born: Guildford, July 16, 1946

Season				
1979-80	23+3(1)	2	5+1	4+3
1980-1	38(5)	1	4(2)	-

1981-2	40(1)	1	5	4(1)
1982-3	22+1(2)	8	5(1)	2
Total	123+4(9)	12	19+1(3)	10+3(1)

Grand total: 172 apps, 13 goals
England cap: 1

BRIAN HORNSBY (WINGER)
Born: Cambridge, September 10, 1954

1972-3	1	-	-	-
1973-4	6+3(3)	-	-	-
1974-5	12(3)	-	-	-
1975-6	4	-	-	-
Total:	23+3(6)	-	-	-

Grand total: 26 apps, 6 goals

PAT HOWARD (CENTRE BACK)
Born: Dodworth, October 7, 1947

1976-7	15+1	-	4	-

ALAN HUDSON (MIDFIELD)
Born: Chelsea, June 21, 1951

1976-7	19	3	-	-
1977-8	17	4	3+1	-
Total:	36	7	3+1	-

England caps: 2 (both with Stoke)

STEPHEN HUGHES (MIDFIELD)
Born: Wokingham, September 18, 1976

1994-5	1	-	-	-
1995-6	-+1	-	-+1	-
1996-7	9+5(1)	2(1)	-	-
1997-8	7+10(2)	3+3	3+2(1)	
1998-9	4+9(1)	2+2	2	2+2(1)
1999-2000	1+1	-+2	-	-+1
Total:	22+26(4)	7+7(1)	5+3(1)	2+3(1)

Grand total: 75 apps, 7 goals

JUNICHI INAMOTO (MIDFIELD)
Born: Osaka, Japan, September 18, 1979

2001-2	-	-	2	-+2

Japan caps: 27, 3 goals

CARLIN ITONGA (FORWARD)
Born: Zaire, December 11, 1982

1981-2	-	-	-+1	-

PAT JENNINGS (GOALKEEPER)
Born: Newry, June 12, 1945

1977-8	42	6	7	-
1978-9	39	11	1	6
1979-80	37	11	7	9
1980-1	31	1	2	-
1981-2	16	1	4	4
1982-3	19	7	4	-
1983-4	38	1	4	-
1984-5	15	-	3	-
Total:	237	38	32	19

Grand total: 326 apps
Northern Ireland caps: 119

FRANCIS JEFFERS (STRIKER)
Born: Liverpool, January 25, 1981

2001-2	2+4(2)	1+1	-	-+2

JOHN JENSEN (MIDFIELD)
Born: Copenhagen, May 3, 1965

1992-3	29+3	4	3	-
1993-4	27	-+1	5	8
1994-5	24(1)	2	1+1	6
1995-6	13+2	2	5+1	-
Total:	93+5(1)	8+1	14+2	14

Grand total: 137 apps, 1 goal
Denmark caps: 69, 4 goals

SIGGI JONSSON (MIDFIELD)
Born: Akranes, Iceland, September 27, 1966

1989-90	-+6(1)	-+1	1	-
1990-1	2	-	-	-
Total:	2+6(1)	-+1	1	-

Iceland caps: 65, 3 goals

NWANKWO KANU (STRIKER)
Born: Owerri, Nigeria, August 1, 1976

1998-9	5+7(6)	-+5(1)	-	-
1999-2000	24+7(12)	-+2	1(1)	9+6(3)
2000-1	13+14(3)	-+1	-	11+3(2)
2001-2	9+14(3)	3+2(2)	2(1)	4+5
Total:	51+42(24)	3+10(3)	3(2)	24+14(5)

Grand total: 147 apps, 34 goals
Nigeria caps: 38, 6 goals

JOHN KAY (RIGHT BACK)
Born: Chester-le-Street, JanuAary 29, 1964

1982-3	7	-	-	-
1983-4	6+1	-	-	-
Total:	13+1	-	-	-

EDDIE KELLY (MIDFIELD)
Born: Glasgow, February 7, 1951

1969-70	14+2(2)	-	-	6+2(1)
1970-1	21+2(4)	-+2(1)	5	4
1971-2	22+1(2)	3	3	3(1)
1972-3	27(1)	7(1)	2	-
1973-4	35+2(1)	3(1)	1	-
1974-5	32(1)	2(1)	2	-
1975-6	17(2)	-	2	-
Total:	168+7(13)	15+2(4)	15	13+2(2)

Grand total: 222 apps, 19 goals

RAY KENNEDY (STRIKER)
Born: Seaton Delaval, July 28, 1951

1969-70	2+2(1)	-	-	-+2(1)
1970-1	41(19)	9(2)	5(2)	8(3)
1971-2	37(12)	6+2(1)	4(2)	6(4)
1972-3	34(9)	7(2)	1	-
1973-4	42(12)	3(1)	1	-
Total:	156+2(53)	25+2(6)	11(4)	14+2(8)

Grand total: 212 apps, 71 goals
England caps: 12, 3 goals

MARTIN KEOWN (CENTRE BACK/MIDFIELD)
Born: Oxford, July 24, 1966

1985-6	22	5	2	-
1992-3	15+1	-	-	-
1993-4	23+10	2+1	3	4+3
1994-5	24+7(1)	1+1	3+2	5+1
1995-6	34	2	5(1)	-
1996-7	33(1)	3	3	2
1997-8	18	7	2	-
1998-9	34(1)	4	-	5(1)
1999-2000	27(1)	2	-	9
2000-1	28	2	-	9(2)
2001-2	21+1	3+1	2	4+2
Total:	279+19(4)	31+3	18+2(1)	38+6(3)

Grand total: 396, 8 goals
England caps: 43, 2 goals

BRIAN KIDD (STRIKER)
Born: Collyhurst, May 29, 1949

1974-5	40(19)	8(3)	2(1)	-
1975-6	37(11)	1	2	-
Total:	77(30)	9(3)	4(1)	-

England caps: 2, 1 goal

CHRIS KIWOMYA (STRIKER)
Born: Huddersfield, December 2, 1969

1994-5	5+9(3)	-	-	1+2

JOHN KOSMINA (STRIKER)
Born: Adelaide, Australia, August 17, 1956

1978-9	-+1	-	-	1+2

Australia caps: 60, 25 goals

LAUREN (MIDFIELD/RIGHT BACK)
Born: Londi Kribi, Cameroon, January 19, 1977

2000-1	15+3(2)	4	-	6+5(1)
2001-2	27(2)	3	-	11
Total:	42+3(4)	7	-	17+5(1)

Cameroon caps: 25, 1 goal

ANDERS LIMPAR (WINGER)
Born: Solna, Sweden, September 24, 1965

1990-1	32+2(11)	5(2)	2	-
1991-2	23+6(4)	-	1	3(1)
1992-3	12+11(2)	2	4	-
1993-4	9+1	-	2	-
Total:	76+20(17)	7(2)	9	3(1)

Grand total: 115 apps, 20 goals
Sweden caps: 58, 6 goals

ANDY LINIGHAN (CENTRE BACK)
Born: Hartlepool, June 8, 1962

1990-1	7+3	3+1	-	-
1991-2	15+2	-	1+1	2(1)
1992-3	19+2(2)	7(1)	4(1)	-
1993-4	20+1	-	4	-1+1
1994-5	13+7(2)	2	2	3

1995-6	17+1	-+1	2	-
1996-7	10+1(1)	-	-	2
Total:	101+17(5)	12+2(1)	13+1(1)	8+1(1)

Grand total: 155 apps, 8 goals

FREDDIE LJUNGBERG (MIDFIELD)
Born: Halmstad, Sweden, April 16, 1977

1998-9	10+6(1)	2+1	2	-
1999-2000	22+4(6)	2	-	11+3(2)
2000-1	25+5(6)	4+1(1)	-	10+3(2)
2001-2	24+1(12)	5(2)	-	8+1(3)
Total:	81+16(25)	13+2(3)	2	29+7(7)

Grand total: 150, 35 goald
Sweden caps: 34, 2 goals

JOHN LUKIC (GOALKEEPER)
Born: Chesterfield, December 11, 1960

1983-4	4	-	-	-
1984-5	27	3	-	-
1985-6	40	5	6	-
1986-7	36	4	9	-
1987-8	40	4	8	-
1988-9	38	2	5	-
1989-90	38	3	4	-
1996-7	15	1	1	-
2000-1	3	-	-	1
Total:	241	22	33	1

Grand total: 297 apps

OLEG LUZHNY (RIGHT BACK)
Born: Kyiv, Ukraine, August 5, 1968

1999-2000	16+5	1	2	6
2000-1	16+3	2	-	8
2001-2	15+3	4	1	3
Total:	47+11	7	3	17

Grand total: 85 apps
Ukraine caps: 46

PAL LYDERSEN (DEFENDER)
Born: Kristiansand, Norway, September 10, 1965

1991-2	5+2	-	-	-
1992-3	7+1	-	1	-
Total:	12+3	-	1	-

Norway caps: 20, 1 goal

BRIAN MCDERMOTT (WINGER)
Born: Slough, April 8, 1961

1978-9	-+2	-	-	-
1979-80	-+1	-	-	-+1
1980-1	16+7(5)	-+1	-	+1
1981-2	9+4(1)	-	3	3+1(1)
1982-3	7+2(4)	-	-	-+1
1983-4	6+7(2)	-	-	-
Total:	38+23(12)	-+1	3+1	3+3(1)-

Grand total: 72 apps, 13 goals

MALCOLM MACDONALD (STRIKER)
Born: Fulham, January 7, 1950

1976-7	41(25)	3(3)	6(1)	-
1977-8	39(15)	6(7)	7(4)	-
1978-9	4(2)	-	1	-+1
Total:	84(42)	9(10)	14(5)	-+1

Grand total: 106 apps, 57 goals
England caps: 14, 6 goals

EDDIE MCGOLDRICK (MIDFIELD)
Born: Islington, April 30, 1965

1993-4	23+3	1+1	4	3+2(1)
1994-5	9+2	-	3+2	1+1
1995-6	-+1	-	-	-
Total:	32+6	1+1	7+2	4+3(1)

Grand total: 56 apps, 1 goal
Ireland caps: 15

BRIAN MCGOVERN (CENTRE BACK)
Born: Dublin, April 28, 1980

1999-2000	-+1	-	-	-

GAVIN MCGOWAN (DEFENDER)
Born: Blackheath, January 16, 1976

1992-3	-+2	-	-	-
1994-5	1	-	-	-
1995-6	1	1	-	-
1996-7	1	-	-	-
1997-8	-+1	-	-	-
Total:	3+3	1	-	-

Grand total: 7 apps

FRANK MCLINTOCK (WING HALF/DEFENDER)
Born: Glasgow, December 28, 1939

1964-5	25(2)	2	-	-
1965-6	36(2)	1	-	-
1966-7	40(9)	3	2(2)	-
1967-8	38(4)	5	8(2)	-
1968-9	37(1)	4	7	-
1969-70	30	-	4	7
1970-1	42(5)	9	5	7(1)
1971-2	37(3)	9	4	5
1972-3	27+2	3(1)	4	-
Total:	312+2(26)	36(1)	34(4)	19(1)

Grand total: 403 apps, 32 goals
Scotland caps: 9, 1 goal

BOB MCNAB (FULL BACK)
Born: Huddersfield, July 20, 1943

1966-7	25+1	1	-	-
1967-8	30	3	5(1)	-
1968-9	42	4	7	-
1969-70	37(2)	1	4(1)	11
1970-1	40	9	5	8
1971-2	20	3	1+1	1+1
1972-3	42(1)	7	3	-
1973-4	23(1)	3	1	-
1974-5	18	8	-	-

Total:	277+1(4)	39	26+1(2)	20+1

Grand total: 365 apps, 6 goals
England caps: 4

DAVID MADDEN (MIDFIELD)
Born: Stepney, January 6, 1963

1983-4	2	-	-	-

STEFAN MALZ
Born: Ludwigshafen, Germany, June 15, 1972

1999-2000	2+3(1)	-	-	-
2000-1	-+1	-+2	-	-
Total:	2+4	-+2	-	-

TERRY MANCINI (CENTRE BACK)
Born: St Pancras, October 4, 1942

1974-5	26	8	-	-
1975-6	26(1)	-	2	-
Total:	52(1)	8	2	-

Ireland caps: 5, 1 goal

ALEX MANNINGER (GOALKEEPER)
Born: Salzburg, Austria, June 4, 1977

1997-8	7	5	4	-
1998-9	6	2	2	-
1999-2000	14+1	1	1	6
2000-1	11	1	-	2
Total:	38+1	9	7	8

Grand total: 63 apps
Austria caps: 10

PETER MARINELLO (WINGER)
Born: Edinburgh, February 26, 1950

1969-70	14(1)	-	-	4
1970-1	1+2	-	-	-+1
1971-2	4+4(1)	-	1	2(1)
1972-3	13(1)	-+1	4(1)	-
Total:	32+6(3)	-+1	5(1)	6+1(1)

Grand total: 51 apps, 5 goals

PAUL MARINER (STRIKER)
Born: Bolton, May 22, 1953

1983-4	15(7)	-	-	-
1984-5	34+2(7)	3(2)	2	-
1985-6	3+6	2+1	1+1	-
Total:	52+8(14)	5+1(2)	3+1(1)	-

Grand total: 70 apps, 17 goals
England caps: 35 (33 with Ipswich), 13 goals

SCOTT MARSHALL (CENTRE BACK)
Born: Edinburgh, May 1, 1973

1992-3	2	-	-	-
1995-6	10+1(1)	-	-	-
1996-7	6+2	-	-	-
1997-8	1+2	-	1+1	-
Total:	19+5(1)	-	1+1	-

Grand total: 26 apps, 1 goal

BRIAN MARWOOD (WINGER)
Born: Seaham Harbour, Durhan, February 5, 1960

Season				
1987-8	4(1)	-	-	-
1988-9	31(9)	2	5(1)	-
1989-90	17(6)	-	1	-
Total:	52(16)	2	6(1)	-

Grand total: 60 apps, 17 goals
England caps: 1

JOHN MATTHEWS (DEFENDER/MIDFIELD)
Born: Camden Town, November 1, 1955

Season				
1974-5	20	4+1(1)	2	-
1975-6	-+1	-	-	-
1976-7	14+3(2)	-+1	1	-
1977-8	4+3	-	3(2)	-
Total:	38+7(2)	4+2(1)	6(2)	-

Grand total: 57 apps, 5 goals

RAPHAEL MEADE (STRIKER)
Born: Islington, November 22, 1962

Season				
1981-2	8+8(4)	-+1	1+1	2+1(1)
1982-3	2+2(2)	1	2	-
1983-4	9+4(5)	1	-	-
1984-5	6+2(3)	-	-	-
Total:	25+16(14)	2+1	3+1(1)	2+1(1)

Grand total: 51 apps, 16 goals

ALBERTO MENDEZ (MIDFIELD)
Born: Nurnberg, Germany, October 24, 1974

Season				
1997-8	1+2	-	2(1)	-
1998-9	-+1	1	1+1	1
2000-1	-	-	-+1	-
Total:	1+3	1	3+2(1)	1

Grand total: 11 apps, 1 goal

PAUL MERSON (STRIKER/MIDFIELD)
Born: Park Royal, March 20, 1968

Season				
1986-7	5+2(3)	-	-	-
1987-8	7+8(5)	1	-+1	-
1988-9	29+8(10)	2(2)	4(2)	-
1989-90	21+8(7)	1+2	2+1	-
1990-1	36+1(13)	8(1)	4(2)	-
1991-2	41+1(12)	1	3(1)	4
1992-3	32+1(6)	8(1)	9(1)	-
1993-4	24+9(7)	2+1	4(2)	8(3)
1994-5	24(4)	-	2(1)	9+1(2)
1995-6	38(5)	2	7	-
1996-7	32(6)	3	3(1)	2(2)
Total:	289+38(78)	28+3(4)	38+2(10)	23+1(7)

Grand total: 422 apps, 99 goals
England caps: 21, 3 goals

ALAN MILLER (GOALKEEPER)
Born: Epping, March 29, 1970

Season				
1992-3	3+1	-	-	-
1993-4	3+1	-	-	-
Total:	6+2	-	-	-

STEPHEN MORROW (DEFENDER)
Born: Carrickfergus, July 2, 1970

1991-2	-+2	-	-	-
1992-3	13+3	2+2	4+1(1)	-
1993-4	7+4	-	1	1
1994-5	11+4(1)	1	1+1(1)	-+4
1995-6	3+1	-	1	-
1996-7	5+9	2	-+2	-
Total:	39+23(1)	5+2	7+4(2)	1+4

Grand total: 85 apps, 3 goals
Northern Ireland caps: 39, 1 goal

JEHAD MUNTASSER (MIDFIELD)
Born: Tripoli, Libya, July 26, 1978

1997-8	-	-	-+1	-

Libya cap: 1, 1 goal

SAMMY NELSON (LEFT BACK)
Born: Belfast: April 1, 1949

1969-70	4	1	-	1+1
1970-1	2+2	-	1	-+1
1971-2	24(1)	6	3	5
1972-3	2+4	-+1	1	-
1973-4	18+1(1)	-	-	-
1974-5	19+1	-	1	-
1975-6	36	1	2	-
1976-7	31+1(3)	3	5	-
1977-8	41(1)	6	7	-
1978-9	33(2)	10	1	6
1979-80	35(2)	6+1(1)	6(1)	7
1980-1	-+1	-	-	-
Total:	245+10(10)	33+2(1)	27(1)	19+2

Grand total: 338 apps, 12 goals
Northern Ireland caps: 51, 1 goal

CHARLIE NICHOLAS (STRIKER)
Born: Glasgow, December 30, 1961

1983-4	41(11)	1(1)	4(1)	-
1984-5	35+3(9)	3(1)	3(2)	-
1985-6	41(10)	5(4)	7(4)	-
1986-7	25+3(4)	2+2(4)	6(3)	-
1987-8	3	-	-	-
Total: 145+6(34)	11+2(10)	20(10)	-	

Grand total: 184 apps, 54 goals
Scotland caps: 20, 5 goals

PETER NICHOLAS (MIDFIELD)
Born: Newport, November 10, 1959

1980-1	8(1)	-	-	-
1981-2	28+3	1	5(1)	4
1982-3	21	7	3(1)	-
Total:	57+3(1)	8	8(2)	4

Grand total: 80 apps, 3 goals
Wales caps: 73

DAVID O'LEARY (CENTRE BACK)
Born: Stoke Newington, May 2, 1958

1975-6	27	1	2	-
1976-7	33(2)	3	4(1)	-

1977-8	41(1)	6(1)	6	-
1978-9	37(2)	11	1	5
1979-80	34(1)	9	6	9
1980-1	24(1)	1	2	-
1981-2	40(1)	1	5	4
1982-3	36(1)	5	7	2
1983-4	36	1	4	-
1984-5	36	3	3	-
1985-6	35	5	7	-
1986-7	39	4	9	-
1987-8	23	4	6(1)	-
1988-9	26	2	-	-
1989-90	28+6(1)	3	4	-
1990-1	11+10(1)	5+1	-+1	-
1991-2	11+14	1	-+1	1
1992-3	6+5	1+3	2	-
Total:	523+35(11)	66+4(1)	68+2(2)	21

Grand total: 719 apps, 14 goals
Ireland caps: 68, 1 goal

DANNY O'SHEA (DEFENDER)
Born: Kennington, March 26, 1963

1982-3	6	-	3	-

MARC OVERMARS (WINGER)
Born: Emst, Holland, March 29, 1973

1997-8	32(12)	8+1(2)	3(2)	2
1998-9	37(6)	6+1(4)	-	4(1)
1999-2000	22+9(7)	1(1)	-+1	11+3(5)
Total:	91+9(25)	15+2(7)	3+1(2)	17+3(6)

Grand total: 141 apps, 40 goals
Holland caps: 72, 15 goals

RAY PARLOUR (MIDFIELD)
Born: Romford, March 7, 1973

1991-2	2+4(1)	-	-	-
1992-3	16+5(1)	4(1)	3+1	-
1993-4	24+3(2)	3	2	-
1994-5	22+8	2	5	7+2
1995-6	20+2	-	3+1	-
1996-7	17+13(2)	3	-+1	1+1
1997-8	34(5)	7(1)	4	2
1998-9	35(6)	7	-	4
1999-2000	29+1(1)	1	2	9+2(3)
2000-1	28+5(4)	3+1	-	9+1(2)
2001-2	25+2	2+2(2)	1	5+3
Total:	252+43(22)	32+3(4)	20+3	37+9(5)

Grand total: 199 apps, 31 goals
England caps: 10

COLIN PATES (CENTRE BACK)
Born: Carshalton, August 10, 1961

1989-90	1+1	-	-	-
1990-1	-+1	-	-	-
1991-2	9+2	-	2	2(1)
1992-3	2+5	-	-	
Total:	12+9	-	2	2(1)

Grand total: 25 apps, 1 goal

JERMAINE PENNANT (WINGER)
Born: Nottingham, January 15, 1983

Season				
1999-2000	-	-	-+1	-
2000-1	-	-	1	-
2001-2	-	-	3	-+2
Total:	-	-	4+1	-+2

Grand total: 7 apps

EMANUEL PETIT (MIDFIELD)
Born: Dieppe, France, September 22, 1970

Season				
1997-8	32(2)	7	3	2
1998-9	26+1(4)	3(2)	-	3
1999-2000	24+2(3)	3	-	9+1
Total:	82+3(9)	13(2)	3	14+1

Grand total: 116 apps, 11 goals
France caps: 59, 6 goals

VLADIMIR PETROVIC (MIDFIELD)
Born: Belgrade, Yugoslavia, July 1, 1955

Season				
1982-3	10+3(2)	6(1)	3	-

Yugoslav caps: 34

ROBERT PIRES (MIDFIELD)
Born: Reims, France, January 29, 1973

Season				
2000-1	29+4(4)	6(3)	-	11+1(1)
2001-2002	27+1(9)	3+2(1)	-	12(3)
Total:	46+5(13)	(+2(4)	-	23+1(4)

France caps: 53, 9 goals

DAVID PLATT (MIDFIELD)
Born: Chadderton, Lancashire, June 10, 1966

Season				
1995-6	27+2(6)	1	2+1	-
1996-7	27+1(4)	1	3(1)	2
1997-8	11+20(3)	1+3	2+2(1)	-+2
Total:	65+23(13)	3+3	7+3(2)	2+2

Grand total: 108 apps, 15 goals
England caps: 62, 27 goals

RICHIE POWLING (DEFENDER/MIDFIELD)
Born: Barking, May 21, 1956

Season				
1973-4	2	-	-	-
1974-5	5+3	1	-	-
1975-6	28+1(1)	1	-	-
1976-7	11+1	-	1	-
1977-8	4(2)	-	1	-
Total:	50+5(3)	2	2	-

Grand total: 59 apps, 3 goals

DAVID PRICE (MIDFIELD)
Born: Caterham, June 23, 1955

Season				
1972-3	-+1	-	-	-
1973-4	3+1	-	-	-
1974-5	-+1	-	-	-
1976-7	6+2(1)	-	-	-
1977-8	38+1(5)	6	6	-
1978-9	39(8)	11(1)	1	6
1979-80	21+1(1)	9	2	5+1(2)

1980-1	9+3(1)	-	2	-
Total:	116+10(16)	26(1)	11	11+1(2)

Grand total: 175 apps, 19 goals

NIALL QUINN (STRIKER)
Born: Dublin, October 6, 1966

1985-6	10+2(1)	2+1	2	-
1986-7	35(8)	4(1)	9(3)	-
1987-8	6+5(2)	1+1	1+2	-
1988-9	2+1(1)	-	-	-
1989-90	6(2)	1(1)	2(1)	-
Total:	59+8(14)	8+2(2)	14+2(4)	-

Grand total: 93 apps, 20 goals
Ireland caps: 91, 21 goals

JOHN RADFORD (STRIKER)
Born: Hemsworth, Yorkshire, February 22, 1947

1963-4	1	-	-	-
1964-5	13(7)	2(2)	-	-
1965-6	32(8)	-	-	-
1966-7	30(4)	3(3)	1	-
1967-8	39(10)	5(2)	8(2)	-
1968-9	31+3(15)	4	6(4)	-
1969-70	39(12)	2(2)	3	11(5)
1970-1	41(15)	9(2)	4(1)	8(3)
1971-2	34(8)	4+1(1)	4(2)	5(3)
1972-3	38(15)	3+1(1)	4(3)	-
1973-4	32(7)	3	1	-
1974-5	29(7)	7(2)	2	-
1975-6	15(3)	-	1	-
1976-7	1+1	-	-	-
Total:	375+4(111)	42+2(15)	34(12)	24(11)

Grand total: 481 apps, 149 goals
England caps: 2

ISAIAH RANKIN (STRIKER)
Born: Islington. May 22, 1978

1997-8	-+1	-	-	-

PAT RICE (RIGHT BACK)
Born: Belfast, March 17, 1949

1967-8	2+4	-	1	-
1969-70	7(1)	-	1	1
1970-1	41	9	5	8
1971-2	42(1)	9(1)	4	6
1972-3	39(2)	7	4	-
1973-4	41(1)	3	1	-
1974-5	32	8	-	-
1975-6	42(1)	1	2	-
1976-7	42(3)	3	6	-
1977-8	38(2)	6	7	-
1978-9	39(1)	11	1	6
1979-80	26	10	4	5+1
1980-1	-+2	-	-	-
Total:	391+6(12)	67(1)	36	26+1

Grand total: 527 apps, 13 goals
Northern Ireland caps: 49

KEVIN RICHARDSON (MIDFIELD)
Born: Newcastle, December 4, 1962

1987-8	24/5(4)	4(1)	6+1(2)	-
1988/9	32+2(1)	2	3+2	-
1989-90	32+1	3	4	-
Total:	88+8(5)	9(1)	13+3(2)	-

Grand total: 121 apps, 8 goals
England cap: 1

ROHAN RICKETTS (MIDFIELD)
Born: Clapham, December 22, 1982

2001-2	-	-	-+1	-

JIMMY RIMMER (GOALKEEPER)
Born: Southport, February 10, 1948

1973-4	1	-	-	-
1974-5	40	8	2	-
1975-6	41	1	2	-
1976-7	42	3	6	-
Total:	124	12	10	

Grand total: 146 apps
England cap: 1

GRAHAM RIX (MIDFIELD)
Born: Askern, October 23, 1957

1976-7	4+3(1)	-	-	-
1977-8	37+2(2)	4+1(1)	7	-
1978-9	39(3)	11	1	6
1979-80	38(4)	11	7	9
1980-1	35(5)	1	4	-
1981-2	39(9)	1	4	4(1)
1982-3	36(6)	8(4)	8	2
1983-4	34(4)	1	3(1)	-
1984-5	18(2)	-	3(1)	-
1985-6	38(3)	4(2)	5	-
1986-7	13+5(2)	-	1+2	-
1987-8	7+3	1+1	2	-
Total:	338+13(41)	42+2(7)	45+2(2)	21(1)

Grand total: 463 apps, 51 goals
England caps: 17

OMER RIZA (STRIKER)
Born: Edmonton, November 8, 1979

1998-9	-	-	-+1	-

JOHN ROBERTS (CENTRE BACK)
Born: Abercynon, Wales, September 11, 1946

1969-70	11(1)	-	2	-
1970-1	18	-	5(1)	5
1971-2	21+2(3)	-	4	4+1
1972-3	6+1	-	1	-
Total:	56+3(4)	-	12(1)	9+1

Grand total: 81 apps, 5 goals
Wales caps: 22

JIMMY ROBERTSON (WINGER)
Born: Cardonald, December 17, 1944

1968-9	18+1(3)	2(1)	-	-

1969-70	27(4)	2	4	5
Total:	45+1(7)	4(1)	4	5

Scotland caps: 1

STEWART ROBSON (RIGHT BACK/MIDFIELD)
Born: Billericay, November 6, 1964

1981-2	20(2)	1	1	-
1982-3	31(2)	8	8(1)	2(1)
1983-4	28(6)	-	4(1)	-
1984-5	40(2)	3	3	-
1985-6	26+1(4)	1(1)	4(1)	-
1986-7	5	-	-	-
Total:	150+1(16)	13(1)	20(3)	2(1)
Grand total:	186 apps, 21 goals			

DAVID ROCASTLE (MIDFIELD, 1967-2001)
Born: Lewisham, May 2, 1967, died: March 31, 2001

1985-6	13+3(1)	5(1)	2+1	-
1986-7	36(2)	4(1)	8(2)	-
1987-8	40(7)	4(2)	8(3)	-
1988-9	38(6)	2	5(1)	-
1989-90	28+5(2)	2+1	4	-
1990-1	13+3(2)	-+1	2	-
1991-2	36+3(4)	1	3	4
Total:	204+14(24)	18+2(4)	32+1(6)	4
Grand total: 275 apps, 34 goals				
England caps: 14				

MATTHEW ROSE (DEFENDER)
Born: Dartford, September 24, 1975

1995-6	1+3	-	-	-
1996-7	1	-	-	-
Total:	2+3	-	-	-

TREVOR ROSS (MIDFIELD)
Born: Ashton-under-Lyne, January 16, 1957

1974-5	1+1	-	-	-
1975-6	17(1)	-	-	-
1976-7	29(4)	3(1)	5(3)	-
1977-8	10	-	1	-
Total:	57+1(5)	3(1)	6(3)	-
Grand total: 67 apps, 9 goals				

WILF ROSTRON (WINGER)
Born: Sunderland, September 29, 1956

1974-5	6(2)	-	-	-
1975-6	2+3	-	1	-
1976-7	4+2	1	-	-
Total:	12+5(2)	1	1	-
Grand total: 19 apps, 2 goals				

KENNY SANSOM (LEFT BACK)
Born: Camberwell, September 26, 1958

Season	League	FA Cup	League Cup	Europe
1980-1	42(3)	1	4	-
1981-2	42	1	5	4
1982-3	40	8	8	2
1983-4	40(1)	1	4	-

1984-5	39(1)	2	3	-
1985-6	42	5	7	-
1986-7	35	4	9	-
1987-8	34(1)	4	8	-
Total:	314(6)	26	48	6

Grand total: 394 apps, 6 goals
Arsenal's most capped player with 86 caps (77 at Arsenal), 1 goal

STEFAN SCHWARZ (MIDFIELD)
Born: Kulldall, Sweden, April 18, 1969

1984-5	34(2)	1	4	10(2)

Sweden caps: 69, 6 goals

DAVID SEAMAN (GOALKEEPER)
Born: Rotherham, September 19, 1963

1990-1	38	8	4	-
1991-2	42	1	3	4
1992-3	39	8	9	-
1993-4	39	3	5	9
1994-5	31	2	6	11
1995-6	38	2	7	-
1996-7	22	2	2	2
1997-8	31	4	1	2
1998-9	32	5	-	6
1999-2000	24	2	1	9
2000-1	24	5	-	10
2001-2	17	1	-	7
Total:	377	43	38	60

Grand total: 518 apps
England caps: 73

IAN SELLEY (MIDFIELD)
Born: Chertsey, June 14, 1974

1992-3	9	3	1	-
1993-4	16+2	-	1+1	5+2(1)
1994-5	10+3	-	3	3(1)
1996-7	-+1	-	-	-
Total:	35+6	3	5+1	8+2(2)

Grand total: 60 apps, 2 goals

PAUL SHAW (MIDFIELD)
Born: Maidenhead, September 4, 1973

1994-5	-+1	-	-	-
1995-6	-+3	-+1	-	-
1996-7	1+7(2)	-	-	-
Total:	1+11(2)	-+1	-	-

Grand total: 13 apps, 2 goals

SILVINHO (LEFT BACK)
Born: Sao Paulo, Brazil, April 12, 1974

1999-2000	23+8(1)	3	2	7+2
2000-1	23+1(2)	1+2	-	6+1(2)
Total:	46+9(4)	4+2	2	13+3(2)

Brazil caps: 6

PETER SIMPSON (CENTRE BACK)
Born: Gorleston, Norfolk, January 13, 1945

1963-4	6	-	-	-

1964-5	6(2)	-	-	-
1965-6	5+3	-	-	-
1966-7	34+2(1)	4	2	-
1967-8	40	5	8(1)	-
1968-9	34	4	7(2)	-
1969-70	39	2	4	12
1970-1	25	9(1)	-	4
1971-2	32+2(4)	9	1	4+1(1)
1972-3	27(1)	7	3	-
1973-4	34+4(2)	3	1	-
1974-5	39+1	7	2	-
1975-6	7+2	-	-	-
1976-7	19	3	3	-
1977-8	6+3	-	1+1	-
Total:	353+17(10)	53(1)	32+1(3)	20+1(1)

Grand total: 477 apps, 15 goals

ALAN SMITH (STRIKER)
Born: Hollywood, Birmingham, November 21, 1962

1987-8	36+3(11)	3(1)	8(4)	-
1988-9	36(23)	2	5(2)	-
1989-90	37+1(10)	2	3+1(3)	-
1990-1	35+2(22)	8(2)	4(3)	-
1991-2	33+6(12)	1(1)	2	4(4)
1992-3	27+4(3)	5+2(1)	7(2)	-
1993-4	21+4(3)	1+1(1)	4+1(1)	7+2(2)
1994-5	17+2(2)	1	3(1)	4(1)
Total:	242+22(87)	23+3(6)	36+2(16)	15+2(7)

Grand total: 345 apps, 115 goals
England caps: 13, 2 goals

BRIAN SPARROW (LEFT BACK)
Born: Bethnal Green, June 24, 1962

1983-4	2	-	-	-

FRANK STAPLETON (STRIKER)
Born: Dublin, July 10, 1956

1974-5	1	-	-	-
1975-6	23+2(4)	1	1+1(1)	-
1976-7	40(13)	3(1)	6(3)	-
1977-8	39(13)	5(4)	7(2)	-
1978-9	41(17)	11(6)	1(1)	6(4)
1979-80	39(14)	11(4)	7(5)	9
1980-1	40(14)	1	4(2)	-
Total:	223+2(75)	32(15)	26+1(14)	15(4)

Grand total: 297 apps, 108 goals
Ireland caps: 71, 20 goals

KEVIN STEAD (DEFENDER)
Born: West Ham, October 2, 1958

1978-9	1+1	-	-	-

IGORS STEPANOVS (CENTRE BACK)
Born: Ogre, Latvia, January 21, 1976

2000-1	9	3	1(1)	-
2001-2	6	1	2+1	3+1
Total:	15	4	3+1(1)	15(4)

Latvia caps: 50, 2 goals

PETER STOREY (RIGHT BACK/MIDFIELD)
Born: Farnham, Surrey, September 7, 1945

1965-6	28	1	-	-
1966-7	34(1)	4	3	-
1967-8	39	5	7	-
1968-9	42	4	7	-
1969-70	39(1)	2	4	11
1970-1	40(2)	9(4)	5	8(2)
1971-2	29(1)	6+1	2	3
1972-3	40(4)	7	4(2)	-
1973-4	41	3	1	-
1974-5	37	7	2	-
1975-6	11	1	-	-
1976-7	7+4	-+1	1+1	-
Total:	387+4(9)	49+2(4)	36+1(2)	22(2)

Grand total: 501 apps, 17 goals
England caps: 19

DAVOR SUKER (STRIKER)
Born: Osijek, Croatia, January 1, 1968

1999-2000	8+14(8)	3	1	3+10(2)

Croatia caps: 69, 45 goals

ALAN SUNDERLAND (STRIKER)
Born: Conisborough, Yorkshire, July 1, 1953

1977-8	23(4)	5(3)	-	-
1978-9	37(9)	11(6)	1	4(3)
1979-80	36+1(14)	11(6)	6(4)	7(4)
1980-1	34(7)	1	4(2)	-
1981-2	38(11)	1	5(1)	2
1982-3	25(6)	5(1)	6(5)	-+1
1983-4	11+1(4)	-	4(1)	-
Total:	204+2(55)	34(16)	26(13)	13+1(7)

Grand total: 280 apps, 91 goals
England cap: 1

SEBASTIAN SVARD (CENTRE BACK)
Born: Denmark, January 15, 1983

2001-2	-	-	-+1	-

Croatia caps: 69, 45 goals

BRIAN TALBOT (MIDFIELD)
Born: Ipswich, July 21, 1953

1978-9	20	6(2)	-	-
1979-80	42(1)	11(2)	7(1)	9
1980-1	40(7)	1	4	-
1981-2	42(7)	1	5	4(1)
1982-3	38+4(9)	7(1)	7	2
1983-4	26+1(6)	-+1	-+1	-
1984-5	37+4(10)	3(2)	3	-
Total:	245+9(40)	29+1(7)	26+1(1)	15(1)

Grand total: 326 apps, 49 goals
England caps: 6

STATHIS TAVLARDIS (CENTRE BACK)
Born: Greece, January 25, 1980

2000-1	-	-	3	-

STUART TAYLOR (GOALKEEPER)
Born: Romford, November 28, 1980

2000-1	-	-	1	1
2001-2	9+1	1	2	1+1
Total:	9+1	1	3	2+1

MICHAEL THOMAS (MIDFIELD)
Born: Lambeth, August 24, 1967

1986-7	12	-+2	2+2	-
1987-8	36+1(9)	2	7(2)	-
1988-9	33+4(7)	2	5	-
1989-90	35+1(5)	2+1	4(3)	-
1990-1	27+4(2)	8(1)	2	-
1991-2	6+4(1)	-	2	1+1
Total:	149+14(24)	14+3(1)	22+2(5)	1+1

Grand total: 206 apps, 30 goals
England caps: 2

MATTHEW UPSON (CENTRE BACK)
Born: Stowmarket, April 18, 1979

1997-8	5	1	2	-
1998-9	-+5	1	2	1
1999-2000	5+3	-	2	1+1
2000-1	-+2	-	1	1
2001-2	10+4	-+1	1	5+1
Total:	20+14	2+1	8	8+2

Grand total: 55 apps

GIOVANNI VAN BRONCKHORST (MIDFIELD/LEFT BACK)
Born: Rotterdam, Holland, February 5, 1975

2001-2002	13+8(1)	2	3	6+1

Holland caps: 26, 2 goals

PAUL VAESSEN (STRIKER)
Born: Bermondsey, October 16, 1961, died August 8, 2001

1978-9	1	-	-	-+2
1979-80	8+6(2)	-	1(2)	1+2(1)
1980-1	5+2(2)	-	-	-
1981-2	9+1(2)	-	-+1	2
Total:	23+9(6)		1+1(2)	3+4(1)

Grand total: 41 apps, 9 goals

PAOLO VERNAZZA (MIDFIELD)
Born: Islington, November 1, 1979

1997-8	1	-	1	-
1998-9	-	-	-	1
1999-2000	1+1	-	2	-+1
2000-1	-+2(1)	-	1	-+1
Total:	2+3(1)	-	4	1+2

Grand total: 12 apps, 1 goal

PATRICK VIEIRA (MIDFIELD)
Born: Dakar, Senegal, June 23, 1976

1996-7	30+1(2)	3	3	1
1997-8	31+2(2)	8+1	2	2
1998-9	34(3)	5(1)	-	3
1999-2000	29+1(2)	2	-	14
2000-1	28+2(5)	5+1(1)	-	12

2001-2	35+1(2)	7	-	11(1)
Total:	187+7(16)	30+2(2)	5	43(1)

Grand total: 274, 19 goals
France caps: 53, 3 goals

NELSON VIVAS (RIGHT BACK)
Born: San Nicolas, Argentina, October 18, 1969

1998-9	10+13	4+2	2(1)	2+3
1999-2000	1+4	-	1	1+3
2000-1	3+9	1+2	1	3+4
Total:	14+26	5+4	4(1)	6+10

Grand total: 69 apps, 1 goal
Argentina caps: 43, 1 goal

MORITZ VOLTZ (MIDFIELD)
Born: Siegen, Germany, January 21, 1983

2000-1	-	-	1	-
2001-2	-	-	-	-
Total:	-	-	1	-

STEVE WALFORD (DEFENDER)
Born: Highgate, January 5, 1958

1977-8	2+3	-	-	-
1978-9	26+7(2)	2+4	-	2+1
1979-80	16+3(1)	3+1	3	1+1
1980-1	20	-	2(1)	-
Total:	64+13(3)	5+5	5(1)	3+2

Grand total: 97 apps, 4 goals

RHYS WESTON (CENTRE BACK)
Born: Rogiet, October 27, 1980

1999-2000	1	-	-+1	-
2000-1	-	-	1	-
Total:	1	-	1+1	-

CHRIS WHYTE (CENTRE BACK)
Born: Islington, September 2, 1961

1981-2	32(2)	1	3	1+1
1982-3	36(3)	4	6	2
1983-4	14+1(2)	-	4	-
1985-6	4+3(1)	-	1	-
Total:	86+4(8)	5	14	3+1

Grand total: 113 apps, 8 goals

STEVE WILLIAMS (MIDFIELD)
Born: Hammersmith, July 12, 1958

1984-5	14+1(1)	3	-	-
1985-6	17	3	3	-
1986-7	33+1(2)	3	7	-
1987-8	29(1)	2	5(1)	-
Total:	93+2(4)	11	15(1)	-

Grand total: 121 apps, 5 goals
England caps: 6

RHYS WILMOT (GOALKEEPER)
Born: Newport, February 21, 1962

1985-6	2	-	1	-
1986-7	6	-	-	-
Total:	8	-	1	-

BOB WILSON (GOALKEEPER)
Born: Chesterfield, October 30, 1941

1963-4	5	-	-	1
1965-6	4	-	-	-
1967-8	13	1	-	-
1968-9	42	4	7	-
1969-70	28	2	2	9
1970-1	42	9	5	8
1971-2	37	7	3	6
1972-3	22	6	-	-
1973-4	41	3	1	-
Total:	234	32	18	24

Grand total: 308 apps
Scotland caps: 2

SYLVAIN WILTORD (STRIKER)
Born: Paris, May 10, 1974

2000-1	20+7(8)	5+1(6)	1	2+11(1)
2001-2	23+10(10)	6+1(2)	3(4)	9+2(1)
Total:	43+17(18)	11+2(8)	4(4)	11+13(2)

France caps: 43

NIGEL WINTERBURN (LEFT BACK)
Born: Nuneaton, December 11, 1963

1987-8	16+1	4	4(1)	-
1988-9	38(3)	2	5(1)	-
1989-90	36	2	4	-
1990-1	38	8	4	-
1991-2	41(1)	1	2	4
1992-3	29(1)	8	7(1)	-
1993-4	34	3	4	9
1994-5	39	2	5	11
1995-6	36(2)	1	7	-
1996-7	38	2	3	2
1997-8	35+1(1)	8	3	2
1998-9	30	6	-	5
1999-2000	19+9	-	1	9+1(1)
Total:	429+11(8)	47	49(3)	42+1(1)

Grand total: 579 apps, 12 goals
England caps: 2

GEORGE WOOD (GOALKEEPER)
Born: Douglas, Lanarkshire, September 26, 1952

1980-1	11	-	2	-
1981-2	26	-	1	-
1982-3	23	1	4	2
Total:	60	1	7	2

Grand total: 70 apps
Scotland caps: 4

TONY WOODCOCK (STRIKER)
Born: Eastwood, Nottingham, December 6, 1955

1982-3	34(14)	8(4)	8(3)	2
1983-4	37(21)	1(1)	4(1)	-
1984-5	27(10)	3(2)	3(1)	-
1985-6	31+2(11)	1+1	5+2	-
Total:	129+2(56)	13+1(7)	20+2(5)	2

Grand total: 169 apps, 68 goals
England caps: 42, 16 goals

CHRISTOPHER WREH (STRIKER)
Born: Monrovia, Liberia, May 14, 1975

1997-8	7+9(3)	2+4(1)	1+2	-+1
1998-9	3+9	-	2	3
1999-2000	-	-	-+1	-
2000-1	-	-	-+1	-
Total: 10+18(3)	2+4(1)	3+3	3+2	

Grand total: 45 apps, 4 goals

IAN WRIGHT (STRIKER)
Born: Woolwich, November 3, 1963

1991-2	30(24)	-	3(2)	-
1992-3	30+1(15)	7(10)	8(5)	-
1993-4	39(23)	3(1)	4(6)	6(4)
1994-5	30+1(18)	2	3(3)	11(9)
1995-6	31(15)	2(1)	7(7)	-
1996-7	30+5(23)	1	3(5)	2(2)
1997-8	22+2(10)	1	1(1)	2
Total:	212+9(128)	16(12)	29(29)	21(15)

Grand total: 287 apps, 184 goals
Arsenal's all-time leading scorer in first-class competitions
England caps: 33, 9 goals

RICHARD WRIGHT (GOALKEEPER)
Born: Ipswich, November 5, 1977

2001-2	12	5	1	4

England caps: 2

WILLIE YOUNG (CENTRE BACK)
Born: Edinburgh, November 25, 1951

1976-7	14(1)	-	-	-
1977-8	35(3)	6(1)	7	-
1978-9	33	10(2)	1	6(1)
1979-80	38(3)	11	6	9(3)
1980-1	40(4)	1	4	-
1981-2	10	-	2(1)	3
Total:	170(11)	28(3)	20(1)	18(4)

Grand total: 236 apps, 19 goals

SEASON-BY-SEASON RECORDS

SEASON 1886-1887

● FRIENDLIES

11 Dec	Eastern W	A	W	6-0
8 Jan	Erith	H	W	6-1
15 Jan	Alexandria U	H	W	11-0
22 Jan	Eastern W	H	W	1-0
29 Jan	Erith	A	W	3-2
5 Feb	Millwall Rov	A	L	0-4
12 Feb	Alexandria U	A	W	6-0
25 Feb	2nd Rifle Brigade	H	D	0-0
12 Mar	Millwall Rov	H	W	3-0
26 Mar	2nd Rifle Brigade	A	L	0-1

● RECORD

P	W	D	L	F	A
10	7	1	2	36	8

SEASON 1887-1888

● FRIENDLIES

30 Sep	Alexandria U	H	W	5-1
14 Oct	Clapton Pilgrims	H	D	2-2
22 Oct	St Lukes			
5 Nov	Grange Institute	H	W	4-0
12 Nov	Deptford Iona	H	D	1-1
19 Nov	Tottenham H	A	L	1-2
26 Nov	Millwall Rov	A	L	0-3
3 Dec	Grange Park	H		
10 Dec	Brixton Ran	H	L	1-2
16 Dec	Shrewsbury Park	A	W	4-0
31 Dec	Forest Gate Alliance	A	L	1-2
14 Jan	Deptford Iona	A	W	3-2
28 Jan	Champion Hill	H	W	6-0
4 Feb	Tottenham H	H	W	6-2
11 Feb	Millwall Rov	H	D	3-3
18 Feb	Erith	H	W	2-1
25 Feb	Forest Gate Alliance	H	D	1-1
3 Mar	Grange Institute	H	W	2-1
10 Mar	Brixton Ran	A	W	9-3
17 Mar	Ascham		W	5-0
30 Mar	Millwall Rov	H	W	3-0
7 Apr	Alexandria U	A	W	3-1*
	*abandoned after 25 mins			

● LONDON SENIOR CUP

8 Oct	Grove House	H	W	3-1
29 Oct	Barnes	H	L	0-4

● JUNIOR MATCHES

10 Nov	Woolwich Pupils	H	W	1-0
& Teachers				

26 Nov	Erith	A	L	0-1
24 Feb	Thistle	A	L	1-2

● 1ST TEAM RECORD

P	W	D	L	F	A
24	14	4	6	66	33

SEASON 1888-1889

● FRIENDLIES

15 Sep	London Scottish	H	D	3-3
22 Sep	Tottenham H	H	L	0-1
29 Sep	Old St Pauls	H	W	7-3
6 Oct	Grove House	H	W	2-0
13 Oct	London Scottish	H	W	4-0
20 Oct	2nd Rifle Brigade	H	L	1-2
27 Oct	Brixton Ran	A	L	1-3
10 Nov	Millwall Rov			
17 Nov	St Lukes	A	D	1-1
1 Dec	Phoenix		D	0-0
22 Dec	St Brides			
5 Jan	Vulcan		D	1-1
12 Jan	Unity		D	0-0
26 Jan	St Lukes	A		
2 Feb	Ilford	A	L	1-2
16 Feb	Millwall Rov			
23 Feb	Ilford	A	L	0-1
2 Mar	London Cal	H	L	1-2
9 Mar	Tottenham H	A	W	1-0
16 Mar	South Eastern Ran	H	L	1-2
23 Mar	Royal Artillery		W	9-0
30 Mar	2nd Rifle Brigade	H	W	2-0
1 Apr	2nd Rifle Brigade		W	6-1
6 Apr	Old St Pauls	A	W	1-0
13 Apr	Millwall Rov		W	3-0
19 Oct	Boston T		L	1-4
20 Apr	Spartan Rov	H	W	6-0
23 Apr	Scots Guards		W	7-2
27 Apr	London Caledonians	H	L	0-1

● LONDON ASSOCIATION CUP

3 Nov	Phoenix	H	W	3-0
24 Nov	Dulwich	H	W	4-2
8 Dec	Old St Pauls	H	W	3-1
19 Jan	Clapton (SF)	*	L	0-2
	*played at Leyton			

● KENT COUNTY CHALLENGE CUP

10 Nov	Horton Kirby	A	W	6-2
29 Dec	Deptford Iona	A	W	5-1
9 Feb	Gravesend	A	D	3-3*
*Arsenal disqualified for refusing to play extra time.				

1ST TEAM RECORD

P	W	D	L	F	A
32	16	6	10	83	40

SEASON 1889-1890

● FRIENDLIES

7 Sep	London Cal	H	D	2-2
14 Sep	Casuals	H	W	6-0
21 Sep	Tottenham H	H	W	10-1
28 Sep	Unity	H	W	8-0
19 Oct	St Marks Coll	A	W	2-1
30 Nov	Great Marlow	A	L	0-2
21 Dec	Ilford	A	W	2-0
25 Dec	Preston Hornets	H	W	5-0
26 Dec	Chatham	A	D	2-2
27 Dec	Reading T	H	W	5-1
4 Jan	Windsor Phoenix	H	W	3-1
18 Jan	Old Harrovians	H	W	2-1
25 Jan	Foxes	H	W	7-2
8 Feb	Chiswick Park	H	D	1-1
1 Mar	Birmingham St Georges	H	L	1-4
15 Mar	Ilford	A	W	4-1
29 Mar	Clapton	A	L	0-2
31 Mar	Mr W.H. Loraine's XI	H	W	3-1
7 Apr	1st Lincs. Regt	H	W	2-1
12 Apr	Great Marlow	H	W	3-1
19 Apr	Chatham	H	W	1-0
26 Apr	Claptonians	H	W	6-1
3 May	London Cal/ Claptonians Comb	H	W	3-2
10 May	Millwall Ath	A	D	3-3

● FA CUP

5 Oct	Lyndhurst (Q1)	H	W	11-0
26 Oct	Thorpe (Q2)	A	D	2-2*
16 Nov	Crusaders (Q3)	H	W	5-2
7 Dec	Swifts (Q4)	H	L	1-5
	*Thorpe withdrew			

● LONDON SENIOR CUP

2 Nov	Unity	H	W	4-1
23 Nov	Foxes	H	W	4-1
14 Dec	St Martins Ath	H	W	6-0
11 Jan	London Cal	H	W	3-1
8 Mar	Old Westminster (F)	*	L	0-1
	*At Kennington Oval			

● LONDON CHARITY CUP

1 Feb	Great Marlow	H	W	4-1
22 Feb	2nd Batt Scots Guards	H	W	3-0
5 Apr	Old Westminsters (F)	*	W	3-1
	*at Leyton			

● KENT SENIOR CUP

12 Oct	5th Northern Fusilliers	H	W	6-1
9 Nov	West Kent	H	W	10-1
14 Dec	Gravesend	H	W	7-2
15 Feb	Chatham	H	W	5-0
22 Mar	Thanet W (F)	*	W	3-0
	*at Chatham			

● SIX-A-SIDE COMPETITION

Run by National Physical Recreation Society at Agricultural Hall

31 May	London Cal	W	15-7

● 1ST TEAM RECORD

P	W	D	L	F	A
41	31	5	5	158	49

SEASON 1890-1891

● FRIENDLIES

6 Sep	93rd Highlanders	H	D	1-1
13 Sep	Casuals	H	W	5-4
20 Sep	Ilford	H	W	6-0
27 Sep	London Cal	H	W	3-1
4 Oct	Chiswick Park	A	W	4-0
11 Oct	93rd Highlanders	H	W	4-1
18 Oct	Old St Marks	A	W	4-0
25 Oct	St Bartholomew's Hospital	H	W	1-0
1 Nov	South Shore (Blackpool)	H	D	2-2
8 Nov	Ilford	A	W	3-0
15 Nov	Clapton	A	L	1-2
22 Nov	Gainsborough Trin	H	W	2-1
1 Dec	Cambridge Univ	H	W	5-1
6 Dec	Casuals	H	D	0-0
24 Jan	Millwall Ath	A	W	1-0
26 Jan	Everton	H	L	0-5
7 Feb	St Bartholomew's Hospital	H	W	5-4
14 Mar	Old Harrovians	H	W	5-1
21 Mar	Sheffield U	H	D	1-1
27 Mar	71st Highland Light Infantry	H	W	3-1
28 Mar	Old Harrovians	H	W	5-0
30 Mar	Heart of Midlothian	H	L	1-5
31 Mar	Nottingham F	H	L	0-5
18 Apr	Clapton	H	W	3-1
25 Apr	Sunderland	H	L	1-3
30 Apr	London Cal	H	D	1-1
2 May	1st Highland Light Infantry	H	W	5-1
3 Jan	London Cal*			
	*abandoned			

● FA CUP

17 Jan	Derby Co (1)	H	L	1-2

● LONDON SENIOR CUP

13 Dec	Old Westminsters	A	W	4-1

31 Jan	Old Westminsters	A	L	4-5*
21 Feb	Casuals	H	W	3-2
28 Feb	Clapton	A‡	W	3-2
7 Mar	St Bart's Hospital	‡	W	6-0
	*(aet)			
	‡at Kennington Oval			

● **LONDON CHARITY CUP**

14 Feb	Crusaders	H	W	1-0
4 Apr	Old Carthusians	A*	D	1-1
7 Apr	Old Carthusians	A*	D	2-2
11 Apr	Old Carthusians	A*	L	1-2
	*at Leyton			

● **1ST TEAM RECORD**

P	W	D	L	F	A
37	22	7	6	98	58

SEASON 1891-1892

● **FRIENDLIES**

5 Sep	Sheffield U	H	L	0-2
12 Sep	Casuals	H	W	2-1
19 Sep	Gainsborough Trin	H	L	1-4
26 Sep	WBA	H	D	1-1
3 Oct	Birmingham St Georges	H	L	1-5
8 Oct	Royal Engineers	H	W	8-0
10 Oct	Crusaders	H	W	4-1
17 Oct	Bootle	A	D	2-2
19 Oct	Sheffield Wed	H	L	1-8
24 Oct	Long Eaton Ran	H	W	3-1
29 Oct	Royal Artillery	H	W	10-0
31 Oct	Clapton	A	W	7-0
5 Nov	Notts Co	A	L	3-4
7 Nov	London Cal	A	W	4-3
12 Nov	Erith	H	W	7-0
14 Nov	Cambridge Univ	H	W	5-1
19 Nov	Woolwich League	H	W	6-1
21 Nov	St Bart's Hospital	H	W	9-0
23 Nov	2nd Scots Guards	H	W	6-0
28 Nov	Canadians	H	D	1-1
30 Nov	Sheffield Wed	A	L	1-5
3 Dec	Canadians	H	W	4-0
5 Dec	Lincoln C	H	W	3-1
10 Dec	2nd Royal West Kent Reg	H	L	1-2
12 Dec	Chiswick Park	H	W	5-1
19 Dec	Preston NE	H	L	0-3
25 Dec	Sheffield U	A	D	3-3
26 Dec	1st Lincolnshire Regt	H	W	6-0
2 Jan	Cowlairs (Glasgow)	H	L	1-2
7 Jan	City Ramblers	H	W	3-0
9 Jan	Crusaders	H	W	4-1
21 Jan	Windsor Phoenix	H	W	3-1
23 Jan	Grimsby T	H	W	4-1
30 Jan	Burton W	H	W	3-1

4 Feb	Sheffield U	H	L	1-4
6 Feb	Cambridge Univ	H	W	2-1
13 Feb	Chatham	H	W	3-2
20 Feb	Burton Swifts	H	W	3-1
25 Feb	Windsor Phoenix	A	W	5-0
27 Feb	Derby Co	H	L	3-4
3 Mar	Borough Road Coll	H	W	5-1
5 Mar	Wolverhampton W	H	L	1-4
10 Mar	Casuals	H	W	3-1
12 Mar	Great Marlow	A	W	5-2
14 Mar	3rd Lanark Rov	H	L	0-1
19 Mar	Highland Light Infantry	H	W	3-2
22 Mar	Preston NE	H	D	3-3
26 Mar	Everton	H	D	2-2
31 Mar	Notts Co	H	L	2-4
2 Apr	Chatham	H	W	5-3
9 Apr	South Shore	H	D	1-1
15 Apr	Small Heath	H	L	1-2
16 Apr	Crewe Alexandra	H	W	2-1
18 Apr	Bootle	H	D	1-1
23 Apr	Clapton	H	W	4-1
26 Apr	Bolton W	H	W	3-2
30 Apr	Glasgow Ran	H	L	2-3

● **FA CUP**

16 Jan	Small Heath (1)		L	1-5

● **1ST TEAM RECORD**

P	W	D	L	F	A
58	33	8	17	183	107

SEASON 1892-1893

● **FRIENDLIES**

2 Sep	Highland Light Infantry	H	W	9-0
7 Sep	Gainsborough Trin	H	W	4-2
8 Sep	2nd Scots Guards	H	W	5-1
10 Sep	Casuals	H	L	2-4
12 Sep	Sheffield U	A	L	0-1
16 Sep	Darlington	H	W	3-2
24 Sep	Crusaders	H	W	4-0
1 Oct	Marlow	H	W	4-0
6 Oct	3rd West Kent Ran	H	W	3-0
8 Oct	Clapton		W	4-1
20 Oct	Sheffield U	H	W	1-0
22 Oct	Staffordshire Regt		W	1-0
27 Oct	Oxford Univ	L		0-4
5 Nov	Lincoln C	H	W	4-0
7 Nov	Fleetwood Ran	L		1-2
12 Nov	Cambridge Univ	H	D	6-6
14 Nov	Sunderland	H	L	0-4
23 Nov	Ipswich T	A	W	5-0
25 Nov	Norfolk Co	A	W	4-1
26 Nov	Clapton	A	W	5-0
3 Dec	WBA	H	W	3-1

12 Dec	Mr F.G. Armitage's XI		W	3-1
17 Dec	Nottingham F	H	L	2-3
23 Dec	Leith Ath	H	W	1-0
25 Dec	Burslem PV	L		1-3
26 Dec	Stockton	W		1-0
27 Dec	Blackpool	H	D	1-1
2 Jan	Glasgow Thistle	H	L	1-2
7 Jan	Middlesbrough Ironopolis	L		0-2
11 Jan	Sussex Martlets	A	W	2-0
14 Jan	Wolverhampton W	H	L	1-3
25 Jan	Oxford Univ	A	L	0-1
28 Jan	Chatham	A	L	1-3
31 Jan	1st Batt Sherwood Foresters	A	W	3-0
3 Feb	Casuals	A	W	4-1
6 Feb	Royal Lancaster Regt	H	W	2-0
9 Feb	Cambridge Univ	A	L	2-4
11 Feb	Small Heath	H	W	3-1
13 Feb	3rd Lanark	H	W	3-0
18 Feb	Millwall Ath	H	W	5-0
25 Feb	Walsall T Swifts	H	W	4-0
27 Feb	Notts Greenhalgh	H	L	1-3
3 Mar	Middlesbrough Ironopolis	H	L	0-2
11 Mar	Dumbarton	H	W	3-1
13 Mar	Aston Villa	H	L	0-1
18 Mar	Middlesbrough Ironopolis	H	W	3-0
25 Mar	Millwall Ath	A	W	1-0
31 Mar	Middlesbrough	H	W	4-1
1 Apr	Accrington Stanley	H	W	3-1
3 Apr	Grimsby T	H	L	3-5
8 Apr	Crusaders	A	W	3-0
15 Apr	Casuals	A	W	2-0
22 Apr	Derby Co	H	D	0-0
24 Apr	London Welsh	H	W	4-2
26 Apr	Sevenoaks	A	W	11-0
28 Apr	Stoke C	H	L	0-1

● FA CUP

15 Oct	Highland Light Infantry (Q1)	H	W	3-0
29 Oct	City Ramblers (Q2)	H	W	10-1
19 Nov	Millwall Ath (Q3)	H	W	3-2
10 Dec	Clapton (Q4)	H	W	5-0
21 Jan	Sunderland (1)	A	L	0-1

● 1ST TEAM RECORD

P	W	D	L	F	A
61	40	3	18	164	75

SEASON 1893-1894

● FOOTBALL LEAGUE (DIVISION 2)

2 Sep	Newcastle U	H	D	2-2
9 Sep	Notts Co	A	L	2-3
11 Sep	Walsall T Swifts	H	W	4-0
25 Sep	Grimsby T	H	W	3-1
30 Sep	Newcastle U	A	L	0-6
21 Oct	Small Heath	A	L	1-4
28 Oct	Liverpool	H	L	0-5
11 Nov	Ardwick	H	W	1-0
13 Nov	Rotherham T	H	W	3-0
18 Nov	Burton Swifts	A	L	2-6
9 Dec	Northwich Victoria	A	D	2-2
25 Dec	Burslem PV	H	W	4-1
26 Dec	Grimsby T	A	L	1-3
30 Dec	Ardwick	A	W	1-0
1 Jan	Liverpool	A	L	0-2
6 Jan	Burslem	A	L	1-2
3 Feb	Lincoln C	A	L	0-3
6 Feb	Rotherham	A	D	1-1
10 Feb	Crewe Alexandra	H	W	3-2
12 Feb	Walsall	A	W	2-1
17 Feb	Lincoln C	H	W	4-0
24 Feb	Middlesbrough Ironopolis	A	W	6-3
3 Mar	Crewe Alexandra	A	D	0-0
10 Mar	Middlesbrough Ironopolis	H	W	1-0
23 Mar	Northwich Victoria	H	W	6-0
24 Mar	Notts Co	H	L	1-2
31 Mar	Small Heath	H	L	1-4
14 Apr	Burton Swifts	H	L	0-2

● FA CUP

14 Oct	Ashford Univ (Q1)	H	W	12-0
4 Nov	Clapton Orient (Q2)	H	W	6-2
25 Nov	Millwall Ath (Q3)	H	W	2-0
16 Dec	2nd Scots Guards (Q4)	A	W	2-1
27 Jan	Sheffield Wed (1)	H	L	1-2

● FRIENDLIES

4 Sep	Doncaster Rov	H	W	4-1
16 Sep	Chatham	H	W	5-0
23 Sep	Middlesbrough Ironopolis	H	W	4-1
7 Oct	Casuals	H	W	5-1
9 Oct	Sunderland	H	L	1-4
12 Oct	London Cal	H	W	10-3
23 Oct	Mr Roston Bourke's XI	H	W	4-3
30 Oct	Wolverhampton W	H	W	1-0
30 Nov	London Cal	A	D	1-1
2 Dec	WBA	A	W	5-0
11 Dec	Preston NE	H	D	1-1*
23 Dec	Crusaders	H	W	7-0
3 Jan	Sussex	A	W	4-1
13 Jan	Accrington Stanley	H	W	2-0
15 Jan	Aston Villa	H	L	1-3
20 Jan	Chatham	A	W	4-0
29 Jan	Blackpool	H	W	5-2
1 Mar	London Cal	H	W	1-0
5 Mar	Luton T	H	W	2-0

12 Mar	Sheffield U	A	W	2-0
17 Mar	Millwall Ath	A	D	2-2
26 Mar	St Mirren	H	L	1-3
2 Apr	Nottingham F	H	L	1-3
7 Apr	Millwall Ath	A	W	4-1
9 Apr	Sheffield U	H	L	0-1
11 Apr	New Brompton	A	W	4-2‡
12 Apr	Westerham District XI	A	W	6-3
16 Apr	Luton T	A	D	3-3
21 Apr	Burnley	H	W	2-0
25 Apr	Corinthians	A°	L	3-4
28 Apr	Stoke	H	D	3-3

*abandoned after 80 minutes
‡abandoned after 85 minutes
° at Leyton

● **POSITION IN FOOTBALL LEAGUE TABLE**

	P	W	D	L	F	A	Pts
1st Liverpool	28	22	0	6	77	18	50
9th Woolwich Arsenal	28	12	4	12	52	55	28

SEASON 1894-1895

● **FOOTBALL LEAGUE (DIVISION 2)**

1 Sep	Lincoln C	A	L	2-5
10 Sep	Grimsby T	H	L	1-3
15 Sep	Burton Swifts	A	L	0-3
22 Sep	Bury	H	W	4-2
29 Sep	Manchester C	H	W	4-2
6 Oct	Lincoln C	H	W	5-2
13 Oct	Newton Heath	A	D	3-3
20 Oct	Rotherham	A	W	2-1
27 Oct	Notts Co	A	D	2-2
3 Nov	Notts Co	H	W	2-1
10 Nov	Walsall T Swifts	A	L	1-4
24 Nov	Newcastle U	A	W	4-2
8 Dec	Darwen	H	W	4-0
15 Dec	Manchester C	A	L	1-4
25 Dec	Burslem PV	H	W	7-0
26 Dec	Grimsby T	A	L	2-4
1 Jan	Darwen	A	L	1-3
7 Jan	Leicester Fosse	A	L	1-3
12 Jan	Newcastle U	H	W	3-2
19 Jan	Burslem PV	A	W	1-0
26 Jan	Burton W	H	D	1-1
9 Feb	Rotherham	H	D	1-1
23 Feb	Burton Swifts	H*	W	3-0
2 Mar	Bury	A	L	0-2
9 Mar	Leicester Fosse	H‡	D	3-3
23 Mar	Crewe Alexandra	A	D	0-0
30 Mar	Newton Heath	H	W	3-2
6 Apr	Crewe Alexandra	H	W	7-0
12 Apr	Walsall T Swifts	H	W	6-1
20 Apr	Burton W	A	L	1-2

*at New Brompton
‡at Leyton

● **FA CUP**

2 Feb	Bolton W (1)	A	L	0-1

● **FRIENDLIES**

3 Sep	Nottingham F	H	W	3-2
8 Sep	Fleetwood Rov	H	W	4-0
17 Sep	WBA	H	L	0-1
24 Sep	Renton	H	W	6-1
4 Oct	Casuals	*	W	8-0
15 Oct	Sunderland	H	W	2-1
29 Oct	Luton T	H	W	5-0
12 Nov	Mr Roston Bourke's XI	H	W	6-2
17 Nov	Casuals	H	W	4-1
21 Nov	Marlow	A	W	4-2
1 Dec	Stoke C	H	W	3-1
3 Dec	St Bernards	H	L	1-2
24 Dec	New Brompton	A	L	0-5
29 Dec	Dresden University	H	W	1-0
5 Jan	Sheppey U	A	W	6-1
11 Feb	Luton T	A	W	2-1
16 Feb	Chatham	A	W	6-0
25 Feb	Liverpool	H‡	W	4-3
6 Mar	Eastbourne	A	W	5-1
13 Mar	Bromley & District	A	W	4-1
16 Mar	Gainsborough Trin	H	W	2-0
20 Mar	Home Park	A	W	2-1
21 Mar	Weymouth Ath	A	W	5-0
25 Mar	Millwall	H	D	1-1
1 Apr	Blackburn Rov	H	D	2-2
8 Apr	Millwall	A	D	0-0§
13 Apr	Dumbarton	H	W	5-1
15 Apr	Small Heath	H	L	3-4
25 Apr	Royal Ordnance	H	L	0-1
27 Apr	Millwall	A	W	3-1
30 Apr	Grimsby T	H	L	0-2

*played at Leyton
‡played at Hornsey
°played at Gravesend
§abandoned after 85 minutes

● **POSITION IN FOOTBALL LEAGUE TABLE**

	P	W	D	L	F	A	Pts
1st Bury	30	23	2	5	78	33	48
8th Woolwich Arsenal	30	14	6	10	75	58	34

SEASON 1895-1896

● **FOOTBALL LEAGUE (DIVISION 2)**

2 Sep	Grimsby T	H	W	3-1
7 Sep	Manchester C	H	L	0-1
14 Sep	Lincoln C	A	D	1-1
21 Sep	Lincoln C	H	W	4-0
28 Sep	Manchester C	A	L	0-1
5 Oct	Rotherham T	H	W	5-0
12 Oct	Burton W	H	W	3-0

19 Oct	Burton Swifts	H	W	5-0
26 Oct	Rotherham T	A	L	0-3
2 Oct	Notts Co	A	W	4-3
9 Nov	Newton Heath	H	W	2-1
16 Nov	Liverpool	H	L	0-2
30 Nov	Newton Heath	A	L	1-5
7 Dec	Leicester Fosse	H	D	1-1
14 Dec	Burton W	A	L	1-4
21 Dec	Burton Swifts	A	L	2-3
23 Dec	Crewe Alexandra	A	W	1-0
25 Dec	Burslem PV	H	W	2-1
4 Jan	Loughborough T	H	W	6-0
11 Jan	Liverpool	A	L	0-3
18 Jan	Newcastle U	A	L	1-3
25 Jan	Leicester Fosse	A	L	0-1
15 Feb	Burslem PV	A	W	2-0
29 Feb	Loughborough T	A	L	1-2
7 Mar	Notts Co	H	W	2-0
14 Mar	Darwen	A	D	1-1
21 Mar	Crewe Alexandra	H	W	7-0
4 Mar	Grimsby T	A	D	1-1
6 Apr	Newcastle U	H	W	2-1
18 Apr	Darwen	H	L	1-3

● FA CUP

2 Feb	Burnley (1)	A	L	1-6

● FRIENDLIES

9 Sep	Millwall Ath	A	W	3-1
23 Sep	Sheffield Wed	H	W	2-1
14 Oct	Everton	H	L	0-2
14 Nov	Royal Ordnance	H	W	3-1
21 Nov	Casuals	A	W	3-0
23 Nov	Barnsley St Peters	H	W	4-1
9 Dec	Sunderland	H	L	1-2
26 Dec	Cliftonville	H	W	10-1
28 Dec	Darlington	H	W	6-2
1 Jan	Hastings	A	W	12-0
20 Jan	Cambridge Univ	H	W	7-1
10 Feb	Royal Ordnance	H	W	6-0
22 Feb	E Stirlingshire	H	W	5-0
24 Feb	Newton Heath	H	W	6-1
2 Mar	Casuals	H	W	4-1
16 Mar	Tottenham H	H	L	1-3
23 Mar	Sheffield U	H	W	3-1
26 Mar	Tottenham H	A	W	3-1
28 Mar	Millwall	A	W	3-1
2 Apr	Stockton	H	W	2-0
3 Apr	Dundee	H	W	3-1
8 Apr	Gravesend	A	W	4-0
11 Apr	Millwall	H	D	2-2
13 Apr	Everton	H	W	2-1
20 Apr	Mr Nat Whittaker's XI	H	W	3-2
25 Apr	Luton T	H	W	5-2
27 Apr	Luton T	A	L	0-2
29 Apr	Chatham	A	W	1-0
30 Apr	Tottenham H	A	L	2-3

● POSITION IN FOOTBALL LEAGUE TABLE

	P	W	D	L	F	A	Pts
1st Liverpool	30	22	2	6	106	32	46
7th Woolwich Arsenal	30	14	4	12	59	42	32

SEASON 1896-1897

● FOOTBALL LEAGUE (DIVISION 2)

5 Sep	Manchester City	A	D	1-1
12 Sep	Walsall	H	D	1-1
14 Sep	Burton W	A	W	3-0
19 Sep	Loughborough T	H	W	2-0
26 Sep	Notts Co	H	L	2-3
12 Oct	Burton W	H	W	3-0
17 Oct	Walsall	A	L	3-5
24 Oct	Gainsborough Trin	H	W	6-1
7 Nov	Notts Co	A	L	4-7
14 Nov	Small Heath	A	L	2-5
28 Nov	Grimsby T	H	W	4-2
5 Dec	Lincoln C	A	W	3-2
12 Dec	Loughborough T	A	L	0-8
19 Dec	Blackpool	H	W	4-2
25 Dec	Lincoln C	H	W	6-2
26 Dec	Gainsborough Trin	A	L	1-4
1 Jan	Darwen	A	L	1-4
4 Jan	Blackpool	A	D	1-1
23 Jan	Newcastle U	A	L	0-2
13 Feb	Leicester Fosse	A	L	3-6
20 Feb	Burton Swifts	H	W	3-0
13 Mar	Burton Swifts	A	W	2-1
22 Mar	Newton Heath	A	D	1-1
29 Mar	Small Heath	H	L	2-3
3 Apr	Newton Heath	H	L	0-2
8 Apr	Grimsby T	A	L	1-3
16 Apr	Newcastle U	H	W	5-1
17 Apr	Leicester Fosse	H	W	2-1
19 Apr	Darwen	H	W	1-0
28 Apr	Manchester City	H	L	1-2

● FA CUP

12 Dec	Leyton (Q)	H	W	5-2
2 Jan	Chatham (Q)	H	W	4-0
16 Jan	Millwall Ath (Q)	A	L	2-4

● UNITED LEAGUE

7 Sep	Rushden	H	W	3-2
3 Oct	Luton T	H	D	2-2
5 Oct	Rushden	A	L	3-5
19 Oct	Wellingborough	H	W	2-1
2 Nov	Kettering T	H	D	1-1
9 Nov	Tottenham H	H	W	2-1
23 Nov	Kettering T	A	W	1-0
30 Nov	Wellingbrough	A	L	1-4
9 Jan	Loughborough T	H	W	5-3
25 Feb	Tottenham H	A	D	2-2

27 Feb	Millwall Ath	H	W	3-1
20 Mar	Luton T	A	L	2-5
7 Apr	Loughborough T	A	L	0-4
24 Apr	Millwall Ath	A	L	1-3

● FRIENDLIES

1 Sep	Rossendale	H	W	4-0
10 Sep	Millwall Ath	A	W	2-1
10 Oct	Millwall Ath	H	L	1-5
26 Oct	Luton T	A	L	1-3
31 Oct	Clyde	H	L	2-3
21 Nov	Millwall Ath	H	D	2-2
7 Dec	Aston Villa	H	L	1-3
30 Jan	Ilkeston	H	W	7-0
8 Feb	Luton T	H	W	5-1
15 Feb	Glasgow Celtic	H	L	4-5
1 Mar	Reading	H	W	6-2
6 Mar	Casuals	A	L	3-5
10 Mar	Reading	A	W	2-1
15 Mar	Southampton St Mary's	H	W	2-1
27 Mar	Nottingham F	H	W	1-0
20 Apr	Norfolk Co	A	L	3-4
26 Apr	Sheffield U	H	D	1-1
28 Mar	Southampton St Mary's	A	W	5-1

● POSITION IN FOOTBALL LEAGUE TABLE

	P	W	D	L	F	A	Pts
1st Notts Co	30	19	4	7	92	43	42
10th Woolwich Arsenal	30	13	4	13	68	70	30

POSITION IN UNITED LEAGUE TABLE

	P	W	D	L	F	A	Pts
1st Millwall	14	11	2	1	43	22	23
3rd Woolwich Arsenal	14	6	5	3	28	34	15

SEASON 1897-1898

● FOOTBALL LEAGUE (DIVISION 2)

1 Sep	Grimsby T	H	W	4-1
4 Sep	Newcastle U	A	L	1-4
6 Sep	Burnley	A	L	0-5
11 Sep	Lincoln C	H	D	2-2
18 Sep	Gainsborough Trin	H	W	4-0
25 Sep	Manchester C	A	L	1-4
2 Oct	Luton T	A	W	2-0
9 Oct	Luton T	H	W	3-0
16 Oct	Newcastle U	H	D	0-0
23 Oct	Leicester Fosse	H	L	0-3
6 Nov	Walsall	A	L	2-3
13 Nov	Walsall	H	W	4-0
27 Nov	Blackpool	H	W	2-1
4 Dec	Leicester Fosse	A	L	1-2
18 Dec	Loughborough T	A	W	3-1
27 Dec	Lincoln C	A	W	3-2
1 Jan	Blackpool	A	D	3-3
8 Jan	Newton Heath	H	W	5-1
15 Jan	Burton Swifts	A	W	2-1
5 Feb	Manchester C	H	D	2-2
12 Feb	Grimsby T	A	W	4-1
26 Feb	Newton Heath	A	L	1-5
5 Mar	Small Heath	H	W	4-2
12 Mar	Darwen	A	W	4-1
19 Mar	Loughborough T	H	W	4-0
26 Mar	Gainsborough Trin	A	L	0-1
2 Apr	Burnley	H	D	1-1
9 Apr	Darwen	H	W	3-1
11 Apr	Burton Swifts	H	W	3-0
23 Apr	Small Heath	A	L	1-2

● FA CUP

30 Oct	St Albans (Q)	H	W	9-0
20 Nov	Sheppey U (Q)	H	W	3-0
11 Dec	New Brompton (Q)	H	W	4-2
29 Jan	Burnley (Q)	A	L	1-3

● UNITED LEAGUE

22 Sep	Loughborough T	A	W	3-1
4 Oct	Kettering T	H	W	4-0
11 Oct	Wellingborough	A	W	3-2
13 Dec	Rushden	H	W	3-1
20 Dec	Southampton	H	D	1-1
25 Dec	Tottenham H	H	L	2-3
10 Jan	Wellingborough	H	W	3-1
22 Jan	Millwall Ath	A	D	2-2
19 Feb	Millwall Ath	H	D	2-2
21 Feb	Luton T	H	D	2-2
28 Mar	Rushden	A	W	3-2
1 Apr	Loughborough T	H	W	4-1
4 Apr	Kettering T	A	W	2-1
8 Apr	Tottenham H	A	D	0-0
13 Apr	Southampton	A	L	0-3
16 Apr	Luton T	A	L	1-2

● FRIENDLIES

15 Sep	Gravesend	A	W	3-1
1 Nov	Reading	H	W	3-1
8 Nov	Blackburn Rov	H	W	3-0
15 Nov	Bristol C	A	L	2-4
9 Feb	Maidstone	A	W	3-0
21 Mar	Bristol C	H	W	3-1
26 Apr	Thames Ironworks	A	D	2-2
28 Apr	Tottenham H	H	W	5-0
30 Apr	Millwall Ath	A	L	0-2

● POSITION IN FOOTBALL LEAGUE TABLE

	P	W	D	L	F	A	Pts
1st Burnley	30	20	8	2	80	24	48
5th Woolwich Arsenal	30	16	5	9	69	49	37

POSITION IN UNITED LEAGUE TABLE

	P	W	D	L	F	A	Pts
1st Luton T	16	13	2	1	49	11	28
3rd Woolwich Arsenal	16	8	5	3	35	24	21

SEASON 1898-1899

● FOOTBALL LEAGUE (DIVISION 2)

3 Sep	Luton T	A	W	1-0
5 Sep	Burslem PV	A	L	0-3
10 Sep	Leicester Fosse	H	W	4-0
17 Sep	Darwen	A	W	4-1
24 Sep	Gainsborough Trin	H	W	5-1
1 Oct	Manchester C	A	L	1-3
15 Oct	Walsall	A	L	1-4
22 Oct	Burton Swifts	H	W	2-1
5 Nov	Small Heath	H	W	2-0
12 Nov	Loughborough T	A	D	0-0
26 Nov	Grimsby T	A	L	0-1
3 Dec	Newton Heath	H	W	5-1
10 Dec	New Brighton	A	L	1-3
17 Dec	Lincoln C	H	W	4-2
24 Dec	Barnsley	A	L	1-2
31 Dec	Luton T	H	W	6-2
7 Jan	Leicester Fosse	A	L	1-2
14 Jan	Darwen	H	W	6-0
21 Jan	Gainsborough Trin	A	W	1-0
4 Feb	Glossop NE	A	L	0-2
11 Feb	Walsall	H	D	0-0
13 Feb	Glossop NE	H	W	3-0
18 Feb	Burton Swifts	A	W	2-1
25 Feb	Burslem PV	H	W	1-0
4 Mar	Small Heath	A	L	1-4
13 Mar	Loughborough T	H	W	3-1
18 Mar	Blackpool	H	W	6-0
22 Mar	Blackpool	A	D	1-1
25 Mar	Grimsby T	H	D	1-1
1 Apr	Newton Heath	A	D	2-2
3 Apr	Manchester C	H	L	0-1
8 Apr	New Brighton	H	W	4-0
15 Apr	Lincoln C	A	L	0-2
22 Apr	Barnsley	H	W	3-0

● FA CUP

28 Jan	Derby Co (1)	H	L	0-6

● CHATHAM CHARITY CUP

18 Jan	Chatham	A	D	1-1
20 Feb	Chatham	H	D	3-3
6 Mar	Chatham	A	L	1-2

● UNITED LEAGUE

14 Sep	Reading	A	D	1-1
3 Oct	Reading	H	W	2-0
8 Oct	Millwall Ath	A	D	1-1
10 Oct	Luton T	H	W	3-2
17 Oct	Rushden	H	W	2-0
24 Oct	Kettering T	A	L	1-2
29 Oct	Southampton	A	L	1-5
31 Oct	Brighton U	H	W	5-2
9 Nov	Bristol C	A	W	2-1
14 Nov	Wellingborough	A	L	0-3
19 Nov	Southampton	H	W	2-1
21 Nov	Rushden	A	W	6-0
12 Dec	Bristol C	H	L	1-3
26 Dec	Millwall Ath	H	L	0-1
27 Dec	Luton T	A	D	1-1
4 Jan	Brighton U	A	D	1-1
6 Feb	Kettering T	H	W	4-2
11 Mar	Tottenham H	H	W	2-1
31 Mar	Wellingborough	H	W	3-0
29 Apr	Tottenham H	A	L	2-3

● FRIENDLIES

1 Sep	Gravesend U	H	L	0-1
19 Sep	Thames Ironworks	H	W	4-0
25 Oct	Gravesend U		W	1-0
23 Nov	Corinthians	A*	L	1-4
28 Nov	Chatham	A	L	1-3
8 Dec	Thames Ironworks	A	W	2-1
25 Jan	Sevenoaks	A	W	7-1
30 Jan	Millwall Ath	H	L	2-4
15 Feb	Gravesend U	A	L	2-3
27 Feb	Clapton	A	W	3-0
9 Mar	Casuals	A	W	3-1
23 Mar	Past XI v Present XI●			1-3
4 Apr	Millwall Ath	A‡	D	0-0
24 Apr	Notts Co	H	W	2-1
26 Apr	Woolwich League		W	3-0

*at Kensington
●testimonial for Adam Hayward
‡at Tufnell Park

● POSITION IN FOOTBALL LEAGUE TABLE

	P	W	D	L	F	A	Pts
1st Manchester C	34	23	6	5	92	35	52
7th Woolwich Arsenal	34	18	5	11	72	41	41

● POSITION IN UNITED LEAGUE TABLE

	P	W	D	L	F	A	Pts
1st Millwall	20	14	3	3	42	19	31
4th Woolwich Arsenal	20	10	4	6	40	30	24

SEASON 1899-1900

● FOOTBALL LEAGUE (DIVISION 2)

2 Sep	Leicester Fosse	H	L	0-2
9 Sep	Luton T	A	W	2-1
16 Sep	Burslem PV	H	W	1-0

23 Sep	Walsall	A	L	0-2
30 Sep	Middlesbrough	H	W	3-0
7 Oct	Chesterfield	A	L	1-3
14 Oct	Gainsborough Trin	H	W	2-1
21 Oct	Bolton W	A	L	0-1
4 Nov	Newton Heath	A	L	0-2
11 Nov	Sheffield Wed	H	L	1-2
25 Nov	Small Heath	H	W	3-0
2 Dec	New Brighton	A	W	2-0
16 Dec	Burton Swifts	H	D	1-1
25 Dec	Lincoln C	A	L	0-5
30 Dec	Leicester Fosse	A	D	0-0
6 Jan	Luton T	H	W	3-1
13 Jan	Burslem PV	A	D	1-1
20 Jan	Walsall	H	W	3-1
3 Feb	Middlesbrough	A	L	0-1
10 Feb	Chesterfield	H	W	2-0
17 Feb	Gainsborough Trin	A	D	1-1
24 Feb	Bolton W	H	L	0-1
3 Mar	Loughborough T	A	W	3-2
10 Mar	Newton Heath	H	W	2-1
12 Mar	Loughborough T	H	W	12-0
17 Mar	Sheffield Wed	A	L	1-3
24 Mar	Lincoln C	H	W	2-1
31 Mar	Small Heath	A	l	1-3
7 Apr	New Brighton	H	W	5-0
14 Apr	Grimsby T	A	L	0-1
16 Apr	Grimsby T	H	W	2-0
21 Apr	Burton Swifts	A	L	0-2
23 Apr	Barnsley	A	L	2-3
28 Apr	Barnsley	H	W	5-1

● FA CUP

28 Oct	New Brompton (Q)	H	D	1-1
1 Nov	New Brompton (QR)	A	D	0-0
6 Nov	New Brompton (QR)	A*	D	2-2
8 Nov	New Brompton (QR)	A‡	D	1-1
14 Nov	New Brompton (QR)	A°	L	0-1
	*at Millwall			
	‡at Tottenham			
	°at Gravesend			

● SOUTHERN DISTRICT COMBINATION

11 Sep	Millwall Ath	A	L	0-1
27 Sep	Reading	A	W	3-0
11 Oct	Southampton	A	L	0-3
23 Oct	Portsmouth	H	L	0-2
30 Oct	Bristol C	H	W	3-0
10 Jan	Bristol C	A	W	3-1
29 Jan	Chatham	H	W	4-0
7 Feb	Portsmouth	A	L	1-3
26 Feb	Chatham	A	W	2-1
5 Mar	Southampton	H	W	1-0
19 Mar	QPR	H	W	5-1
26 Mar	Reading	H	D	1-1
2 Apr	Millwall Ath	H	L	0-1
9 Apr	QPR	A	L	0-3
17 Apr	Tottenham H	H	L	2-4

24 Apr	Tottenham H	H	W	2-1*
	*abandoned after 65 minutes			

● FRIENDLIES

4 Sep	Stoke C		W	5-3
2 Oct	Aston Villa		W	1-0
29 Nov	Eastbourne		W	2-1
9 Dec	Southampton		D	1-1
23 Dec	Swindon T		W	2-1
27 Jan	Bedminster		W	3-0
19 Feb	Derby Co		L	0-1
13 Apr	Burnley		W	2-0

● POSITION IN FOOTBALL LEAGUE TABLE

	P	W	D	L	F	A	Pts
1st Sheffield Wed	34	25	4	5	84	22	54
8th Woolwich Arsenal	34	16	4	14	61	43	36

● POSITION IN SOUTHERN DISTRICT COMBINATION LEAGUE

	P	W	D	L	F	A	Pts
1st Millwall Ath	16	12	2	2	30	10	26
4th Woolwich Arsenal	15	7	1	7	25	21	15

(Excluding unfinished match against Tottenham on 24 April)

SEASON 1900-1901

● FOOTBALL LEAGUE (DIVISION 2)

1 Sep	Gainsborough Trin	H	W	2-1
8 Sep	Walsall	H	D	1-1
15 Sep	Burton Swifts	A	L	0-1
22 Sep	Barnsley	H	L	1-2
29 Sep	Chesterfield	H	W	1-0
6 Oct	Blackpool	A	D	1-1
13 Oct	Stockport Co	H	W	2-0
20 Oct	Small Heath	A	L	1-2
27 Oct	Grimsby T	H	D	1-1
3 Nov	Leicester Fosse	H	W	2-1
10 Nov	Newton Heath	H	W	2-1
17 Nov	Glossop NE	A	W	1-0
24 Nov	Middlesbrough	H	W	1-0
1 Dec	Burnley	A	L	0-3
8 Dec	Burslem PV	H	W	3-0
15 Dec	Leicester Fosse	A	L	0-1
22 Dec	New Brighton	H	W	2-1
24 Dec	Walsall	A	L	0-1
29 Dec	Gainsborough Trin	A	L	0-1
12 Jan	Burton Swifts	H	W	3-1
19 Jan	Barnsley	A	L	0-3
26 Jan	Lincoln C	A	D	3-3
16 Feb	Stockport Co	A	L	1-3
19 Feb	Chesterfield	A	W	1-0
2 Mar	Grimsby T	A	L	0-1
9 Mar	Lincoln C	H	D	0-0
16 Mar	Newton Heath	A	L	0-1

23 Mar	Glossop NE	H	W	2-0
30 Mar	Middlesbrough	A	D	1-1
6 Apr	Burnley	H	W	3-1
8 Apr	Blackpool	H	W	3-1
13 Apr	Burslem PV	A	L	0-1
22 Apr	Small Heath	H	W	1-0
27 Apr	New Brighton	A	L	0-1

● FA CUP

5 Jan	Darwen (Q)	A	W	2-0
9 Feb	Blackburn Rov (1)	H	W	2-0
23 Feb	WBA (2)	H	L	0-1

● FRIENDLIES

1 Oct	Aston Villa	H	W	3-0
21 Nov	Southampton	A	L	1-4
25 Dec	West Ham U	H	W	1-0
26 Dec	Newcastle U	H	D	1-1
1 Jan	Newcastle U	A	L	1-5
4 Mar	Southern League XI	H	W	2-1
1 Apr	Millwall	H	D	1-1
5 Apr	Nottingham F	H	D	1-1
20 Apr	Notts Co	H	W	3-0
25 Apr	West Ham U	A	D	0-0

● POSITION IN FOOTBALL LEAGUE TABLE

	P	W	D	L	F	A	Pts
1st Grimsby T	34	20	9	5	60	33	49
7th Woolwich	34	15	6	13	39	35	36
Arsenal							

SEASON 1901-1902

● FOOTBALL LEAGUE (DIVISION 2)

2 Sep	Barnsley	H	W	2-1
4 Sep	Leicester Fosse	H	W	2-0
14 Sep	Preston NE	A	L	0-2
21 Sep	Burnley	H	W	4-0
28 Sep	Burslem PV	A	L	0-1
5 Oct	Chesterfield	H	W	3-2
12 Oct	Gainsborough Trin	A	D	2-2
19 Oct	Middlesbrough	H	L	0-3
26 Oct	Bristol C	A	W	3-0
9 Nov	Stockport Co	A	D	0-0
16 Nov	Newton Heath	H	W	2-0
23 Nov	Glossop NE	A	W	1-0
30 Nov	Doncaster Rov	H	W	1-0
7 Dec	Lincoln C	A	D	0-0
21 Dec	Burton U	H	L	0-1
25 Dec	Blackpool	H	D	0-0
26 Dec	Burslem PV	H	W	3-1
28 Dec	Barnsley	A	L	0-2
4 Jan	Leicester Fosse	A	L	1-2
11 Jan	Preston NE	H	D	0-0
18 Jan	Burnley	A	D	0-0
1 Feb	Chesterfield	A	W	3-1
8 Feb	Gainsborough Trin	H	W	5-0
15 Feb	Middlesbrough	A	L	0-1

22 Feb	Bristol C	H	W	2-0
1 Mar	Blackpool	A	W	3-1
8 Mar	Stockport Co	H	W	3-0
15 Mar	Newton Heath	A	W	1-0
22 Mar	Glossop NE	H	W	4-0
29 Mar	Doncaster Rov	A	L	0-1
31 Mar	WBA	H	W	2-1
5 Apr	Lincoln C	H	W	2-0
12 Apr	WBA	A	L	1-2
19 Apr	Burton U	A	L	0-2

● FA CUP

14 Dec	Luton T (Q)	H	D	1-1
18 Dec	Luton T (QR)	A	W	2-0
25 Jan	Newcastle U (1)	H	L	0-2

● SOUTHERN PROFESSIONAL CHARITY CUP

7 Apr	Portsmouth	A	W	2-1
23 Apr	Tottenham H (SF)	H	D	0-0
29 Apr	Tottenham H (SF)	A	L	1-2

● LONDON LEAGUE

16 Sep	Tottenham H	H	L	0-2
30 Sep	Millwall	H	D	1-1
21 Oct	West Ham U	H	L	0-1
4 Nov	Tottenham H	A	L	0-5
3 Feb	QPR	A	D	2-2
17 Feb	QPR	H	W	3-0
24 Feb	Millwall	A	L	1-2
28 Mar	West Ham U	A	W	2-0

● FRIENDLIES

2 Nov	Reading	H	W	1-0
18 Nov	Southampton	H	L	0-1
1 Apr	Blackburn Rov	H	W	2-0
25 Apr	Plymouth Arg	A	W	4-1
26 Apr	WBA	H*	L	0-1
	*at Exeter			

● POSITION IN FOOTBALL LEAGUE TABLE

	P	W	D	L	F	A	Pts
1st WBA	34	25	5	4	82	29	55
4th Woolwich	34	18	6	10	50	26	42
Arsenal							

● POSITION IN LONDON LEAGUE TABLE

	P	W	D	L	F	A	Pts
1st West Ham U	8	5	1	2	19	9	11
5th Woolwich	8	2	2	4	9	13	6
Arsenal							

SEASON 1902-1903

● FOOTBALL LEAGUE (DIVISION 2)

6 Sep	Preston NE	A	D	2-2
13 Sep	Burslem PV	H	W	3-0
20 Sep	Barnsley	A	D	1-1

27 Sep	Gainsborough Trin	H	W	6-1
4 Oct	Bristol C	A	L	0-1
11 Oct	Bristol C	H	W	2-1
18 Oct	Glossop NE	A	W	2-1
25 Oct	Manchester U	H	L	0-1
1 Nov	Manchester C	H	W	1-0
8 Nov	Blackpool	H	W	2-1
15 Nov	Burnley	A	W	3-0
22 Nov	Doncaster Rov	A	W	1-0
29 Nov	Lincoln C	H	W	2-1
6 Dec	Small Heath	A	L	0-2
20 Dec	Manchester C	A	L	1-4
25 Dec	Burton Un	A	L	1-2
27 Dec	Burnley	H	W	5-1
1 Jan	Stockport Co	A	W	1-0
3 Jan	Preston NE	H	W	3-1
10 Jan	Burslem PV	A	D	1-1
17 Jan	Barnsley	H	W	4-0
24 Jan	Gainsborough Trin	A	W	1-0
31 Jan	Burton Un	H	W	3-0
14 Feb	Glossop NE	H	D	0-0
28 Feb	Stockport Co	H	W	3-1
7 Mar	Blackpool	A	D	0-0
9 Mar	Manchester U	A	L	0-3
14 Mar	Chesterfield	A	D	2-2
21 Mar	Doncaster Rov	H	W	3-0
28 Mar	Lincoln C	A	D	2-2
4 Apr	Small Heath	H	W	6-1
10 Apr	Chesterfield	H	W	3-0
11 Apr	Leicester Fosse	A	W	2-0
13 Apr	Leicester Fosse	H	D	0-0

● FA CUP

13 Dec	Brentford*	A	D	1-1
17 Dec	Brentford(R)*	H	W	5-0
7 Feb	Sheffield U (1)	H	L	1-3
	*supplementary round			

● SOUTHERN PROFESSIONAL CHARITY CUP

| 9 Feb | Millwall Ath | H | L | 2-3 |

● LONDON LEAGUE

1 Sep	West Ham U	A	W	3-1
15 Sep	QPR	H	W	3-1
27 Oct	QPR	A	W	2-0
10 Nov	Brentford	H	W	3-0
17 Nov	Tottenham H	H	W	2-1
1 Dec	Tottenham H	A	L	0-1
26 Dec	Millwall	A	L	0-3
21 Feb	West Ham U	H	L	0-1
23 Mar	Brentford	A	W	1-0
18 Apr	Millwall	H	L	0-2

● FRIENDLIES

| 8 Sep | New Brompton | A | W | 3-2 |
| 18 Mar | Brighton & HA | A | W | 3-1 |

14 Apr	Northampton T	A	D	1-1
20 Apr	Bristol C	A	W	2-1
25 Apr	Chesterfield	H	W	1-0

● POSITION IN FOOTBALL LEAGUE TABLE

		P	W	D	L	F	A	Pts
1st	Manchester C	34	25	4	5	95	29	54
3rd	Woolwich Arsenal	34	20	8	6	66	30	48

● POSITION IN LONDON LEAGUE TABLE

		P	W	D	L	F	A	Pts
1st	Tottenham H	10	7	1	2	19	4	15
3rd	Woolwich Arsenal	10	6	0	4	14	10	12

SEASON 1903-1904

● FOOTBALL LEAGUE (DIVISION 2)

5 Sep	Blackpool	H	W	3-0
12 Sep	Gainsborough Trin	A	W	2-0
19 Sep	Burton U	H	W	8-0
26 Sep	Bristol C	A	W	4-0
3 Oct	Manchester U	H	W	4-0
10 Oct	Glossop NE	A	W	3-1
24 Oct	Burslem PV	A	W	3-2
26 Oct	Leicester Fosse	H	W	8-0
31 Oct	Barnsley	A	L	1-2
7 Nov	Lincoln C	H	W	4-0
21 Nov	Chesterfield	H	W	6-0
28 Nov	Bolton W	A	L	1-2
19 Dec	Grimsby T	H	W	5-1
25 Dec	Bradford C	H	W	4-1
26 Dec	Leicester Fosse	A	D	0-0
1 Jan	Stockport Co	A	D	0-0
2 Jan	Blackpool	A	D	2-2
9 Jan	Gainsborough Trin	H	W	6-0
16 Jan	Burton U	A	L	1-3
30 Jan	Manchester U	A	L	0-1
27 Feb	Barnsley	H	W	3-0
29 Feb	Burnley	H	W	4-0
5 Mar	Lincoln C	A	W	2-0
12 Mar	Stockport Co	H	W	5-2
14 Mar	Bristol C	H	W	2-0
19 Mar	Chesterfield	A	L	0-1
26 Mar	Bolton W	H	W	3-0
1 Apr	Preston NE	A	D	0-0
2 Apr	Burnley	A	L	0-1
4 Apr	Glossop NE	H	W	2-1
9 Apr	Preston NE	H	D	0-0
16 Apr	Grimsby T	A	D	2-2
19 Apr	Bradford C	A	W	3-0
25 Apr	Burslem PV	H	D	0-0

● FA CUP

| 12 Dec | Bristol Rov* | A | D | 1-1 |

15 Dec	Bristol Rov (R)*	H	D	1-1
21 Dec	Bristol Rov (R)*	A‡	W	1-0
6 Feb	Fulham (1)	H	W	1-0
20 Feb	Manchester C (2)	H	L	0-2
	*supplementary round			
	‡at Tottenham H			

● **SOUTHERN PROFESSIONAL CHARITY CUP**

12 Oct	West Ham U	H	W	1-0
18 Jan	Reading (SF)	*	W	3-1
28 Apr	Millwall Ath (F)	H	L	1-2
	*at Tottenham			

● **LONDON LEAGUE**

1 Sep	Tottenham H	A	W	1-0
7 Sep	Fulham	H	W	2-0
14 Sep	West Ham U	H	W	4-1
14 Nov	Tottenham H	H	D	1-1
23 Nov	Brentford	A	D	1-1
7 Dec	Millwall	H	L	1-3
11 Jan	QPR	H	W	6-2
8 Feb	Brentford	H	W	3-2
22 Feb	West Ham U	A	W	4-2
7 Mar	Millwall	A	L	0-3
21 Mar	QPR	A	L	1-3
30 Apr	Fulham	A	L	0-1

● **FRIENDLIES**

| 17 Oct | Luton T | | D | 2-2 |
| 30 Nov | Army | | W | 4-0 |

● **POSITION IN FOOTBALL LEAGUE TABLE**

	P	W	D	L	F	A	Pts
1st Preston NE	34	20	10	4	62	24	50
2nd Woolwich Arsenal	34	21	7	6	91	22	49

● **POSITION IN LONDON LEAGUE TABLE**

	P	W	D	L	F	A	Pts
1st Millwall Ath	12	11	1	0	38	8	23
3rd Woolwich Arsenal	12	6	2	4	24	19	14

SEASON 1904-1905

● **FOOTBALL LEAGUE (DIVISION 1)**

3 Sep	Newcastle U	A	L	0-3
10 Sep	Preston NE	H	D	0-0
17 Sep	Middlesbrough	A	L	0-1
24 Sep	Wolverhampton W	H	W	2-0
1 Oct	Bury	A	D	1-1
8 Oct	Aston Villa	H	W	1-0
15 Oct	Blackburn Rov	A	D	1-1
22 Oct	Nottingham F	H	L	0-3
29 Oct	Sheffield Wed	A	W	3-0
5 Nov	Sunderland	H	D	0-0
12 Nov	Stoke C	H	W	2-1
19 Nov	Derby Co	A	D	0-0
3 Dec	Small Heath	A	L	1-2
10 Dec	Manchester C	H	W	1-0
17 Dec	Notts Co	A	W	5-1
24 Dec	Sheffield U	H	W	1-0
26 Dec	Aston Villa	A	L	1-3
27 Dec	Nottingham F	A	W	3-0
28 Dec	Sheffield U	A	L	0-4
31 Dec	Newcastle U	H	L	0-2
7 Jan	Preston NE	A	L	0-3
14 Jan	Middlesbrough	H	D	1-1
21 Jan	Wolverhampton W	A	L	1-4
28 Jan	Bury	H	W	2-1
11 Feb	Blackburn Rov	H	W	2-0
25 Feb	Sheffield Wed	H	W	3-0
4 Mar	Sunderland	A	D	1-1
11 Mar	Stoke C	A	L	0-2
18 Mar	Derby Co	H	D	0-0
1 Apr	Small Heath	H	D	1-1
5 Apr	Everton	A	L	0-1
8 Apr	Manchester C	A	L	0-1
15 Apr	Notts Co	H	L	1-2
22 Apr	Everton	H	W	2-1

● **FA CUP**

| 4 Feb | Bristol C (1) | H | D | 0-0 |
| 8 Feb | Bristol C (1R) | A | L | 0-1 |

● **SOUTHERN PROFESSIONAL CHARITY CUP**

| 10 Oct | Tottenham H | H | L | 1-3 |

● **FRIENDLIES**

1 Sep	Bristol C	H	W	3-2
12 Sep	West Ham U	A	D	1-1
31 Oct	Cambridge Univ	H	W	3-0
22 Nov	Cambridge Univ	A	W	4-3
5 Dec	Parisian XI	H	W	26-1
18 Feb	Corinthians	A*	L	1-2
27 Feb	Queens Park (Glasgow)	H	W	6-1
25 Mar	Burnley	H	W	3-0
12 Apr	Southend Ath	A	W	2-0
21 Apr	New Brompton	H	W	3-1
24 Apr	Dundee	H	W	3-0
26 Apr	Ipswich T	A	W	3-1
27 Apr	Norwich C	A	L	1-2
29 Apr	Sheffield U	A	L	2-3
	*at Leyton			

● **POSITION IN FOOTBALL LEAGUE TABLE**

	P	W	D	L	F	A	Pts
1st Newcastle U	34	23	2	9	72	33	48
10th Woolwich Arsenal	34	12	9	13	36	40	33

SEASON 1905-1906

● FOOTBALL LEAGUE (DIVISION 1)

2 Sep	Liverpool	H	W	3-1
9 Sep	Sheffield U	A	L	1-3
16 Sep	Notts Co	H	D	1-1
18 Sep	Preston NE	H	D	2-2
23 Sep	Stoke C	A	L	1-2
30 Sep	Bolton W	H	D	0-0
7 Oct	Wolverhampton W	A	W	2-0
14 Oct	Blackburn Rov	A	L	0-2
21 Oct	Sunderland	H	W	2-0
28 Oct	Birmingham	A	L	1-2
4 Nov	Everton	H	L	1-2
11 Nov	Derby Co	A	L	1-5
18 Nov	Sheffield Wed	H	L	0-2
25 Nov	Nottingham F	A	L	1-3
2 Dec	Manchester C	H	W	2-0
9 Dec	Bury	A	L	0-2
16 Dec	Middlesbrough	H	D	2-2
23 Dec	Preston NE	A	D	2-2
25 Dec	Newcastle U	H	W	4-3
27 Dec	Aston Villa	A	L	1-2
30 Dec	Liverpool	A	L	0-3
1 Jan	Bolton W	A	L	1-6
6 Jan	Sheffield U	H	W	5-1
20 Jan	Notts Co	A	L	0-1
27 Jan	Stoke C	H	L	1-2
10 Feb	Wolverhampton W	H	W	2-1
17 Feb	Blackburn Rov	H	W	3-2
3 Mar	Birmingham	H	W	5-0
17 Mar	Derby Co	H	W	1-0
21 Mar	Everton	A	W	1-0
24 Mar	Sheffield Wed	A	L	2-4
2 Apr	Nottingham F	H	W	3-1
7 Apr	Manchester C	A	W	2-1
13 Apr	Aston Villa	H	W	2-1
14 Apr	Bury	H	W	4-0
16 Apr	Newcastle U	A	D	1-1
21 Apr	Middlesbrough	A	L	0-2
25 Apr	Sunderland	A	D	2-2

● FA CUP

13 Jan	West Ham U (1)	H	D	1-1
18 Jan	West Ham U (1R)	A	W	3-2
3 Feb	Watford (2)	H	W	3-0
24 Feb	Sunderland (3)	H	W	5-0
10 Mar	Manchester U (4)	A	W	3-2
31 Mar	Newcastle U (SF)	*	L	0-2
	*at Stoke			

● SOUTHERN PROFESSIONAL CHARITY CUP

9 Oct	West Ham U	H	W	3-2
9 Apr	Tottenham H	A	D	0-0
28 Apr	Tottenham H(R)	H	W	5-0
30 Apr	Reading (F)	A*	W	1-0
	*at Fulham			

● FRIENDLIES

21 Sep	Faversham Ran	A	W	9-0
18 Oct	Corinthians	A*	L	1-2
30 Oct	Oxford Univ	H	W	3-1
26 Dec	Corinthians	H	D	1-1
15 Jan	Cambridge Univ	H	W	4-2
22 Jan	Oxford Univ	A	W	4-0
18 Apr	West Hartlepool	A	W	4-0
	*at Fulham			

● POSITION IN FOOTBALL LEAGUE TABLE

	P	W	D	L	F	A	Pts
1st Liverpool	38	23	5	10	79	46	51
12th Woolwich Arsenal	38	15	7	16	62	64	37

SEASON 1906-1907

● FOOTBALL LEAGUE (DIVISION 1)

1 Sep	Manchester C	A	W	4-1
3 Sep	Bury	A	L	1-4
8 Sep	Middlesbrough	H	W	2-0
15 Sep	Preston NE	A	W	3-0
22 Sep	Newcastle U	H	W	2-0
29 Sep	Aston Villa	A	D	2-2
6 Oct	Liverpool	H	W	2-1
13 Oct	Bristol C	A	W	3-1
20 Oct	Notts Co	H	W	1-0
27 Oct	Sheffield U	A	L	2-4
3 Nov	Bolton W	H	D	2-2
10 Nov	Manchester U	A	L	0-1
17 Nov	Stoke C	H	W	2-1
24 Nov	Blackburn Rov	A	W	3-2
1 Dec	Sunderland	H	L	0-1
8 Dec	Birmingham	A	L	1-5
15 Dec	Everton	H	W	3-1
22 Dec	Derby Co	A	D	0-0
26 Dec	Bury	H	W	3-1
29 Dec	Manchester C	H	W	4-1
1 Jan	Sheffield Wed	A	D	1-1
5 Jan	Middlesbrough	A	L	3-5
19 Jan	Preston NE	H	W	1-0
26 Jan	Newcastle U	A	L	0-1
9 Feb	Liverpool	A	L	0-4
16 Feb	Bristol City	H	L	1-2
2 Mar	Sheffield U	H	L	0-1
16 Mar	Manchester U	H	W	4-0
27 Mar	Bolton W	A	L	0-3
28 Mar	Sheffield Wed	H	W	1-0
30 Mar	Blackburn Rov	H	W	2-0
1 Apr	Aston Villa	H	W	3-1
6 Apr	Sunderland	A	W	3-2
10 Apr	Everton	A	L	1-2
13 Apr	Birmingham	H	W	2-1
15 Apr	Stoke C	A	L	0-2
17 Apr	Notts Co	A	L	1-4
27 Apr	Derby Co	H	W	3-2

FA CUP

12 Jan	Grimsby T (1)	A	D	1-1
16 Jan	Grimsby T (1R)	H	W	3-0
2 Feb	Bristol C (2)	H	W	2-1
23 Feb	Bristol Rov (3)	H	W	1-0
9 Mar	Barnsley (4)	A	W	2-1
23 Mar	Sheffield Wed (SF)	*	L	1-3
	*at Birmingham			

SOUTHERN PROFESSIONAL CHARITY CUP

10 Dec	Millwall Ath	H	L	1-2

FRIENDLIES

12 Sep	Reading	A	W	1-0
19 Sep	West Norwood	A*	W	1-0
5 Nov	Oxford Univ	H	W	7-1
19 Nov	Leyton	A	W	3-1
3 Dec	Cambridge Univ	A	W	3-1
25 Dec	Glasgow Celtic	H	L	0-2
14 Jan	Cambridge Univ	H	W	6-3
	*at Herne Hill			

ON TOUR

5 May	Racing Club, Brussels	A	W	2-1
7 May	The Hague	A	W	6-3
9 May	BFC Pruessen, Berlin	A	W	9-1
12 May	SK Slavia, Prague	A	W	7-5
16 May	SK Slavia, Prague	A	W	4-2
18 May	Comb Vienna Team	A	W	4-2
19 May	Budapest Turnaklub	A	D	2-2
20 May	Magyar TKK	A	W	9-0

POSITION IN FOOTBALL LEAGUE TABLE

	P	W	D	L	F	A	Pts
1st Newcastle U	38	22	7	9	74	46	51
7th Woolwich Arsenal	38	20	4	14	66	59	44

SEASON 1907-1908

FOOTBALL LEAGUE (DIVISION 1)

2 Sep	Notts Co	H	D	1-1
7 Sep	Bristol C	H	L	0-4
9 Sep	Bury	A	L	2-3
14 Sep	Notts Co	A	L	0-2
21 Sep	Manchester C	H	W	2-1
28 Sep	Preston NE	A	L	0-3
5 Oct	Bury	H	D	0-0
12 Oct	Aston Villa	A	W	1-0
19 Oct	Liverpool	H	W	2-1
26 Oct	Middlesbrough	A	D	0-0
2 Nov	Sheffield U	H	W	5-1
9 Nov	Chelsea	A	L	1-2
16 Nov	Nottingham F	H	W	3-1
23 Nov	Manchester U	A	L	2-4
30 Nov	Blackburn Rov	H	W	2-0
7 Dec	Bolton W	A	L	1-3

14 Dec	Birmingham	H	D	1-1
21 Dec	Everton	A	D	1-1
25 Dec	Newcastle U	H	D	2-2
28 Dec	Sunderland	H	W	4-0
31 Dec	Sheffield Wed	A	L	0-6
1 Jan	Sunderland	A	L	2-5
4 Jan	Bristol C	A	W	2-1
18 Jan	Manchester C	A	L	0-4
25 Jan	Preston NE	H	D	1-1
8 Feb	Aston Villa	H	L	0-1
15 Feb	Liverpool	A	L	1-4
22 Feb	Middlesbrough	H	W	4-1
29 Feb	Sheffield U	A	D	2-2
7 Mar	Chelsea	H	D	0-0
14 Mar	Nottingham F	A	L	0-1
21 Mar	Manchester U	H	W	1-0
28 Mar	Blackburn Rov	A	D	1-1
4 Apr	Bolton W	H	D	1-1
11 Apr	Birmingham	A	W	2-1
17 Apr	Newcastle U	A	L	1-2
18 Apr	Everton	H	W	2-1
20 Apr	Sheffield Wed	H	D	1-1

FA CUP

11 Jan	Hull C (1)	H	D	0-0
16 Jan	Hull C (1R)	A	L	1-4

SOUTHERN PROFESSIONAL CHARITY CUP

23 Sep	Reading	H	L	0-1

FRIENDLIES

16 Sep	Barnsley	H	W	1-0
14 Oct	Rest of Kent	A	W	3-1
26 Dec	Liverpool	H	D	2-2
1 Feb	Tottenham H	A	W	1-0

ON TOUR

21 Apr	Hearts	A	L	1-3
22 Apr	Raith Rovers	A	L	0-1
23 Apr	Aberdeen	A	L	1-4
25 Apr	Dundee	A	L	1-2
27 Apr	Motherwell	A	D	1-1
28 Apr	Rangers	A	D	1-1
29 Apr	Morton	A	L	0-1
30 Apr	Kilmarnock	A	W	2-1

POSITION IN FOOTBALL LEAGUE TABLE

	P	W	D	L	F	A	Pts
1st Manchester U	38	23	6	9	81	48	52
14th Woolwich Arsenal	38	12	12	14	51	63	36

SEASON 1908-1909

FOOTBALL LEAGUE (DIVISION 1)

2 Sep	Everton	H	L	0-4
5 Sep	Notts Co	A	L	1-2

7 Sep	Everton	A	W	3-0
12 Sep	Newcastle U	H	L	1-2
19 Sep	Bristol C	A	L	1-2
26 Sep	Preston NE	H	W	1-0
3 Oct	Middlesbrough	A	D	1-1
10 Oct	Manchester C	H	W	3-0
17 Oct	Liverpool	A	D	2-2
24 Oct	Bury	H	W	4-0
28 Oct	Chelsea	A	W	2-1
31 Oct	Sheffield U	A	D	1-1
7 Nov	Aston Villa	H	L	0-1
14 Nov	Nottingham F	A	W	1-0
21 Nov	Sunderland	H	L	0-4
5 Dec	Blackburn Rov	H	L	0-1
12 Dec	Bradford C	A	L	1-4
19 Dec	Manchester U	H	L	0-1
25 Dec	Leicester Fosse	A	D	1-1
26 Dec	Leicester Fosse	H	W	2-1
28 Dec	Sheffield Wed	A	L	2-6
2 Jan	Notts Co	H	W	1-0
9 Jan	Newcastle U	H	L	1-3
23 Jan	Bristol C	H	D	1-1
30 Jan	Preston NE	A	D	0-0
13 Feb	Manchester C	A	D	2-2
20 Feb	Liverpool	H	W	5-0
27 Feb	Bury	A	D	1-1
13 Mar	Aston Villa	A	L	1-2
17 Mar	Middlesbrough	H	D	1-1
20 Mar	Nottingham F	H	L	1-2
27 Mar	Sunderland	A	L	0-1
1 Apr	Sheffield U	H	W	1-0
3 Apr	Chelsea	H	D	0-0
10 Apr	Blackburn Rov	A	W	3-1
12 Apr	Sheffield Wed	H	W	2-0
17 Apr	Bradford C	H	W	1-0
27 Apr	Manchester U	A	W	4-1

● FA CUP

16 Jan	Croydon Common (1)	*	D	1-1
20 Jan	Croydon Common (1R)	H	W	2-0
6 Feb	Millwall (2)	H	D	1-1
10 Feb	Millwall (2R)	A	L	0-1
	*at Crystal Palace			

● LONDON FA CHALLENGE CUP

28 Sep	Fulham	A	W	1-0
9 Nov	Crystal Place	H	W	2-1
22 Feb	Clapton Orient (SF)	A*	L	1-2
	*at Tottenham H			

● LONDON PROFESSIONAL
FOOTBALLERS ASSOCIATION
CHARITY FUND

| 7 Dec | Chelsea | H | W | 1-0 |

● FRIENDLIES

| 7 Oct | Rest of Kent | A | W | 3-0 |
| 22 Oct | Ryde | A | W | 2-0 |

| 10 Mar | Hastings | A | W | 3-1 |
| 9 Apr | Exeter | A | L | 2-3 |

● POSITION IN FOOTBALL LEAGUE TABLE

	P	W	D	L	F	A	Pts
1st Newcastle U	38	24	5	9	65	41	53
6th Woolwich Arsenal	38	14	10	14	52	49	38

SEASON 1909-1910

● FOOTBALL LEAGUE (DIVISION 1)

1 Sep	Aston Villa	A	L	1-5
4 Sep	Sheffield U	H	D	0-0
11 Sep	Middlesbrough	A	L	2-5
18 Sep	Bolton W	A	L	0-3
25 Sep	Chelsea	H	W	3-2
2 Oct	Blackburn Rov	A	L	0-7
7 Oct	Notts Co	A	L	1-5
9 Oct	Nottingham F	H	L	0-1
16 Oct	Sunderland	A	L	2-6
23 Oct	Everton	H	W	1-0
30 Oct	Manchester U	A	L	0-1
6 Nov	Bradford C	H	L	0-1
13 Nov	Sheffield Wed	A	D	1-1
20 Nov	Bristol C	H	D	2-2
27 Nov	Bury	A	W	2-1
4 Dec	Tottenham H	H	W	1-0
11 Dec	Preston NE	A	W	4-3
18 Dec	Notts Co	H	L	1-2
25 Dec	Newcastle U	H	L	0-3
27 Dec	Liverpool	H	D	1-1
1 Jan	Liverpool	A	L	1-5
8 Jan	Sheffield U	A	L	0-2
22 Jan	Middlesbrough	H	W	3-0
29 Jan	Bolton W	H	W	2-0
12 Feb	Blackburn Rov	H	L	0-1
26 Feb	Sunderland	H	L	1-2
2 Mar	Nottingham F	A	D	1-1
7 Mar	Everton	A	L	0-1
12 Mar	Manchester U	H	D	0-0
19 Mar	Bradford C	A	W	1-0
25 Mar	Newcastle U	A	D	1-1
26 Mar	Sheffield Wed	H	L	0-1
28 Mar	Chelsea	A	W	1-0
2 Apr	Bristol C	A	W	1-0
9 Apr	Bury	H	D	0-0
11 Apr	Aston Villa	H	W	1-0
16 Apr	Tottenham H	A	D	1-1
23 Apr	Preston NE	H	L	1-3

● FA CUP

| 15 Jan | Watford (1) | H | W | 3-0 |
| 5 Feb | Everton (2) | A | L | 0-5 |

● LONDON FA CHALLENGE CUP

| 20 Sep | Bromley | H | W | 4-0 |

In annual records figures in brackets are goal totals

11 Oct	West Ham U	H	L	0-1

● LONDON PROFESSIONAL FOOTBALLERS ASSOCIATION CHARITY FUND

1 Nov	Tottenham H	A	L	0-3

● FOORD FLOOD RELIEF FUND

25 Nov	Shorncliffe Garrison District XI *at Folkestone	*	W	5-2

● FRIENDLIES

22 Sep	Rest of Kent	A	W	3-2
28 Oct	Barnsley	A	L	2-3
19 Feb	Fulham	H	D	2-2
5 Mar	Millwall	A	D	3-3
28 Apr	Colchester	A	W	3-2
30 Apr	Ilford	A	L	2-3

● POSITION IN FOOTBALL LEAGUE TABLE

	P	W	D	L	F	A	Pts
1st Aston Villa	38	23	7	8	84	42	53
18th Woolwich Arsenal	38	11	9	18	37	67	31

SEASON 1910-1911

● FOOTBALL LEAGUE (DIVISION 1)

1 Sep	Manchester U	H	L	1-2
3 Sep	Bury	A	D	1-1
10 Sep	Sheffield U	H	D	0-0
17 Sep	Aston Villa	A	L	0-3
24 Sep	Sunderland	H	D	0-0
1 Oct	Oldham Ath	H	D	0-0
8 Oct	Bradford C	A	L	0-3
15 Oct	Blackburn Rov	H	W	4-1
22 Oct	Nottingham F	A	W	3-2
29 Oct	Manchester C	H	L	0-1
5 Nov	Everton	A	L	0-2
12 Nov	Sheffield Wed	H	W	1-0
19 Nov	Bristol C	A	W	1-0
26 Nov	Newcastle U	H	L	1-2
3 Dec	Tottenham H	A	L	1-3
10 Dec	Middlesbrough	H	L	0-2
17 Dec	Preston NE	A	L	1-4
24 Dec	Notts Co	H	W	2-1
26 Dec	Manchester U	A	L	0-5
31 Dec	Bury	H	W	3-2
7 Jan	Sheffield U	A	L	2-3
28 Jan	Sunderland	A	D	2-2
11 Feb	Bradford C	H	D	0-0
18 Feb	Blackburn Rov	A	L	0-1
25 Feb	Nottingham F	H	W	3-2
4 Mar	Manchester C	A	D	1-1
6 Mar	Oldham Ath	A	L	0-3
11 Mar	Everton	H	W	1-0

15 Mar	Aston Villa	H	D	1-1
18 Mar	Sheffield Wed	A	D	0-0
25 Mar	Bristol C	H	W	3-0
1 Apr	Newcastle U	A	W	1-0
8 Apr	Tottenham H	H	W	2-0
14 Apr	Liverpool	H	D	0-0
15 Apr	Middlesbrough	A	D	1-1
17 Apr	Liverpool	A	D	1-1
22 Apr	Preston NE	H	W	2-0
29 Apr	Notts Co	A	W	2-0

● FA CUP

14 Jan	Clapton Orient (1)			*
16 Jan	Clapton Orient (1)	A	W	2-1
4 Feb	Swindon T (2) *match abandoned – fog	A	L	0-1

● LONDON FA CHALLENGE CUP

19 Sep	QPR	H	W	3-0
10 Oct	Millwall	A	L	0-1

● LONDON PROFESSIONAL FOOTBALLERS ASSOCIATION CHARITY FUND

26 Sep	Fulham	A	W	3-2

● POSITION IN FOOTBALL LEAGUE TABLE

	P	W	D	L	F	A	Pts
1st Manchester U	38	22	8	8	72	40	52
10th Woolwich Arsenal	38	13	12	13	41	49	38

SEASON 1911-1912

● FOOTBALL LEAGUE (DIVISION 1)

2 Sep	Liverpool	H	D	2-2
9 Sep	Aston Villa	A	L	1-4
16 Sep	Newcastle U	H	W	2-0
23 Sep	Sheffield U	A	L	1-2
30 Sep	Oldham Ath	H	D	1-1
7 Oct	Bolton W	A	D	2-2
14 Oct	Bradford C	H	W	2-0
21 Oct	Preston NE	A	W	1-0
28 Oct	Manchester C	A	D	3-3
4 Nov	Everton	H	L	0-1
11 Nov	WBA	A	D	1-1
18 Nov	Sunderland	H	W	3-0
25 Nov	Blackburn Rov	A	L	0-4
2 Dec	Sheffield Wed	H	L	0-2
9 Dec	Bury	A	L	1-3
16 Dec	Middlesbrough	H	W	3-1
23 Dec	Notts Co	A	L	1-3
25 Dec	Tottenham H	A	L	0-5
26 Dec	Tottenham H	H	W	3-1
30 Dec	Liverpool	A	L	1-4
1 Jan	Manchester U	A	L	0-2
6 Jan	Aston Villa	H	D	2-2

20 Jan	Newcastle U	A	W	2-1
27 Jan	Sheffield U	H	W	3-1
10 Feb	Bolton W	H	W	3-0
17 Feb	Bradford C	A	D	1-1
24 Feb	Middlesbrough	A	W	2-0
2 Mar	Manchester C	H	W	7-0
9 Mar	Oldham Ath	A	D	0-0
16 Mar	WBA	H	L	0-2
23 Mar	Sunderland	A	L	0-1
27 Mar	Everton	A	L	0-1
5 Apr	Manchester U	H	W	2-1
5 Apr	Sheffield Wed	A	L	0-3
6 Apr	Preston NE	H	W	4-1
8 Apr	Bury	H	W	1-0
22 Apr	Blackburn Rov	H	W	5-1
27 Apr	Notts Co	H	L	0-3

● FA CUP

13 Jan	Bolton W (1)	A	L	0-1

● LONDON FA CHALLENGE CUP

18 Sep	QPR	A	W	2-0
16 Oct	Chelsea	H	L	2-3

● LONDON PROFESSIONAL FOOTBALLERS ASSOCIATION CHARITY FUND

4 Sep	Chelsea	A	D	2-2
30 Oct	Chelsea	H	W	1-0

● TITANIC DISASTER FUND MATCH

29 Apr	Tottennham *at White City	H*	W	3-0

● FRIENDLIES

25 Mar	West Ham U	H	W	3-0
20 Apr	Glasgow Ran	A	D	0-0

● ON TOUR

17 May	Hertha Berlin	A	W	5-0
12 May	Viktoria 89	A	D	2-2
16 May	Deutscher FC (Prague)	A	W	4-1
19 May	Ferencvaros	A	W	6-0
22 May	Grazer AK	A	W	6-0
24 May	Tottenham H	*	W	4-0
26 May	Rapid Vienna	A	W	8-2
27 May	Wiener Sport Club	A	W	5-0
29 May	SpVgg Furth *in Vienna	A	W	2-1

● POSITION IN FOOTBALL LEAGUE TABLE

	P	W	D	L	F	A	Pts
1st Blackburn Rov	38	20	9	9	60	43	49
10th Woolwich Arsenal	38	15	8	15	55	59	38

SEASON 1912-1913

● FOOTBALL LEAGUE (DIVISION 1)

2 Sep	Manchester U	H	D	0-0
7 Sep	Liverpool	A	L	0-3
14 Sep	Bolton W	H	L	1-2
16 Sep	Aston Villa	H	L	0-3
21 Sep	Sheffield U	A	W	3-1
28 Sep	Newcastle U	H	D	1-1
5 Oct	Oldham Ath	A	D	0-0
12 Oct	Chelsea	H	L	0-1
19 Oct	Sunderland	H	L	1-3
26 Oct	Bradford PA	A	L	1-3
2 Nov	Manchester C	H	L	0-4
9 Nov	WBA	A	L	1-2
16 Nov	Everton	H	D	0-0
23 Nov	Sheffield Wed	A	L	0-2
30 Nov	Blackburn Rov	H	L	0-1
7 Dec	Derby Co	A	L	1-4
14 Dec	Tottenham H	L	H	0-3
21 Dec	Middlesbrough	A	L	0-2
25 Dec	Notts Co	H	D	0-0
26 Dec	Notts Co	A	L	1-2
28 Dec	Liverpool	H	D	1-1
1 Jan	Sunderland	A	L	1-4
4 Jan	Bolton W	A	L	1-5
18 Jan	Sheffield U	H	L	1-3
25 Jan	Newcastle U	A	L	1-3
8 Feb	Oldham Ath	H	D	0-0
15 Feb	Chelsea	A	D	1-1
1 Mar	Bradford PA	H	D	1-1
8 Mar	Manchester C	A	W	1-0
15 Mar	WBA	H	W	1-0
21 Mar	Manchester U	A	L	0-2
22 Mar	Everton	A	L	0-3
24 Mar	Aston Villa	A	L	1-4
29 Mar	Sheffield Wed	H	L	2-5
5 Apr	Blackburn	A	D	1-1
12 Apr	Derby Co	H	L	1-2
19 Apr	Tottenham H	A	D	1-1
26 Apr	Middlesbrough	H	D	1-1

● FA CUP

11 Jan	Croydon Common (I)	A	D	0-0
15 Jan	Croydon Common (1R)	H	W	2-1
1 Feb	Liverpool (2)	H	L	1-4

● LONDON FA CHALLENGE CUP

23 Sep	Clapton Orient	A	L	2-4

● LONDON PROFESSIONAL FOOTBALLERS ASSOCIATION CHARITY FUND

30 Sep	Chelsea	A	W	3-1

● KENT SENIOR SHIELD

16 Oct	Crystal Palace	A	L	0-1

SEASON 1912-1913

In annual records figures in brackets are goal totals

● POSITION IN FOOTBALL LEAGUE TABLE

	P	W	D	L	F	A	Pts
1st Sunderland	38	25	4	9	86	43	54
20th Woolwich Arsenal	38	3	12	23	26	74	18

ARSENAL AT HIGHBURY

SEASON 1913-1914

● FOOTBALL LEAGUE (DIVISION 2)

6 Sep	Leicester C	H	W	2-1
13 Sep	Wolverhampton W	A	W	2-1
15 Sep	Notts Co	H	W	3-0
20 Sep	Hull C	H	D	0-0
27 Sep	Barnsley	A	L	0-1
4 Oct	Bury	H	L	0-1
11 Oct	Huddersfield	A	W	2-1
18 Oct	Lincoln C	H	W	3-0
25 Oct	Blackpool	A	D	1-1
1 Nov	Nottingham F	H	W	3-2
8 Nov	Fulham	A	L	1-6
15 Nov	Grimsby T	A	D	1-1
22 Nov	Birmingham	H	W	1-0
29 Nov	Bristol C	A	D	1-1
6 Dec	Leeds C	H	W	1-0
13 Dec	Clapton Orient	A	L	0-1
20 Dec	Glossop	H	W	2-0
25 Dec	Bradford PA	A	W	3-2
26 Dec	Bradford PA	H	W	2-0
27 Dec	Leicester C	A	W	2-1
1 Jan	Notts Co	A	L	0-1
3 Jan	Wolverhampton W	H	W	3-1
17 Jan	Hull C	A	W	2-1
24 Jan	Barnsley	H	W	1-0
7 Feb	Bury	A	D	1-1
14 Feb	Huddersfield T	H	L	0-1
21 Feb	Lincoln C	A	L	2-5
28 Feb	Blackpool	H	W	2-1
7 Mar	Nottingham F	A	D	0-0
14 Mar	Fulham	H	W	2-0
28 Mar	Birmingham	A	L	0-2
4 Apr	Bristol C	A	D	1-1
10 Apr	Stockport Co	H	W	4-0
11 Apr	Leeds C	A	D	0-0
13 Apr	Stockport Co	H	W	4-0
18 Apr	Clapton Orient	H	D	2-2
23 Apr	Grimsby T	H	W	2-0
25 Apr	Glossop	A	W	2-0

● FA CUP

10 Jan	Bradford C (1)	A	L	0-2

● LONDON FA CHALLENGE CUP

22 Sep	QPR	H	D	1-1
29 Sep	QPR	A	W	3-2

20 Oct	Chelsea	A	W	1-0
10 Nov	Tottenham H	A*	L	1-2
	*at Chelsea			

● LONDON PROFESSIONAL FOOTBALLERS ASSOCIATION CHARITY FUND

27 Oct	West Ham U	A	L	2-3

● FRIENDLIES

1 Sep	QPR	A	W	2-0
31 Jan	Everton	H	L	1-2

● POSITION IN FOOTBALL LEAGUE TABLE

	P	W	D	L	F	A	Pts
1st Notts Co	38	23	7	8	77	36	53
3rd Arsenal	38	20	9	9	54	38	49

SEASON 1914-1915

● FOOTBALL LEAGUE (DIVISION 2)

1 Sep	Glossop	H	W	3-0
5 Sep	Wolverhampton W	A	L	0-1
8 Sep	Glossop	A	W	4-0
12 Sep	Fulham	H	W	3-0
19 Sep	Stockport Co	A	D	1-1
26 Sep	Hull C	H	W	2-1
3 Oct	Leeds C	A	D	2-2
10 Oct	Clapton Orient	H	W	2-1
17 Oct	Blackpool	H	W	2-0
24 Oct	Derby Co	A	L	0-4
31 Oct	Lincoln C	H	D	1-1
7 Nov	Birmingham	A	L	0-3
14 Nov	Grimsby T	H	W	6-0
18 Nov	Nottingham F	A	D	1-1
21 Nov	Huddersfield T	A	L	0-3
28 Nov	Bristol C	H	W	3-0
5 Dec	Bury	A	L	1-3
12 Dec	Preston NE	H	L	1-2
25 Dec	Leicester C	A	W	4-1
26 Dec	Leicester C	H	W	6-0
1 Jan	Barnsley	A	L	0-1
2 Jan	Wolverhampton W	H	W	5-1
16 Jan	Fulham	A	W	1-0
23 Jan	Stockport Co	H	W	3-1
6 Feb	Leeds C	H	W	2-0
13 Feb	Clapton Orient	A	L	0-1
20 Feb	Blackpool	A	W	2-0
27 Feb	Derby Co	H	L	1-2
6 Mar	Lincoln C	A	L	0-1
13 Mar	Birmingham	H	W	1-0
20 Mar	Grimsby T	A	L	0-1
27 Mar	Huddersfield T	H	L	0-3
2 Apr	Hull C	A	L	0-1
3 Apr	Bristol C	A	D	1-1
5 Apr	Barnsley	H	W	1-0

10 Apr	Bury	H	W	3-1
17 Apr	Preston NE	A	L	0-3
24 Apr	Nottingham F	H	W	7-0

● FA CUP

9 Jan	Merthyr Tydfil (1)	H*	W	3-0
30 Jan	Chelsea (2)	A	L	0-1
	*by arrangement			

● LONDON FA CHALLENGE CUP

21 Sep	Tufnell Park	H	W	6-0
19 Oct	QPR	H	W	2-1
9 Nov	Crystal Palace	A*	W	2-0
7 Dec	Millwall Ath (F)	A‡	L	1-2
	*at Chelsea			
	‡at New Cross			

● LONDON PROFESSIONAL FOOTBALLERS ASSOCIATION CHARITY FUND

2 Nov	West Ham U	H	W	1-0

● FRIENDLY

19 Dec	Swindon T		L	1-2

● POSITION IN FOOTBALL LEAGUE TABLE

	P	W	D	L	F	A	Pts
1st Derby Co	38	23	8	7	71	33	53
5th Arsenal	38	19	5	14	69	41	43

No League football was played throughout the rest of the First World War. After the war, the First Division was increased from 20 to 22 clubs, and Arsenal were elected to one of the new places.

SEASON 1919-1920

● FOOTBALL LEAGUE (DIVISION 1)

30 Aug	Newcastle U	H	L	0-1
1 Sep	Liverpool	A	W	3-2
6 Sep	Newcastle U	A	L	1-3
8 Sep	Liverpool	H	W	1-0
13 Sep	Sunderland	A	D	1-1
20 Sep	Sunderland	H	W	3-2
27 Sep	Blackburn Rov	A	D	2-2
4 Oct	Blackburn Rov	H	L	0-1
11 Oct	Everton	A	W	3-2
18 Oct	Everton	H	D	1-1
25 Oct	Bradford C	H	L	1-2
1 Nov	Bradford C	A	D	1-1
8 Nov	Bolton W	H	D	2-2
15 Nov	Bolton W	A	D	2-2
22 Nov	Notts Co	H	W	3-1
29 Nov	Notts Co	A	D	2-2
6 Dec	Chelsea	H	D	1-1
13 Dec	Chelsea	A	L	1-3

20 Dec	Sheffield Wed	H	W	3-1
25 Dec	Derby Co	A	L	1-2
26 Dec	Derby Co	H	W	1-0
27 Dec	Sheffield Wed	A	W	2-1
3 Jan	Manchester C	H	D	2-2
17 Jan	Manchester C	A	L	1-4
24 Jan	Aston Villa	H	L	0-1
7 Feb	Oldham Ath	H	W	3-2
11 Feb	Aston Villa	A	L	1-2
14 Feb	Oldham Ath	A	L	0-3
21 Feb	Manchester U	H	L	0-3
28 Feb	Manchester U	A	W	1-0
6 Mar	Sheffield U	A	L	0-2
13 Mar	Sheffield U	H	W	3-0
20 Mar	Middlesbrough	A	L	0-1
27 Mar	Middlesbrough	H	W	2-1
3 Apr	Burnley	A	L	1-2
5 Apr	WBA	H	W	1-0
6 Apr	WBA	A	L	0-1
10 Apr	Burnley	H	W	2-0
17 Apr	Preston NE	A	D	1-1
24 Apr	Preston NE	H	D	0-0
28 Apr	Bradford PA	A	D	0-0
1 May	Bradford PA	H	W	3-0

● FA CUP

10 Jan	Rochdale (1)	H	W	4-2
31 Jan	Bristol C (2)	A	L	0-1

APPEARANCES (Goals) Baker 17; Blyth 29(5); Bradshaw 33(2); Buckley 23(1); Burgess 7(1); Butler 21(1); Coopland 1; Cownley 4; Dunn 16; Graham 22(5); Greenaway 3; Groves 29(5); Hardinge 13(3); Hutchins 18; Lewis 5(1); McKinnon 4(1); North 4(1); Pagnam 25(13); Pattison 1; Peart 5; Rutherford 36(3); Shaw 33; Toner 15(1); Voysey 5; White 29(15); Whittaker 1; Williamson 26; Total: 27 players (56)

● POSITION IN LEAGUE TABLE

	P	W	D	L	F	A	Pts
1st WBA	42	28	4	10	104	47	60
10th Arsenal	42	15	12	15	56	58	42

SEASON 1920-1921

● FOOTBALL LEAGUE (DIVISION 1)

28 Aug	Aston Villa	A	L	0-5
30 Aug	Manchester U	H	W	2-0
4 Sep	Aston Villa	H	L	0-1
6 Sep	Manchester U	A	D	1-1
11 Sep	Manchester C	H	W	2-1
18 Sep	Manchester C	A	L	1-3
25 Sep	Middlesbrough	H	D	2-2
2 Oct	Middlesbrough	A	L	1-2
9 Oct	Bolton W	H	D	0-0

16 Oct	Bolton W	A	D	1-1
23 Oct	Derby Co	A	D	1-1
30 Oct	Derby Co	H	W	2-0
6 Nov	Blackburn Rov	A	D	2-2
13 Nov	Blackburn Rov	H	W	2-0
20 Nov	Huddersfield T	A	W	4-0
27 Nov	Huddersfield T	H	W	2-0
4 Dec	Chelsea	A	W	2-1
11 Dec	Chelsea	H	D	1-1
18 Dec	Bradford C	A	L	1-3
25 Dec	Everton	A	W	4-2
27 Dec	Everton	H	D	1-1
1 Jan	Bradford C	H	L	1-2
15 Jan	Tottenham H	A	L	1-2
22 Jan	Tottenham H	H	W	3-2
29 Jan	Sunderland	H	L	1-2
5 Feb	Sunderland	A	L	1-5
12 Feb	Oldham Ath	A	D	1-1
19 Feb	Oldham Ath	H	D	2-2
26 Feb	Preston NE	A	W	1-0
12 Mar	Burnley	A	L	0-1
19 Mar	Burnley	H	D	1-1
26 Mar	Sheffield U	H	L	2-6
28 Mar	WBA	H	W	2-1
29 Mar	WBA	A	W	4-3
2 Apr	Sheffield U	A	D	1-1
9 Apr	Bradford PA	H	W	2-1
16 Apr	Bradford PA	A	W	1-0
23 Apr	Newcastle U	H	D	1-1
25 Apr	Preston NE	H	W	2-1
30 Apr	Newcastle U	A	L	0-1
2 May	Liverpool	H	L	0-0
7 May	Liverpool	A	L	0-3

● FA CUP

8 Jan	QPR (1)	A	L	0-2

APPEARANCES (Goals) Baker 37(2); Blyth W 40(7); Bradshaw 21; Buckley 4(1); Burgess 4; Butler 6; Cownley 1; Dunn 9; Graham 30(5); Groves 13(1); Hopkins 8(2); Hutchins 39; McKenzie 5(1); McKinnon 37(2); North 8(2); Pagnam 25(14); Paterson 20; Pattison 6; Peart 1; Rutherford 32(7); Shaw 28; Smith 10(1); Toner 12(3); Walden 2(1); White 26(10); Whittaker 5; Willamson 33; Total: 27 players (59)

● POSITION IN LEAGUE TABLE

	P	W	D	L	F	A	Pts
1st Burnley	42	23	6	13	79	36	59
9th Arsenal	42	15	13	14	59	63	44

SEASON 1921-1922

● FOOTBALL LEAGUE (DIVISION 1)

27 Aug	Sheffield U	H	L	1-2
29 Aug	Preston NE	A	L	2-3
3 Sep	Sheffield U	A	L	1-4
5 Sep	Preston NE	H	W	1-0
10 Sep	Manchester C	A	L	0-2
17 Sep	Manchester C	H	L	0-1
24 Sep	Everton	A	D	1-1
1 Oct	Everton	H	W	1-0
8 Oct	Sunderland	A	L	0-1
15 Oct	Sunderland	H	L	1-2
22 Oct	Huddersfield T	A	L	0-2
29 Oct	Huddersfield T	H	L	1-3
5 Nov	Birmingham	A	W	1-0
12 Nov	Birmingham	H	W	5-2
19 Nov	Bolton W	A	L	0-1
3 Dec	Blackburn Rov	A	W	1-0
10 Dec	Blackburn Rov	H	D	1-1
12 Dec	Bolton W	H	D	1-1
17 Dec	Oldham Ath	A	L	1-2
24 Dec	Oldham Ath	H	L	0-1
26 Dec	Cardiff C	H	D	0-0
27 Dec	Cardiff C	A	L	3-4
31 Dec	Chelsea	A	W	2-0
14 Jan	Chelsea	H	W	1-0
21 Jan	Burnley	H	D	0-0
4 Feb	Newcastle U	H	W	2-1
11 Feb	Newcastle U	A	L	1-3
20 Feb	Burnley	A	L	0-1
25 Feb	Liverpool	A	L	0-4
11 Mar	Manchester U	A	L	0-1
18 Mar	Aston Villa	A	L	0-2
22 Mar	Liverpool	H	W	1-0
25 Mar	Aston Villa	H	W	2-0
1 Apr	Middlesbrough	H	D	2-2
5 Apr	Manchester U	H	W	3-1
8 Apr	Middlesbrough	A	L	2-4
15 Apr	Tottenham H	A	L	0-2
17 Apr	WBA	A	W	3-0
18 Apr	WBA	H	D	2-2
22 Apr	Tottenham H	H	W	1-0
29 Apr	Bradford C	A	W	2-0
6 May	Bradford C	H	W	1-0

● FA CUP

7 Jan	QPR (1)	H	D	0-0
11 Jan	QPR (1R)	A	W	2-1
28 Jan	Bradford C (2)	A	W	3-2
18 Feb	Leicester C (3)	H	W	3-0
4 Mar	Preston NE (4)	H	D	1-1
8 Mar	Preston NE (4R)	A	L	1-2

APPEARANCES (Goals) Baker 32(4); Blyth 25(1); Boreham 22(10); Bradshaw 32(2); Burgess 2; Butler 25(2); Cownley 10; Creegan 5; Dunn 1; Earle 1; Graham 21(3); Henderson 5; Hutchins 37; Hopkins 11(3); Maxwell 1; Milne 4; McKenzie 3; McKinnon 17; North 11(3); Paterson 2; Pattison 2; Rutherford 36(1); Shaw 6; Toner

24(1); Turnbull 5; Voysey 1; Whittaker 36(1); White 35(14); Williamson 41; Young 9(2) ;
Total: 30 players (47)

● **POSITION IN LEAGUE TABLE**

	P	W	D	L	F	A	Pts
1st Liverpool	42	22	13	7	63	36	57
17th Arsenal	42	15	7	20	47	56	37

SEASON 1922-1923

● **FOOTBALL LEAGUE (DIVISION 1)**

26 Aug	Liverpool	A	L	2-5
28 Aug	Burnley	H	D	1-1
2 Sep	Liverpool	H	W	1-0
4 Sep	Burnley	A	L	1-4
9 Sep	Cardiff C	A	L	1-4
16 Sep	Cardiff C	H	W	2-1
23 Sep	Tottenham H	A	W	2-1
30 Sep	Tottenham H	H	L	0-2
2 Oct	Sheffield U	A	L	1-2
7 Oct	WBA	H	W	3-1
14 Oct	WBA	A	L	0-7
21 Oct	Newcastle U	A	D	1-1
28 Oct	Newcastle U	H	L	1-2
4 Nov	Everton	A	L	0-1
11 Nov	Everton	H	L	1-2
18 Nov	Sunderland	A	D	3-3
25 Nov	Sunderland	H	L	2-3
2 Dec	Birmingham	A	L	2-3
9 Dec	Birmingham	H	W	1-0
16 Dec	Huddersfield T	H	D	1-1
23 Dec	Huddersfield T	A	L	0-4
25 Dec	Bolton W	A	L	1-4
26 Dec	Bolton W	H	W	5-0
30 Dec	Stoke C	H	W	3-0
1 Jan	Blackburn Rov	A	W	5-0
6 Jan	Stoke C	A	L	0-1
20 Jan	Manchester C	H	W	1-0
27 Jan	Manchester C	A	D	0-0
3 Feb	Nottingham F	A	L	1-2
10 Feb	Nottingham F	H	W	2-0
17 Feb	Chelsea	A	D	0-0
24 Feb	Chelsea	H	W	3-1
3 Mar	Middlesbrough	A	L	0-2
10 Mar	Middlesbrough	H	W	3-0
17 Mar	Oldham Ath	H	W	2-0
24 Mar	Oldham Ath	A	D	0-0
31 Mar	Aston Villa	H	W	2-0
2 Apr	Blackburn Rov	H	D	1-1
7 Apr	Aston Villa	A	D	1-1
14 Apr	Preston NE	H	D	1-1
21 Apr	Preston NE	A	W	2-1
28 Apr	Sheffield U	H	W	2-0

● **FA CUP**

13 Jan	Liverpool (1)	A	D	0-0
17 Jan	Liverpool (1R)	H	L	1-4

APPEARANCES (Goals) Baker 29(6); Blyth 31(9); Boreham 27(8); Bradshaw 17; Butler 18; Clark 2; Dunn 17; Earle 1(1); Elvey 1; Graham 17(1); Henderson 2; Hopkins 2(2); Hutchins 10(1); John 24; Kennedy 24; McKenzie 7 (1); Milne 31; Mackie 23; Paterson 26; Robson 20; Roe 4(1); Rutherford 26(1); Toner 7; Townrow 1; Turnbull 35(20); Voysey 18(4); White 11(1); Whittaker 13 (1); Willamson 5; Young 13(3); o/g 1; Total: 30 players (61)

● **POSITION IN LEAGUE TABLE**

	P	W	D	L	F	A	Pts
1st Liverpool	42	26	8	8	70	31	60
11th Arsenal	42	16	10	16	61	62	42

SEASON 1923-1924

● **FOOTBALL LEAGUE (DIVISION 1)**

25 Aug	Newcastle U	H	L	1-4
27 Aug	West Ham U	A	L	0-1
1 Sep	Newcastle U	A	L	0-1
8 Sep	WBA	A	L	0-4
10 Sep	West Ham U	H	W	4-1
15 Sep	WBA	H	W	1-0
22 Sep	Birmingham	A	W	2-0
29 Sep	Birmingham	H	D	0-0
6 Oct	Manchester C	A	L	0-1
13 Oct	Manchester C	H	L	1-2
20 Oct	Bolton W	A	W	2-1
27 Oct	Bolton W	H	D	0-0
3 Nov	Middlesbrough	H	W	2-1
10 Nov	Middlesbrough	A	D	0-0
17 Nov	Tottenham H	H	D	1-1
24 Nov	Tottenham H	A	L	0-3
1 Dec	Blackburn Rov	H	D	2-2
8 Dec	Blackburn Rov	A	L	0-2
15 Dec	Huddersfield T	H	L	1-3
22 Dec	Huddersfield T	A	L	1-6
26 Dec	Notts Co	A	W	2-1
27 Dec	Notts Co	H	D	0-0
29 Dec	Chelsea	H	W	1-0
5 Jan	Chelsea	A	D	0-0
19 Jan	Cardiff C	H	L	1-2
26 Jan	Cardiff C	A	L	0-4
9 Feb	Sheffield U	A	L	1-3
16 Feb	Aston Villa	H	L	0-1
25 Feb	Sheffield U	H	L	1-3
1 Mar	Liverpool	H	W	3-1
12 Mar	Aston Villa	A	L	1-2
15 Mar	Nottingham F	A	L	1-2
22 Mar	Nottingham F	H	W	1-0
2 Apr	Liverpool	A	D	0-0
5 Apr	Burnley	H	W	2-0
12 Apr	Sunderland	H	W	2-0
18 Apr	Everton	A	L	1-3

In annual records figures in brackets are goal totals

19 Apr	Sunderland	A	D	1-1
21 Apr	Everton	H	L	0-1
26 Apr	Preston NE	A	W	2-0
28 Apr	Burnley	A	L	1-4
3 May	Preston NE	H	L	1-2

● FA CUP

12 Jan	Luton T (1)	H	W	4-1
2 Feb	Cardiff (2)	A	L	0-1

APPEARANCES (Goals) Baker 21(1); Blyth 27(3); Boreham 2; Butler 24; Clark 2; Earle 2(2); Graham 25(1); Haden 31(3); John 15; Jones 2; Kennedy 29; Mackie 31; Milne 36(1); Neil 11(2); Paterson 21; Ramsay 11(3); Robson 42; Rutherford 22 (2); Toner 3; Townrow 7(2); Turnbull 18(6); Voysey 10(2); Wallington 1; Whittaker 8; Woods 36(9); Young 25(2) o/g 1; Total: 26 players (40)

● POSITION IN LEAGUE TABLE

	P	W	D	L	F	A	Pts
1st Huddersfield	42	23	11	8	60	33	57
19th Arsenal	42	12	9	21	40	63	33

SEASON 1924-1925

● FOOTBALL LEAGUE (DIVISION 1)

30 Aug	Nottingham F	A	W	2-0
1 Sep	Manchester C	H	W	1-0
6 Sep	Liverpool	H	W	2-0
13 Sep	Newcastle U	A	D	2-2
17 Sep	Manchester C	A	L	0-2
20 Sep	Sheffield U	H	W	2-0
27 Sep	West Ham U	A	L	0-1
4 Oct	Blackburn Rov	H	W	1-0
11 Oct	Huddersfield T	A	L	0-4
13 Oct	Bury	H	L	0-1
18 Oct	Aston Villa	H	D	1-1
25 Oct	Tottenham H	H	W	1-0
1 Nov	Bolton W	A	L	1-4
8 Nov	Notts Co	H	L	0-1
15 Nov	Everton	A	W	3-2
22 Nov	Sunderland	H	D	0-0
29 Nov	Cardiff C	A	D	1-1
6 Dec	Preston NE	H	W	4-0
13 Dec	Burnley	A	L	0-1
20 Dec	Leeds U	H	W	6-1
25 Dec	Birmingham	A	L	1-2
26 Dec	Birmingham	H	L	0-1
27 Dec	Nottingham F	H	W	2-1
3 Jan	Liverpool	A	L	1-2
17 Jan	Newcastle U	H	L	0-2
24 Jan	Sheffield U	A	L	1-2
7 Feb	Blackburn Rov	A	L	0-1
14 Feb	Huddersfield T	H	L	0-5
28 Feb	Tottenham H	A	L	0-2

7 Mar	Bolton W	H	W	1-0
14 Mar	Notts Co	A	L	1-2
21 Mar	Everton	H	W	3-1
23 Mar	West Ham U	H	L	1-2
28 Mar	Sunderland	A	L	0-2
1 Apr	Aston Villa	A	L	0-4
4 Apr	Cardiff C	H	D	1-1
11 Apr	Preston NE	A	L	0-2
13 Apr	WBA	A	L	0-2
14 Apr	WBA	H	W	2-0
18 Apr	Burnley	H	W	5-0
25 Apr	Leeds U	A	L	0-1
2 May	Bury	A	L	0-2

● FA CUP

14 Jan	West Ham U (1)	A	D	0-0
21 Jan	West Ham U (1R)	H	D	2-2
26 Jan	West Ham U (1R)	A*	L	0-1
	* at Chelsea			

APPEARANCES (Goals) Baker 32(2); Blyth 17(1); Brain 28(12); Butler 39(3); Clark 2; Cock 2; Haden 15(1); Hoar 19(1); Hughes 1; John 39(1); Kennedy 40; Lewis 16; Mackie 19; Milne 32; Neil 16(2); Ramsey 30(6) Robson 26; Roe 1; Rutherford 20(2); Toner 26(1); Turnbull 1; Whittaker 1; Woods 32(12); Young 8(2); Total: 24 players (46)

● POSITION IN LEAGUE TABLE

	P	W	D	L	F	A	Pts
1st Huddersfield	42	21	16	5	69	28	58
20th Arsenal	42	14	5	23	46	58	33

SEASON 1925-1926

● FOOTBALL LEAGUE (DIVISION 1)

29 Aug	Tottenham H	H	L	0-1
31 Aug	Leicester C	H	D	2-2
5 Sep	Manchester U	A	W	1-0
7 Sep	Leicester C	A	W	1-0
12 Sep	Liverpool	H	D	1-1
19 Sep	Burnley	A	D	2-2
21 Sep	West Ham U	H	W	3-2
26 Sep	Leeds U	H	W	4-1
3 Oct	Newcastle U	A	L	0-7
5 Oct	West Ham U	A	W	4-0
10 Oct	Bolton W	H	L	2-3
17 Oct	Cardiff C	H	W	5-0
24 Oct	Sheffield U	A	L	0-4
31 Oct	Everton	H	W	4-1
7 Nov	Manchester C	A	W	5-2
14 Nov	Bury	H	W	6-1
21 Nov	Blackburn Rov	A	W	3-2
28 Nov	Sunderland	H	W	2-0
5 Dec	Huddersfield T	A	D	2-2
12 Dec	WBA	H	W	1-0

19 Dec	Birmingham	A	L	0-1
25 Dec	Notts Co	H	W	3-0
26 Dec	Notts Co	A	L	1-4
1 Jan	Tottenham H	A	D	1-1
16 Jan	Manchester U	H	W	3-2
23 Jan	Liverpool	A	L	0-3
3 Feb	Burnley	H	L	1-2
6 Feb	Leeds U	A	L	2-4
13 Feb	Newcastle U	H	W	3-0
23 Feb	Cardiff C	A	D	0-0
13 Mar	Everton	A	W	3-2
17 Mar	Sheffield U	H	W	4-0
20 Mar	Manchester C	H	W	1-0
27 Mar	Bury	A	D	2-2
2 Apr	Aston Villa	A	L	0-3
3 Apr	Blackburn Rov	H	W	4-2
5 Apr	Aston Villa	H	W	2-0
10 Apr	Sunderland	A	L	1-2
17 Apr	Huddersfield T	H	W	3-1
24 Apr	WBA	A	L	1-2
28 Apr	Bolton W	A	D	1-1
1 May	Birmingham	H	W	3-0

● FA CUP

9 Jan	Wolves (3)	A	D	1-1
13 Jan	Wolves (3R)	H	W	1-0
30 Jan	Blackburn Rov (4)	H	W	3-1
20 Feb	Aston Villa (5)	A	D	1-1
24 Feb	Aston Villa (5R)	H	W	2-0
6 Mar	Swansea T (6)	A	L	1-2

APPEARANCES (Goals) Baker 31(6); Blyth 40(7); Brain 41(34); Buchan 39(19); Butler 41; Cock 1; Haden 25(2); Harper 19; Hoar 21(3); Hulme 15(2); John 29; Kennedy 16; Lawson 13(2); Lewis 14; Mackie 35; Milne 5; Neil 27(6); Parker 7(3); Paterson 1(1); Ramsey 16; Robson 9; J.Rutherford 3; J.J.Rutherford 1; Seddon 1; Toner 2; Voysey 1; Woods 2; Young 7; o/g 3; Total: 28 players (87)

● POSITION IN LEAGUE TABLE

	P	W	D	L	F	A	Pts
1st Huddersfield	42	23	11	8	92	60	57
2nd Arsenal	42	22	8	12	87	63	52

SEASON 1926-1927

● FOOTBALL LEAGUE (DIVISION 1)

28 Aug	Derby Co	H	W	2-1
1 Sep	Bolton W	H	W	2-1
4 Sep	Sheffield U	A	L	0-4
6 Sep	Bolton W	A	D	2-2
11 Sep	Leicester C	H	D	2-2
15 Sep	Manchester U	A	D	2-2
18 Sep	Liverpool	H	W	2-0
25 Sep	Leeds U	A	L	1-4
2 Oct	Newcastle U	H	D	2-2
9 Oct	Burnley	A	L	0-2
16 Oct	West Ham U	H	D	2-2
23 Oct	Sheffield Wed	H	W	6-2
30 Oct	Everton	A	L	1-3
6 Nov	Blackburn Rov	H	D	2-2
13 Nov	Huddersfield T	A	D	3-3
20 Nov	Sunderland	H	L	2-3
27 Nov	WBA	A	W	3-1
4 Dec	Bury	H	W	1-0
11 Dec	Birmingham	A	D	0-0
18 Dec	Tottenham H	H	L	2-4
27 Dec	Cardiff C	A	L	0-2
28 Dec	Manchester U	H	W	1-0
1 Jan	Cardiff C	H	W	3-2
15 Jan	Derby Co	A	W	2-0
22 Jan	Sheffield U	H	D	1-1
5 Feb	Liverpool	A	L	0-3
10 Feb	Leicester C	A	L	1-2
12 Feb	Leeds	H	W	1-0
26 Feb	Burnley	H	W	6-2
7 Mar	West Ham U	A	L	0-7
12 Mar	Sheffield Wed	A	L	2-4
19 Mar	Everton	H	L	1-2
2 Apr	Huddersfield T	H	L	0-2
6 Apr	Newcastle U	A	L	1-6
9 Apr	Sunderland	A	L	1-5
15 Apr	Aston Villa	H	W	2-1
16 Apr	WBA	H	W	4-1
18 Apr	Aston Villa	A	W	3-2
28 Apr	Blackburn Rov	A	W	2-1
30 Apr	Birmingham	H	W	3-0
4 May	Bury	A	L	2-3
7 May	Tottenham H	A	W	4-0

● FA CUP

8 Jan	Sheffield U (3)	A	W	3-2
29 Jan	Port Vale (4)	A	D	2-2
2 Feb	Port Vale (4R)	H	W	1-0
19 Feb	Liverpool (5)	H	W	2-0
5 Mar	Wolves (6)	H	W	2-1
26 Mar	Southampton (SF)	*	W	2-1
23 Apr	Cardiff (F)	‡	L	0-1
	*at Chelsea			
	‡at Wembley			

APPEARANCES (Goals) Baker 23; Barley 3(1); Blyth 33(2); Bowen 1; Brain 37(31); Buchan 33(14); Butler 31(1); Cope 11; Haden 17(4); Harper 23; Hoar 16(2); Hulme 37(8); John 41(3); Kennedy 11; Lambert 16(1); Lee 7; Lewis 17; Milne 6; Moody 2; Parker 42(4); Peel 9; Ramsey 12(2); Roberts 2; Seddon 17; Shaw 5(1); Tricker 4(3); Young 6; Total: 27 players (77)

● POSITION IN LEAGUE TABLE

	P	W	D	L	F	A	Pts
1st Newcastle U	42	25	6	11	96	58	56
11th Arsenal	42	17	9	16	77	86	43

SEASON 1927-1928

• FOOTBALL LEAGUE (DIVISION 1)

27 Aug	Bury	A	L	1-5
31 Aug	Burnley	H	W	4-1
3 Sep	Sheffield U	H	W	6-1
5 Sep	Burnley	A	W	2-1
10 Sep	Aston Villa	A	D	2-2
17 Sep	Sunderland	H	W	2-1
24 Sep	Derby Co	A	L	0-4
1 Oct	West Ham U	H	D	2-2
8 Oct	Portsmouth	A	W	3-2
15 Oct	Leicester C	H	D	2-2
22 Oct	Sheffield Wed	A	D	1-1
29 Oct	Bolton W	H	L	1-2
5 Nov	Blackburn Rov	A	L	1-4
12 Nov	Middlesbrough	H	W	3-1
19 Nov	Birmingham	A	D	1-1
3 Dec	Huddersfield T	A	L	1-2
10 Dec	Newcastle U	H	W	4-1
17 Dec	Manchester U	A	L	1-4
24 Dec	Everton	H	W	3-2
27 Dec	Liverpool	A	W	2-0
31 Dec	Bury	H	W	3-1
2 Jan	Tottenham H	H	D	1-1
7 Jan	Sheffield U	A	L	4-6
21 Jan	Aston Villa	H	L	0-3
4 Feb	Derby Co	H	L	3-4
11 Feb	West Ham U	A	D	2-2
25 Feb	Leicester C	A	L	2-3
7 Mar	Liverpool	H	W	6-3
10 Mar	Bolton W	A	D	1-1
14 Mar	Sunderland	A	L	1-5
17 Mar	Blackburn Rov	H	W	3-2
28 Mar	Portsmouth	H	L	0-2
31 Mar	Birmingham	H	D	2-2
6 Apr	Cardiff C	H	W	3-0
7 Apr	Tottenham H	A	L	0-2
9 Apr	Cardiff C	A	D	2-2
14 Apr	Huddersfield T	H	D	0-0
18 Apr	Middlesbrough	A	D	2-2
21 Apr	Newcastle U	A	D	1-1
28 Apr	Manchester U	H	L	0-1
2 May	Sheffield Wed	H	D	1-1
5 May	Everton	A	D	3-3

● FA CUP

14 Jan	WBA (3)	H	W	2-0
28 Jan	Everton (4)	H	W	4-3
18 Feb	Aston Villa (5)	H	W	4-1
3 Mar	Stoke C (6)	H	W	4-1

24 Mar	Blackburn R (SF)	*	L	0-1
	*at Leicester			

APPEARANCES (Goals) Baker 37 (2); Barley 2; Blyth 39(7); Brain 39(25); Buchan 30 (16); Butler 38; Clark 1; Cope 24; Hapgood 3; Hoar 38(9); Hulme 36(8); John 39(1); Kennedy 2; Lambert 16(3); Lewis 33; Moody 4; Parker 42(4); Paterson 5; Peel 13; Roberts 3; Seddon 4; Shaw 6(3); Thompson 1; Tricker 7(2); Own goals 2 Total: 24 players (82)

● POSITION IN LEAGUE TABLE

	P	W	D	L	F	A	Pts
1st Everton	42	20	13	9	102	66	53
10th Arsenal	42	13	15	14	82	86	41

SEASON 1928-1929

● FOOTBALL LEAGUE (DIVISION 1)

25 Aug	Sheffield Wed	A	L	2-3
29 Aug	Derby Co	H	L	1-3
1 Sep	Bolton W	H	W	2-0
8 Sep	Portsmouth	A	L	0-2
15 Sep	Birmingham	H	D	0-0
22 Sep	Manchester C	A	L	1-4
26 Sep	Derby Co	A	D	0-0
29 Sep	Huddersfield	H	W	2-0
6 Oct	Everton	A	L	2-4
13 Oct	West Ham U	H	L	2-3
20 Oct	Newcastle U	A	W	3-0
27 Oct	Liverpool	H	D	4-4
3 Nov	Cardiff C	A	D	1-1
10 Nov	Sheffield U	H	W	2-0
17 Nov	Bury	A	L	0-1
24 Nov	Aston Villa	H	L	2-5
1 Dec	Leicester C	A	D	1-1
8 Dec	Manchester U	H	W	3-1
15 Dec	Leeds U	A	D	1-1
22 Dec	Burnley	H	W	3-1
25 Dec	Blackburn Rov	A	L	2-5
26 Dec	Sunderland	H	D	1-1
29 Dec	Sheffield Wed	H	D	2-2
1 Jan	Sunderland	A	L	1-5
5 Jan	Bolter W	A	W	2-1
19 Jan	Portsmouth	H	W	4-0
2 Feb	Manchester C	H	D	0-0
9 Feb	Huddersfield	A	W	1-0
23 Feb	West Ham U	A	W	4-3
9 Mar	Liverpool	A	W	4-2
13 Mar	Birmingham	A	D	1-1
16 Mar	Cardiff C	H	W	2-1
23 Mar	Sheffield U	A	D	2-2
29 Mar	Blackburn Rov	H	W	1-0
30 Mar	Bury	H	W	7-1
2 Apr	Newcastle U	H	L	1-2

6 Apr	Aston Villa	A	L	2-4
13 Apr	Leicester C	H	D	1-1
20 Apr	Manchester U	A	L	1-4
22 Apr	Everton	H	W	2-0
27 Apr	Leeds U	H	W	1-0
4 May	Burnley	A	D	3-3

● FA CUP

12 Jan	Stoke C (3)	H	W	2-1
26 Jan	Mansfield T (4)	H	W	2-0
16 Feb	Swindon T (5)	A	D	0-0
20 Feb	Swindon T (5R)	H	W	1-0
2 Mar	Aston Villa (6)	A	L	0-1

APPEARANCES (Goals) Baker 31; Barley 3; Blyth 21(1); Brain 37(19); Butler 22; Cope 23; Hapgood 17; Hoar 6(1); Hulme 41(6); Jack 31(25); John 34(1); C.Jones 39 (6); Lambert 6(1); Lewis 32; Parker 42(3); Parkin 5(3); Paterson 10; Peel 24 (5); Roberts 20; Thompson 17(5); Tricker 1; Own goals 1; Total: 21 players (77)

● POSITION IN LEAGUE TABLE

	P	W	D	L	F	A	Pts
1st Sheffield Wed	42	21	10	11	86	62	52
9th Arsenal	42	16	13	13	77	72	45

SEASON 1929-1930

● FOOTBALL LEAGUE (DIVISION 1)

31 Aug	Leeds U	H	W	4-0
4 Sep	Manchester C	A	L	1-3
7 Sep	Sheffield Wed	A	W	2-0
11 Sep	Manchester C	H	W	3-2
14 Sep	Burnley	H	W	6-1
21 Sep	Sunderland	A	W	1-0
25 Sep	Aston Villa	A	L	2-5
28 Sep	Bolton W	H	L	1-2
5 Oct	Everton	A	D	1-1
12 Oct	Derby Co	H	D	1-1
19 Oct	Grimsby T	H	W	4-1
26 Oct	Manchester U	A	L	0-1
2 Nov	West Ham U	H	L	0-1
9 Nov	Birmingham	A	W	3-2
23 Nov	Blackburn Rov	A	D	1-1
27 Nov	Middlesbrough	H	L	1-2
30 Nov	Newcastle U	H	L	0-1
14 Dec	Huddersfield T	H	W	2-0
16 Dec	Sheffield U	A	L	1-4
21 Dec	Liverpool	A	L	0-1
25 Dec	Portsmouth	A	W	1-0
26 Dec	Portsmouth	H	L	1-2
28 Dec	Leeds U	A	L	0-2
4 Jan	Sheffield W	H	L	2-3
18 Jan	Burnley	A	D	2-2

1 Feb	Bolton W	A	D	0-0
8 Feb	Everton	H	W	4-0
19 Feb	Derby Co	A	L	1-4
22 Feb	Grimsby T	A	D	1-1
8 Mar	West Ham U	A	L	2-3
12 Mar	Manchester U	H	W	4-2
15 Mar	Birmingham	H	W	1-0
29 Mar	Blackburn Rov	H	W	4-0
2 Apr	Liverpool	H	L	0-1
5 Apr	Newcastle U	A	D	1-1
9 Apr	Middlesbrough	A	D	1-1
12 Apr	Sheffield U	H	W	8-1
18 Apr	Leicester	H	D	1-1
19 Apr	Huddersfield	A	D	2-2
21 Apr	Leicester C	A	D	6-6
28 Apr	Sunderland	H	L	0-1
3 May	Aston Villa	H	L	2-4

● FA CUP

11 Jan	Chelsea (3)	H	W	2-0
25 Jan	Birmingham (4)	H	D	2-2
29 Jan	Birmingham (4R)	A	W	1-0
15 Feb	Middlesbrough (5)	A	W	2-0
1 Mar	West Ham U (6)	A	W	3-0
22 Mar	Hull C (SF)	*	D	2-2
26 Mar	Hull C (SFR)	‡	W	1-0
26 Apr	Huddersfield T (F)	°	W	2-0

*at Leeds
‡at Aston Villa
°at Wembley

APPEARANCES (Goals) Baker 19; Bastin 21(7); Brain 6; Butler 2; Cope 1; Halliday 15(8); Hapgood 38; Haynes 13; Hulme 37(14); Humpish 3; Jack 33(13); James 31(6); John 34; Johnstone 7(3); C.Jones 31(2) Lambert 20(18); Lewis 30; Parker 41(3); Peel 1; Preedy 12; Roberts 26; Seddon 24; Thompson 5(1); Williams 12(3); own goals 1; Total: 24 players (78)

● POSITION IN LEAGUE TABLE

	P	W	D	L	F	A	Pts
1st Sheffield Wed	42	26	8	8	105	57	60
14th Arsenal	42	14	11	17	78	66	39

SEASON 1930-1931

● FOOTBALL LEAGUE (DIVISION 1)

30 Aug	Blackpool	A	W	4-1
1 Sep	Bolton W	A	W	4-1
6 Sep	Leeds U	H	W	3-1
10 Sep	Blackburn Rov	H	W	3-2
13 Sep	Sunderland	A	W	4-1
15 Sep	Blackburn Rov	A	D	2-2
20 Sep	Leicester C	H	W	4-1

27 Sep	Birmingham	A	W	4-2
4 Oct	Sheffield U	H	D	1-1
11 Oct	Derby Co	A	L	2-4
18 Oct	Manchester U	A	W	2-1
25 Oct	West Ham U	H	D	1-1
1 Nov	Huddersfield T	A	D	1-1
8 Nov	Aston Villa	H	W	5-2
15 Nov	Sheffield Wed	A	W	2-1
22 Nov	Middlesbrough	H	W	5-3
29 Nov	Chelsea	A	W	5-1
13 Dec	Liverpool	A	D	1-1
20 Dec	Newcastle U	H	L	1-2
25 Dec	Manchester C	A	W	4-1
26 Dec	Manchester C	H	W	3-1
27 Dec	Blackpool	H	W	7-1
17 Jan	Sunderland	H	L	1-3
28 Jan	Grimsby T	H	W	9-1
31 Jan	Birmingham	H	D	1-1
5 Feb	Leicester C	A	W	7-2
7 Feb	Sheffield U	A	D	1-1
14 Feb	Derby Co	H	W	6-3
21 Feb	Manchester U	H	W	4-1
28 Feb	West Ham U	A	W	4-2
7 Mar	Huddersfield T	H	D	0-0
11 Mar	Leeds U	A	W	2-1
14 Mar	Aston Villa	A	L	1-5
21 Mar	Sheffield W	H	W	2-0
28 Mar	Middlesbrough	A	W	5-2
3 Apr	Portsmouth	A	D	1-1
4 Apr	Chelsea	H	W	2-1
6 Apr	Portsmouth	H	D	1-1
11 Apr	Grimsby T	A	W	1-0
18 Apr	Liverpool	H	W	3-1
25 Apr	Newcastle U	A	W	3-1
2 May	Bolton W	H	W	5-0

● FA CUP

10 Jan	Aston Villa (3)	H	D	2-2
14 Jan	Aston Villa (3R)	A	W	3-1
24 Jan	Chelsea (4)	A	L	1-2

● FA CHARITY SHIELD

8 Oct	Sheffield Wed	*	W	2-1
	*at Chelsea			

APPEARANCES (Goals) Baker 1; Bastin 42(28); Brain 16(4); Cope 1; Hapgood 38; Harper 19; Haynes 2; Hulme 32(14); Jack 35(31); James 40(5); John 40(2); Johnstone 2(1); C.Jones 24(1); Keizer 12; Lambert 34(38); Male 3; Parker 41; Preedy 11; Roberts 40 (1); Seddon 18; Thompson 2; Williams 9(2); Total: 22 players (127)

● POSITION IN LEAGUE TABLE

	P	W	D	L	F	A	Pts
1st Arsenal	42	28	10	4	127	59	66

SEASON 1931-1932

● FOOTBALL LEAGUE (DIVISION 1)

29 Aug	WBA	H	L	0-1
31 Aug	Blackburn Rov	A	D	1-1
5 Sep	Birmingham	A	D	2-2
9 Sep	Portsmouth	H	D	3-3
12 Sep	Sunderland	H	W	2-0
16 Sep	Portsmouth	A	W	3-0
19 Sep	Manchester C	A	W	3-1
26 Sep	Everton	H	W	3-2
3 Oct	Grimsby T	A	L	1-3
10 Oct	Blackpool	A	W	5-1
17 Oct	Bolton W	H	D	1-1
24 Oct	Leicester C	A	W	2-1
31 Oct	Aston Villa	H	D	1-1
7 Nov	Newcastle U	A	L	2-3
14 Nov	West Ham U	H	W	4-1
21 Nov	Chelsea	A	L	1-2
28 Nov	Liverpool	H	W	6-0
5 Dec	Sheffield Wed	A	W	3-1
12 Dec	Huddersfield T	H	D	1-1
19 Dec	Middlesbrough	A	W	5-2
25 Dec	Sheffield U	A	L	1-4
26 Dec	Sheffield U	H	L	0-2
2 Jan	WBA	A	L	0-1
16 Jan	Birmingham	H	W	3-0
30 Jan	Manchester C	H	W	4-0
6 Feb	Everton	A	W	3-1
17 Feb	Grimsby T	H	W	4-0
20 Feb	Blackpool	H	W	2-0
2 Mar	Bolton W	A	L	0-1
5 Mar	Leicester C	H	W	2-1
19 Mar	Newcastle U	H	W	1-0
25 Mar	Derby Co	H	W	2-1
26 Mar	West Ham U	A	D	1-1
28 Mar	Derby Co	A	D	1-1
3 Apr	Chelsea	H	D	1-1
6 Apr	Sunderland	A	L	0-2
9 Apr	Liverpool	A	L	1-2
16 Apr	Sheffield Wed	H	W	3-1
25 Apr	Aston Villa	A	D	1-1
27 Apr	Huddersfield T	A	W	2-1
30 Apr	Middlesbrough	H	W	5-0
7 May	Blackburn Rov	H	W	4-0

● FA CUP

9 Jan	Darwen (3)	H	W	11-1
23 Jan	Plymouth (4)	H	W	4-2
13 Feb	Portsmouth (5)	A	W	2-0
27 Feb	Huddersfield T (6)	A	W	1-0
12 Mar	Manchester C (SF)	*	W	1-0
23 Apr	Newcastle U (F)	‡	L	1-2
	*at Aston Villa			
	‡at Wembley			

● **FA CHARITY SHIELD**

7 Oct	WBA	*	W	1-0

*at Aston Villa

APPEARANCES (Goals) Bastin 40(15); Beasley 3; Coleman 6(1); L.Compton 4; Cope 1; Hapgood 41; Harper 2; Haynes 7; Hulme 40(14); Jack 34(21); James 32(2); John 38(3); C.Jones 37; Lambert 36(22); Male 9; Moss 27; Parker 38; Parkin 9(7); Preedy 13; Roberts 35; Seddon 5; Stockill 3(1); Thompson 1; Williams 1; o/g 4; Total: 24 players (90)

● **POSITION IN LEAGUE TABLE**

	P	W	D	L	F	A	Pts
1st Everton	42	26	4	12	116	64	56
2nd Arsenal	42	22	10	10	90	48	54

SEASON 1932-1933

● **FOOTBALL LEAGUE (DIVISION 1)**

27 Aug	Birmingham	A	W	1-0
31 Aug	WBA	H	L	1-2
3 Sep	Sunderland	H	W	6-1
10 Sep	Manchester C	A	W	3-2
14 Sep	WBA	A	D	1-1
17 Sep	Bolton W	H	W	3-2
24 Sep	Everton	H	W	2-1
1 Oct	Blackpool	A	W	2-1
8 Oct	Derby Co	H	D	3-3
15 Oct	Blackburn Rov	A	W	3-2
22 Oct	Liverpool	A	W	3-2
24 Oct	Leicester C	H	W	8-2
5 Nov	Wolverhampton W	A	W	7-1
12 Nov	Newcastle U	H	W	1-0
19 Nov	Aston Villa	A	L	3-5
26 Nov	Middlesbrough	H	W	4-2
3 Dec	Portsmouth	A	W	3-1
10 Dec	Chelsea	H	W	4-1
17 Dec	Huddersfield T	A	W	1-0
24 Dec	Sheffield U	H	W	9-2
26 Dec	Leeds U	H	L	1-2
27 Dec	Leeds U	A	D	0-0
31 Dec	Birmingham	H	W	3-0
2 Jan	Sheffield Wed	A	L	2-3
7 Jan	Sunderland	A	L	2-3
21 Jan	Manchester C	H	W	2-1
1 Feb	Bolton W	A	W	4-0
4 Feb	Everton	A	D	1-1
11 Feb	Blackpool	H	D	1-1
22 Feb	Derby Co	A	D	2-2
25 Feb	Blackburn Rov	H	W	8-0
4 Mar	Liverpool	H	L	0-1
11 Mar	Leicester C	A	D	1-1
18 Mar	Wolverhampton W	H	L	1-2
25 Mar	Newcastle U	A	L	1-2
1 Apr	Aston Villa	H	W	5-0
8 Apr	Middlesbrough	A	W	4-3
14 Apr	Sheffield Wed	H	W	4-2
15 Apr	Portsmouth	H	W	2-0
22 Apr	Chelsea	A	W	3-1
29 Apr	Huddersfield T	H	D	2-2
6 May	Sheffield U	A	L	1-3

● **FA CUP**

14 Jan	Walsall (3)	A	L	0-2

APPEARANCES (Goals) Bastin 42(33); Bowden 7(2); Coleman 27(24); L.Compton 4; Cope 4; Hapgood 38; Haynes 6; Hill 26(1); Hulme 40(20); Jack 34(18); James 40(3); John 37; C.Jones 16; Lambert 12(14); Male 35; Moss 41; Parker 5; Parkin 5; Preedy 1; Roberts 36; Sidey 2; Stockill 4(3); Total: 22 players (118)

● **POSITION IN LEAGUE TABLE**

	P	W	D	L	F	A	Pts
1st Arsenal	42	25	8	9	118	61	58

SEASON 1933-1934

● **FOOTBALL LEAGUE (DIVISION 1)**

26 Aug	Birmingham	H	D	1-1
2 Sep	Sheffield Wed	A	W	2-1
6 Sep	WBA	H	W	3-1
9 Sep	Manchester C	H	D	1-1
13 Sep	WBA	A	L	0-1
16 Sep	Tottenham H	A	D	1-1
23 Sep	Everton	A	L	1-3
30 Sep	Middlesbrough	H	W	6-0
7 Oct	Blackburn Rov	A	D	2-2
14 Oct	Newcastle U	H	W	3-0
21 Oct	Leicester C	H	W	2-0
28 Oct	Aston Villa	A	W	3-2
4 Nov	Portsmouth	H	D	1-1
11 Nov	Wolverhampton W	A	W	1-0
18 Nov	Stoke C	H	W	3-0
25 Nov	Huddersfield T	A	W	1-0
2 Dec	Liverpool	H	W	2-1
9 Dec	Sunderland	A	L	0-3
16 Dec	Chelsea	H	W	2-1
23 Dec	Sheffield U	A	W	3-1
25 Dec	Leeds U	A	W	1-0
26 Dec	Leeds U	H	W	2-0
30 Dec	Birmingham	A	D	0-0
6 Jan	Sheffield Wed	H	D	1-1
20 Jan	Manchester C	A	L	1-2
31 Jan	Tottenham H	H	L	1-3
3 Feb	Everton	H	L	1-2
10 Feb	Middlesbrough	A	W	2-0
21 Feb	Blackburn Rov	H	W	2-1
24 Feb	Newcastle U	A	W	1-0

8 Mar	Leicester C	A	L	1-4
10 Mar	Aston Villa	H	W	3-2
24 Mar	Wolverhampton W	H	W	3-2
30 Mar	Derby Co	H	W	1-0
31 Mar	Stoke C	A	D	1-1
2 Apr	Derby Co	A	W	4-2
7 Apr	Huddersfield T	H	W	3-1
14 Apr	Liverpool	A	W	3-2
18 Apr	Portsmouth	A	L	0-1
21 Apr	Sunderland	H	W	2-1
28 Apr	Chelsea	A	D	2-2
5 May	Sheffield U	H	W	2-0

● FA CUP

13 Jan	Luton T (3)	A	W	1-0
27 Jan	Crystal Pal (4)	H	W	7-0
17 Feb	Derby Co (5)	H	W	1-0
3 Mar	Aston Villa (6)	H	L	1-2

● FA CHARITY SHIELD

18 Oct	Everton	A	W	3-0

APPEARANCES (Goals) Bastin 38(13);
Beasley 23(10); Birkett 15(5); Bowden
32(13); Coleman 12(1); Cox 2; Dougall 5;
Drake 10(7); Dunne 21(9); Hapgood 40;
Haynes 1; Hill 25; Hulme 8(5); Jack 14(5);
James 22(3) John 31(1); C.Jones 29;
Lambert 3(1); Male 42; Moss 37; Parkin 5;
Roberts 30(1); Sidey 12; Wilson 5; o/g 1;
Total: 24 players (75)

● IN LEAGUE TABLE

	P	W	D	L	F	A	Pts
1st Arsenal	42	25	9	8	75	47	59

SEASON 1934-1935

● FOOTBALL LEAGUE (DIVISION 1)

25 Aug	Portsmouth	A	D	3-3
1 Sep	Liverpool	H	W	8-1
5 Sep	Blackburn Rov	H	W	4-0
8 Sep	Leeds U	A	D	1-1
15 Sep	WBA	H	W	4-3
17 Sep	Blackburn Rov	A	L	0-2
22 Sep	Sheffield Wed	A	D	0-0
29 Sep	Birmingham	H	W	5-1
6 Oct	Stoke C	A	D	2-2
13 Oct	Manchester C	H	W	3-0
20 Oct	Tottenham H	H	W	5-1
27 Oct	Sunderland	A	L	1-2
3 Nov	Everton	H	W	2-0
10 Nov	Grimsby T	A	D	2-2
17 Nov	Aston Villa	H	L	1-2
24 Nov	Chelsea	A	W	5-2
1 Dec	Wolverhampton W	H	W	7-0
8 Dec	Huddersfield T	A	D	1-1
15 Dec	Leicester C	H	W	8-0
22 Dec	Derby Co	A	L	1-3
25 Dec	Preston NE	H	W	5-3
26 Dec	Preston NE	A	L	1-2
29 Dec	Portsmouth	H	D	1-1
5 Jan	Liverpool	A	W	2-0
19 Jan	Leeds U	H	W	3-0
30 Jan	WBA	A	W	3-0
2 Feb	Sheffield Wed	H	W	4-1
9 Feb	Birmingham	A	L	0-3
20 Feb	Stoke C	H	W	2-0
23 Feb	Manchester C	A	D	1-1
6 Mar	Tottenham H	A	W	6-0
9 Mar	Sunderland	H	D	0-0
16 Mar	Everton	A	W	2-0
23 Mar	Grimsby T	H	D	1-1
30 Mar	Aston Villa	A	W	3-1
6 Apr	Chelsea	H	D	2-2
13 Apr	Wolverhampton W	A	D	1-1
19 Apr	Middlesbrough	H	W	8-0
20 Apr	Huddersfield T	H	W	1-0
22 Apr	Middlesbrough	H	W	1-0
27 Apr	Leicester C	A	W	5-3
4 May	Derby Co	H	L	0-1

● FA CUP

12 Jan	Brighton & HA (2)	A	W	2-0
26 Jan	Leicester C (3)	H	W	1-0
16 Feb	Reading (4)	A	W	1-0
2 Mar	Sheffield Wed (5)	A	L	1-2

● FA CHARITY SHIELD

28 Nov	Manchester C	H	W	4-0

APPEARANCES (Goals) Bastin 36 (20);
Beasley 20(6); Birkett 4(2); Bowden 24(14);
L.Compton 5(1); Copping 31; Crayston 37(3);
Davidson 11(2); Dougall 8(1); Drake 41(42);
Dunne 1; Hapgood 34(1); Hill 15(3); Hulme
16(8); James 30(4); John 9; Kirchen 7(2);
Male 39; Marshall 4; Moss 33(1); Roberts
36; Rogers 5(2); Sidey 6; Trim 1; Wilson 9;
o/g 3 Total: 25 players (115)

● POSITION IN LEAGUE TABLE

	P	W	D	L	F	A	Pts
1st Arsenal	42	23	12	7	115	46	58

SEASON 1935-1936

● FOOTBALL LEAGUE (DIVISION 1)

31 Aug	Sunderland	H	W	3-1
3 Sep	Grimsby T	A	L	0-1
7 Sep	Birmingham	A	D	1-1
11 Sep	Grimsby T	H	W	6-0
14 Sep	Sheffield Wed	H	D	2-2
18 Sep	Leeds U	A	D	1-1

21 Sep	Manchester C	H	L	2-3
28 Sep	Stoke C	A	W	3-0
5 Oct	Blackburn Rov	H	W	5-1
12 Oct	Chelsea	A	D	1-1
19 Oct	Portsmouth	A	L	1-2
26 Oct	Preston NE	H	W	2-1
2 Nov	Brentford	A	L	1-2
9 Nov	Derby Co	H	D	1-1
16 Nov	Everton	A	W	2-0
23 Nov	Wolverhampton W	H	W	4-0
30 Nov	Huddersfield T	A	D	0-0
9 Dec	Middlesbrough	H	W	2-0
14 Dec	Aston Villa	A	W	7-1
25 Dec	Liverpool	A	W	1-0
26 Dec	Liverpool	H	L	1-2
28 Dec	Sunderland	A	L	4-5
4 Jan	Birmingham	H	D	1-1
18 Jan	Sheffield Wed	A	L	2-3
1 Feb	Stoke C	H	W	1-0
8 Feb	Blackburn Rov	A	W	1-0
22 Feb	Portsmouth	H	L	2-3
4 Mar	Derby Co	A	W	4-0
7 Mar	Huddersfield T	H	D	1-1
11 Mar	Manchester City	A	L	0-1
14 Mar	Preston NE	A	L	0-1
25 Mar	Everton	H	D	1-1
28 Mar	Wolverhampton W	A	D	2-2
1 Apr	Bolton W	H	D	1-1
4 Apr	Brentford	H	D	1-1
10 Apr	WBA	H	W	4-0
11 Apr	Middlesbrough	A	D	2-2
13 Apr	WBA	A	L	0-1
18 Apr	Aston Villa	H	W	1-0
27 Apr	Chelsea	H	D	1-1
29 Apr	Bolton W	A	L	1-2
2 May	Leeds U	H	D	2-2

● FA CUP

11 Jan	Bristol Rov (3)	A	W	5-1
25 Jan	Liverpool (4)	A	W	2-0
15 Feb	Newcastle U (5)	A	D	3-3
19 Feb	Newcastle U (5R)	H	W	3-0
29 Feb	Barnsley (6)	H	W	4-1
21 Mar	Grimsby T (SF)	*	W	1-0
	(at Huddersfield)			
25 Apr	Sheffield U (F)	‡	W	1-0
	*at Huddersfield			
	‡at Wembley			

● FA CHARITY SHIELD

| 23 Oct | Sheffield Wed | H | L | 0-1 |

APPEARANCES (Goals) Bastin 31(11); Beasley 26(2); Bowden 22 (6); Cartwright 5; L.Compton 12(1); Copping 33; Cox 5(1); Crayston 36(5); Davidson 13; Dougall 8(3); Drake 26(24); Dunne 6(1); Hapgood 33; Hill 10; Hulme 21(6); James 17(2); John 6; Joy 2; Kirchen 6(3); Male 35; Milne 14 (6); Moss 5; Parkin 1(1); Roberts 26(1); Rogers 11(3); Sidey 11; Tuckett 2; Westcott 2(1); Wilson 37; o/g 1; Total: 29 players (78)

● POSITION IN LEAGUE TABLE

	P	W	D	L	F	A	Pts
1st Sunderland	42	25	11	6	109	74	56
6th Arsenal	42	15	15	12	78	48	45

SEASON 1936-1937

● FOOTBALL LEAGUE (DIVISION 1)

29 Aug	Everton	H	W	3-2
3 Sep	Brentford	A	L	0-2
5 Sep	Huddersfield T	A	D	0-0
9 Sep	Brentford	H	D	1-1
12 Sep	Sunderland	H	W	4-1
19 Sep	Wolverhampton W	A	L	2-4
26 Sep	Derby Co	H	D	2-2
3 Oct	Manchester U	A	L	0-2
10 Oct	Sheffield Wed	H	D	1-1
17 Oct	Charlton Ath	A	W	2-0
24 Oct	Grimsby T	H	D	0-0
31 Oct	Liverpool	A	L	1-2
7 Nov	Leeds U	H	W	4-1
14 Nov	Birmingham	A	W	3-1
21 Nov	Middlesbrough	H	W	5-3
28 Nov	WBA	A	W	4-2
5 Dec	Manchester C	H	L	1-3
12 Dec	Portsmouth	A	W	5-1
19 Dec	Chelsea	H	W	4-1
25 Dec	Preston NE	H	W	4-1
26 Dec	Everton	A	D	1-1
28 Dec	Preston NE	A	W	3-1
1 Jan	Bolton W	A	W	5-0
2 Jan	Huddersfield T	H	D	1-1
9 Jan	Sunderland	A	D	1-1
23 Jan	Wolverhampton W	H	W	2-1
3 Feb	Derby Co	A	L	4-5
6 Feb	Manchester U	H	D	1-1
13 Feb	Sheffield Wed	A	D	0-0
24 Feb	Charlton Ath	H	D	1-1
27 Feb	Grimsby T	A	W	3-1
10 Mar	Liverpool	H	W	1-0
13 Mar	Leeds U	A	W	4-3
20 Mar	Birmingham	H	D	1-1
26 Mar	Stoke C	H	D	0-0
27 Mar	Middlesbrough	A	D	1-1
29 Mar	Stoke C	A	D	0-0
3 Apr	WBA	H	W	2-0
10 Apr	Manchester City	A	L	0-2
17 Apr	Portsmouth	H	W	4-0
24 Apr	Chelsea	A	L	0-2
1 May	Bolton W	H	D	0-0

● FA CUP

16 Jan	Chesterfield (3)	A	W	5-1
30 Jan	Manchester U (4)	H	W	5-0
20 Feb	Burnley (5)	A	W	7-1
6 Mar	WBA (6)	A	L	1-3

● FA CHARITY SHIELD

28 Oct	Sunderland	A	L	1-2

APPEARANCES (Goals) Bastin 33(5); Beasley 7(1); Biggs 1; Boulton 21; Bowden 28(6); Cartwright 2; D.Compton 14(4); L.Compton 15; Copping 38; Crayston 30(1); Davidson 28(9); Drake 26(20); Hapgood 32(1); Hulme 3 James 19(1); John 5; Joy 6; Kirchen 33(18); Male 37; Milne 19(9); Nelson 8(3); Roberts 30(1); Sidey 6 Swindin 19; Wilson 2; o/g 1; Total: 25 players (80)

● POSITION IN LEAGUE TABLE

	P	W	D	L	F	A	Pts
1st Manchester C	42	22	13	7	107	61	57
3rd Arsenal	42	18	16	8	80	49	52

SEASON 1937-1938

● FOOTBALL LEAGUE (DIVISION 1)

28 Aug	Everton	A	W	4-1
1 Sep	Huddersfield T	H	W	3-1
4 Sep	Wolverhampton W	H	W	5-0
8 Sep	Huddersfield T	A	L	1-2
11 Sep	Leicester C	A	D	1-1
15 Sep	Bolton W	A	L	0-1
18 Sep	Sunderland	H	W	4-1
25 Sep	Derby Co	A	L	0-2
2 Oct	Manchester C	H	W	2-1
9 Oct	Chelsea	A	D	2-2
16 Oct	Portsmouth	H	D	1-1
23 Oct	Stoke C	A	D	1-1
30 Oct	Middlesbrough	H	L	1-2
6 Nov	Grimsby T	A	L	1-2
13 Nov	WBA	H	D	1-1
20 Nov	Charlton Ath	A	W	3-0
27 Nov	Leeds U	H	W	4-1
4 Dec	Birmingham	A	W	2-1
11 Dec	Preston NE	H	W	2-0
18 Dec	Liverpool	A	L	0-2
25 Dec	Blackpool	A	L	1-2
27 Dec	Blackpool	H	W	2-1
1 Jan	Everton	H	W	2-1
15 Jan	Wolverhampton W	A	L	1-3
29 Jan	Sunderland	A	D	1-1
2 Feb	Leicester C	H	W	3-1
5 Feb	Derby Co	H	W	3-0
16 Feb	Manchester C	A	W	2-1
19 Feb	Chelsea	H	W	2-0
26 Feb	Portsmouth	A	D	0-0
5 Mar	Stoke C	H	W	4-0
12 Mar	Middlesbrough	A	L	1-2
19 Mar	Grimsby T	H	W	5-1
26 Mar	WBA	A	D	0-0
2 Apr	Charlton Ath	H	D	2-2
9 Apr	Leeds U	A	W	1-0
15 Apr	Brentford	H	L	0-2
16 Apr	Birmingham	H	D	0-0
18 Apr	Brentford	A	L	0-3
23 Apr	Preston NE	A	W	3-1
30 Apr	Liverpool	H	W	1-0
7 May	Bolton W	H	W	5-0

● FA CUP

8 Jan	Bolton W (3)	H	W	3-1
22 Jan	Wolverhampton W (4)	A	W	2-1
12 Feb	Preston NE (5)	H	L	0-1

APPEARANCES (Goals) Bastin 38(15); Biggs 2; Boulton 15; Bowden 10(1); Bremner 2(1); Carr 11(7); Cartwright 6(2); Collett 5; D.Compton 7(1); L.Compton 9(1); Copping 38; Crayston 31(4); Davidson 5(2); Drake 27(17); Drury 11; Griffiths 9(5); Hapgood 41; Hulme 7(2); Hunt 18(3); L.Jones 28 (3); Joy 26; Kirchen 19(6); Lewis 4(2); Male 34; Milne 16(4); Roberts 13; Sidey 3; Swindin 17; Wilson 10; o/g 1; Total: 29 players (77)

● POSITION IN LEAGUE TABLE

	P	W	D	L	F	A	Pts
1st Arsenal	42	21	10	11	77	44	52

SEASON 1938-1939

● FOOTBALL LEAGUE (DIVISION 1)

27 Aug	Portsmouth	H	W	2-0
3 Sep	Huddersfield T	A	D	1-1
8 Sep	Brentford	A	L	0-1
10 Sep	Everton	H	L	1-2
14 Sep	Derby Co	H	L	1-2
17 Sep	Wolverhampton W	A	W	1-0
24 Sep	Aston Villa	H	D	0-0
1 Oct	Sunderland	A	D	0-0
8 Oct	Grimsby T	H	W	2-0
15 Oct	Chelsea	A	L	2-4
22 Oct	Preston NE	H	W	1-0
29 Oct	Bolton W	A	D	1-1
5 Nov	Leeds U	H	L	2-3
12 Nov	Liverpool	A	D	2-2
19 Nov	Leicester C	H	D	0-0
26 Nov	Middlesbrough	A	D	1-1
3 Dec	Birmingham	H	W	3-1
10 Dec	Manchester U	A	L	0-1

17 Dec	Stoke C	H	W	4-1
24 Dec	Portsmouth	A	D	0-0
27 Dec	Charlton Ath	A	L	0-1
31 Dec	Huddersfield T	H	W	1-0
14 Jan	Everton	A	L	0-2
21 Jan	Charlton Ath	H	W	2-0
28 Jan	Aston Villa	A	W	3-1
1 Feb	Wolverhampton W	H	D	0-0
4 Feb	Sunderland	H	W	2-0
18 Feb	Chelsea	H	W	1-0
21 Feb	Grimsby T	A	L	1-2
25 Feb	Preston NE	A	L	1-2
4 Mar	Bolton W	H	W	3-1
11 Mar	Leeds U	A	L	2-4
18 Mar	Liverpool	H	W	2-0
25 Mar	Leicester C	A	W	2-0
1 Apr	Middlesbrough	H	L	1-2
7 Apr	Blackpool	A	L	0-1
8 Apr	Birmingham	A	W	2-1
10 Apr	Blackpool	H	W	2-1
15 Apr	Manchester U	H	W	2-1
22 Apr	Stoke C	A	L	0-1
29 Apr	Derby Co	A	W	2-1
6 May	Brentford	H	W	2-0

● FA CUP

7 Jan	Chelsea (3)	A	L	1-2

● FA CHARITY SHIELD

26 Sep	Preston NE	H	W	2-1

APPEARANCES (Goals) Bastin 23(3); Bremner 13(3); Carr 1; Cartwright 3; Collett 9; D.Compton 1; L.Compton 18(2); Copping 26; Crayston 34(3); Cumner 12(2); Curtis 2; Drake 38(14); Drury 23(3); Farr 2(1); Fields 3; Hapgood 38; B.Jones 30(4); L.Jones 18; Joy 39; Kirchen 27(9); Lewis 15(7); Male 28; Marks 2; Nelson 9(1); Pryde 4; Pugh 1; Swindin 21; Walsh 3; Wilson 19; o/g 3;Total: 29 players (55)

● POSITION IN LEAGUE TABLE

	P	W	D	L	F	A	Pts
1st Everton	42	27	5	10	88	52	59
5th Arsenal	42	19	9	14	55	41	47

SEASON 1939-1940

● FOOTBALL LEAGUE (DIVISION 1)
(Before outbreak of Second World War)

26 Aug	Wolverhampton W	A	D	2-2
30 Aug	Blackburn Rov	H	W	1-0
2 Sep	Sunderland	H	W	5-2
15 Oct	Chelsea	A	L	2-4

● FOOTBALL LEAGUE JUBILEE FUND MATCH

21 Aug	Tottenham H	H	D	1-1

Scorers: (Football League) Drake 4, Bastin 1, Drury 1, Lewis 1, Kirchen 1. (Jubilee Fund Match) Drury 1

SEASON 1946-47

● FOOTBALL LEAGUE (DIVISION 1)

31 Aug	Wolverhampton W	A	L	1-6
4 Sep	Blackburn Rov	H	L	1-3
7 Sep	Sunderland	A	D	2-2
11 Sep	Everton	A	L	2-3
14 Sep	Aston Villa	A	W	2-0
17 Sep	Blackburn Rov	A	W	2-1
21 Sep	Derby Co	H	L	0-1
28 Sep	Manchester U	A	L	2-5
5 Oct	Blackpool	A	L	1-2
12 Oct	Brentford	H	D	2-2
19 Oct	Stoke C	H	W	1-0
26 Oct	Chelsea	A	L	1-2
2 Nov	Sheffield U	H	L	2-3
9 Nov	Preston NE	A	L	0-2
16 Nov	Leeds U	H	W	4-2
23 Nov	Liverpool	A	L	2-4
30 Nov	Bolton W	H	D	2-2
7 Dec	Middlesbrough	A	L	0-2
14 Dec	Charlton Ath	H	W	1-0
21 Dec	Grimsby T	A	D	0-0
25 Dec	Portsmouth	H	W	2-1
26 Dec	Portsmouth	A	W	2-0
28 Dec	Wolverhampton W	H	D	1-1
4 Jan	Sunderland	A	W	4-1
18 Jan	Aston Villa	H	L	0-2
1 Feb	Manchester U	H	W	6-2
8 Feb	Blackpool	H	D	1-1
22 Feb	Stoke C	A	L	1-3
1 Mar	Chelsea	H	L	1-2
15 Mar	Preston NE	H	W	4-1
22 Mar	Leeds U	A	D	1-1
4 Apr	Huddersfield T	H	L	1-2
5 Apr	Bolton W	A	W	3-1
7 Apr	Huddersfield T	A	D	0-0
12 Apr	Middlesbrough	H	W	4-0
19 Apr	Charlton Ath	A	D	2-2
26 Apr	Grimsby T	H	W	5-3
10 May	Derby Co	A	W	1-0
24 May	Liverpool	H	L	1-2
26 May	Brentford	A	W	1-0
31 May	Everton	H	W	2-1
7 June	Sheffield U	A	L	1-2

● FA CUP

11 Jan	Chelsea (3)	A	D	1-1
15 Jan	Chelsea (3R)	H	D	1-1
20 Jan	Chelsea (3R)	*	L	0-2
	*at Tottenham			

APPEARANCES (Goals) Barnes 26; Bastin 6; Calverley 11; Collett 6 D.Compton 1(1); L.Compton 36; Curtis 11; Drury 4; Fields 8; Grant 2; Gudmundsson 2; Hodges 2; Jones 26(1); Joy 13; Lewis 28(29); Logie 35 (8); Male 15; McPherson 37(6); Mercer 25; Morgan 2; Nelson 10; O'Flanagan 14(3); Platt 4; Rooke 24(21); Rudkin 5(2); Scott 28; Sloan 30(1) Smith 3; Swindin 38; Wade 2; Waller 8; Total: 31 players (72)

● POSITION IN LEAGUE

	P	W	D	L	F	A	Pts
1st Liverpool	42	25	7	10	84	52	57
13th Arsenal	42	16	9	17	72	70	41

SEASON 1947-1948

● FOOTBALL LEAGUE (DIVISION 1)

23 Aug	Sunderland	H	W	3-1
27 Aug	Charlton Ath	A	W	4-2
30 Aug	Sheffield U	A	W	2-1
3 Sep	Charlton Ath	H	W	6-0
6 Sep	Manchester U	H	W	2-1
10 Sep	Bolton W	H	W	2-0
13 Sep	Preston NE	A	D	0-0
20 Sep	Stoke C	H	W	3-0
27 Sep	Burnley	A	W	1-0
4 Oct	Portsmouth	H	D	0-0
11 Oct	Aston Villa	H	W	1-0
18 Oct	Wolverhampton W	A	D	1-1
25 Oct	Everton	H	D	1-1
1 Nov	Chelsea	A	D	0-0
8 Nov	Blackpool	H	W	2-1
15 Nov	Blackburn Rov	A	W	1-0
22 Nov	Huddersfield T	H	W	2-0
29 Nov	Derby Co	A	L	0-1
6 Dec	Manchester C	H	D	1-1
13 Dec	Grimsby T	A	W	4-0
20 Dec	Sunderland	A	D	1-1
25 Dec	Liverpool	A	W	3-1
27 Dec	Liverpool	H	L	1-2
1 Jan	Bolton W	A	W	1-0
3 Jan	Sheffield U	H	W	3-2
17 Jan	Manchester U	A	D	1-1
31 Jan	Preston NE	H	W	3-0
7 Feb	Stoke C	A	D	0-0
14 Feb	Burnley	H	W	3-0
28 Feb	Aston Villa	A	L	2-4
6 Mar	Wolverhampton W	H	W	5-2
13 Mar	Everton	A	W	2-0
20 Mar	Chelsea	H	L	0-2
26 Mar	Middlesbrough	H	W	7-0
27 Mar	Blackpool	A	L	0-3
29 Mar	Middlesbrough	A	D	1-1
3 Apr	Blackburn Rov	H	W	2-0
10 Apr	Huddersfield T	A	D	1-1
17 Apr	Derby Co	H	L	1-2
21 Apr	Portsmouth	D	0-0	
24 Apr	Manchester C	A	D	0-0
1 May	Grimsby T	H	W	8-0

● FA CUP

10 Jan	Bradford C (3)	H	L	0-1

APPEARANCES (Goals) Barnes 35;
D.Compton 14(6); L.Compton 35; Fields 6;
Forbes 11(2); Jones 7(1); Lewis 28(14); Logie
39(8); Macaulay 40; Male 8; McPherson
29(5); Mercer 40; Rooke 42(33); Roper 40(10);
Scott 39; Sloan 3; L.Smith 1; Swindin 42;
Wade 3; o/g 2; Total: 19 players (81)

● **POSITION IN LEAGUE**

	P	W	D	L	F	A	Pts
1st Arsenal	42	23	13	6	81	32	59

SEASON 1948-1949

● **FOOTBALL LEAGUE (DIVISION 1)**

21 Aug	Huddersfield T	A	D	1-1
25 Aug	Stoke C	H	W	3-0
28 Aug	Manchester U	H	L	0-1
30 Aug	Stoke C	A	L	0-1
4 Sep	Sheffield U	A	D	1-1
8 Sep	Liverpool	H	D	1-1
11 Sep	Aston Villa	H	W	3-1
15 Sep	Liverpool	A	W	1-0
18 Sep	Sunderland	A	D	1-1
25 Sep	Wolverhampton W	H	W	3-1
2 Oct	Bolton W	A	L	0-1
9 Oct	Burnley	H	W	3-1
16 Oct	Preston NE	A	D	1-1
23 Oct	Everton	H	W	5-0
30 Oct	Chelsea	A	W	1-0
6 Nov	Birmingham C	H	W	2-0
13 Nov	Middlesbrough	A	W	1-0
20 Nov	Newcastle U	H	L	0-1
27 Nov	Portsmouth	A	L	1-4
4 Dec	Manchester C	H	D	1-1
11 Dec	Charlton Ath	A	L	3-4
18 Dec	Huddersfield T	H	W	3-0
25 Dec	Derby Co	H	D	3-3
27 Dec	Derby Co	A	L	1-2
1 Jan	Manchester U	A	L	0-2
15 Jan	Sheffield U	H	W	5-3
22 Jan	Aston Villa	A	L	0-1
5 Feb	Sunderland	H	W	5-0
19 Feb	Wolverhampton W	A	W	3-1
26 Feb	Bolton W	H	W	5-0
5 Mar	Burnley	A	D	1-1
12 Mar	Preston NE	H	D	0-0
19 Mar	Newcastle U	A	L	2-3
2 Apr	Birmingham C	A	D	1-1
9 Apr	Middlesbrough	H	D	1-1
15 Apr	Blackpool	A	D	1-1
16 Apr	Everton	A	D	0-0
18 Apr	Blackpool	H	W	2-0
23 Apr	Chelsea	H	L	1-2
27 Apr	Manchester C	A	W	3-0
4 May	Portsmouth	H	W	3-2
7 May	Charlton Ath	H	W	2-0

● **FA CUP**

8 Jan	Tottenham H (3)	H	W	3-0
29 Jan	Derby Co (4)	A	L	0-1

● **FA CHARITY SHIELD**

6 Oct	Manchester U	H	W	4-3

APPEARANCES (Goals) Barnes 40;
D.Compton 6(2); L.Compton 40; Daniel 1;
Fields 1; Forbes 25(4); Jones 8(1); Lewis
25(16); Lishman 23(12); Logie 35(11);
Macaulay 39(1); McPherson 33(5); Mercer
33; Platt 10; Rooke 22(14); Roper 31(5);
Scott 12; L.Smith 32; Swindin 32; Vallance
14(2); o/g 1; Total: players 20 (74)

● **POSITION IN LEAGUE TABLE**

	P	W	D	L	F	A	Pts
1st Portsmouth	42	25	8	9	84	42	58
5th Arsenal	42	18	13	11	74	44	49

SEASON 1949-1950

● **FOOTBALL LEAGUE (DIVISION 1)**

20 Aug	Burnley	H	L	0-1
24 Aug	Chelsea	A	W	2-1
27 Aug	Sunderland	A	L	2-4
31 Aug	Chelsea	H	L	2-3
3 Sep	Liverpool	H	L	1-2
7 Sep	WBA	A	W	2-1
10 Sep	Huddersfield T	A	D	2-2
14 Sep	WBA	H	W	4-1
17 Sep	Bolton W	A	D	2-2
24 Sep	Birmingham C	H	W	4-2
1 Oct	Derby Co	A	W	2-1
8 Oct	Everton	H	W	5-2
15 Oct	Middlesbrough	A	D	1-1
22 Oct	Blackpool	H	W	1-0
29 Oct	Newcastle U	A	W	3-0
5 Nov	Fulham	H	W	2-1
12 Nov	Manchester C	A	W	2-0
19 Nov	Charlton Ath	H	L	2-3
26 Nov	Aston Villa	A	D	1-1
3 Dec	Wolverhampton W	H	D	1-1
10 Dec	Portsmouth	A	L	1-2
17 Dec	Burnley	A	D	0-0
24 Dec	Sunderland	H	W	5-0
26 Dec	Manchester U	A	L	0-2
27 Dec	Manchester U	H	D	0-0
31 Dec	Liverpool	A	L	0-2
14 Jan	Huddersfield T	H	W	1-0
21 Jan	Bolton W	H	D	1-1
4 Feb	Birmingham C	A	L	1-2
18 Feb	Derby Co	H	W	1-0
25 Feb	Everton	A	W	1-0
8 Mar	Middlesbrough	H	D	1-1
11 Mar	Charlton Ath	A	D	1-1
25 Mar	Fulham	A	D	2-2

29 Mar	Aston Villa	H	L	1-3
1 Apr	Manchester C	H	W	4-1
8 Apr	Blackpool	A	L	1-2
10 Apr	Stoke C	H	W	6-0
15 Apr	Newcastle U	H	W	4-2
22 Apr	Wolverhampton W	A	L	0-3
3 May	Portsmouth	H	W	2-0
6 May	Stoke C	A	W	5-2

● **FA CUP**

7 Jan	Sheffield Wed (3)	H	W	1-0
28 Jan	Swansea T (4)	H	W	2-1
11 Feb	Burnley (5)	H	W	2-0
4 Mar	Leeds U (6)	H	W	1-0
18 Mar	Chelsea (SF)	*	D	2-2
22 Mar	Chelsea (SFR)	*	W	1-0
29 Apr	Liverpool (F)	‡	W	2-0
	*at Tottenham H			
	‡at Wembley			

APPEARANCES (Goals) Barnes 38(5); D.Compton 11(1); L.Compton 35; Cox 32(3); Daniel 6; Forbes 23(2); Goring 29(21); Kelly 1; Lewis 31(19); Lishman 14(9); Logie 34(7); Macaulay 24; McPherson 27(3); Mercer 35; Platt 19; Roper 27(7); Scott 15; Shaw 5; L.Smith 31; Swindin 23; Vallance 1; Wade 1 o/g 2; Total: 22 players (79)

● **POSITION IN LEAGUE**

	P	W	D	L	F	A	Pts
1st Portsmouth	42	22	9	11	74	38	53
6th Arsenal	42	19	11	12	79	55	49

SEASON 1950-1951

● **FOOTBALL LEAGUE (DIVISION 1)**

19 Aug	Burnley	A	W	1-0
23 Aug	Chelsea	H	D	0-0
26 Aug	Tottenham H	H	D	2-2
30 Aug	Chelsea	A	W	1-0
2 Sep	Sheffield Wed	H	W	3-0
6 Sep	Everton	H	W	2-1
9 Sep	Middlesbrough	A	L	1-2
13 Sep	Everton	A	D	1-1
16 Sep	Huddersfield T	H	W	6-2
23 Sep	Newcastle U	A	L	1-2
30 Sep	WBA	H	W	3-0
7 Oct	Charlton	A	W	3-1
14 Oct	Manchester U	H	W	3-0
21 Oct	Aston Villa	A	D	1-1
28 Oct	Derby	H	W	3-1
4 Nov	Wolverhampton W	A	W	1-0
11 Nov	Sunderland	H	W	5-1
18 Nov	Liverpool	A	W	3-1
25 Nov	Fulham	H	W	5-1
2 Dec	Bolton W	A	L	0-3
9 Dec	Blackpool	H	D	4-4

16 Dec	Burnley	H	L	0-1
23 Dec	Tottenham H	A	L	0-1
25 Dec	Stoke C	H	L	0-3
26 Dec	Stoke C	A	L	0-1
30 Dec	Sheffield Wed	A	W	2-0
13 Jan	Middlesbrough	H	W	3-1
20 Jan	Huddersfield T	A	D	2-2
3 Feb	Newcastle U	H	D	0-0
17 Feb	WBA	A	L	0-2
24 Feb	Charlton Ath	H	L	2-5
3 Mar	Manchester U	A	L	1-3
10 Mar	Aston Villa	H	W	2-1
17 Mar	Derby Co	A	L	2-4
23 Mar	Portsmouth	H	L	0-1
24 Mar	Wolverhampton W	H	W	2-1
26 Mar	Portsmouth	A	D	1-1
31 Mar	Sunderland	A	W	2-0
7 Apr	Liverpool	H	L	1-2
14 Apr	Fulham	A	L	2-3
21 Apr	Bolton W	H	D	1-1
2 May	Blackpool	A	W	1-0

● **FA CUP**

6 Jan	Carlisle (3)	H	D	0-0
11 Jan	Carlisle (3R)	A	W	4-1
27 Jan	Northampton T (4)	H	W	3-2
10 Feb	Manchester U (5)	A	L	0-1

APPEARANCES (Goals) Barnes 35(3); Bowen 7; L.Compton 36; Cox 13(2); Daniel 5; Fields 1; Forbes 32(4); Goring 34(15); Holton 10(5); Kelsey 4; Lewis 14(8); Lishman 26(17); Logie 39 (9); McPherson 26; Marden 11(2); Mercer 31; Milton 1; Platt 17; Roper 34(7); Scott 17; Shaw 16; L.Smith 32; Swindin 21 og 1; Total: 23 players (73)

● **POSITION IN LEAGUE**

	P	W	D	L	F	A	Pts
1st Tottenham H	42	25	10	7	82	44	60
5th Arsenal	42	19	9	14	73	56	47

SEASON 1951-1952

● **FOOTBALL LEAGUE (DIVISION 1)**

18 Aug	Huddersfield T	H	D	2-2
22 Aug	Chelsea	A	W	3-1
25 Aug	Wolverhampton W	A	L	1-2
29 Aug	Chelsea	H	W	2-1
1 Sep	Sunderland	H	W	3-0
5 Sep	Liverpool	H	D	0-0
8 Sep	Aston Villa	A	L	0-1
12 Sep	Liverpool	A	D	0-0
15 Sep	Derby Co	H	W	3-1
22 Sep	Manchester C	A	W	2-0

29 Sep	Tottenham H	H	D	1-1
6 Oct	Preston NE	A	L	0-2
13 Oct	Burnley	H	W	1-0
20 Oct	Charlton Ath	A	W	3-1
27 Oct	Fulham	H	W	4-3
3 Nov	Middlesbrough	A	W	3-0
10 Nov	WBA	H	W	6-3
17 Nov	Newcastle U	A	L	0-2
24 Nov	Bolton W	H	W	4-2
1 Dec	Stoke C	A	L	1-2
8 Dec	Manchester U	H	L	1-3
15 Dec	Huddersfield T	A	W	3-2
22 Dec	Wolverhampton W	H	D	2-2
25 Dec	Portsmouth	H	W	4-1
26 Dec	Portsmouth	A	D	1-1
29 Dec	Sunderland	A	L	1-4
5 Jan	Aston Villa	H	W	2-1
19 Jan	Derby Co	A	W	2-1
26 Jan	Manchester C	H	D	2-2
9 Feb	Tottenham H	A	W	2-1
16 Feb	Preston NE	H	D	3-3
1 Mar	Burnley	A	W	1-0
13 Mar	Charlton Ath	H	W	2-1
15 Mar	Fulham	A	D	0-0
22 Mar	Middlesbrough	H	W	3-1
11 Apr	Blackpool	A	D	0-0
12 Apr	Bolton W	A	L	1-2
14 Apr	Blackpool	H	W	4-1
16 Apr	Newcastle U	H	D	1-1
19 Apr	Stoke C	H	W	4-1
21 Apr	WBA	A	L	1-3
26 Apr	Manchester U	A	L	1-6

● FA CUP

12 Jan	Norwich C (3)	A	W	5-0
2 Feb	Barnsley (4)	H	W	4-0
23 Feb	Leyton Orient (5)	A	W	3-0
8 Mar	Luton T (6)	A	W	3-2
5 Apr	Chelsea (SF)	*	D	1-1
7 Apr	Chelsea (SFR)	*	W	3-0
3 May	Newcastle U (F)	‡	L	0-1

*at Tottenham H
‡at Wembley

APPEARANCES (Goals) Barnes 41 (2); Bowen 8; Chenhall 3; L.Compton 4; Cox 25(3); Daniel 34; Forbes 38(2); Goring 16(4); Holton 28(17); Lewis 9(8); Lishman 38(23); Logie 34(4); Marden 7(2); Mercer 36; Milton 20(5); Robertson 1; Roper 30(9); Scott 4; Shaw 8; L.Smith 28; Swindin 42; Wade 8; o/g 1 Total: 22 players (80)

● POSITION IN LEAGUE

	P	W	D	L	F	A	Pts
1st Manchester U	42	23	11	8	95	52	57
3rd Arsenal	42	21	11	10	80	61	53

SEASON 1952-1953

● FOOTBALL LEAGUE (DIVISION 1)

23 Aug	Aston Villa	A	W	2-1
27 Aug	Manchester U	H	W	2-1
30 Aug	Sunderland	H	L	1-2
3 Sep	Manchester U	A	D	0-0
6 Sep	Wolverhampton W	A	D	1-1
10 Sep	Portsmouth	H	W	3-1
13 Sep	Charlton Ath	H	L	3-4
17 Sep	Portsmouth	A	D	2-2
20 Sep	Tottenham H	A	W	3-1
27 Sep	Derby Co	A	L	0-2
4 Oct	Blackpool	H	W	3-1
11 Oct	Sheffield Wed	H	D	2-2
25 Oct	Newcastle U	H	W	3-0
1 Nov	WBA	A	L	0-2
8 Nov	Middlesbrough	H	W	2-1
15 Nov	Liverpool	A	W	5-1
22 Nov	Manchester C	H	W	3-1
29 Nov	Stoke C	A	D	1-1
13 Dec	Burnley	A	D	1-1
20 Dec	Aston Villa	H	W	3-1
25 Dec	Bolton W	A	W	6-4
3 Jan	Sunderland	A	L	1-3
17 Jan	Wolverhampton W	H	W	5-3
24 Jan	Charlton Ath	A	D	2-2
7 Feb	Tottenham H	H	W	4-0
18 Feb	Derby Co	H	W	6-2
21 Feb	Blackpool	A	L	2-3
2 Mar	Sheffield Wed	A	W	4-1
7 Mar	Cardiff C	H	L	0-1
14 Mar	Newcastle U	A	D	2-2
19 Mar	Preston NE	H	D	1-1
21 Mar	WBA	H	D	2-2
28 Mar	Middlesbrough	A	L	0-2
3 Apr	Chelsea	A	D	1-1
4 Apr	Liverpool	H	W	5-3
6 Apr	Chelsea	H	W	2-0
11 Apr	Manchester C	A	W	4-2
15 Apr	Bolton W	H	W	4-1
18 Apr	Stoke C	H	W	3-1
22 Apr	Cardiff C	A	D	0-0
25 Apr	Preston NE	A	L	0-2
1 May	Burnley	H	W	3-2

● FA CUP

10 Jan	Doncaster Rov (3)	H	W	4-0
31 Jan	Bury (4)	H	W	6-2
14 Feb	Burnley (5)	A	W	2-0
28 Feb	Blackpool (6)	H	L	1-2

APPEARANCES (Goals) Bowen 2; Chenhall 13; Cox 9(1); Daniel 41(5); Dodgin 1; Forbes 33(1); Goring 29(10); Holton 21(19); Kelsey 25; Lishman 39(22); Logie 32(10); Marden 8(4); Mercer 28(2); Milton 25(7); Oakes 2(1);

Figures shown as 2 etc. refer to goals scored by individual players

Platt 3; Roper 41(14); Shaw 25; L.Smith 31;
Swindin 14; Wade 40; o/g 1; Total: 21
players (97)

● POSITION IN LEAGUE

	P	W	D	L	F	A	Pts
1st Arsenal	42	21	12	9	97	64	54

SEASON 1953-1954

● FOOTBALL LEAGUE (DIVISION 1)

19 Aug	WBA	A	L	0-2
22 Aug	Huddersfield T	H	D	0-0
24 Aug	Sheffield U	A	L	0-1
29 Aug	Aston Villa	A	L	1-2
1 Sep	Sheffield U	H	D	1-1
5 Sep	Wolverhampton W	H	L	2-3
8 Sep	Chelsea	H	L	1-2
12 Sep	Sunderland	A	L	1-7
15 Sep	Chelsea	A	W	2-0
19 Sep	Manchester C	H	D	2-2
26 Sep	Cardiff C	A	W	3-0
3 Oct	Preston NE	H	W	3-2
10 Oct	Tottenham H	A	W	4-1
17 Oct	Burnley	H	L	2-5
24 Oct	Charlton Ath	A	W	5-1
31 Oct	Sheffield Wed	H	W	4-1
7 Nov	Manchester U	A	D	2-2
14 Nov	Bolton W	H	W	4-3
21 Nov	Liverpool	A	W	2-1
28 Nov	Newcastle U	H	W	2-1
5 Dec	Middlesbrough	A	L	0-2
12 Dec	WBA	H	D	2-2
19 Dec	Huddersfield T	A	D	2-2
26 Dec	Blackpool	A	D	2-2
28 Dec	Blackpool	H	D	1-1
16 Jan	Wolverhampton W	A	W	2-0
23 Jan	Sunderland	H	L	1-4
6 Feb	Manchester C	A	D	0-0
13 Feb	Cardiff C	H	D	1-1
24 Feb	Preston NE	A	W	1-0
27 Feb	Tottenham H	H	L	0-3
6 Mar	Burnley	A	L	1-2
13 Mar	Charlton Ath	H	D	3-3
20 Mar	Sheffield Wed	A	L	1-2
27 Mar	Manchester U	H	W	3-1
3 Apr	Bolton W	A	L	1-3
6 Apr	Aston Villa	H	D	1-1
10 Apr	Liverpool	H	W	3-0
16 Apr	Portsmouth	H	W	3-0
17 Apr	Newcastle U	A	L	2-5
19 Apr	Portsmouth	A	D	1-1
24 Apr	Middlesbrough	H	W	3-1

● FA CUP

9 Jan	Aston Villa (3)	H	W	5-1
30 Jan	Norwich C (4)	H	L	1-2

● FA CHARITY SHIELD

12 Oct	Blackpool	H	W	3-1

APPEARANCES (Goals) Barnes 19(1);
Bowen 10; Dickson 24(1); Dodgin 39; Evans
10; Forbes 30(4); Goring 9; Holton 32(17);
Kelsey 39; Lawton 9(1); Lishman 39(18);
Logie 35(8); Marden 9(3); Mercer 19;
Milton 21(3); Roper 39(12); Shaw 2; L.Smith
7; Sullivan 1; Swindin 2; Tapscott 5(5);
Tilley 1; Wade 18; Walsh 10; Ward 3; Wills
30; o/g 2; Total: 26 players (75)

● POSITION IN LEAGUE

	P	W	D	L	F	A	Pts
1st Wolverhampton W	42	25	7	10	96	56	57
12th Arsenal	42	15	13	14	75	73	43

SEASON 1954-1955

● FOOTBALL LEAGUE (DIVISION 1)

21 Aug	Newcastle U	H	L	1-3
25 Aug	Everton	A	L	0-1
28 Aug	WBA	A	L	1-3
31 Aug	Everton	H	W	2-0
4 Sep	Tottenham H	H	W	2-0
8 Sep	Manchester C	A	L	1-2
11 Sep	Sheffield U	H	W	4-0
14 Sep	Manchester C	H	L	2-3
18 Sep	Preston NE	A	L	1-3
25 Sep	Burnley	H	W	4-0
2 Oct	Leicester C	A	D	3-3
9 Oct	Sheffield Wed	A	W	2-1
16 Oct	Portsmouth	H	L	0-1
23 Oct	Aston Villa	A	L	1-2
30 Oct	Sunderland	H	L	1-3
6 Nov	Bolton W	A	D	2-2
13 Nov	Huddersfield T	H	L	3-5
20 Nov	Manchester U	A	L	1-2
27 Nov	Wolverhampton W	H	D	1-1
4 Dec	Blackpool	A	D	2-2
11 Dec	Charlton Ath	H	W	3-1
18 Dec	Newcastle U	A	L	1-5
25 Dec	Chelsea	H	W	1-0
27 Dec	Chelsea	A	D	1-1
1 Jan	WBA	H	D	2-2
15 Jan	Tottenham H	A	W	1-0
5 Feb	Preston NE	H	W	2-0
12 Feb	Burnley	A	L	0-3
19 Feb	Leicester C	H	D	1-1
26 Feb	Sheffield Wed	H	W	3-2
5 Mar	Charlton Ath	A	D	1-1
12 Mar	Aston Villa	H	W	2-0
19 Mar	Sunderland	A	W	1-0
26 Mar	Bolton W	H	W	3-0
2 Apr	Huddersfield T	A	W	1-0

8 Apr	Cardiff C	H	W	2-0
9 Apr	Blackpool	H	W	3-0
11 Apr	Cardiff C	A	W	2-1
16 Apr	Wolverhampton W	A	L	1-3
18 Apr	Sheffield U	A	D	1-1
23 Apr	Manchester U	H	L	2-3
30 Apr	Portsmouth	A	L	1-2

● FA CUP

| 8 Jan | Cardiff C (3) | H | W | 1-0 |
| 29 Jan | Wolverhampton W (4) | A | L | 0-1 |

APPEARANCES (Goals) Barnes 25; Bloomfield 19(4);Bowen 21: Danny Clapton 16; Dickson 4; Dodgin 3; Evans 21; Forbes 20(1); Fotheringham 27; Goring 41(1); Guthrie 2; Haverty 6; Herd 3(1); Holton 8; Kelsey 38; Lawton 18(6); Lishman 32(19); Logie 13(3); Marden 7; Milton 8(3); Oakes 9; Roper 35(17); Shaw 1; Sullivan 2; Swallow 1; Tapscott 37(13); Wade 14; Walsh 6; Wilkinson 1; Wills 24(1); Total: players 30 (69)

● POSITION IN LEAGUE

	P	W	D	L	F	A	Pts
1st Chelsea	42	20	12	10	81	57	52
9th Arsenal	42	17	9	16	69	63	43

SEASON 1955-1956

● FOOTBALL LEAGUE (DIVISION 1)

20 Aug	Blackpool	A	L	1-3
23 Aug	Cardiff C	H	W	3-1
27 Aug	Chelsea	H	D	1-1
31 Aug	Manchester C	A	D	2-2
3 Sep	Bolton W	A	L	1-4
6 Sep	Manchester C	H	D	0-0
10 Sep	Tottenham H	A	L	1-3
17 Sep	Portsmouth	H	L	1-3
24 Sep	Sunderland	A	L	1-3
1 Oct	Aston Villa	H	W	1-0
8 Oct	Everton	A	D	1-1
15 Oct	Newcastle U	H	W	1-0
22 Oct	Luton T	A	D	0-0
29 Oct	Charlton Ath	H	L	2-4
5 Nov	Manchester U	A	D	1-1
12 Nov	Sheffield U	H	W	2-1
19 Nov	Preston NE	A	W	1-0
26 Nov	Burnley	H	L	0-1
3 Dec	Birmingham C	A	L	0-4
10 Dec	WBA	H	W	2-0
17 Dec	Blackpool	H	W	4-1
24 Dec	Chelsea	A	L	0-2
26 Dec	Wolverhampton W	A	D	3-3
27 Dec	Wolverhampton W	H	D	2-2
31 Dec	Bolton W	H	W	3-1
14 Jan	Tottenham H	H	L	0-1

21 Jan	Portsmouth	A	L	2-5
4 Feb	Sunderland	H	W	3-1
11 Feb	Aston Villa	A	D	1-1
21 Feb	Everton	H	W	3-2
25 Feb	Newcastle U	A	L	0-2
6 Mar	Preston NE	H	W	3-2
10 Mar	Charlton Ath	A	L	0-2
17 Mar	Manchester U	H	D	1-1
24 Mar	Sheffield U	A	W	2-0
31 Mar	Luton T	H	W	3-0
2 Apr	Huddersfield T	H	W	2-0
3 Apr	Huddersfield T	A	W	1-0
7 Apr	Burnley	A	W	1-0
14 Apr	Birmingham C	H	W	1-0
21 Apr	WBA	A	L	1-2
28 Apr	Cardiff C	A	W	2-1

● FA CUP

7 Jan	Bedford T (3)	H	D	2-2
12 Jan	Bedford T (3R)	A	W	2-1
28 Jan	Aston Villa (4)	H	W	4-1
18 Feb	Charlton Ath (5)	A	W	2-0
3 Mar	Birmingham C (6)	H	L	1-3

APPEARANCES (Goals) Barnes 8; Bloomfield 32(3); Bowen 22; Charlton 19; Danny Clapton 39(2); Dickson 1; Dodgin 15; Evans 42; Forbes 5; Fotheringham 25; Goring 37; Groves 15(8); Haverty 8(2); Herd 5(2); Holton 31(8); Kelsey 32; Lawton 8(6); Lishman 15(5); Nutt 8(1); Roper 16(4); Sullivan 10; Swallow 1(1); Tapscott 31(17); Tiddy 21; Walsh 1; Wills 15; o/g 1; Total: 26 players (60)

● POSITION IN LEAGUE TABLE

	P	W	D	L	F	A	Pts
1st Manchester U	42	25	10	7	83	51	60
5th Arsenal	42	18	10	14	60	61	46

SEASON 1956-1957

● FOOTBALL LEAGUE (DIVISION 1)

18 Aug	Cardiff C	H	D	0-0
21 Aug	Burnley	H	W	2-0
25 Aug	Birmingham C	A	L	2-4
28 Aug	Burnley	A	L	1-3
1 Sep	WBA	H	W	4-1
4 Sep	Preston NE	H	L	1-2
8 Sep	Portsmouth	A	W	3-2
10 Sep	Preston NE	A	L	0-3
15 Sep	Newcastle U	H	L	0-1
22 Sep	Sheffield Wed	A	W	4-2
29 Sep	Manchester U	H	L	1-2
6 Oct	Manchester C	H	W	7-3
13 Oct	Charlton Ath	A	W	3-1
20 Oct	Tottenham H	H	W	3-1
27 Oct	Everton	A	L	0-4

3 Nov	Aston Villa	H	W	2-1	
10 Nov	Wolverhampton W	A	L	2-5	
17 Nov	Bolton W	H	W	3-0	
24 Nov	Leeds U	A	D	3-3	
1 Dec	Sunderland	H	D	1-1	
8 Dec	Luton T	A	W	2-1	
15 Dec	Cardiff C	A	W	3-2	
22 Dec	Birmingham C	H	W	4-0	
25 Dec	Chelsea	A	D	1-1	
26 Dec	Chelsea	H	W	2-0	
29 Dec	WBA	A	W	2-0	
12 Jan	Portsmouth	H	D	1-1	
19 Jan	Newcastle U	A	L	1-3	
2 Feb	Sheffield Wed	H	W	6-3	
9 Feb	Manchester U	A	L	2-6	
23 Feb	Everton	H	W	2-0	
9 Mar	Luton T	H	L	1-3	
13 Mar	Tottenham H	A	W	3-1	
16 Mar	Aston Villa	A	D	0-0	
20 Mar	Manchester C	A	W	3-2	
23 Mar	Wolverhampton W	H	D	0-0	
30 Mar	Bolton W	A	L	1-2	
6 Apr	Leeds U	H	W	1-0	
13 Apr	Sunderland	A	L	0-1	
19 Apr	Blackpool	H	D	1-1	
20 Apr	Charlton Ath	H	W	3-1	
22 Apr	Blackpool	A	W	4-2	

● FA CUP

5 Jan	Stoke C (3)	H	W	4-2	
26 Jan	Newport (4)	A	W	2-0	
16 Feb	Preston NE (5)	A	D	3-3	
19 Feb	Preston NE (5R)	H	W	2-1	
2 Mar	WBA (6)	A	D	2-2	
5 Mar	WBA (6R)	H	L	1-2	

APPEARANCES (Goals) Barnwell 1; Bloomfield 42(10); Bowen 30(2); Charlton 40; Danny Clapton 39(2); Dodgin 41; Evans 40(4); Goring 13; Groves 5(2); Haverty 28(8); Herd 22(12); Holton 39(10); Kelsey 30; Nutt 1; Roper 4(3); Sullivan 12; Swallow 4; Tapscott 38(25); Tiddy 15(6); Wills 18; o/g 1; Total: 20 players (85)

● POSITION IN LEAGUE

	P	W	D	L	F	A	Pts
1st Manchester U	42	28	8	6	103	54	64
5th Arsenal	42	21	8	13	85	69	50

SEASON 1957-1958

● FOOTBALL LEAGUE (DIVISION 1)

24 Aug	Sunderland	A	W	1-0	
27 Aug	WBA	H	D	2-2	
31 Aug	Luton T	H	W	2-0	
4 Sep	WBA	A	W	2-1	
7 Sep	Blackpool	A	L	0-1	
10 Sep	Everton	H	L	2-3	
14 Sep	Leicester C	H	W	3-1	
21 Sep	Manchester U	A	L	2-4	
28 Sep	Leeds U	H	W	2-1	
2 Oct	Aston Villa	H	W	4-0	
5 Oct	Bolton W	A	W	1-0	
12 Oct	Tottenham H	A	L	1-3	
16 Oct	Everton	A	D	2-2	
19 Oct	Birmingham C	H	L	1-3	
26 Oct	Chelsea	A	D	0-0	
2 Nov	Manchester C	H	W	2-1	
9 Nov	Nottingham F	A	L	0-4	
16 Nov	Portsmouth	H	W	3-2	
23 Nov	Sheffield Wed	A	L	0-2	
30 Nov	Newcastle U	H	L	2-3	
7 Dec	Burnley	A	L	1-2	
14 Dec	Preston NE	H	W	4-2	
21 Dec	Sunderland	H	W	3-0	
26 Dec	Aston Villa	A	L	0-3	
28 Dec	Luton T	A	L	0-4	
11 Jan	Blackpool	H	L	2-3	
18 Jan	Leicester C	A	W	1-0	
1 Feb	Manchester U	H	L	4-5	
18 Feb	Bolton W	H	L	1-2	
22 Feb	Tottenham H	H	D	4-4	
1 Mar	Birmingham C	A	L	1-4	
8 Mar	Chelsea	H	W	5-4	
15 Mar	Manchester C	A	W	4-2	
19 Mar	Leeds U	A	L	0-2	
22 Mar	Sheffield Wed	H	W	1-0	
29 Mar	Portsmouth	A	L	4-5	
7 Apr	Wolverhampton W	H	L	0-2	
8 Apr	Wolverhampton W	A	W	2-1	
12 Apr	Newcastle U	A	D	3-3	
19 Apr	Burnley	H	D	0-0	
21 Apr	Nottingham Forest	H	D	1-1	
26 Apr	Preston NE	A	L	0-3	

● FA CUP

4 Jan	Northampton T (3)	A	L	1-3	

APPEARANCES (Goals) Biggs 2; Bloomfield 40(16); Bowen 30; Charlton 36; Danny Clapton 28(5); Dodgin 23; Evans 32; Fotheringham 19; Goring 10; Groves 30(10); Haverty 15; Herd 39(24); Holton 26(4); Kelsey 38; Le Roux 5; Nutt 21(3); Petts 9; Standen 1; Sullivan 3; Swallow 7(3); Tapscott 8(2); Tiddy 12(2); Ward 10; Wills 18(1); o/g 3; Total: 24 players (73)

● POSITION IN LEAGUE TABLE

	P	W	D	L	F	A	Pts
1st Wolverhampton W	42	28	8	6	103	47	64
12th Arsenal	42	16	7	19	73	85	39

SEASON 1958-1959

● FOOTBALL LEAGUE (DIVISION 1)

23 Aug	Preston NE	A	L	1-2
26 Aug	Burnley	H	W	3-0
30 Aug	Leicester C	H	W	5-1
2 Sep	Burnley	A	L	1-3
6 Sep	Everton	A	W	6-1
9 Sep	Bolton W	H	W	6-1
13 Sep	Tottenham H	H	W	3-1
17 Sep	Bolton W	A	L	1-2
20 Sep	Manchester C	H	W	4-1
27 Sep	Leeds U	A	L	1-2
4 Oct	WBA	H	W	4-3
11 Oct	Manchester U	A	D	1-1
18 Oct	Wolverhampton W	H	D	1-1
22 Oct	Aston Villa	A	W	2-1
25 Oct	Blackburn Rov	A	L	2-4
1 Nov	Newcastle U	H	W	3-2
8 Nov	West Ham U	A	D	0-0
15 Nov	Nottingham F	H	W	3-1
22 Nov	Chelsea	A	W	3-0
29 Nov	Blackpool	H	L	1-4
6 Dec	Portsmouth	A	W	1-0
13 Dec	Aston Villa	H	L	1-2
20 Dec	Preston NE	H	L	1-2
26 Dec	Luton T	A	L	3-6
27 Dec	Luton T	H	W	1-0
3 Jan	Leicester C	A	W	3-2
17 Jan	Everton	H	W	3-1
31 Jan	Tottenham H	A	W	4-1
7 Feb	Manchester C	A	D	0-0
21 Feb	WBA	A	D	1-1
24 Feb	Leeds U	H	W	1-0
28 Feb	Manchester U	H	W	3-2
7 Mar	Wolverhampton W	A	L	1-6
14 Mar	Blackburn Rov	H	D	1-1
21 Mar	Newcastle U	A	L	0-1
28 Mar	West Ham U	H	L	1-2
4 Apr	Nottingham F	A	D	1-1
11 Apr	Chelsea	H	D	1-1
14 Apr	Birmingham C	A	L	1-4
18 Apr	Blackpool	A	W	2-1
25 Apr	Portsmouth	H	W	5-2
4 May	Birmingham C	H	W	2-1

● FA CUP

10 Jan	Bury (3)	A	W	1-0
24 Jan	Colchester U (4)	A	D	2-2
28 Jan	Colchester U (4R)	H	W	4-0
14 Feb	Sheffield U (5)	H	D	2-2
18 Feb	Sheffield U (5R)	A	L	0-3

APPEARANCES (Goals) Barnwell 16(3); Biggs 2(1); Bloomfield 29(10); Bowen 16; Charlton 4; Danny Clapton 39(6); Docherty 38(1); Dodgin 39; Evans 37(5); Fotheringham 1; Goring 2; Goulden 1; Goy 2; Groves 33(10); Haverty 10(3); Henderson 21(12); Herd 26(15); Holton 3(3); Julians 10(5); Kelsey 27; McCullough 10; Nutt 16(6); Petts 3; Standen 13; Ward G 31(4) Wills 33(1); o/g 3; Total: 26 players (88)

● POSITION IN LEAGUE

	P	W	D	L	F	A	Pts
1st Wolverhampton W	42	28	5	9	110	49	61
3rd Arsenal	42	21	8	13	88	68	50

SEASON 1959-1960

● FOOTBALL LEAGUE (DIVISION 1)

22 Aug	Sheffield Wed	H	L	0-1
26 Aug	Nottingham F	A	W	3-0
29 Aug	Wolverhampton W	A	D	3-3
1 Sep	Nottingham F	H	D	1-1
5 Sep	Tottenham H	H	D	1-1
9 Sep	Bolton W	A	W	1-0
12 Sep	Manchester C	H	W	3-1
15 Sep	Bolton W	H	W	2-1
19 Sep	Blackburn Rov	A	D	1-1
26 Sep	Blackpool	H	W	2-1
3 Oct	Everton	A	L	1-3
10 Oct	Manchester U	A	L	2-4
17 Oct	Preston NE	H	L	0-3
24 Oct	Leicester C	A	D	2-2
31 Oct	Birmingham C	H	W	3-0
7 Nov	Leeds U	A	L	2-3
14 Nov	West Ham U	H	L	1-3
21 Nov	Chelsea	A	W	3-1
28 Nov	WBA	H	L	2-4
5 Dec	Newcastle U	A	L	1-4
12 Dec	Burnley	H	L	2-4
19 Dec	Sheffield Wed	A	L	1-5
26 Dec	Luton T	H	L	0-3
28 Dec	Luton T	A	W	1-0
2 Jan	Wolverhampton W	H	D	4-4
16 Jan	Tottenham H	A	L	0-3
23 Jan	Manchester C	A	W	2-1
6 Feb	Blackburn Rov	H	W	5-2
13 Feb	Blackpool	A	L	1-2
20 Feb	Everton	H	W	2-1
27 Feb	Newcastle U	H	W	1-0
5 Mar	Preston NE	A	W	3-0
15 Mar	Leicester C	H	D	1-1
19 Mar	Burnley	A	L	2-3
26 Mar	Leeds U	H	D	1-1
2 Apr	West Ham U	A	D	0-0
9 Apr	Chelsea	H	L	1-4
15 Apr	Fulham	H	W	2-0
16 Apr	Birmingham C	A	L	0-3
18 Apr	Fulham	A	L	0-3
23 Apr	Manchester U	H	W	5-2
30 Apr	WBA	A	L	0-1

Figures shown as 2 etc. refer to goals scored by individual players

● **FA CUP**

9 Jan	Rotherham U (3)	A	D	2-2
13 Jan	Rotherham U (3R)	H	D	1-1
18 Jan	Rotherham U (3R)	*	L	0-2
	*at Sheffield Wed			

APPEARANCES (Goals) Barnwell 28(7); Bloomfield 36(10); Charles 20(8); Danny Clapton 23(7); Denis Clapton D 3; Docherty 24; Dodgin 30; Evans 7(1); Everitt 5; Groves 30(1); Haverty 35(8); Henderson 31(7); Herd 31(14); Julians 8(2); Kelsey 22; Magill 17; McCullough 33; Nutt 3; Petts 7; Snedden 1; Standen 20; Ward 15(1); Wills 33(1); o/g 1; Total: 23 players (68)

● **POSITION IN LEAGUE**

	P	W	D	L	F	A	Pts
1st Burnley	42	24	7	11	85	61	55
13th Arsenal	42	15	9	18	68	80	39

SEASON 1960-1961

● **FOOTBALL LEAGUE (DIVISION 1)**

20 Aug	Burnley	A	L	2-3
23 Aug	Preston NE	H	W	1-0
27 Aug	Nottingham F	H	W	3-0
30 Aug	Preston NE	A	L	0-2
3 Sep	Manchester C	A	D	0-0
6 Sep	Birmingham C	H	W	2-0
10 Sep	Tottenham H	H	L	2-3
14 Sep	Birmingham C	A	L	0-2
17 Sep	Newcastle U	H	W	5-0
24 Sep	Cardiff C	A	L	0-1
1 Oct	WBA	H	W	1-0
8 Oct	Leicester C	A	L	1-2
15 Oct	Aston Villa	H	W	2-1
22 Oct	Blackburn Rov	A	W	4-2
29 Oct	Manchester U	H	W	2-1
5 Nov	West Ham U	A	L	0-6
12 Nov	Chelsea	H	L	1-4
19 Nov	Blackpool	A	D	1-1
26 Nov	Everton	H	W	3-2
3 Dec	Wolverhampton W	A	L	3-5
10 Dec	Bolton W	H	W	5-1
17 Dec	Burnley	H	L	2-5
23 Dec	Sheffield Wed	A	D	1-1
26 Dec	Sheffield Wed	H	D	1-1
31 Dec	Nottingham Forest	A	W	5-3
14 Jan	Manchester C	H	W	5-4
21 Jan	Tottenham H	A	L	2-4
4 Feb	Newcastle U	A	D	3-3
11 Feb	Cardiff C	H	L	2-3
18 Feb	WBA	A	W	3-2
25 Feb	Leicester C	H	L	1-3
4 Mar	Aston Villa	A	D	2-2
11 Mar	Blackburn Rov	H	D	0-0
18 Mar	Manchester U	A	D	1-1
25 Mar	West Ham U	H	D	0-0
31 Mar	Fulham	A	D	2-2
1 Apr	Bolton W	A	D	1-1
3 Apr	Fulham	H	W	4-2
8 Apr	Blackpool	H	W	1-0
15 Apr	Chelsea	A	L	1-3
22 Apr	Wolverhampton W	H	L	1-5
29 Apr	Everton	A	L	1-4

● **FA CUP**

7 Jan	Sunderland (3)	A	L	1-2

APPEARANCES (Goals) Bacuzzi 13; Barnwell 26(6); Bloomfield 12(1); Charles 19(3); Danny Clapton 18(2); Denis Clapton 1; Docherty 21; Eastham 19(5); Everitt 4(1); Griffiths 1; Groves 32; Haverty 12(4); Henderson 39(10); Herd 40(29); Kane 4(1); Kelsey 37; Magill 6; McClelland 4; McCullough 41; Neill 14(1); O'Neill 2; Petts 1; Skirton 16(3); Snedden 23; Standen 1; Strong 19(10); Ward 9(1); Wills 24; Young 4; Total: 29 players (77)

● **POSITION IN LEAGUE**

	P	W	D	L	F	A	Pts
1st Tottenham H	42	31	4	7	115	55	66
11th Arsenal	42	15	11	16	77	85	41

SEASON 1961-1962

● **FOOTBALL LEAGUE (DIVISION 1)**

19 Aug	Burnley	H	D	2-2
23 Aug	Leicester C	A	W	1-0
26 Aug	Tottenham H	A	L	3-4
29 Aug	Leicester C	H	D	4-4
2 Sep	Bolton W	A	L	1-2
9 Sep	Manchester C	H	W	3-0
16 Sep	WBA	A	L	0-4
20 Sep	Sheffield Wed	A	D	1-1
23 Sep	Birmingham C	H	D	1-1
30 Sep	Everton	A	L	1-4
7 Oct	Blackpool	H	W	3-0
14 Oct	Blackburn Rov	A	D	0-0
21 Oct	Manchester U	H	W	5-1
28 Oct	Cardiff C	A	D	1-1
4 Nov	Chelsea	H	L	0-3
11 Nov	Aston Villa	A	L	1-3
14 Nov	Sheffield Wed	H	W	1-0
18 Nov	Nottingham F	H	W	2-1
25 Nov	Wolverhampton W	A	W	3-2
2 Dec	West Ham U	H	D	2-2
9 Dec	Sheffield U	A	L	1-2
16 Dec	Burnley	A	W	2-0
23 Dec	Tottenham H	H	W	2-1

26 Dec	Fulham	H	W	1-0
13 Jan	Bolton W	H	L	1-2
20 Jan	Manchester C	A	L	2-3
3 Feb	WBA	H	L	0-1
10 Feb	Birmingham C	A	L	0-1
24 Feb	Blackpool	A	W	1-0
3 Mar	Blackburn Rov	H	D	0-0
17 Mar	Cardiff C	H	D	1-1
24 Mar	Chelsea	A	W	3-2
31 Mar	Aston Villa	H	L	4-5
7 Apr	Nottingham F	A	L	2-5
11 Apr	Fulham	A	L	2-5
14 Apr	Wolverhampton W	H	W	3-1
16 Apr	Manchester U	A	W	3-2
20 Apr	Ipswich T	A	D	2-2
21 Apr	West Ham U	A	D	3-3
23 Apr	Ipswich T	H	L	0-3
28 Apr	Sheffield U	H	W	2-0
1 May	Everton	H	L	2-3

● FA CUP

6 Jan	Bradford C (3)	H	W	3-0
31 Jan	Manchester U (4)	A	L	0-1

APPEARANCES (Goals) Armstrong 4(1); Bacuzzi 22; Barnwell 14(3); Brown 41; Charles 21(15); Clamp 18; Danny Clapton 5(1); Clarke 1; Eastham 38(6); Griffiths 14(2); Groves 16; Henderson 12; Kelsey 35; MacLeod 37(6); Magill 21; McClelland 4; McCullough 40; McKechnie 3; Neill 20; Petts 12; Skirton 38(19); Snedden 15; Strong 20(12); Ward 11; o/g 2; Total: 24 players (71)

● POSITION IN LEAGUE

	P	W	D	L	F	A	Pts
1st Ipswich T	42	24	8	10	93	67	56
10th Arsenal	42	16	11	15	71	72	43

SEASON 1962-1963

● FOOTBALL LEAGUE (DIVISION 1)

18 Aug	Leyton Orient	A	W	2-1
21 Aug	Birmingham C	H	W	2-0
25 Aug	Manchester U	H	L	1-3
29 Aug	Birmingham C	A	D	2-2
1 Sep	Burnley	A	L	1-2
4 Sep	Aston Villa	H	L	1-2
8 Sep	Sheffield Wed	H	L	1-2
10 Sep	Aston Villa	A	L	1-3
15 Sep	Fulham	A	W	3-1
22 Sep	Leicester C	H	D	1-1
29 Sep	Bolton W	A	L	0-3
6 Oct	Tottenham H	A	D	4-4
13 Oct	West Ham U	H	D	1-1

27 Oct	Wolverhampton W	H	W	5-4
3 Nov	Blackburn Rov	A	D	5-5
10 Nov	Sheffield U	H	W	1-0
14 Nov	Liverpool	A	L	1-2
17 Nov	Nottingham F	A	L	0-3
24 Nov	Ipswich T	H	W	3-1
1 Dec	Manchester C	A	W	4-2
8 Dec	Blackpool	H	W	2-0
15 Dec	Leyton Orient	H	W	2-0
9 Feb	Leicester C	A	L	0-2
16 Feb	Bolton W	H	W	3-2
23 Feb	Tottenham H	H	L	2-3
2 Mar	West Ham U	A	W	4-0
9 Mar	Liverpool	H	D	2-2
23 Mar	Blackburn Rov	H	W	3-1
26 Mar	Everton	H	W	4-3
30 Mar	Ipswich T	A	D	1-1
6 Apr	Nottingham F	H	D	0-0
8 Apr	Wolverhampton W	A	L	0-1
12 Apr	WBA	H	W	3-2
13 Apr	Sheffield U	A	D	3-3
15 Apr	WBA	A	W	2-1
20 Apr	Manchester C	H	L	2-3
24 Apr	Everton	A	D	1-1
27 Apr	Blackpool	A	L	2-3
		A	W	3-2
11 May	Burnley	H	L	2-3
14 May	Fulham	H	W	3-0
18 May	Sheffield Wed	A	W	3-2

● FA CUP

30 Jan	Oxford U (3)	H	W	5-1
12 Mar	Sheffield Wed (4)	H	W	2-0
19 Mar	Liverpool (5)	H	L	1-2

APPEARANCES (Goals) Anderson 5(1); Armstrong 16(2); Bacuzzi (6); Baker 39(29); Barnwell 34(2); Brown 38(1); Clamp 4(1); Clarke 5; Court 6(3); Eastham 33(4); Groves 9; MacLeod 33(9); Magill 36; McClelland 33; McCullough 42(3); McKechnie 9; Neill 17; Sammels 2(1); Skirton 28(10) Smithson 2; Snedden 27; Strong 36(18); Ward 2; o/g 2; Total: 23 players (86)

● POSITION IN LEAGUE

	P	W	D	L	F	A	Pts
1st Everton	42	25	11	6	84	42	61
7th Arsenal	42	18	10	14	86	77	46

SEASON 1963-1964

● FOOTBALL LEAGUE (DIVISION 1)

24 Aug	Wolverhampton W	H	L	1-3
27 Aug	WBA	H	W	3-2
31 Aug	Leicester C	A	L	2-7

4 Sep	WBA	A	L	0-4
7 Sep	Bolton W	H	W	4-3
10 Sep	Aston Villa	H	W	3-0
14 Sep	Fulham	A	W	4-1
21 Sep	Manchester U	H	W	2-1
28 Sep	Burnley	A	W	3-0
2 Oct	Everton	A	L	1-2
5 Oct	Ipswich T	H	W	6-0
9 Oct	Stoke C	A	W	2-1
15 Oct	Tottenham H	H	D	4-4
19 Oct	Aston Villa	A	L	1-2
26 Oct	Nottingham F	H	W	4-2
2 Nov	Sheffield U	A	D	2-2
5 Nov	Birmingham C	H	W	4-1
9 Nov	West Ham U	H	D	3-3
16 Nov	Chelsea	A	L	1-3
23 Nov	Blackpool	H	W	5-3
30 Nov	Blackburn Rov	A	L	1-4
7 Dec	Liverpool	H	D	1-1
10 Dec	Everton	H	W	6-0
14 Dec	Wolverhampton W	A	D	2-2
21 Dec	Leicester C	H	L	0-1
28 Dec	Birmingham C	A	W	4-1
11 Jan	Bolton W	A	D	1-1
18 Jan	Fulham	H	D	2-2
1 Feb	Manchester U	A	L	1-3
8 Feb	Burnley	H	W	3-2
18 Feb	Ipswich T	A	W	2-1
22 Feb	Tottenham H	A	L	1-3
29 Feb	Stoke C	H	D	1-1
7 Mar	Nottingham F	A	L	0-2
14 Mar	Chelsea	H	L	2-4
21 Mar	West Ham U	A	D	1-1
24 Mar	Sheffield Wed	H	D	1-1
28 Mar	Sheffield U	H	L	1-3
30 Mar	Sheffield Wed	A	W	4-0
4 Apr	Blackpool	A	W	1-0
11 Apr	Blackburn Rov	H	D	0-0
18 Apr	Liverpool	A	L	0-5

● FA CUP
4 Jan	Wolverhampton W (3)	H	W	2-1
25 Jan	WBA (4)	A	D	3-3
29 Jan	WBA (4R)	H	W	2-0
15 Feb	Liverpool (5)	H	L	0-1

● INTER-CITIES FAIRS CUP
25 Sep	Staevnet (1/1)	A	W	7-1
22 Oct	Staevnet (1/2)	H	L	2-3*
15 Nov	Standard Liege (2/1)	H	D	1-1
18 Dec	Standard Liege (2/2)	A	L	1-3‡
	*won 9-4 on agg			
	‡lost 2-4 on agg			

APPEARANCES (Goals) Anderson 10(3);
Armstrong 28(3); Bacuzzi 5; Baker 39(26);
Barnwell 19(2); Brown 22(1); Clarke 5;

Court 8(1); Eastham 38(10); Furnell 21;
Groves 15; MacLeod 30(7); Magill 35;
McClelland 5; McCullough 40(1);
McKechnie 11; Meill 11(1); Radford 1;
Simpson 6; Skirton 15(7); Snedden 14;
Strong 38(26); Ure 41(1); Wilson 5; o/g 1;
Total 24 players (90)

● POSITION IN LEAGUE
	P	W	D	L	F	A	Pts
1st Liverpool	42	26	5	11	92	45	57
8th Arsenal	42	17	11	14	90	82	45

SEASON 1964-1965

● FOOTBALL LEAGUE (DIVISION 1)
22 Aug	Liverpool	A	L	2-3
25 Aug	Sheffield Wed	H	D	1-1
29 Aug	Aston Villa	H	W	3-1
2 Sep	Sheffield Wed	A	L	1-2
5 Sep	Wolverhampton W	A	W	1-0
8 Sep	Blackburn Rov	H	D	1-1
12 Sep	Sunderland	H	W	3-1
16 Sep	Blackburn Rov	A	W	2-1
19 Sep	Leicester C	A	W	3-2
26 Sep	Chelsea	H	L	1-3
6 Oct	Nottingham F	H	L	0-3
10 Oct	Tottenham H	A	L	1-3
17 Oct	Burnley	H	W	3-2
24 Oct	Sheffield U	A	L	0-4
31 Oct	Everton	H	W	3-1
7 Nov	Birmingham C	A	W	3-2
11 Nov	Leeds U	A	L	1-3
14 Nov	West Ham U	H	L	0-3
21 Nov	WBA	A	D	0-0
28 Nov	Manchester U	H	L	2-3
5 Dec	Fulham	A	W	4-3
12 Dec	Liverpool	H	D	0-0
19 Dec	Aston Villa	A	L	1-3
26 Dec	Stoke C	H	W	3-2
28 Dec	Stoke C	A	L	1-4
2 Jan	Wolverhampton W	H	W	4-1
16 Jan	Sunderland	A	W	2-0
23 Jan	Leicester C	H	W	4-3
6 Feb	Chelsea	A	L	1-2
13 Feb	Leeds U	H	L	1-2
20 Feb	Fulham	H	W	2-0
23 Feb	Tottenham H	H	W	3-1
27 Feb	Burnley	A	L	1-2
6 Mar	Sheffield U	H	D	1-1
13 Mar	Nottingham F	A	L	0-3
27 Mar	West Ham U	A	L	1-2
3 Apr	WBA	H	D	1-1
6 Apr	Birmingham C	H	W	3-0
16 Apr	Blackpool	A	D	1-1
19 Apr	Blackpool	H	W	3-1

| 24 Apr | Everton | A | L | 0-1 |
| 26 Apr | Manchester U | A | L | 1-3 |

● FA CUP
| 9 Jan | Darlington (3) | A | W | 2-0 |
| 30 Jan | Peterborough U (4) | A | L | 1-2 |

APPEARANCES (Goals) Anderson 10(2); Armstrong 40(4); Baker 42 (25); Baldwin 1; Burns 24; Clarke 15; Court 33(3); Eastham 42(10); Ferry 11; Furnell 18; Howe 40; MacLeod 1; Magill 1; McCullough 30; McLintock 25(2); Neill 29(1); Radford 13(7); Sammels 17(5); Simpson 6(2); Skirton 22(3); Snedden 3; Strong 12(3); Tawse 5; Ure 22(1); Total: 24 players (69)

● POSITION IN LEAGUE TABLE
	P	W	D	L	F	A	Pts
1st Manchester U	42	26	7	9	89	39	61
13th Arsenal	42	17	18	7	69	75	41

SEASON 1965-1966

● FOOTBALL LEAGUE (DIVISION 1)
21 Aug	Stoke C	H	W	2-1
25 Aug	Northampton T	A	D	1-1
28 Aug	Burnley	A	D	2-2
4 Sep	Chelsea	H	L	1-3
7 Sep	Nottingham F	A	W	1-0
11 Sep	Tottenham H	A	D	2-2
14 Sep	Nottingham F	H	W	1-0
18 Sep	Everton	A	L	1-3
25 Sep	Manchester U	H	W	4-2
28 Sep	Northampton T	H	D	1-1
2 Oct	Newcastle U	A	W	1-0
9 Oct	Fulham	H	W	2-1
16 Oct	Blackpool	A	L	3-5
23 Oct	Blackburn Rov	H	D	2-2
30 Oct	Leicester C	A	L	1-3
6 Nov	Sheffield U	H	W	6-2
13 Nov	Leeds U	A	L	0-2
20 Nov	West Ham U	H	W	3-2
4 Dec	Aston Villa	H	D	3-3
11 Dec	Liverpool	A	L	2-4
27 Dec	Sheffield Wed	A	L	0-4
28 Dec	Sheffield Wed	H	W	5-2
1 Jan	Fulham	A	L	0-1
15 Jan	Blackburn Rov	A	L	1-2
29 Jan	Stoke C	A	W	3-1
5 Feb	Burnley	H	D	1-1
19 Feb	Chelsea	A	D	0-0
5 Mar	Blackpool	H	D	0-0
8 Mar	Tottenham H	H	D	1-1
12 Mar	Everton	H	L	0-1
19 Mar	Manchester U	A	L	1-2
26 Mar	Newcastle U	H	L	1-3

5 Apr	WBA	H	D	1-1
11 Apr	WBA	A	D	4-4
16 Apr	West Ham U	A	L	1-2
20 Apr	Sunderland	A	W	2-0
23 Apr	Sunderland	H	D	1-1
25 Apr	Sheffield U	A	L	0-3
30 Apr	Aston Villa	A	L	0-3
5 May	Leeds U	H	L	0-3
7 May	Leicester C	H	W	1-0

● FA CUP
| 22 Jan | Blackburn Rov (3) | A | L | 0-3 |

APPEARANCES (Goals) Armstrong 39(6); Baker 24(13); Baldwin 8(5); Burns 7; Court 38(1); Eastham 37(6); Furnell 31; Howe 29(1); McCullough 17; McGill 2; McLintock 36(2); Neill 39; Neilson 2; Pack 1; Radford 32(8); Sammels 32(6); Simpson 8; Skirton 24(9); Storey 28; Ure 21; Walley 9(1); Wilson 4; o/g 4; Total: 22 players (62)

● POSITION IN LEAGUE TABLE
	P	W	D	L	F	A	Pts
1st Liverpool	42	26	7	9	79	34	61
14th Arsenal	42	12	17	13	62	75	37

SEASON 1966-1967

● FOOTBALL LEAGUE (DIVISION 1)
20 Aug	Sunderland	A	W	3-1
23 Aug	West Ham U	H	W	2-1
27 Aug	Aston Villa	H	W	1-0
29 Aug	West Ham U	A	D	2-2
3 Sep	Tottenham H	A	L	1-3
6 Sep	Sheffield Wed	H	D	1-1
10 Sep	Manchester C	A	D	1-1
17 Sep	Blackpool	H	D	1-1
24 Sep	Chelsea	A	L	1-3
1 Oct	Leicester C	H	L	2-4
8 Oct	Newcastle U	H	W	2-0
15 Oct	Leeds U	A	L	1-3
22 Oct	WBA	H	L	2-3
29 Oct	Manchester U	A	L	0-1
5 Nov	Leeds U	H	L	0-1
12 Nov	Everton	A	D	0-0
19 Nov	Fulham	H	W	1-0
26 Nov	Nottingham F	A	L	1-2
3 Dec	Burnley	H	D	0-0
10 Dec	Sheffield U	A	D	1-1
17 Dec	Sunderland	H	W	2-0
26 Dec	Southampton	H	W	4-1
27 Dec	Southampton	A	L	1-2
31 Dec	Aston Villa	A	W	1-0
7 Jan	Tottenham H	H	L	0-2
14 Jan	Manchester C	H	W	1-0
21 Jan	Blackpool	A	W	3-0

Figures shown as 2 etc. refer to goals scored by individual players

Date	Opponent			Score
4 Feb	Chelsea	H	W	2-1
11 Feb	Leicester C	A	L	1-2
25 Feb	Newcastle U	A	L	1-2
3 Mar	Manchester U	H	D	1-1
18 Mar	WBA	A	W	1-0
25 Mar	Sheffield U	H	W	2-0
27 Mar	Liverpool	A	D	0-0
28 Mar	Liverpool	H	D	1-1
1 Apr	Stoke C	A	D	2-2
19 Apr	Fulham	A	D	0-0
22 Apr	Nottingham F	H	D	1-1
25 Apr	Everton	H	W	3-1
29 Apr	Burnley	A	W	4-1
6 May	Stoke C	H	W	3-1
13 May	Sheffield Wed	A	D	1-1

● FA CUP

28 Jan	Bristol Rov (3)	A	W	3-0
18 Feb	Bolton W (4)	A	D	0-0
22 Feb	Bolton W (4R)	H	W	3-0
11 Mar	Birmingham C (5)	A	L	0-1

● FOOTBALL LEAGUE CUP

13 Sep	Gillingham (2)	H	D	1-1
21 Sep	Gillingham (2R)	A	D	1-1
28 Sep	Gillingham (2R)	H	W	5-0
5 Oct	West Ham U (3)	H	L	1-3

APPEARANCES (Goals) Armstrong 40(7); Addison 17(4); Baldwin 8(2); Boot 4(2); Coakley 9(1); Court 13; Furnell 42; Graham 33(11); Howe 1; McNab 26; McGill 8; McLintock 40(9); Neill 34; Neilson 12(2); Radford 30(4); Sammels 42(10); Simpson 36(1); Skirton 2(2); Storey 34(1); Ure 37; Walley 4; Woodward 3; o/g 2; Total: 22 players (58)

● POSITION IN LEAGUE TABLE

	P	W	D	L	F	A	Pts
1st Manchester U	42	24	6	12	84	45	60
7th Arsenal	42	16	12	14	58	47	46

SEASON 1967-1968

● FOOTBALL LEAGUE (DIVISION 1)

19 Aug	Stoke C	H	W	2-0
22 Aug	Liverpool	A	L	0-2
26 Aug	Nottingham F	A	L	0-2
28 Aug	Liverpool	H	W	2-0
2 Sep	Coventry C	H	D	1-1
6 Sep	WBA	A	W	3-1
9 Sep	Sheffield U	A	W	4-2
16 Sep	Tottenham H	H	W	4-0
23 Sep	Manchester C	H	W	1-0
30 Sep	Newcastle U	A	L	1-2
7 Oct	Manchester U	A	L	0-1
14 Oct	Sunderland	H	W	2-1
23 Oct	Wolverhampton W	A	L	2-3
28 Oct	Fulham	H	W	5-3
4 Nov	Leeds U	A	L	1-3
11 Nov	Everton	H	D	2-2
18 Nov	Leicester C	A	D	2-2
25 Nov	West Ham U	H	D	0-0
2 Dec	Burnley	A	L	0-1
16 Dec	Stoke C	A	W	1-0
23 Dec	Nottingham F	H	W	3-0
26 Dec	Chelsea	A	L	1-2
30 Dec	Chelsea	H	D	1-1
6 Jan	Coventry C	A	D	1-1
13 Jan	Sheffield U	H	D	1-1
20 Jan	Tottenham H	A	L	0-1
3 Feb	Manchester C	A	D	1-1
10 Feb	Newcastle U	H	D	0-0
24 Feb	Manchester U	H	L	0-2
16 Mar	Wolverhampton W	H	L	0-2
23 Mar	Fulham	A	W	3-1
29 Mar	West Ham U	A	D	1-1
6 Apr	Everton	A	L	0-2
10 Apr	Southampton	A	L	0-2
13 Apr	Leicester C	H	W	2-1
15 Apr	Southampton	H	L	0-3
20 Apr	Sunderland	A	L	0-2
27 Apr	Burnley	H	W	2-0
30 Apr	Sheffield Wed	H	W	3-2
4 May	Sheffield Wed	A	W	2-1
7 May	Leeds U	H	W	4-3
11 May	WBA	H	W	2-1

● FA CUP

27 Jan	Shrewsbury T (3)	A	D	1-1
30 Jan	Shrewsbury T (3R)	H	W	2-0
17 Feb	Swansea T (4)	A	W	1-0
9 Mar	Birmingham C (5)	H	D	1-1
12 Mar	Birmingham C (5R)	A	L	1-2

● FOOTBALL LEAGUE CUP

12 Sep	Coventry C (2)	A	W	2-1
11 Oct	Reading (3)	H	W	1-0
1 Nov	Blackburn Rov (4)	H	W	2-1
29 Nov	Burnley (5)	A	D	3-3
5 Dec	Burnley (5R)	H	W	2-1
17 Jan	Huddersfield T (SF)	H	W	3-2
6 Feb	Huddersfield T (SF)	A	W	3-1
2 Mar	Leeds U (F)	*	L	0-1
	*at Wembley			

APPEARANCES (Goals) Addison 11(5); Armstrong 42(5); Court 16(3); Davidson 1; Furnell 29; Gould 16(6); Graham 38(16); Jenkins 3; Johnston 18(3); McLintock 38(4); McNab 30; Neill 38(2); Radford 39(10); Rice 6; Sammels 35(4); Simpson 40; Storey 39; Ure 21; Wilson 13; o/g 2; Total: 19 players (60)

● POSITION IN LEAGUE TABLE

	P	W	D	L	F	A	Pts
1st Manchester C	42	26	10	6	86	43	58
9th Arsenal	42	17	15	10	60	56	44

SEASON 1968-1969

● FOOTBALL LEAGUE (DIVISION 1)

10 Aug	Tottenham H	A	W	2-1
13 Aug	Leicester C	H	W	3-0
17 Aug	Liverpool	H	D	1-1
21 Aug	Wolverhampton	A	D	0-0
24 Aug	Ipswich T	A	W	2-1
27 Aug	Manchester C	H	W	4-1
31 Aug	QPR	H	W	2-1
7 Sep	Southampton	A	W	2-1
14 Sep	Stoke C	H	W	1-0
21 Sep	Leeds U	A	L	0-2
28 Sep	Sunderland	H	D	0-0
5 Oct	Manchester U	A	D	0-0
9 Oct	Manchester C	A	D	1-1
12 Oct	Coventry C	H	W	2-1
19 Oct	WBA	A	L	0-1
26 Oct	West Ham U	H	D	0-0
9 Nov	Newcastle U	H	D	0-0
16 Nov	Nottingham F	A	W	2-0
23 Nov	Chelsea	H	L	0-1
30 Nov	Burnley	A	W	1-0
7 Dec	Everton	H	W	3-1
14 Dec	Coventry C	A	W	1-0
21 Dec	WBA	H	W	2-0
26 Dec	Manchester U	H	W	3-0
11 Jan	Sheffield Wed	H	W	2-0
18 Jan	Newcastle U	A	L	1-2
1 Feb	Nottingham F	H	D	1-1
15 Feb	Burnley	H	W	2-0
18 Feb	Ipswich T	H	L	0-2
1 Mar	Sheffield Wed	A	W	5-0
22 Mar	QPR	A	W	1-0
24 Mar	Tottenham H	H	W	1-0
29 Mar	Southampton	H	D	0-0
31 Mar	Liverpool	A	D	1-1
5 Apr	Sunderland	A	D	0-0
7 Apr	Wolverhampton W	H	W	3-1
8 Apr	Leicester C	A	D	0-0
12 Apr	Leeds U	H	L	1-2
14 Apr	Chelsea	A	L	1-2
19 Apr	Stoke C	A	W	3-1
21 Apr	West Ham U	A	W	2-1
29 Apr	Everton	A	L	0-1

● FA CUP

4 Jan	Cardiff C (3)	A	D	0-0
7 Jan	Cardiff C (3R)	H	W	2-0
25 Jan	Charlton Ath (4)	H	W	2-0
12 Feb	WBA (5)	A	D	0-1

● FOOTBALL LEAGUE CUP

4 Sep	Sunderland (2)	H	W	1-0
25 Sep	Scunthorpe U (3)	A	W	6-1
15 Oct	Liverpool (4)	H	W	2-1
29 Oct	Blackpool (5)	H	W	5-1
20 Nov	Tottenham H (SF)	H	W	1-0
4 Dec	Tottenham H (SF)	A	D	1-1
15 Mar	Swindon T (F)	*	L	1-3‡

*at Wembley
‡aet, 1-1 at 90 mins

APPEARANCES (Goals) Armstrong 29(5);
Court 40(6); Gould 38(10); Graham 26(4);
Jenkins 14(3); Johnston 3; McLintock 37(1);
McNab 42; Neill 22(2); Radford 34(15);
Robertson 19(3); Sammels 36(4); Simpson
34; Storey 42; Ure 23; Wilson 42; o/g 3;
Total: 16 players (56)

● POSITION IN LEAGUE TABLE

	P	W	D	L	F	A	Pts
1st Leeds U	42	27	2	13	66	26	67
4th Arsenal	42	22	8	12	56	27	56

SEASON 1969-1970

● FOOTBALL LEAGUE (DIVISION 1)

9 Aug	Everton	H	L	0-1
13 Aug	Leeds U	A	D	0-0
16 Aug	WBA	A	W	1-0
19 Aug	Leeds U	H	D	1-1
23 Aug	Nottingham F	H	W	2-1
25 Aug	West Ham U	A	D	1-1
30 Aug	Newcastle U	A	L	1-3
6 Sep	Sheffield Wed	H	D	0-0
13 Sep	Burnley	A	W	1-0
16 Sep	Tottenham H	H	L	2-3
20 Sep	Manchester U	H	D	2-2
27 Sep	Chelsea	A	L	0-3
4 Oct	Coventry C	H	L	0-1
7 Oct	WBA	H	D	1-1
11 Oct	Stoke C	A	D	0-0
18 Oct	Sunderland	A	D	1-1
25 Oct	Ipswich T	H	D	0-0
1 Nov	Crystal Pal	A	W	5-1
8 Nov	Derby Co	H	W	4-0
15 Nov	Wolverhampton W	A	L	0-2
22 Nov	Manchester C	H	D	1-1
29 Nov	Liverpool	A	W	1-0
6 Dec	Southampton	H	D	2-2
13 Dec	Burnley	H	W	3-2
20 Dec	Sheffield Wed	A	D	1-1
26 Dec	Nottingham F	A	D	1-1
27 Dec	Newcastle U	H	D	0-0
10 Jan	Manchester U	A	L	1-2
17 Jan	Chelsea	H	L	0-3

31 Jan	Coventry C	A	L	0-2
7 Feb	Stoke C	H	D	0-0
14 Feb	Everton	A	D	2-2
18 Feb	Manchester C	A	D	1-1
21 Feb	Derby Co	A	L	2-3
28 Feb	Sunderland	H	W	3-1
14 Mar	Liverpool	H	W	2-1
21 Mar	Southampton	A	W	2-0
28 Mar	Wolverhampton W	H	D	2-2
30 Mar	Crystal Pal	H	W	2-0
31 Mar	Ipswich T	A	L	1-2
4 Apr	West Ham U	H	W	2-1
2 May	Tottenham H	A	L	0-1

● FA CUP

3 Jan	Blackpool (3)	H	D	1-1
15 Jan	Blackpool (3R)	A	L	2-3

● FOOTBALL LEAGUE CUP

2 Sep	Southampton (2)	A	D	1-1
4 Sep	Southampton (2R)	H	W	2-0
24 Sep	Everton (3)	H	D	0-0
1 Oct	Everton (3R)	A	L	0-1

● EUROPEAN FAIRS CUP

9 Sep	Glentoran (1/1)	H	W	3-0
29 Sep	Glentoran (1/2)	A	L	0-1
20 Oct	Sporting Lisbon (2/1)	A	D	0-0
26 Nov	Sporting Lisbon (2/2)	H	W	3-0
17 Dec	Rouen (3/1)	A	D	0-0
13 Jan	Rouen (3/2)	H	W	1-0
11 Mar	Dinamo Bacau (4/1)	A	W	2-0
18 Mar	Dinamo Bacau (4/2)	H	W	7-1
8 Apr	Ajax (SF/1)	H	W	3-0
15 Apr	Ajax (SF/2)	A	L	0-1
22 Apr	Anderlecht (F/1)	A	L	1-3
28 Apr	Anderlecht (F/2)	H	W	3-0

APPEARANCES (Goals) Armstrong 17(3); Barnett 11; Court 21; George 28(6); Gould 11; Graham 36(7); Kelly 16(2); Kennedy 4(1); Marinello 14(1); McLintock 30; McNab 37(2); Neill 17(1); Nelson 4; Radford 39(12); Rice 7(1); Roberts 11(1); Robertson 27(4); Sammels 36(8); Simpson 39 Storey 39(1); Ure 3; Webster 3; Wilson 28; o/g 1; Total: 23 players (51)

● POSITION IN LEAGUE TABLE

	P	W	D	L	F	A	Pts
1st Everton	42	29	5	8	72	34	66
12th Arsenal	42	12	12	18	51	49	42

SEASON 1970-1971

FOOTBALL LEAGUE (DIVISION 1)

15 Aug   Everton   A   D   2-2
Wilson, Rice, McNab, Kelly, Roberts, McLintock, Armstrong, Storey, Radford, George 1, Graham 1,
Marinello for George

17 Aug   West Ham U   A   D   0-0
Wilson, Storey, McNab, Kelly, McLintock, Roberts, Armstrong, Radford, Kennedy, Marinello,
Graham

22 Aug   Manchester U   H   W   4-0
Wilson, Rice, McNab, Kelly, McLintock, Roberts, Armstrong, Storey, Radford 3, Kennedy, Graham 1,
Marinello for Radford

25 Aug   Huddersfield T   H   W   1-0
Wilson, Rice, McNab, Kelly, McLintock, Roberts, Armstrong, Storey, Radford, Kennedy 1, Graham,
Nelson for Radford

29 Aug   Chelsea   A   L   1-2
Wilson, Rice, McNab, Kelly 1, McLintock, Roberts, Armstrong, Storey, Nelson, Kennedy, Graham

1 Sep   Leeds U   H   D   0-0
Wilson, Rice, McNab, Kelly, McLintock, Roberts, Armstrong, Storey, Radford, Kennedy, Graham

5 Sep   Tottenham H   H   W   2-0
Wilson, Rice, McNab, Kelly, McLintock, Roberts, Armstrong 2, Storey, Radford, Kennedy, Graham,
Nelson for McLintock

12 Sep   Burnley   A   W   2-1
Wilson, Rice, McNab, Kelly, McLintock, Roberts, Armstrong, Storey, Radford 1, Kennedy 1, Graham

19 Sep   W B A   H   W   6-2
Wilson, Rice, McNab, Kelly, McLintock, Roberts, Armstrong 1, Storey, Radford, Kennedy 2, Graham
2, o/g Cantello

26 Sep   Stoke C   A   L   0-5
Wilson, Rice, McNab, Kelly, McLintock, Roberts, Armstrong, Storey, Radford, Kennedy, Graham

3 Oct   Nottingham F   H   W   4-0
Wilson, Rice, McNab, Kelly, McLintock, Roberts, Armstrong 1, Storey, Radford, Kennedy 3, Graham

10 Oct   Newcastle U   A   D   1-1
Wilson, Rice, McNab, Kelly, McLintock, Roberts, Armstrong 1, Storey, Radford, Kennedy, Graham 1

17 Oct   Everton   H   W   4-0
Wilson, Rice, McNab, Kelly 1, McLintock, Roberts, Armstrong 1, Storey 1, Radford, Kennedy 2,
Graham

24 Oct   Coventry C   A   W   3-1
Wilson, Rice, McNab, Kelly, McLintock, Roberts, Armstrong, Storey, Radford 1, Kennedy 1, Graham 1

31 Oct   Derby Co   H   W   2-0
Wilson, Rice, McNab, Kelly, McLintock, Roberts, Armstrong, Storey, Radford 1, Kennedy 1, Graham

7 Nov   Blackpool   A   W   1-0
Wilson, Rice, McNab, Kelly, McLintock, Roberts, Armstrong, Storey, Radford 1, Kennedy, Graham

14 Nov   Crystal Pal   H   D   1-1
Wilson, Rice, McNab, Kelly, McLintock, Roberts, Armstrong, Storey, Radford 1, Kennedy, Graham

21 Nov   Ipswich T   A   W   1-0
Wilson, Rice, McNab, Kelly, McLintock, Simpson, Armstrong 1, Storey, Radford, Kennedy, Sammels

28 Nov   Liverpool   H   W   2-0
Wilson, Rice, McNab, Kelly, McLintock, Simpson, Armstrong, Storey, Radford 1, Kennedy,
Sammels, Graham 1 for Kelly

5 Dec   Manchester C   A   W   2-0
Wilson, Rice, McNab, Graham, McLintock, Simpson, Armstrong1, Storey, Radford 1, Kennedy,
Sammels

12 Dec   Wolverhampton W   H   W   2-1
Wilson, Rice, McNab, Storey, McLintock, Simpson, Armstrong, Sammels, Radford 1, Kennedy,
Graham 1

19 Dec   Manchester U   A   W   3-1
Wilson, Rice, McNab, Storey, McLintock 1, Simpson, Armstrong, Sammels, Radford, Kennedy 1,
Graham 1

Figures shown as 2 etc. refer to goals scored by individual players

26 Dec   Southampton   H   D   0-0
Wilson, Rice, McNab, Storey, McLintock, Simpson, Armstrong, Sammels, Radford, Kennedy, Graham

9 Jan   West Ham U   H   W   2-0
Wilson, Rice, Nelson, Storey, McLintock, Simpson, Armstrong, Sammels, Radford, Kennedy 1, Graham 1

16 Jan   Huddersfield T   A   L   1-2
Wilson, Rice, McNab, Storey, McLintock, Simpson, Armstrong, Sammels, Radford, Kennedy 1, Graham

30 Jan   Liverpool   A   L   0-2
Wilson, Rice, McNab, Storey, McLintock, Simpson, Armstrong, Sammels, Radford, Kennedy, Graham

6 Feb   Manchester C   H   W   1-0
Wilson, Rice, McNab, Storey, McLintock, Simpson, Armstrong, Sammels, Radford 1, Kennedy, George

20 Feb   Ipswich T   H   W   3-2
Wilson, Rice, McNab, Storey, McLintock 1, Simpson, Armstrong, Sammels, Radford 1, Kennedy, George 1

27 Feb   Derby Co   A   L   0-2
Wilson, Rice, McNab, Storey, McLintock, Simpson, Armstrong, Sammels, Radford, Kennedy, George, Graham for Rice

2 Mar   Wolverhampton W   A   W   3-0
Wilson, Rice, McNab, Storey, McLintock, Simpson, Armstrong 1, Sammels, Radford 1, Kennedy 1, George

13 Mar   Crystal Pal   A   W   2-0
Wilson, Rice, McNab, Storey, McLintock, Simpson, Armstrong, Graham 1, Radford, Kennedy, George, Sammels 1 for George

20 Mar   Blackpool   H   W   1-0
Wilson, Rice, McNab, Storey 1, McLintock, Simpson, Armstrong, Graham, Radford, Kennedy, George

3 Apr   Chelsea   H   W   2-0
Wilson, Rice, McNab, Storey, McLintock, Simpson, Armstrong, Graham, Radford, Kennedy 2, George, Kelly for Armstrong

6 Apr   Coventry C   H   W   1-0
Wilson, Rice, McNab, Storey, McLintock, Simpson, Armstrong, Graham, Radford, Kennedy 1, George

10 Apr   Southampton   A   W   2-1
Wilson, Rice, McNab, Storey, McLintock 1, Simpson, Armstrong, Graham, Radford 1, Kennedy, George

13 Apr   Nottingham F   A   W   3-0
Wilson, Rice, McNab, Storey, McLintock 1, Simpson, Armstrong, Graham, Radford, Kennedy 1, George 1

17 Apr   Newcastle U   H   W   1-0
Wilson, Rice, McNab, Storey, McLintock, Simpson, Armstrong, Graham, Radford, Kennedy, George 1

20 Apr   Burnley   H   W   1-0
Wilson, Rice, Roberts, Kelly, McLintock, Simpson, Armstrong, Graham, Radford, Kennedy, George 1

24 Apr   WBA   A   D   2-2
Wilson, Rice, McNab, Storey, McLintock 1, Simpson, Armstrong, Graham, Radford 1, Kennedy, George, Sammels for Rice

26 Apr   Leeds U   A   L   0-1
Wilson, Rice, McNab, Storey, McLintock, Simpson, Armstrong, Graham, Radford, Kennedy, George

1 May   Stoke C   H   W   1-0
Wilson, Rice, McNab, Storey, McLintock, Simpson, Armstrong, Graham, Radford, Kennedy, George, Kelly 1 for Storey

3 May   Tottenham H   A   W   1-0
Wilson, Rice, McNab Kelly, McLintock, Simpson, Armstrong, Graham, Radford, Kennedy 1, George

FA CUP
6 Jan   Yeovil T (3)   A   W   3-0
Wilson, Rice, McNab, Storey, McLintock, Simpson, Armstrong, Sammels, Radford 2, Kennedy 1, Graham, Kelly for McNab

23 Jan   Portsmouth (4)   A   D   1-1
Wilson, Rice, McNab, Storey 1, McLintock, Simpson, Armstrong, Sammels, Radford, Kennedy, Graham, George for Rice

1 Feb   Portsmouth (4R)   H   W   3-2
Wilson, Rice, McNab, Storey 1, McLintock, Simpson 1, Armstrong, Sammels, Radford, Kennedy, George1

17 Feb   Manchester C (5)   A   W   2-1
Wilson, Rice, McNab, Storey, McLintock, Simpson, Armstrong, Sammels, Radford, Kennedy, George 2

6 Mar   Leicester C (6)   A   D   0-0
Wilson, Rice, McNab, Storey, McLintock, Simpson, Armstrong, Sammels, Radford, Kennedy, George

15 Mar   Leicester C (6R)   H   W   1-0
Wilson, Rice, McNab, Storey, McLintock, Simpson, Armstrong, Graham, Radford, Kennedy, George 1

27 Mar   Stoke C (SF)   D   2-2
Wilson, Rice, McNab, Storey 2, McLintock, Simpson, Armstrong, Graham, Radford, Kennedy, George, Sammels for George (at Sheffield Wed)

31 Mar   Stoke C (SFR)   W   2-0
Wilson, Rice, McNab, Storey, McLintock, Simpson, Armstrong, Graham 1, Radford, Kennedy 1, George (at Birmingham)

8 May   Liverpool (F)   W   2-1
Wilson, Rice, McNab, Storey, McLintock, Simpson, Armstrong, Graham 1, Radford, Kennedy, Kelly 1 for Storey (at Wembley, aet, 0-0 at 90 mins

FOOTBALL LEAGUE CUP

8 Sep   Ipswich T (2)   A   D   0-0
Wilson, Rice, McNab, Kelly, McLintock, Roberts, Armstrong, Storey, Nelson, Kennedy, Graham

28 Sep   Ipswich T (2R)   H   W   4-0
Wilson, Rice, McNab, Kelly, McLintock, Roberts 1, Armstrong, Storey, Radford 1, Kennedy 2, Graham

6 Oct   Luton T (3)   A   W   1-0
Wilson, Rice, McNab, Kelly, McLintock, Roberts, Armstrong, Storey, Radford, Kennedy, Graham 1

28 Oct   Crystal Pal (4)   A   D   0-0
Wilson, Rice, McNab, Kelly, McLintock, Roberts, Armstrong, Storey, Radford 1, Kennedy, Graham

9 Nov   Crystal Pal (4R)   H   L   0-2
Wilson, Rice, McNab, Kelly, McLintock, Roberts, Armstrong, Storey, Radford, Kennedy, Graham

EUROPEAN FAIRS CUP

16 Sep   Lazio Roma (1/1)   A   D   2-2
Wilson, Rice, McNab, Kelly, McLintock, Roberts, Armstrong, Storey, Radford 2, Kennedy, Graham

23 Sep   Lazio Roma (1/2)   H   W   2-0
Wilson, Rice, McNab, Kelly, McLintock, Roberts, Armstrong 1, Storey, Radford 1, Kennedy, Graham, Nelson for Graham

21 Oct   Sturm Graz (2/1)   A   L   0-1
Wilson, Rice, McNab, Kelly, McLintock, Roberts, Armstrong, Storey, Radford, Kennedy, Graham

4 Nov   Sturm Graz (2/2)   H   W   2-0
Wilson, Rice, McNab, Kelly, McLintock, Roberts, Armstrong, Storey 1, Radford, Kennedy 1, Graham

2 Dec   Beveren Waas (3/1)   H   W   4-0
Wilson, Rice, McNab, Sammels 1, McLintock, Simpson, Armstrong, Storey, Radford 2, Kennedy, Graham 1

16 Dec   Beveren Waas (3/2)   A   D   0-0
Wilson, Rice, McNab, Storey, Roberts, Simpson, Armstrong, Sammels, Radford, Kennedy, Graham, Marinello for Armstrong, George for Radford

9 Mar   FC Koln (4/1)   H   W   2-1
Wilson, Rice, McNab, Storey 1, McLintock 1, Simpson, Armstrong, George, Radford, Kennedy, Graham

23 Mar   FC Koln (4)   A   L   0-1
Wilson, Rice, McNab, Storey, McLintock, Simpson, Armstrong, Graham, Radford, Kennedy, George

APPEARANCES (Goals) Armstrong 42(7); George 17(5); Graham 38(11);Kelly 23(4); Kennedy 41(19); Marinello 3; McLintock 42(5); McNab 40; Nelson 4; Radford 41(15); Rice 41; Roberts 18; Sammels 15(1); Simpson 25; Storey 40(2); Wilson 42; o/g 2; Total: 16 players (71)

POSITION IN LEAGUE TABLE

	Pld	W	D	L	F	A	Pts
1st Arsenal	42	29	7	6	71	29	65

SEASON 1971-1972

FOOTBALL LEAGUE (DIVISION 1)

14 Aug   Chelsea   H   W   3-0
Wilson, Rice, McNab, Storey, McLintock1, Simpson, Armstrong, Kelly, Radford1, Kennedy 1, Graham
17 Aug   Huddersfield T   A   W   1-0
Wilson, Rice, McNab, Storey, McLintock 1, Simpson, Armstrong, Kelly, Radford, Kennedy 1, Graham
20 Aug   Manchester U   A   L   1-3
Wilson, Rice, McNab, Storey, McLintock 1, Simpson, Armstrong, Kelly, Radford, Kennedy, Graham
(Liverpool)
24 Aug   Sheffield U   H   L   0-1
Wilson, Rice, McNab, Storey, McLintock, Simpson, Armstrong, Kelly, Radford, Kennedy, Graham
28 Aug   Stoke C   H   L   0-1
Wilson, Rice, McNab, Storey, McLintock, Simpson, Armstrong, Kelly, Radford, Kennedy, Graham, Roberts for Rice
4 Sep   WBA   A   W   1-0
Wilson, Rice, McNab, Storey, McLintock, Roberts 1, Armstrong, Kelly, Radford, Kennedy, Graham
11 Sep   Leeds U   H   W   2-0
Wilson, Rice, McNab, Storey 1, McLintock, Roberts, Armstrong, Simpson, Radford, Kennedy, Graham 1
18 Sep   Everton   A   L   1-2
Wilson, Rice, McNab, Storey, McLintock, Roberts, Armstrong, Simpson, Radford, Kennedy 1, Graham, Kelly for McLintock
25 Sep   Leicester C   H   W   3-0
Wilson, Rice 1, Nelson, Storey, Simpson, Roberts, Armstrong, Kelly, Radford 2, Kennedy, Graham, George for Storey
2 Oct   Southampton   A   W   1-0
Wilson, Rice, Nelson, McLintock, Simpson 1, Roberts, Armstrong, Kelly, Radford, Kennedy, Graham, George for Storey
9 Oct   Newcastle U   H   W   4-2
Wilson, Rice, Nelson, McLintock, Simpson, George, Armstrong 1, Kelly 1, Radford, Kennedy 1, Graham 1, Davies for Radford
16 Oct   Chelsea   A   W   2-1
Wilson, Rice, Nelson, McLintock, Roberts, George, Armstrong, Kelly, Radford, Kennedy 2, Graham, Simpson for Kelly
23 Oct   Derby Co   A   L   1-2
Wilson, Rice, Nelson, Kelly, McLintock, Roberts, Armstrong, George, Radford, Kennedy, Graham 1, Simpson for Kelly
30 Oct   Ipswich T   H   W   2-1
Wilson, Rice, Nelson, Storey, Roberts, McLintock, Armstrong, George 1, Radford, Kennedy, Graham. o/g Sivell
6 Nov   Liverpool   A   L   2-3
Wilson, Rice, Nelson, Storey, Roberts, McLintock, Armstrong, George, Radford, Kennedy 1, Graham, o/g Smith
13 Nov   Manchester C   H   L   1-2
Wilson, Rice, Nelson 1, Storey, Roberts, McLintock, Armstrong, George, Radford, Kennedy, Graham
20 Nov   Wolverhampton W   A   L   1-5
Wilson, Rice, Nelson, Storey, Roberts, McLintock, Armstrong, George, Radford, Kennedy 1, Graham

24 Nov   Tottenham H   A   D   1-1
Wilson, Rice, McNab, Storey, Roberts, McLintock, Armstrong, Kelly, Radford, Kennedy 1, Graham
27 Nov   Crystal Pal   H   W   2-1
Wilson, Rice, McNab, Storey, Roberts, McLintock, Armstrong, Kelly 1, Radford 1, Kennedy, Graham
4 Dec   West Ham U   A   D   0-0
Wilson, Rice, McNab, Storey, McLintock, Simpson, Armstrong, Kelly, Radford, Kennedy, Graham
11 Dec   Coventry C   H   W   2-0
Wilson, Rice, McNab, Storey, Simpson, Armstrong, Kelly, Radford 2, Kennedy, Graham,
Marinello for Simpson
18 Dec   W B A   H   W   2-0
Wilson, Rice, McNab, Storey, McLintock, Roberts 2, Armstrong, Kelly, Radford, Kennedy, Graham
27 Dec   Nottingham F   A   D   1-1
Wilson, Rice, McNab, Kelly, McLintock, Simpson, Armstrong, Ball, Radford, Kennedy, Graham 1
1 Jan   Everton   H   D   1-1
Wilson, Rice, McNab, Kelly, Roberts, Simpson 1, Armstrong, Ball, Radford, Kennedy, Graham,
George for Armstrong
8 Jan   Stoke C   A   D   0-0
Wilson, Rice, McNab, Kelly, McLintock, Simpson, Armstrong, Ball, Radford, Kennedy, Graham
22 Jan   Huddersfield T   H   W   1-0
Wilson, Rice, Nelson, Kelly, McLintock, Simpson, Armstrong 1, Ball, Radford, Kennedy, Graham
29 Jan   Sheffield U   A   W   5-0
Wilson, Rice, Nelson, Roberts, McLintock, Simpson 1, Armstrong, Ball, George 2, Kennedy 1, Graham 1
12 Feb   Derby Co   H   W   2-0
Wilson, Rice, Nelson, Kelly, McLintock, Simpson, Armstrong, Ball, George 2, Kennedy, Graham
19 Feb   Ipswich T   A   W   1-0
Wilson, Rice, Nelson, Kelly, McLintock, Simpson, Armstrong, Ball, George 1, Kennedy, Graham
4 Mar   Manchester C   A   L   0-2
Wilson, Rice, Nelson, Storey, McLintock, Simpson, Armstrong, Ball, George, Radford, Graham,
Batson for George
25 Mar   Leeds U   A   L   0-3
Wilson, Rice, Nelson, Storey, McLintock, Simpson, Armstrong, Ball, George, Kennedy, Roberts,
Marinello for Roberts
28 Mar   Southampton   H   W   1-0
Wilson, Rice, Nelson, Storey, McLintock, Simpson, Armstrong, Ball, George, Kennedy, Marinello 1
1 Apr   Nottingham F   H   W   3-0
Wilson, Rice, Nelson, Storey, Roberts, Simpson, Armstrong, Ball, George 1, Kennedy 1, Marinello,
Graham 1 for Kennedy
4 Apr   Leicester C   A   D   0-0
Wilson, Rice, Nelson, Storey, McLintock, Simpson, Armstrong, Ball, George, Graham, Marinello
8 Apr   Wolverhampton W   H   W   2-1
Wilson, Rice, Nelson, Storey, McLintock, Simpson, Marinello, Ball, George, Kennedy, Graham 2,
Armstrong for Marinello
11 Apr   Crystal Pal   A   D   2-2
Wilson, Rice, Nelson, Storey, Roberts, Simpson, Armstrong, Ball 1, Radford 1, George, Graham
22 Apr   West Ham U   H   W   2-1
Barnett, Rice, McNab, Storey, McLintock, Simpson, Armstrong, Ball 2, Radford, George, Graham,
Baston for McLintock
25 Apr   Manchester U   H   W   3-0
Barnett, Rice, McNab, Roberts, McLintock, Simpson 1, Armstrong, Nelson, Radford 1, Kennedy 1,
Graham, Marinello for Graham
2 May   Coventry C   A   W   1-0
Barnett, Rice, McNab, Roberts, McLintock 1, Simpson, Armstrong, Ball, Radford, George, Graham
8 May   Liverpool   H   D   0-0
Barnett, Rice, Nelson, Roberts, McLintock, Simpson, Armstrong, Ball, Radford, Kennedy, Graham,
Roberts for Rice
11 May   Tottenham H   H   L   0-2
Barnett, Rice, McNab, Nelson, McLintock, Roberts, Armstrong, Simpson, Radford, Kennedy,
Graham, Marinello for Simpson

FA CUP

15 Jan   Swindon T (3)   A   W   2-0
Wilson, Rice, Nelson, Kelly, McLintock, Simpson, Armstrong 1, Ball 1, Radford, Kennedy, Graham
5 Feb   Reading (4)   A   W   2-1
Wilson, Rice 1, Nelson, Kelly, McLintock, Simpson, Armstrong 1, Ball, George Kennedy, Graham
26 Feb   Derby Co (5)   A   D   2-2
Wilson, Rice, Nelson, Kelly, McLintock, Simpson, Armstrong, Ball, George 2, Kennedy, Graham, Storey for Kelly
29 Feb   Derby Co (5R)   H   D   0-0
Wilson, Rice, Nelson, Storey, McLintock, Simpson, Armstrong, Ball, George Kennedy, Graham, Radford for Kennedy
13 Mar   Derby Co (5R)   W   1-0
Wilson, Rice, Nelson, Storey, McLintock, Simpson, Armstrong, Ball, George Kennedy 1, Graham (at Leicester)
18 Mar   Leyton Orient (6)   A   W   1-0
Wilson, Rice, Nelson, Storey, McLintock, Simpson, Armstrong, Ball 1, George Kennedy, Graham
15 Apr   Stoke C (SF)   D   1-1
Wilson, Rice, McNab Storey, McLintock, Simpson, Armstrong 1, Ball, Radford, George, Graham, Kennedy for Wilson (Radford went in goal) (at Villa Park)
19 Apr   Stoke C (SFR)   W   2-1
Barnett, Rice, McNab Storey, McLintock, Simpson, Armstrong, Ball, Radford 1, George 1, Graham (at Everton)
6 May   Leeds U (F)   L   0-1
Barnett, Rice, McNab Storey, McLintock, Simpson, Armstrong, Ball, Radford, George, Graham, Kennedy for Radford (at Wembley)

FOOTBALL LEAGUE CUP

8 Sep   Barnsley (2)   H   W   1-0
Wilson, Rice, McNab, Storey, McLintock, Roberts, Marinello, Kelly, Radford, Kennedy 1, Graham
6 Oct   Newcastle U (3)   H   W   4-0
Wilson, Rice, Nelson, McLintock, Simpson, Roberts, Armstrong, Kelly, Radford 2, Kennedy 1, Graham 1
26 Oct   Sheffield U (4)   H   D   0-0
Barnett, Rice, Nelson, Storey, Roberts, McLintock, Armstong, George, Radford, Kennedy, Graham
8 Nov   Sheffield U (4R)   A   L   0-2
Wilson, Rice, Nelson, Kelly, Roberts, McLintock, Armstong, George, Radford, Kennedy, Graham, McNab for McLintock

EUROPEAN CUP

15 Sep   St't Drammen (1/1)   A   W   3-1
Wilson, Rice, Simpson 1, McLintock, McNab, Roberts, Kelly 1, Marinello 1, Graham, Radford, Kennedy, Davies for Marinello
29 Sep   St't Drammen (1/2)   H   W   4-0
Wilson, Rice, Nelson, Kelly, Simpson, Roberts, Armstrong 1, George, Radford 2, Kennedy 1, Graham
20 Oct   Gr'pers Zurich (2/1)   A   W   2-0
Wilson, Rice, Nelson, McLintock, Roberts, George, Armstrong, Kelly, Radford, Kennedy 1, Graham 1
3 Nov   Gr'pers Zurich (2/2)   H   W   3-0
Wilson, Rice, Nelson, Storey, Roberts, McLintock, Armstrong, George 1, Radford 1, Kennedy 1, Graham, Simpson for Roberts, McNab for McLintock
8 Mar   Ajax Ams'dam (3/1)   A   L   1-2
Wilson, Rice, Nelson, Storey, McLintock, Simpson, Armstrong, George, Radford, Kennedy 1, Graham
22 Mar   Ajax Ams'dam (3/2)   H   L   0-1
Wilson, Rice, Nelson, Storey, McLintock, Simpson, Armstong, George, Marinello, Kennedy, Graham, Roberts for Nelson

APPEARANCES (Goals) Armstrong 42(2); Ball 18(3); Batson 2; Barnett 5; Davies 1; George 23(7); Graham 40(8); Kelly 23(2); Kennedy 37(12); McNab 20; McLintock 3 (3); Marinello 8(1); Nelson 24(1); Radford 34(8); Rice 42(1); Roberts 23(3); Simpson 34(4); Storey 29(1); Wilson 37; o/g 2; Total: 19 players (58)

POSITION IN LEAGUE TABLE

	Pld	W	D	L	F	A	Pts
1st Derby Co	42	24	10	8	69	33	58
5th Arsenal	42	23	8	12	58	40	52

SEASON 1972-1973

FOOTBALL LEAGUE (DIVISION 1)

12 Aug Leicester C   A   W   1-0
Barnett, Rice, McNab, Storey, McLintock, Simpson, Armstrong, Ball 1, Radford, Kennedy, Graham

15 Aug Wolverhampton W   H   W   5-2
Barnett, Rice, McNab 1, Storey, McLintock, Simpson 1, Armstrong, Ball, Radford 2, Kennedy 1, Graham, Roberts for Simpson

19 Aug Stoke C   H   W   2-0
Barnett, Rice, McNab, Storey, McLintock, Roberts, Armstrong, Ball, Radford, Kennedy 2, Graham

22 Aug Coventry C   A   D   1-1
Barnett, Rice 1, McNab, Storey, McLintock, Simpson, Armstrong, Ball, Radford, Kennedy, Graham

26 Aug Manchester U   A   D   0-0
Barnett, Rice, McNab, Storey, McLintock, Simpson, Armstrong, Ball, George, Kennedy, Graham

29 Aug West Ham U   H   W   1-0
Barnett, Rice, McNab, Storey, McLintock, Simpson, Armstrong, Ball 1, Radford, Kennedy, Graham, George for Armstrong

2 Sep   Chelsea   H   D   1-1
Barnett, Rice, McNab, Storey, McLintock, Simpson, Armstrong, Ball, Radford, Kennedy, Graham, George for Armstrong, o/g Webb

9 Sep   Newcastle U   A   L   1-2
Barnett, Rice, McNab, Storey, McLintock, Roberts, Marinello, Ball, Radford, Kennedy 1, Graham

16 Sep Liverpool   H   D   0-0
Barnett, Rice, McNab, Storey, McLintock, Roberts, Marinello, Ball, Radford, Kennedy, Graham

23 Sep Norwich C   A   L   2-3
Barnett, Rice, McNab, Storey 1, McLintock, Roberts, Marinello, Ball, Radford 1, Kennedy, Graham

26 Sep Birmingham C   H   W   2-0
Barnett, Rice, McNab, Storey 1, McLintock, Roberts, Marinello, Ball, Radford, Kennedy, George 1

30 Sep Southampton   H   W   1-0
Barnett, Rice, McNab, Storey, McLintock, Roberts, Marinello, Ball, Radford, Kennedy, George, Graham 1 for Kennedy

7 Oct   Sheffield U   A   L   0-1
Barnett, Rice, McNab, Storey, McLintock, Blockley, Marinello, Ball, Radford, Graham, George

14 Oct Ipswich T   H   W   1-0
Barnett, Rice, McNab, Storey, McLintock, Blockley, Marinello, Ball, Radford, Graham 1, George

21 Oct Crystal Pal   A   W   3-2
Barnett, Rice 1, McNab, Storey, McLintock, Blockley, Marinello, Kelly, Radford 1, Graham, George 1, Nelson for Kelly

28 Oct Manchester C   H   D   0-0
Barnett, Rice, McNab, Storey, McLintock, Blockley, Marinello, Kelly, Radford, George, Graham

4 Nov   Coventry C   H   L   0-2
Barnett, Rice, McNab, Storey, McLintock, Blockley, Marinello, Ball, Radford, George, Kelly, Graham for Kelly

17 Nov Wolverhampton W   A   W   3-1
Barnett, Rice, McNab, Storey, McLintock, Blockley, Marinello 1, Ball, Radford 2, George, Kelly

18 Nov Everton   H   W   1-0
Barnett, Rice, McNab, Storey, Simpson, Blockley, Marinello, Ball, Radford 1, George, Kelly

25 Nov Derby Co   A   L   0-5
Wilson, Rice, McNab, Storey, McLintock, Simpson, Marinello, Ball, Radford, George, Kelly, Armstrong for Marinello

2 Dec   Leeds U   H   W   2-1
Wilson, Rice, McNab, Storey, Blockley, Simpson, Armstrong, Ball 1, Radford 1, Kennedy, Kelly

9 Dec   Tottenham H   A   W   2-1
Wilson, Rice, McNab, Storey 1, Blockley, Simpson, Armstrong, Ball, Radford 1, Kennedy, Kelly,
McLintock for Simpson
16 Dec   WBA   H   W   2-1
Barnett, Rice, McNab, Storey, McLintock, Simpson, Armstrong, Ball, Radford 1, Kennedy, Kelly,
George for Rice, o/g Nisbet
23 Dec   Birmingham C   A   D   1-1
Wilson, Nelson, McNab, Storey, Blockley, Simpson, Armstrong, Ball, Radford, Kennedy, Kelly 1
26 Dec   Norwich C   H   W   2-0
Wilson, Nelson, McNab, Storey, Blockley, Simpson, Armstrong, Ball 1, Radford 1, Kennedy, Kelly,
George for Nelson
30 Dec   Stoke C   A   D   0-0
Wilson, Rice, McNab, Storey, Blockley, Simpson, Armstrong, Ball, Radford, Kennedy, Kelly
6 Jan   Manchester U   H   W   3-1
Wilson, Rice, McNab, Storey, Blockley, Simpson, Armstrong 1, Ball 1, Radford, Kennedy 1, Kelly
20 Jan   Chelsea   A   W   1-0
Wilson, Rice, McNab, Storey, Blockley, Simpson, Armstrong, Ball, Radford, Kennedy 1, Kelly,
McLintock for Kelly
27 Jan   Newcastle U   H   D   2-2
Wilson, Rice, McNab, Storey, Blockley, Simpson, Armstrong, Ball 1, Radford, Kennedy 1, Kelly,
George for Armstrong
10 Feb   Liverpool   A   W   2-0
Wilson, Rice, McNab, Storey, Blockley, Simpson, Armstrong, Ball 1, Radford 1, Kennedy, Kelly,
George for Radford
17 Feb   Leicester C   H   W   1-0
Wilson, Rice, McNab, Storey, Blockley, McLintock, Armstrong, Ball, Radford, Kennedy, Kelly,
George for Blockley, o/g Manley
28 Feb   W B A   A   L   0-1
Wilson, Rice, McNab, Batson, McLintock, George, Armstrong, Ball, Radford, Kennedy, Kelly
3 Mar   Sheffield U   H   W   3-2
Wilson, Rice, McNab, George 2, McLintock, Batson, Armstrong, Ball 1, Radford, Kennedy, Kelly
10 Mar   Ipswich T   A   W   2-1
Wilson, Rice, McNab, Storey, McLintock, Simpson, Armstrong, Ball 1, Radford 1, Kennedy, Kelly
24 Mar   Manchester C   A   W   2-1
Wilson, Rice, McNab, Storey, McLintock, Simpson, Armstrong, Ball, George1, Kennedy 1, Kelly,
Nelson for Kelly
26 Mar   Crystal Pal   H   W   1-0
Wilson, Rice, McNab, Storey, McLintock, Simpson, Armstrong, Ball 1, George, Kennedy, Kelly
31 Mar   Derby Co   H   L   0-1
Wilson, Rice, McNab, Storey, McLintock, Simpson, Armstrong, Ball, George, Kennedy, Kelly,
Nelson for McLintock
14 Apr   Tottenham H   H   D   1-1
Wilson, Rice, McNab, Storey 1, Blockley, Simpson, Armstrong, Ball, Radford, Kennedy, Kelly,
George for Kelly
21 Apr   Everton   A   D   0-0
Wilson, Rice, McNab, Storey, Blockley, Simpson, Armstrong, Ball, Radford, Kennedy, Kelly, George
for Blockley
23 Apr   Southampton   A   D   2-2
Wilson, Rice, McNab, Storey, Kelly, Simpson, Armstrong, Ball, Radford 1, George 1, Kennedy
28 Apr   West Ham U   A   W   2-1
Wilson, Rice, McNab, Storey, Kelly, Simpson, Armstrong, Ball, Radford 1, Kennedy 1, George
9 May   Leeds U   A   L   1-6
Wilson, Batson, McNab, Storey, Blockley, Simpson, Armstrong 1, Ball, Radford, Kennedy, Hornsby,
Price for Hornsby

FA CUP
13 Jan   Leicester C (3)   H   D   2-2
Wilson, Rice, McNab, Storey, Blockley, Simpson, Armstrong 1, Ball, Radford, Kennedy 1, Kelly

17 Jan   Leicester C (3R)   A   W   2-1
Wilson, Rice, McNab, Storey, Blockley, Simpson, Armstrong, Ball, Radford 1, Kennedy, Kelly 1
3 Feb   Bradford C (4)   H   W   2-0
Wilson, Rice, McNab, Storey, Blockley, Simpson, Armstrong, Ball 1, George 1, Kennedy, Kelly,
Marinello for George
24 Feb   Carlisle U (5)   A   W   2-1
Barnett, Rice, McNab, Storey, McLintock 1, Simpson, Armstrong, Ball 1, Radford, Kennedy, Kelly,
Nelson for Storey
17 Mar   Chelsea (6)   A   D   2-2
Wilson, Rice, McNab, Storey, McLintock, Simpson, Armstrong, Ball 1, George 1, Kennedy, Kelly
20 Mar   Chelsea (6R)   H   W   2-1
Wilson, Rice, McNab, Storey, McLintock, Simpson, Armstrong, Ball 1, George, Kennedy 1, Kelly
7 Apr   Sunderland (SF)   A   L   1-2
Wilson, Rice, McNab, Storey, Blockley, Simpson, Armstrong, Ball, George 1, Kennedy, Kelly,
Radford for Blockley (at Sheffield Wed)

FOOTBALL LEAGUE CUP
Sep   Everton (2)   H   W   1-0
Barnett, Rice, McNab, Storey 1, McLintock, Simpson, Marinello, Ball, Radford, Kennedy, Graham
3 Oct   Rotherham U (3)   H   W   5-0
Barnett, Rice, Nelson, Storey 1, McLintock, Roberts, Marinello 1, Ball, Radford 2, Graham, George 1
31 Oct   Sheffield U (4)   A   W   2-1
Barnett, Rice, McNab, Storey, McLintock, Simpson, Marinello, Kelly, Radford 1, Graham, George 1
21 Nov   Norwich C (5)   H   L   0-3
Barnett, Rice, McNab, Storey, Simpson, Roberts, Kelly, Ball, Radford, George, Kelly

APPEARANCES (Goals) Armstrong 30(2); Ball 40(10); Barnett 20; Batson 3; Blockley 20; George 27(6);
Graham 16(2); Hornsby 1; Kelly 27(1); Kennedy 34(9); McLintock 29; McNab 42(1); Marinello 13(1);
Nelson 6; Price 1; Radford 38(15); Rice 39(2); Roberts 7; Simpson 27(1); Storey 40(4); Wilson 22; o/g 3;
Total: 21 players (57)

POSITION IN LEAGUE TABLE

	Pld	W	D	L	F	A	Pts
1st Liverpool	42	25	10	7	72	42	60
2nd Arsenal	42	23	11	8	57	43	57

SEASON 1973-1974

FOOTBALL LEAGUE (DIVISION 1)
25 Aug   Manchester U   H   W   3-0
Wilson, Rice, McNab, Price, Blockley, Simpson, Armstrong, Ball 1, Radford 1, Kennedy 1, George,
Hornsby for Radford
28 Aug   Leeds U   H   L   1-2
Wilson, Rice, McNab, Storey, Blockley 1, Simpson, Armstrong, Ball, Radford, Kennedy, George,
Price for Simpson
1 Sep   Newcastle U   A   D   1-1
Wilson, Rice, McNab, Price, Blockley, Storey, Armstrong, Ball, Kelly, Radford, Kennedy 1
4 Sep   Sheffield U   A   L   0-5
Wilson, Rice, McNab, Batson, Blockley, Storey, Armstrong, Ball, Kelly, Radford, Kennedy
8 Sep   Leicester C   H   L   0-2
Wilson, Rice, McNab, Storey, Blockley, Simpson, Kelly, Ball, Radford, Radford, Kennedy, Armstrong
for Kelly
11 Sep   Sheffield U   H   W   1-0
Wilson, Rice, McNab, Storey, Blockley, Simpson, Armstrong, Ball, Radford, Radford, Kennedy 1, Kelly
15 Sep   Norwich C   A   W   4-0
Wilson, Rice, McNab 1, Storey, Blockley, George 1, Armstrong, Ball 1, Radford 1, Kennedy, Kelly

22 Sep   Stoke C   H   W   2-1
Wilson, Rice, McNab, Storey, Blockley, Simpson, Armstrong, Ball 1, Radford 1, Kennedy, George, Kelly for George

29 Sep   Everton   A   L   0-1
Wilson, Rice, McNab, Storey, Blockley, Simpson, Armstrong, Ball, Radford, Kennedy, George, Kelly for George

6 Oct   Birmingham C   H   W   1-0
Wilson, Rice, McNab, Storey, Blockley, Simpson, Armstrong, Chambers, Radford, Kennedy 1, Kelly, Brady for Blockley

13 Oct   Tottenham H   A   L   0-2
Wilson, Rice, McNab, Storey, Simpson, Kelly, Armstrong, George, Radford, Kennedy, Brady, Batson for Radford

20 Oct   Ipswich T   H   D   1-1
Wilson, Rice, McNab, Storey, Simpson 1, Kelly, Armstrong, George, Batson, Kennedy, Price

27 Oct   QPR   A   L   0-2
Wilson, Rice, McNab, Storey, Simpson, Kelly, Armstrong, George, Batson, Kennedy, Powling

3 Nov   Liverpool   H   L   0-2
Wilson, Rice, McNab, Storey, Simpson, Powling, Armstrong, George, Radford, Kennedy, Kelly, Batson for Kelly

10 Nov   Manchester C   A   W   2-1
Wilson, Rice, McNab, Storey, Simpson, Kelly 1, Ball, George, Hornsby 1, Kennedy, Armstrong

17 Nov   Chelsea   H   D   0-0
Wilson, Rice, McNab, Storey, Simpson, Kelly, Ball, George, Hornsby, Kennedy, Armstrong

24 Nov   West Ham U   A   W   3-1
Wilson, Rice, McNab, Storey, Simpson, Kelly, Ball 2, George 1, Hornsby, Kennedy, Armstrong

1 Dec   Coventry C   H   D   2-2
Wilson, Rice, McNab, Storey, Simpson, Kelly, Ball, George, Hornsby 1, Kennedy, Armstrong, Nelson1 for Kelly

4 Dec   Wolverhampton W   H   D   2-2
Wilson, Rice, McNab, Storey, Simpson, Kelly, Ball, George 1, Radford, Kennedy, Armstrong, Hornsby1 for George

8 Dec   Derby Co   A   D   1-1
Wilson, Rice, McNab, Storey, Simpson, Kelly, Ball, Blockley, Radford, Kennedy, Armstrong (o/g Newton)

15 Dec   Burnley   A   L   1-2
Wilson, Rice, Nelson, Storey, Simpson, Kelly, Ball, Blockley, Radford 1, Kennedy, Armstrong

22 Dec   Everton   H   W   1-0
Wilson, Rice, McNab, Storey, Blockley, Simpson, Armstrong, Ball1, Homsby, Kennedy, Kelly

26 Dec   Southampton   A   D   1-1
Wilson, Rice, Nelson, Storey, Blockley, Simpson, Armstrong, Ball 1, Radford, Kennedy, Kelly, Homsby for Kelly

29 Dec   Leicester C   A   L   0-2
Wilson, Rice, Nelson, Storey, Blockley, Simpson, Armstrong, Ball, Radford, Kennedy, Hornsby

1 Jan   Newcastle U   H   L   0-1
Wilson, Rice, Nelson, Storey, Blockley, Simpson, Armstrong, Ball, Radford, Kennedy, Kelly

12 Jan   Norwich C   H   W   2-0
Wilson, Rice, Storey, Kelly, Blockley, Simpson, Armstrong, Ball 2, Radford, Kennedy, Brady

19 Jan   Manchester U   A   D   1-1
Wilson, Rice, McNab, Storey, Blockley, Simpson, Armstrong, Ball, Radford, Kennedy 1, Kelly

2 Feb   Burnley   H   D   1-1
Wilson, Rice, Storey, Kelly, Blockley, Simpson, Armstrong, Ball 1, Radford, Kennedy, Brady

5 Feb   Leeds U   A   L   1-3
Wilson, Rice, Nelson, Storey, Simpson, Kelly, Armstrong, Ball 1, Radford, Kennedy, Brady

16 Feb   Tottenham H   H   L   0-1
Wilson, Rice, Nelson, Storey, Simpson, Kelly, Armstrong, Ball, Radford, Kennedy, Brady

23 Feb   Birmingham C   A   L   1-3
Wilson, Rice, Nelson, Storey, Simpson, Kelly, George, Ball, Radford, Kennedy 1, Brady

2 Mar   Southampton   H   W   1-0
Wilson, Rice, Nelson, Storey, Simpson, Kelly, George, Ball 1, Radford, Kennedy, Armstrong
16 Mar   Ipswich T   A   D   2-2
Wilson, McNab, Nelson, Storey, Simpson, Kelly, George, Brady, Radford, Kennedy 1, Armstrong
23 Mar   Manchester C   H   W   2-0
Wilson, Rice, Nelson, Storey, Simpson, Kelly, George, Ball, Radford 2, Kennedy, Armstrong
30 Mar   Stoke C   A   D   0-0
Wilson, Rice, Nelson, Storey, Blockley, Kelly, Armstrong, Ball, Radford, Kennedy, George, Simpson
for Kelly
6 Apr   West Ham U   H   D   0-0
Wilson, Rice, Nelson, Storey, Blockley, Kelly, Armstrong, Ball, Radford, Kennedy, George
13 Apr   Chelsea   A   W   3-1
Wilson, Rice, Nelson, Storey, Blockley, Kelly, Armstrong, Ball, Radford 1, Kennedy 2, George,
Simpson for Kelly
15 Apr   Wolverhampton W   A   L   1-3
Wilson, Rice, Nelson, Storey, Blockley, Simpson, Armstrong, Ball, Radford, Kennedy 1, George,
Brady for Radford
20 Apr   Derby Co   H   W   2-0
Wilson, Rice 1, Nelson, Storey, Blockley, Kelly, Armstrong, Ball 1, George 1, Kennedy, Brady,
Simpson for George
24 Apr   Liverpool   A   W   1-0
Rimmer, Rice, Nelson, Storey, Blockley, Kelly, Armstrong, Ball, Radford, Kennedy 1, Brady, Simpson
for Blockley
27 Apr   Coventry   A   D   3-3
Wilson, Rice 1, Nelson, Storey, Simpson, Kelly, Armstrong, Ball, Radford 1, Kennedy 1, George
30 Apr   QPR   H   D   1-1
Wilson, Rice, Nelson, Storey, Simpson, Kelly, Armstrong, Ball, Radford, Kennedy, George, Brady 1
for Ball

FA CUP
5 Jan   Norwich C (3)   A   W   1-0
Wilson, Rice, McNab, Storey, Blockley, Simpson, Kelly 1, Ball, Radford, Kennedy, Armstrong
26 Jan   Aston Villa (4)   H   D   1-1
Wilson, Rice, McNab, Storey, Blockley, Simpson, Armstrong, Ball, Radford, Kennedy 1, Kelly
30 Jan   Aston Villa (4R)   A   L   0-2
Wilson, Rice, McNab, Storey, Blockley, Simpson, Armstrong, Ball, Radford, Kennedy, Kelly, Brady
for McNab

FOOTBALL LEAGUE CUP
2 Oct   Tranmere Rov (2)   H   L   0-1
Wilson, Rice, McNab, Storey, Blockley, Simpson, Armstrong, Ball, Radford, Kennedy, Kelly,
Chambers for Ball

FA CUP (1972-73) THIRD PLACE PLAY-OFF
18 Aug   Wolverhampton W   H   L   1-3
Wilson, Batson, McNab, Price, Blockley, Simpson, Chambers, Ball, Radford, Kennedy, Hornsby 1

APPEARANCES (Goals) Armstrong 41; Ball 36(13); Batson 5; Blockley 26(1); Brady 13(1); Chambers
1; George 28(5); Homsby 9(3); Kelly 37(1); Kennedy 42(12); McNab 23(1); Nelson 19(1); Powling 2;
Price 4; Radford 32(7); Rice 41(1); Rimmer 1; Simpson 38(2); Storey 41; Wilson 41; o/g 1; Total: 20
players (49)

POSITION IN LEAGUE TABLE

	Pld	W	D	L	F	A	Pts
1st Leeds U	42	24	14	4	66	31	62
5th Arsenal	42	14	14	14	49	51	42

SEASON 1974-1975

FOOTBALL LEAGUE (DIVISION 1)

17 Aug   Leicester C   A   W   1-0
Rimmer, Matthews, Nelson, Storey, Simpson, Kelly, Armstrong, Brady, Radford, George, Kidd 1, Price for Kelly

20 Aug   Ipswich T   H   L   0-1
Rimmer, Storey, Nelson, Kelly, Simpson, Matthews, Armstrong, Hornsby, Radford, Kidd, Brady

24 Aug   Manchester C   H   W   4-0
Rimmer, Rice, Nelson, Kelly, Simpson, Storey, Matthews, George, Radford 2, Kidd 2, Brady, Armstrong for Simpson

27 Aug   Ipswich T   A   L   0-3
Rimmer, Rice, Nelson, Kelly, Simpson, Matthews, Brady, George, Radford, Kidd, Storey

31 Aug   Everton   A   L   1-2
Rimmer, Rice, Nelson, Storey, Simpson, Kelly, Blockley, Brady, Radford, George, Kidd 1, Powling for Kelly

7 Sep   Burnley   H   L   0-1
Rimmer, Rice, Nelson, Storey, Blockley, Matthews, Armstrong, Brady, Radford, George, Kidd, Simpson for Rice

14 Sep   Chelsea   A   D   0-0
Rimmer, Kelly, Simpson, Storey, Blockley, Matthews, Armstrong, George, Radford, Kidd, Brady

21 Sep   Luton T   H   D   2-2
Rimmer, Simpson, Nelson, Storey, Blockley, Matthews, Armstrong, Kelly, Radford, Kidd 2, Brady

28 Sep   Birmingham C   A   L   1-3
Rimmer, Storey, Simpson, Kelly, Blockley, Matthews, George 1, Ball, Radford, Kidd, Brady

5 Oct   Leeds U   A   L   0-2
Rimmer, Storey, Simpson, Kelly, Blockley, Matthews, Armstrong, Ball, Radford, Kidd, Brady, Powling for Blockley

12 Oct   QPR   H   D   2-2
Rimmer, Storey, Simpson, Kelly Powling, Matthews, Armstrong, Ball, Radford 1, Kidd 1, Brady

16 Oct   Manchester C   A   L   1-2
Rimmer, Storey, Simpson, Nelson, Powling, Kelly, Ball, Brady, Radford 1, Kidd, Armstrong

19 Oct   Tottenham H   A   L   0-2
Rimmer, Storey, Nelson, Kelly, Powling, Simpson, Armstrong, Ball, Radford, Brady, Kidd

26 Oct   West Ham U   H   W   3-0
Rimmer, Storey, McNab, Kelly, Mancini, Simpson, Rice, Ball, Radford 1, Brady 1, Kidd 1, Armstrong for Rice

2 Nov   Wolverhampton W   H   D   0-0
Rimmer, Storey, McNab, Kelly, Mancini, Simpson, Rice, Ball, Radford1, Brady1, Kidd

9 Nov   Liverpool   A   W   3-1
Rimmer, Rice, McNab, Kelly, Mancini, Simpson, Storey, Ball 2, Radford, Kidd, Brady 1

16 Nov   Derby Co   H   W   3-1
Rimmer, Rice, McNab, Kelly, Mancini, Simpson, Storey, Ball 2, Radford, Kidd 1, Brady

23 Nov   Coventry C   A   L   0-3
Rimmer, Rice, McNab, Kelly, Simpson, Powling, Armstrong, Ball, Radford, Kidd, Brady, George for Brady

30 Nov   Middlesbrough   H   W   2-0
Rimmer, Rice, McNab, Kelly, Simpson, Powling, George, Ball 1, Radford, Kidd, Brady 1

7 Dec   Carlisle U   A   L   1-2
Rimmer, Rice, McNab, Kelly, Simpson, Mancini, Storey, Ball, Radford, Kidd 1, Cropley

14 Dec   Leicester C   H   D   0-0
Rimmer, Rice, McNab, Kelly, Mancini, Simpson, Storey, Ball, Radford, Kidd, Cropley

21 Dec   Stoke C   A   W   2-0
Rimmer, Rice, McNab, Kelly, Mancini, Simpson, Storey, Ball, Radford, Kidd 2, Cropley

26 Dec   Chelsea   H   L   1-2
Rimmer, Rice, McNab, Kelly, Mancini, Simpson, Storey, Ball 1, Radford, Kidd, Cropley

28 Dec   Sheffield U   A   D   1-1
Rimmer, Rice, McNab, Kelly, Mancini, Simpson, Storey, Ball, George 1, Kidd, Cropley, Armstrong for Kelly
11 Jan   Carlisle U   H   W   2-1
Rimmer, Rice, McNab, Kelly, Mancini, Simpson, Armstrong, Ball, Radford 1, Kidd, Cropley 1
18 Jan   Middlesbrough   A   D   0-0
Rimmer, Rice, McNab, Kelly, Mancini, Simpson, Armstrong, Ball, Storey, Kidd, Cropley
1 Feb   Liverpool   H   W   2-0
Rimmer, Rice, McNab, Matthews, Mancini, Simpson, Armstrong, Ball 2, Brady, Kidd, Storey, Ross for Ball
8 Feb   Wolverhampton W   A   L   0-1
Rimmer, Rice, McNab, Ross, Mancini, Simpson, Armstrong, Brady, Radford, Kidd, Storey
22 Feb   Derby Co   A   L   1-2
Rimmer, Rice, McNab, Storey, Mancini, Simpson, Armstrong, Ball, Radford 1, Kidd, Brady
1 Mar   Everton   H   L   0-2
Rimmer, Rice, McNab, Storey, Mancini, Simpson, Armstrong, Ball, Radford, Kidd, Brady
15 Mar   Birmingham C   H   D   1-1
Rimmer, Rice, Nelson, Storey, Mancini, Simpson Matthews, Armstrong, Ball, Radford, Kidd 1, Brady
18 Mar   Newcastle U   H   W   3-0
Rimmer, Rice, Nelson, Rostron1, Simpson, Matthews, Armstrong, Ball 1, Hornsby, Kidd 1, Brady
22 Mar   Burnley   A   D   3-3
Rimmer, Rice, Nelson, Matthews, Simpson, Matthews, Rostron 1, Ball, Hornsby 2, Kidd, Brady, Powling for Matthews
25 Mar   Luton T   A   L   0-2
Rimmer, Rice, Nelson, Storey, Simpson, Matthews, Rostron, Ball, Radford, Hornsby, Brady
29 Mar   Stoke C   H   D   1-1
Rimmer, Rice, McNab, Storey, Kelly1, Simpson, Matthews, Ball, Stapleton, Rostron, Hornsby, Brady for Stapleton
31 Mar   Sheffield U   H   W   1-0
Rimmer, Rice, Nelson, Storey, Mancini, Simpson, Matthews, Kelly, Hornsby, Kidd 1, Armstrong
8 Apr   Coventry C   H   W   2-0
Rimmer, Rice, Nelson, Storey, Mancini, Simpson, Matthews, Kelly, Hornsby, Kidd 2, Armstrong
12 Apr   Leeds U   H   L   1-2
Rimmer, Rice, Nelson, Storey, Mancini, Simpson, Matthews, Kelly, Hornsby, Kidd 1, Armstrong, Brady for Nelson
19 Apr   QPR   A   D   0-0
Rimmer, Rice, Nelson, Storey, Mancini, Simpson, Ball, Kelly, Hornsby, Kidd, Armstrong
23 Apr   Newcastle U   A   L   1-3
Rimmer, Rice, Matthews, Storey, Mancini, Brady, Ball, Kelly, Hornsby 1, Kidd, Rostron, Nelson for Kelly
26 Apr   Tottenham H   H   W   1-0
Barnett, Rice, Nelson, Storey, Mancini, Simpson, Ball, Brady, Hornsby, Kidd 1, Armstrong
28 Apr   West Ham U   A   L   0-1
Barnett, Storey, Nelson, Kelly, Mancini, Matthews, Ball, Brady, Hornsby, Kidd, Rostron

FA CUP
4 Jan   York C (3)   H   D   1-1
Rimmer, Rice, McNab, Kelly1, Mancini, Powling, Storey, Ball, Armstrong, Kidd, Cropley
7 Jan   York C (3R)   A   W   3-1
Rimmer, Rice, McNab, Kelly, Simpson, Mancini, Armstrong, Ball, Radford, Kidd 3, Cropley
25 Jan   Coventry (4)   A   D   1-1
Rimmer, Rice, McNab, Storey, Mancini, Simpson, Armstrong, Ball 1, Radford, Kidd, George, Matthews for George
29 Jan   Coventry (4R)   H   W   3-0
Rimmer, Rice, McNab, Matthews 1, Mancini, Simpson, Armstrong 2, Ball, Radford, Kidd, Storey, Brady for Radford
15 Feb   Leicester C (5)   H   D   0-0
Rimmer, Rice, McNab, Storey, Mancini, Simpson, Armstrong, Ball, Radford, Kidd, Brady

19 Feb   Leicester C (5R)   A   D   1-1
Rimmer, Rice, McNab, Storey, Mancini, Simpson, Armstrong, Ball, Radford 1, Kidd, Matthews, Brady for Matthews
24 Feb   Leicester C (5R)   A   W   1-0
Rimmer, Rice, McNab, Storey, Mancini, Simpson, Armstrong, Ball, Radford 1, Kidd, Matthews, Brady for Matthews
8 Mar   West Ham U (6)   H   L   0-2
Rimmer, Rice, McNab, Storey, Mancini, Simpson, Matthews, Ball, Radford, Kidd, Brady, Armstrong for Radford

FOOTBALL LEAGUE CUP
10 Sep   Leicester C (2)   H   D   1-1
Rimmer, Kelly, Simpson, Storey, Blockley, Mathews, Armstrong, George, Radford, Kidd 1, Brady
18 Sep   Leicester C (2R)   A   L   1-2
Rimmer, Simpson, Nelson, Storey, Blockley, Mathews, Armstrong, Kelly, Radford, Kidd, Brady 1

LEAGUE APPEARANCES (Goals) Armstrong 24; Ball 30(9); Barnett 2; Blockley 6; Brady 32(3); Cropley 7(1); George 10(2); Hornsby 12(3); Kelly 32(1); Kidd 40(19); Mancini 26; McNab 18; Matthews 20; Nelson 20; Powling 8; Price 1; Radford 29(7); Rice 32; Rimmer 40; Ross 2; Rostron 6(2); Simpson 40; Stapleton 1; Storey 37; Total 24 players (47)

POSITION IN LEAGUE TABLE
	Pld	W	D	L	F	A	Pts
1st Derby Co	42	21	11	10	67	49	53
16th Arsenal	42	13	11	18	47	49	37

SEASON 1975-1976

FOOTBALL LEAGUE (DIVISION 1)
16 Aug   Burnley   A   D   0-0
Rimmer, Rice, Nelson, Kelly, Mancini, O'Leary, Armstrong, Cropley, Hornsby, Kidd, Brady
19 Aug   Sheffield U   A   W   3-1
Rimmer, Rice 1, Nelson, Kelly, Mancini, O'Leary, Armstrong, Cropley, Hornsby, Kidd 1, Brady 1
23 Aug   Stoke C   H   L   0-1
Rimmer, Rice, Nelson, Kelly, Mancini, O'Leary, Armstrong, Cropley, Hornsby, Kidd, Brady
26 Aug   Norwich C   H   W   2-1
Rimmer, Rice, Storey, Kelly 1, Mancini, O'Leary, Armstrong, Cropley, Ball 1, Kidd, Brady
30 Aug   Wolverhampton W   A   D   0-0
Rimmer, Rice, Nelson, Kelly, Mancini, O'Leary, Ball, Cropley, Radford, Kidd, Brady
6 Sep   Leicester C   H   D   1-1
Rimmer, Rice, Nelson, Kelly, Mancini, O'Leary, Ball, Cropley, Stapleton 1, Kidd, Brady
13 Sep   Aston Villa   A   L   0-2
Rimmer, Rice, Nelson, Kelly, Mancini, O'Leary, Ball, Cropley, Stapleton, Kidd, Brady
20 Sep   Everton   H   D   2-2
Rimmer, Rice, Nelson, Kelly, Mancini, O'Leary, Ball, Cropley, Stapleton 1, Kidd 1, Brady
27 Sep   Tottenham H   A   D   0-0
Rimmer, Rice, Nelson, Kelly, Mancini, O'Leary, Ball, Cropley, Stapleton, Kidd, Rostron, Brady for Rostron
4 Oct   Manchester C   H   L   2-3
Rimmer, Rice, Nelson, Kelly, Simpson, O'Leary, Ball 1, Cropley 1, Stapleton, Kidd, Brady, Rostron for Kelly
11 Oct   Coventry C   H   W   5-0
Rimmer, Rice, Nelson, Powling, Simpson, O'Leary, Ball 1, Cropley 2, Stapleton, Kidd 2, Brady, Rostron for Cropley
18 Oct   Manchester U   A   L   1-3
Rimmer, Rice, Nelson, Kelly 1, O'Leary, Simpson, Ball, Cropley, Stapleton, Kidd, Brady
25 Oct   Middlesbrough   H   W   2-1
Rimmer, Rice, Nelson, Kelly, O'Leary, Simpson, Ball, Cropley 1, Stapleton 1, Kidd, Brady, Powling for Kelly

1 Nov **Newcastle U** **A** **L** **0-2**
Rimmer, Rice, Nelson, Kelly, O'Leary, Simpson, Ball, Powling, Stapleton, Kidd, Brady

8 Nov **Derby Co** **H** **L** **0-1**
Rimmer, Rice, Storey, Kelly, O'Leary, Powling, Ball, Cropley, Stapleton, Hornsby, Brady

15 Nov **Birmingham C** **A** **L** **1-3**
Rimmer, Rice, Storey, Kelly, O'Leary, Powling, Ball 1, Cropley, Stapleton, Kidd, Brady, Matthews for Cropley

22 Nov **Manchester U** **H** **W** **3-1**
Rimmer, Rice, Kelly, Storey Nelson, O'Leary, Ball 1, Armstrong 1, Stapleton, Kidd, Brady, (o/g Greenhoff)

29 Nov **West Ham U** **A** **L** **0-1**
Rimmer, Rice, Nelson, Storey, O'Leary, Powling, Ball, Armstrong, Stapleton, Kidd, Brady

2 Dec **Liverpool** **A** **D** **2-2**
Rimmer, Rice, Storey, Nelson, O'Leary, Powling, Ball 1, Armstrong, Stapleton, Kidd 1, Brady

6 Dec **Leeds U** **H** **L** **1-2**
Rimmer, Rice, Nelson, Storey, O'Leary, Powling, Armstrong, Ball, Stapleton, Kidd, Brady 1

13 Dec **Stoke C** **A** **L** **1-2**
Barnett, Rice, Nelson, Storey, O'Leary, Powling, Armstrong 1, Ball, Stapleton, Kidd, Brady, Simpson for Nelson

20 Dec **Burnley** **H** **W** **1-0**
Rimmer, Rice, Simpson, Kelly, Mancini, Powling, Armstrong, Ball, Radford 1, Kidd, Brady, Stapleton for Brady

26 Dec **Ipswich T** **A** **L** **0-2**
Rimmer, Rice Kelly, Storey, O'Leary, Powling, Armstrong, Ball, Radford, Kidd, Brady

27 Dec **QPR** **H** **W** **2-0**
Rimmer, Rice, Nelson, Storey, O'Leary, Powling, Armstrong, Ball 1, Stapleton, Kidd 1, Brady

10 Jan **Aston Villa** **H** **D** **0-0**
Rimmer, Rice, Nelson, Powling, O'Leary, Mancini, Armstrong, Ball, Stapleton, Kidd, Brady

17 Jan **Leicester C** **A** **L** **1-2**
Rimmer, Rice, Nelson, Ross1, O'Leary, Mancini, Armstrong, Ball, Stapleton, Kidd, Brady

31 Jan **Sheffield U** **H** **W** **1-0**
Rimmer, Rice, Nelson, Ross, Mancini, Powling, Armstrong, Ball, Stapleton, Kidd, Brady 1, Rostron for Nelson

7 Feb **Norwich C** **A** **L** **1-3**
Rimmer, Rice, Storey, Ross, Mancini, Simpson, Armstrong, Ball, Stapleton, Kidd 1, Brady

18 Feb **Derby Co** **A** **L** **0-2**
Rimmer, Rice, Nelson, Ross, Mancini, Powling, Armstrong, Ball, Radford, Kidd, Brady

21 Feb **Birmingham C** **H** **W** **1-0**
Rimmer, Rice, Nelson, Ross, Mancini, Powling, Armstrong, Ball, Radford, Kidd, Brady 1, Simpson for Brady

24 Feb **Liverpool** **H** **W** **1-0**
Rimmer, Rice, Nelson, Ross, Mancini, Powling, Armstrong, Ball, Radford 1, Kidd, Brady

28 Feb **Middlesbrough** **A** **W** **1-0**
Rimmer, Rice, Nelson, Ross, Mancini, Powling, Armstrong, Ball, Radford 1, Kidd, Brady

13 Mar **Coventry C** **A** **D** **1-1**
Rimmer, Rice, Nelson, Ross, Mancini, Powling 1, Armstrong, Ball, Radford, Kidd, Brady

16 Mar **Newcastle U** **H** **D** **0-0**
Rimmer, Rice, Nelson, Ross, Mancini, Powling, Armstrong, Ball, Radford, Kidd, Brady

20 Mar **West Ham U** **H** **W** **6-1**
Rimmer, Rice, Nelson, Ross, Mancini, Powling, Armstrong 1, Ball 2, Radford, Kidd 3, Brady, Stapleton for Rice

27 Mar **Leeds U** **A** **L** **0-3**
Rimmer, Rice, Nelson, Ross, Mancini, Powling, Armstrong, Ball, Radford, Kidd, Brady

3 Apr **Tottenham H** **H** **L** **0-2**
Rimmer, Rice, Nelson, Ross, Mancini, Powling, Armstrong, Ball, Radford, Kidd, Brady

10 Apr **Everton** **A** **D** **0-0**
Rimmer, Rice, Nelson, Ross, Mancini, Powling, Armstrong, Ball, Radford, Cropley, Brady

13 Apr Wolverhampton W   H   W   2-1
Rimmer, Rice, Nelson, Ross, Mancini 1, Powling, Armstrong, Ball, Radford, Cropley, Brady 1
17 Apr Ipswich T   H   L   1-2
Rimmer, Rice, Nelson, Ross, O'Leary, Powling, Rostron, Ball, Stapleton 1, Cropley, Brady
19 Apr QPR   A   L   1-2
Rimmer, Rice, Nelson, Ross, O'Leary, Powling, Kidd 1, Ball, Radford, Cropley, Brady, Armstrong for Radford
24 Apr Manchester C   A   L   1-3
Rimmer, Rice, Nelson, Ross, Mancini, Powling, Armstrong 1, Ball, Stapleton, Cropley, Brady

FA CUP
3 Jan Wolverhampton W (3) A   L   0-3
Rimmer, Rice, Nelson, Storey, O'Leary, Powling, Armstrong, Ball, Stapleton, Kidd, Brady

FOOTBALL LEAGUE CUP
9 Sep Everton (2)   A   D   2-2
Rimmer, Rice, Nelson, Kelly, Mancini, O'Leary, Ball, Cropley 1, Radford, Kidd, Brady, Stapleton 1 for Mancini
23 Sep Everton (2R)   H   L   0-1
Rimmer, Rice, Nelson, Kelly, Mancini, O'Leary, Ball, Cropley, Stapleton, Kidd, Rostron

APPEARANCES (Goals) Armstrong 29(4); Ball 39(9); Barnett 1; Brady 42(5); Cropley 20(4); Hornsby 4; Kelly 17(2); Kidd 37(11); Mancini 26(1); Matthews 1; Nelson 36;- O'Leary 27; Powling 29(1); Radford 15(3); Rice 42(1); Rimmer 41; Ross 17(1); Rostron 5; Simpson 9; Stapleton 25(4); Storey 11; o/g 1; Total 21 players (47)

POSITION IN LEAGUE TABLE

	Pld	W	D	L	F	A	Pts
1st Liverpool	42	23	14	5	66	31	60
17th Arsenal	42	13	10	19	47	53	36

SEASON 1976-1977

FOOTBALL LEAGUE (DIVISION 1)
21 Aug Bristol C   H   L   0-1
Rimmer, Rice, Nelson, Ross, O'Leary, Simpson, Ball, Armstrong, Macdonald, Radford, Cropley, Storey for Cropley
25 Aug Norwich C   A   W   3-1
Rimmer, Rice, Nelson 1, Ross, O'Leary, Simpson, Ball, Armstrong, Macdonald 1, Stapleton 1, Brady
28 Aug Sunderland   A   D   2-2
Rimmer, Rice, Nelson, Ross 1, O'Leary, Simpson, Ball, Armstrong, Macdonald 1, Stapleton, Brady
4 Sep Manchester C   H   D   0-0
Rimmer, Rice, Nelson, Ross, O'Leary, Simpson, Ball, Brady, Macdonald, Stapleton, Armstrong, Cropley for Stapleton
11 Sep West Ham U   A   W   2-0
Rimmer, Rice, Nelson, Ross 1, O'Leary, Howard, Simpson, Ball, Brady, Cropley, Stapleton 1, Armstrong, Storey for O'Leary
18 Sep Everton   H   W   3-1
Rimmer, Rice, Nelson, Ross, Howard, Powling, Ball, Brady 1, Macdonald 1, Stapleton 1, Armstrong
25 Sep Ipswich T   A   L   1-3
Rimmer, Rice, Nelson, Ross, O'Leary, Howard, Ball, Brady, Macdonald, Stapleton, Armstrong, (o/g Hunter)
2 Oct QPR   H   W   3-2
Rimmer, Rice 1, Nelson, Ross, O'Leary, Howard, Ball, Brady 1, Macdonald, Stapleton 1, Armstrong, Storey for Nelson
16 Oct Stoke C   H   W   2-0
Rimmer, Rice 1, Storey, Ross, O'Leary, Howard, Ball, Brady, Macdonald 1, Stapleton, Armstrong, Radford for Stapleton

20 Oct Aston Villa   A L   1-5
Rimmer, Rice, Storey, Ross, O'Leary, Howard, Ball 1, Brady, Macdonald, Stapleton, Armstrong
23 Oct Leicester C   A L   1-4
Rimmer, Rice, Storey, Ross, O'Leary, Matthews, Ball, Brady, Macdonald, Stapleton 1, Armstrong
30 Oct Leeds U   A L   1-2
Rimmer, Rice, Nelson, Ross, Simpson, Howard, Matthews1, Brady, Macdonald, Stapleton, Armstrong
6 Nov   Birmingham C   H W   4-0
Rimmer, Rice, Nelson 1, Ross 1, O'Leary, Simpson, Matthews, Brady, Macdonald 1, Stapleton 1, Armstrong, Storey for O'Leary
20 Nov Liverpool   H D   1-1
Rimmer, Rice, Nelson, Ross, O'Leary, Simpson, Ball, Brady, Macdonald, Stapleton, Armstrong 1
27 Nov Coventry C   A W   2-1
Rimmer, Rice, Nelson, Ross, O'Leary, Simpson, Ball, Brady, Macdonald 1, Stapleton 1, Armstrong
4 Dec   Newcastle U   H W   5-3
Rimmer, Rice, Nelson, Ross 1, O'Leary, Howard, Ball, Brady, Macdonald 3, Stapleton 1, Armstrong, Matthews for Rice
15 Dec Derby Co   A D   0-0
Rimmer, Rice, Nelson, Ross, O'Leary, Simpson, Storey, Brady, Macdonald, Stapleton, Armstrong
18 Dec Manchester U   H W   3-1
Rimmer, Rice Powling, Ross, O'Leary, Simpson, Storey, Brady 1, Macdonald 2, Stapleton, Armstrong, Rostron for Stapleton
27 Dec Tottenham H   A D   2-2
Rimmer, Rice Powling, Ross, O'Leary, Simpson, Storey, Brady, Macdonald 2, Stapleton, Rostron
3 Jan   Leeds U   H D   1-1
Rimmer, Rice 1 Powling, Ross, O'Leary, Simpson Hudson, Brady, Macdonald, Stapleton, Armstrong
15 Jan Norwich C   H W   1-0
Rimmer, Rice, Nelson, Ross, O'Leary, Simpson Hudson, Brady, Macdonald 1, Stapleton, Armstrong
18 Jan Birmingham C   A D   3-3
Rimmer, Rice, Nelson, Ross, O'Leary, Simpson Hudson, Brady, Macdonald 3, Stapleton, Armstrong
22 Jan Bristol C   A L   0-2
Rimmer, Rice, Nelson, Storey, O'Leary, Simpson Hudson, Brady, Macdonald, Stapleton, Rostron
5 Feb   Sunderland   H D   0-0
Rimmer, Rice, Nelson, Ross, O'Leary, Simpson Hudson, Brady, Macdonald, Stapleton, Rostron
12 Feb Manchester C   A L   0-1
Rimmer, Rice, Nelson, Ross, O'Leary, Simpson Hudson, Brady, Macdonald, Stapleton, Howard, Matthews for O'Leary
15 Feb Middlesbrough   A L   0-3
Rimmer, Rice, Nelson, Ross, Howard, Simpson, Matthews, Hudson, Macdonald, Stapleton, Rostron, Powling for Howard
19 Feb West Ham U   H L   2-3
Rimmer, Rice, Nelson, Ross, Powling, Simpson, Hudson, Brady 1, Macdonald, Stapleton 1, Armstrong
1 Mar   Everton   A L   1-2
Rimmer, Rice, Nelson, Ross, Howard, Powling, Brady, Hudson, Macdonald 1, Stapleton, Armstrong
5 Mar   Ipswich T   H L   1-4
Rimmer, Rice, Young, Ross, Howard, Powling, Brady, Matthews, Macdonald 1, Stapleton, Armstrong, Nelson for Matthews
8 Mar   W B A   H L   1-2
Rimmer, Rice, Nelson, Price, Young, Howard, Brady, Powling, Macdonald 1, Stapleton, Armstrong
12 Mar QPR   A L   1-2
Rimmer, Rice, Nelson, Powling, Young 1, Howard, Brady, Hudson, Macdonald, Stapleton, Armstrong, Price for Hudson
23 Mar Stoke C   A D   1-1
Rimmer, Rice, Nelson, Powling, Young, O'Leary, Brady, Hudson, Macdonald, Price 1, Armstrong
2 Apr   Leicester C   H W   3-0
Rimmer, Rice, Nelson, Powling, O'Leary 2, Young, Rix 1, Price, Macdonald, Stapleton, Armstrong, Matthews for Powling
9 Apr   WBA   A W   2-0
Rimmer, Rice, Matthews, Price, O'Leary, Young, Rix, Hudson, Macdonald 1, Stapleton 1, Armstrong

11 Apr   Tottenham H   H   W   1-0
Rimmer, Rice, Matthews, Price, O'Leary, Young, Rix, Hudson, Macdonald 1, Stapleton, Armstrong,
Brady for Rix
16 Apr   Liverpool   A   L   0-2
Rimmer, Rice, Matthews, Price, O'Leary, Young, Brady, Hudson, Macdonald, Stapleton, Armstrong
23 Apr   Coventry C   H   W   2-0
Rimmer, Rice, Matthews, Ross, O'Leary, Young, Brady, Hudson, Macdonald 1, Stapleton 1,
Armstrong, Rix for Ross
25 Apr   Aston Villa   H   W   3-0
Rimmer, Rice, Nelson1, Matthews, O'Leary, Young, Brady, Hudson, Macdonald 1, Stapleton,
Armstrong 1
30 Apr   Newcastle U   A   W   2-0
Rimmer, Rice, Nelson, Matthews 1, O'Leary, Young, Brady, Hudson, Macdonald 1, Stapleton,
Armstrong, Howard for O'Leary
3 May   Derby Co   H   D   0-0
Rimmer, Rice, Nelson, Matthews, O'Leary, Young, Brady, Hudson, Macdonald, Stapleton,
Armstrong, Rix for Young
7 May   Middlesbrough   H   D   1-1
Rimmer, Rice, Nelson, Matthews, O'Leary, Young, Brady, Hudson, Rix, Macdonald, Stapleton 1,
Armstrong, Price for Matthews
14 May   Manchester U   A   L   2-3
Rimmer, Rice, Nelson, Matthews, O'Leary, Young, Brady 1, Hudson, Macdonald, Stapleton 1,
Armstrong, Rix for Young

FA CUP
8 Jan   Notts Co (3)   A   W   1-0
Rimmer, Rice, Nelson, Ross 1, O'Leary, Simpson, Hudson, Brady, Macdonald, Stapleton, Armstrong
29 Jan   Coventry C (4)   H   W   3-1
Rimmer, Rice, Nelson, Ross, O'Leary, Simpson, Hudson, Brady, Macdonald, Stapleton 1, Armstrong,
Storey for Macdonald
26 Feb   Middlesbrough (5)   A   L   1-4
Rimmer, Rice, Nelson, Ross, O'Leary, Simpson, Brady, Hudson, Macdonald 1, Stapleton, Armstrong,
Matthews for O'Leary

FOOTBALL LEAGUE CUP
31 Aug   Carlisle U (2)   H   W   3-2
Rimmer, Rice, Nelson, Ross 2, O'Leary, Simpson, Ball, Brady, Macdonald 1, Stapleton, Armstrong
21 Sep   Blackpool (3)   A   D   1-1
Rimmer, Rice, Nelson, Ross, Powling, Howard, Ball, Brady, Macdonald, Stapleton, Armstrong 1
28 Sep   Blackpool (3R)   H   D   0-0
Rimmer, Rice, Nelson, Ross, O'Leary, Howard, Ball, Brady, Macdonald, Stapleton, Armstrong,
Storey for Nelson
5 Oct   Blackpool (3R)   H   W   2-0
Rimmer, Rice, Storey, Matthews, O'Leary 1, Howard, Ball, Brady, Macdonald, Stapleton 1,
Armstrong
26 Oct   Chelsea (4)   H   W   2-1
Rimmer, Rice, Nelson, Ross 1, Simpson, Howard, Ball, Brady, Macdonald, Stapleton 1, Armstrong
1 Dec   QPR (5)   A   L   1-2
Rimmer, Rice, Nelson, Ross, O'Leary, Simpson, Ball, Brady, Macdonald, Stapleton 1, Armstrong

APPEARANCES (Goals) Armstrong 37(2); Ball 14(1); Brady 38(5); Cropley 3; Howard 16;Hudson 19;
Macdonald 41(25); Matthews 17(2); Nelson 32(3); O'Leary 33(2); Powling 12; Price 8(1); Radford 2;
Rice 42(3); Rimmer 42; Rix 7(1); Ross 29(4); Rostron 6; Simpson 19; Stapleton 40(13); Storey 11; Young
14(1); o/g 1; Total 22 players (64)

POSITION IN LEAGUE TABLE
	Pld	W	D	L	F	A	Pts
1st Liverpool	42	23	11	8	62	33	57
8th Arsenal	42	16	11	15	64	59	43

SEASON 1977-1978

FOOTBALL LEAGUE (DIVISION 1)

20 Aug Ipswich T   A L 0-1
Jennings, Rice, Nelson, Ross, Young, O'Leary, Powling, Brady, Macdonald, Stapleton, Rix, Price for Brady

23 Aug Everton   H W 1-0
Jennings, Rice, Nelson, Powling 1, O'Leary, Young, Brady, Ross, Macdonald, Stapleton, Rix

27 Aug Wolverhampton W   A D 1-1
Jennings, Rice, Nelson, Powling 1, Young, O'Leary, Ross, Brady, Macdonald, Price, Rix

3 Sep Nottingham F   H W 3-0
Jennings, Rice, Nelson, Powling, O'Leary, Young, Brady 1, Ross, Macdonald, Stapleton 2, Rix

10 Sep Aston Villa   A L 0-1
Jennings, Rice, Nelson, Hudson, O'Leary, Young, Brady, Ross, Macdonald, Stapleton, Rix

17 Sep Leicester C   H W 2-1
Jennings, Rice, Nelson, Price, O'Leary, Young, Brady, Ross, Macdonald 1, Stapleton 1, Rix

24 Sep Norwich C   A L 0-1
Jennings, Rice, Nelson, Price, O'Leary, Simpson, Matthew, Ross, Macdonald, Stapleton, Rix, Walford for Matthews

1 Oct West Ham U   H W 3-0
Jennings, Rice 1, Nelson, Price, O'Leary, Simpson, Brady 1, Ross, Macdonald, Stapleton 1, Rix

4 Oct Liverpool   H D 0-0
Jennings, Rice, Nelson, Price, O'Leary, Simpson, Brady, Ross, Macdonald, Stapleton, Rix, Matthews for Ross

8 Oct Manchester C   A L 1-2
Jennings, Rice, Nelson, Price, O'Leary, Simpson, Brady, Matthews, Macdonald 1, Stapleton, Rix

15 Oct QPR   H W 1-0
Jennings, Rice, Nelson, Price, O'Leary, Young, Hudson, Macdonald 1, Stapleton, Rix

22 Oct Bristol C   A W 2-0
Jennings, Rice, Nelson, Price, Young, Simpson, Hudson, Macdonald 1, Stapleton, Rix 1

29 Oct Birmingham C   H D 1-1
Jennings, Rice 1, Nelson, Price, O'Leary, Simpson, Hudson, Ross, Macdonald, Stapleton, Rix, Heeley for Price

5 Nov Manchester U   A W 2-1
Jennings, Rice , Nelson, Price, O'Leary, Young, Brady, Sunderland, Macdonald 1, Stapleton 1, Rix

12 Nov Coventry C   H D 1-1
Jennings, Rice , Nelson, Price, O'Leary, Young, Brady, Sunderland, Macdonald, Stapleton, Rix, (o/g Coop)

19 Nov Newcastle U   A W 2-1
Jennings, Rice , Nelson, Price, O'Leary, Young, Brady, Sunderland 1, Hudson, Stapleton 1, Rix

26 Nov Derby Co   H L 1-3
Jennings, Rice, Nelson 1, Price, O'Leary, Young, Brady, Sunderland, Macdonald, Stapleton, Rix

3 Dec Middlesbrough   A W 1-0
Jennings, Rice, Nelson , Price, O'Leary, Young, Brady, Sunderland, Macdonald, Stapleton, Rix, (o/g Cooper)

10 Dec Leeds U   H D 1-1
Jennings, Rice, Nelson , Price, O'Leary, Young 1, Brady, Sunderland, Macdonald, Stapleton, Rix

17 Dec Coventry C   A W 2-1
Jennings, Rice, Nelson , Price, O'Leary, Young, Brady, Sunderland, Macdonald, Stapleton 2, Rix

26 Dec Chelsea   H W 3-0
Jennings, Rice, Nelson , Price 1, O'Leary 1, Young, Brady, Sunderland, Macdonald, Stapleton, Rix 1, Simpson for Stapleton

27 Dec WBA   A W 3-1
Jennings, Rice, Nelson , Price, O'Leary, Young, Brady 1, Sunderland 1, Macdonald 1, Stapleton, Rix

31 Dec Everton   A L 0-2
Jennings, Rice, Nelson , Price, O'Leary, Young, Brady, Sunderland, Macdonald, Stapleton, Rix, Simpson for , Macdonald

2 Jan   Ipswich T   H   W   1-0
Jennings, Rice, Nelson , Price 1, O'Leary, Young, Brady, Sunderland, Macdonald, Heeley, Rix, Simpson for Heeley
14 Jan   Wolverhampton W   H   W   3-1
Jennings, Rice, Nelson , Price, O'Leary, Young, Brady 1, Sunderland, Macdonald 1, Stapleton 1, Rix
21 Jan   Nottingham F   A   L   0-2
Jennings, Rice, Nelson, Price, O'Leary, Young, Brady, Sunderland, Macdonald, Stapleton, Rix
4 Feb   Aston Villa   H   L   0-1
Jennings, Rice, Nelson, Price, O'Leary, Young, Brady, Sunderland, Macdonald, Hudson, Rix
11 Feb   Leicester C   A   D   1-1
Jennings, Rice, Nelson, Price, O'Leary, Young, Brady 1, Sunderland, Macdonald, Stapleton, Rix
25 Feb   West Ham U   A   D   2-2
Jennings, Rice, Nelson , Price, O'Leary, Young, Brady, Sunderland, Macdonald 2, Stapleton, Rix, Walford for Rix
28 Feb   Norwich C   H   D   0-0
Jennings, Rice, Nelson, Price, O'Leary, Young, Brady, Sunderland, Macdonald, Stapleton, Hudson, Heeley for Macdonald
4 Mar   Manchester C   H   W   3-0
Jennings, Rice, Nelson, Price 1, O'Leary, Young 1, Brady, Sunderland 1, Hudson, Stapleton, Heeley, Walford for Price
18 Mar   Bristol C   H   W   4-1
Jennings, Rice, Nelson, Price 1, O'Leary, Young, Brady, Sunderland 1, Macdonald, Stapleton 2, Hudson, Rix for Sunderland
21 Mar   Birmingham C   A   D   1-1
Jennings, Rice, Nelson, Price, O'Leary, Young, Brady 1, Sunderland, Macdonald, Stapleton, Hudson
25 Mar   W B A   H   W   4-0
Jennings, Rice, Nelson, Price, O'Leary, Young 1, Brady, Sunderland, Macdonald 3, Stapleton, Hudson, Rix for Sunderland
27 Mar   Chelsea   A   D   0-0
Jennings, Rice, Nelson, Price, O'Leary, Young, Brady, Rix, Macdonald, Stapleton, Hudson
1 Apr   Manchester U   H   W   3-1
Jennings, Rice, Nelson, Price, O'Leary, Young, Brady 1, Rix, Macdonald 2, Stapleton, Hudson
11 Apr   QPR   A   L   1-2
Jennings, Rice, Nelson, Price, O'Leary, Young, Brady 1, Hudson, Macdonald, Stapleton, Rix, Matthews for Young
15 Apr   Newcastle U   H   W   2-1
Jennings, Rice, Nelson, Price 1, O'Leary, Walford, Brady 1, Rix, Macdonald, Stapleton, Hudson
22 Apr   Leeds U   A   W   3-1
Jennings, Devine, Nelson, Price, O'Leary, Young, Brady, Rix, Macdonald 1, Stapleton 1, Matthews, o/g Hart
25 Apr   Liverpool   A   L   0-1
Jennings, Devine, Nelson , Price, O'Leary, Young, Brady, Rix, Macdonald, Stapleton, Hudson, Matthews for Brady
29 Apr   Middlesbrough   H   W   1-0
Jennings, Devine, Nelson , Price, O'Leary, Young, Sunderland, Hudson, Macdonald, Stapleton 1, Rix
9 May   Derby Co   A   L   0-3
Jennings, Price, Matthews, Harvey, O'Leary, Walford, Heeley, Hudson, Sunderland, Stapleton, Rix

FA CUP
7 Jan   Sheffield U (3)   A   W   5-0
Jennings, Rice, Nelson, Price, O'Leary 1, Young, Brady, Sunderland, Macdonald 2, Stapleton 2, Rix
28 Jan   Wolverhampton W (4) H   W   2-1
Jennings, Rice, Nelson, Price, O'Leary, Young, Brady, Sunderland 1, Macdonald 1, Hudson, Rix
18 Feb   Walsall (5)   H   W   4-1
Jennings, Rice, Nelson, Price, O'Leary, Young, Brady, Sunderland 1, Macdonald 1, Stapleton 2, Rix
11 Mar   Wrexham (6)   A   W   3-2
Jennings, Rice, Nelson, Price, O'Leary, Young 1, Brady, Sunderland 1, Macdonald 1, Stapleton, Hudson

8 Apr   **Leyton Orient (SF)**   **A** **W** **3-0**
Jennings, Rice, Nelson, Price, O'Leary, Young , Brady, Rix1, Macdonald 2, Stapleton, Hudson (at Chelsea)
6 May   **Ipswich T (F)**   **A** **L** **0-1**
Jennings, Rice, Nelson, Price, O'Leary, Young, Brady, Sunderland, Macdonald, Stapleton, Hudson, Rix for Brady (at Wembley)

FOOTBALL LEAGUE CUP
30 Aug   **Manchester U (2)**   **H** **W** **3-2**
Jennings, Rice, Nelson, Powling, O'Leary, Young, Brady 1, Ross, Macdonald 2, Stapleton, Rix
25 Oct   **Southampton (3)**   **H** **W** **2-0**
Jennings, Rice, Nelson, Price, Young, Simpson, Brady 1, Hudson, Macdonald, Stapleton 1, Rix
29 Nov   **Hull C (4)**   **H** **W** **5-1**
Jennings, Rice, Nelson, Price, O'Leary, Young, Brady 1, Matthews 2, Macdonald 1, Stapleton 1, Rix, Simpson for O'Leary
18 Jan   **Manchester C (5)**   **A** **D** **0-0**
Jennings, Rice, Nelson, Price, O'Leary, Young, Brady , Matthews, Macdonald, Stapleton, Rix
24 Jan   **Manchester C (5R)**   **H** **W** **1-0**
Jennings, Rice, Nelson, Price, O'Leary, Young, Brady 1, Matthews, Macdonald, Stapleton, Rix, Hudson for Matthews
7 Feb   **Liverpool (SF/1)**   **A** **L** **1-2**
Jennings, Rice, Nelson, Price, O'Leary, Young, Brady, Hudson, Macdonald 1, Stapleton, Rix
14 Feb   **Liverpool (SF/2)**   **H** **D** **0-0**
Jennings, Rice, Nelson, Price, O'Leary, Young, Brady, Hudson, Macdonald, Stapleton, Rix

APPEARANCES (Goals) Brady 39 (9); Devine 3; Harvey 1; Heeley 5; Hudson 17; Jennings 42; Macdonald 39 (15); Matthews 7; Nelson 41 (1); O'Leary 41 (1); Powling 4 (2); Price 39 (5); Rice 38 (2); Rix 39 (2); Ross 10; Simpson 9; Stapleton 39 (13); Sunderland 23 (4); Walford 5; Young 35 (3); o/g; 3; Total: 20 players (60)

POSITION IN LEAGUE TABLE

	Pld	W	D	L	F	A	Pts
1st Nottingham F	42	25	14	3	69	24	64
5th Arsenal	42	21	10	11	60	37	52

SEASON 1978-1979

FOOTBALL LEAGUE (DIVISION 1)
19 Aug   **Leeds U**   **H** **D** **2-2**
Jennings, Devine, Nelson, Price, O'Leary, Young, Brady 2, Sunderland, Macdonald, Stapleton, Harvey, Kosmina for Price
22 Aug   **Manchester C**   **A** **D** **1-1**
Barron, Rice, Nelson, Price, O'Leary, Young, Devine, Sunderland, Macdonald 1, Stapleton, Walford
26 Aug   **Everton**   **A** **L** **0-1**
Barron, Rice, Nelson, Price, O'Leary, Young, Brady, Sunderland, Macdonald, Stapleton, Devine, Walford for Devine
2 Sep   **QPR**   **H** **W** **5-1**
Jennings, Rice, Nelson, Price, O'Leary, Young, Brady 1, Sunderland, Walford, Stapleton 2, Rix 2
9 Sep   **Nottingham F**   **A** **L** **1-2**
Jennings, Rice, Nelson, Price, O'Leary, Young, Brady 1, Sunderland, Walford, Stapleton , Rix, Harvey for O'Leary
16 Sep   **Bolton W**   **H** **W** **1-0**
Jennings, Rice, Nelson, Price, Walford, Young, Brady , Sunderland, Stapleton 1, Heeley, Rix
23 Sep   **Manchester U**   **H** **D** **1-1**
Jennings, Rice, Nelson, Price 1, O'Leary, Young, Brady , Sunderland, Stapleton, Walford, Rix, Heeley for Walford

30 Sep   Middlesbrough   A   W   3-2
Jennings, Rice, Nelson, Price 1, O'Leary 1, Young, Brady, Sunderland, Stapleton, Devine, Rix,
Walford 1 for Devine
7 Oct   Aston Villa   H   D   1-1
Jennings, Rice, Nelson, Price, O'Leary, Young, Brady, Sunderland 1, Stapleton, Walford, Rix
14 Oct   Wolverhampton W   A   L   0-1
Jennings, Rice, Nelson, Price, O'Leary, Young, Brady, Sunderland, Stapleton, Walford, Rix, Stead
for Sunderland
21 Oct   Southampton   H   W   1-0
Jennings, Rice, Nelson, Stead, Gatting, Young, Brady 1, Stapleton, Walford, Rix
28 Oct   Bristol C   A   W   3-1
Jennings, Rice, Nelson, Price, O'Leary, Young, Brady 2, Gatting, , Stapleton 1, Heeley, Rix, Walford
for O'Leary
4 Nov   Ipswich T   H   W   4-1
Jennings, Rice, Nelson1, Price, O'Leary, Young, Brady, Sunderland, Stapleton 3, Gatting, Rix.
11 Nov   Leeds U   A   W   1-0
Jennings, Rice, Nelson, Price, O'Leary, Young, Brady, Sunderland, Stapleton, Gatting 1, Rix
18 Nov   Everton   H   D   2-2
Jennings, Rice, Nelson, Price, O'Leary, Young, Brady 2, Sunderland, Stapleton, Gatting, Rix
25 Nov   Coventry C   A   D   1-1
Jennings, Rice, Nelson, Price, O'Leary, Young, Brady , Sunderland, Stapleton 1, Walford, Rix,
Heeley for Price
2 Dec   Liverpool   H   W   1-0
Jennings, Rice, Nelson, Price 1, O'Leary, Young, Brady , Sunderland, Stapleton, Gatting, Rix
9 Dec   Norwich C   A   D   0-0
Jennings, Rice, Nelson, Price , O'Leary, Young, Brady , Sunderland, Stapleton, Gatting, Rix, Walford
for Nelson
16 Dec   Derby Co   H   W   2-0
Jennings, Rice, Walford, Price 1, O'Leary, Young, Brady, Sunderland, Stapleton 1, Gatting, Rix
23 Dec   Tottenham H   A   W   5-0
Jennings, Rice, Walford, Price, O'Leary, Young, Brady 1, Sunderland 3, Stapleton 1, Gatting, Rix
26 Dec   WBA   H   L   1-2
Jennings, Rice, Walford, Price , O'Leary, Young, Brady 1, Sunderland, Stapleton, Gatting, Rix
30 Dec   Birmingham C   H   W   3-1
Jennings, Rice 1, Walford, Price, O'Leary, Young, Brady, Sunderland 1, Stapleton 1, Gatting, Rix
13 Jan   Nottingham F   H   W   2-1
Jennings, Walford, Nelson, Talbot, O'Leary, Young, Brady, Sunderland, Stapleton 1, Price 1, Rix
3 Feb   Manchester U   A   W   2-0
Jennings, Rice, Nelson, Talbot, O'Leary, Young, Brady, Sunderland 2, Stapleton, Price, Rix
10 Feb   Middlesbrough   H   D   0-0
Jennings, Rice, Nelson, Talbot, O'Leary, Young, Brady, Sunderland, Stapleton, Price, Rix
13 Feb   QPR   A   W   2-0
Jennings, Rice, Nelson, Talbot, O'Leary, Young, Brady 1, Sunderland, Stapleton, Price 1, Rix,
Walford for Young
24 Feb   Wolverhampton W   H   L   0-1
Jennings, Rice, Gatting, Talbot, O'Leary, Walford, Brady, Sunderland, Stapleton, Price, Rix
3 Mar   Southampton   A   L   0-2
Jennings, Rice, Nelson, Talbot, O'Leary, Walford, Brady, Gatting, Stapleton, Price, Rix, Heeley for
Gatting
10 Mar   Bristol C   H   W   2-0
Jennings, Rice, Nelson, Talbot, O'Leary, Walford, Brady, Heeley, Stapleton 1, Price, Rix 1,
McDermott for Heeley
17 Mar   Ipswich T   A   L   0-2
Jennings, Rice, Nelson, Talbot, O'Leary, Walford, Brady, Sunderland, Stapleton, Price, Rix, Gatting
for Price
24 Mar   Manchester C   H   D   1-1
Jennings, Rice, Nelson, Talbot, O'Leary, Young, Heeley, Sunderland 1, Stapleton, Price , Rix,
McDermott for Young

26 Mar   Bolton W   A   L   2-4
Jennings, Rice, Nelson, Talbot, O'Leary, Walford, Gatting, Sunderland, Stapleton, Price 1, Rix,
Heeley 1 for Talbot
3 Apr   Coventry C   H   D   1-1
Jennings, Rice, Nelson 1, Talbot, O'Leary, Young, Gatting, Sunderland, Stapleton, Heeley, Rix,
Walford for Heeley
7 Apr   Liverpool   A   L   0-3
Jennings, Rice, Walford, Talbot, O'Leary, Young, Gatting, Sunderland, Stapleton, Price, Rix, Brignall
for Stapleton
10 Apr   Tottenham H   H   W   1-0
Jennings, Rice, Walford, Talbot, O'Leary, Young, Brady, Sunderland, Stapleton 1, Price, Rix
14 Apr   WBA   A   D   1-1
Jennings, Rice, Nelson, Talbot, O'Leary, Walford, Brady 1, Sunderland, Stapleton, Price, Rix,
Gatting for Rix
16 Apr   Chelsea   H   W   5-2
Jennings, Rice, Nelson, Talbot, O'Leary 1, Walford, Brady, Sunderland 1, Stapleton 2, Price 1, Rix
21 Apr   Derby Co   A   L   0-2
Jennings, Rice, Walford, Talbot, Gatting, Young, Brady, Sunderland, Stapleton, Price, Rix
25 Apr   Aston Villa   A   L   1-5
Jennings, Rice, Walford, Talbot, Gatting, Devine, Brady, Sunderland, Stapleton 1, Price, Rix
28 Apr   Norwich C   H   D   1-1
Jennings, Devine, Nelson, Talbot, Gatting, , Walford 1, Brady , Sunderland, Stapleton, Price, Rix
5 May   Birmingham C   A   D   0-0
Barron, Rice, Nelson, Talbot, O'Leary, Young, Brady, Sunderland, Stapleton, Price, Rix, Walford for
Barron, Price moved to goal
14 May   Chelsea   A   D   1-1
Jennings, Barron, Rice, Nelson, Talbot, O'Leary, Young, Brady, Vaessen, Macdonald 1, Devine, Rix

FA CUP

6 Jan   Sheffield Wed (3)   A   D   1-1
Jennings, Rice, Walford, Price, O'Leary, Young, Brady, Sunderland 1, Stapleton, Gatting, Rix
9 Jan   Sheffield Wed (3R)   H   D   1-1
Jennings, Rice, Nelson, Price, O'Leary, Young, Brady 1, Sunderland, Stapleton, Gatting, Rix
15 Jan   Sheffield Wed (3R)   D   2-2
Jennings, Rice, Nelson, Price, O'Leary, Young, Brady 1, Sunderland 1, Stapleton, Gatting, Rix (at
Leicester C)
17 Jan   Sheffield Wed (3R)   D   3-3
Jennings, Rice, Nelson, Price, O'Leary, Young 1, Brady, Sunderland, Stapleton 2, Gatting, Rix (at
Leicester C)
22 Jan   Sheffield Wed (3R)   W   2-0
Jennings, Rice, Nelson, Price, O'Leary, Young, Brady, Sunderland, Stapleton 1, Gatting 1, Rix,
Walford for Nelson (at Leicester C)
27 Jan   Notts County (4)   H   W   2-0
Jennings, Rice, Nelson, Talbot 1, O'Leary, Young 1, Brady, Sunderland, Stapleton, Price, Rix
26 Feb   Nottingham F (5)   A   W   1-0
Jennings, Rice, Nelson, Talbot, O'Leary, Walford, Brady, Sunderland, Stapleton 1, Price, Rix
19 Mar   Southampton (6)   A   D   1-1
Jennings, Rice, Nelson, Talbot, O'Leary, Young, Brady, Sunderland, Stapleton, Price 1, Rix, Walford
for Price
21 Mar   Southampton (6R)   H   W   2-0
Jennings, Rice, Nelson, Talbot, O'Leary, Young, Brady, Sunderland 2, Stapleton, Price, Rix, Walford
for Brady
31 Mar   Wolverhampton W (SF) W   2-0
Jennings, Rice, Nelson, Talbot, O'Leary, Young, Gatting Sunderland 1, Stapleton 1, Price , Rix (at
Aston Villa)
12 May   Manchester U (F)   W   3-2
Jennings, Rice, Nelson, Talbot 1, O'Leary, Young, Brady, Sunderland 1, Stapleton 1, Price , Rix,
Walford for Price (at Wembley)

FOOTBALL LEAGUE CUP
29 Aug   Rotherham U (2)   A   L   1-3
Jennings, Rice, Nelson, Price, O'Leary, Young, Brady, Sunderland, Macdonald, Stapleton 1, Rix

UEFA CUP
13 Sep   L'motive Leipzig (1/1)   H   W   3-0
Jennings, Rice, Nelson, Price, Walford, Young, Brady, Sunderland 1, Stapleton 2, Harvey, Rix, Gatting/Heeley for Brady/Harvey
27 Sep   L'motive Leipzig (1/2)   A   W   4-1
Jennings, Rice, Nelson, Price, O'Leary, Young, Brady 1, Sunderland 1, Stapleton 2, Devine, Rix, Vaessen/Walford for Price/Young
18 Oct   Hajduk Split (2/1)   A   L   1-2
Jennings, Rice, Nelson, Price, O'Leary, Young, Brady 1, Heeley, Stapleton, Kosmina, Rix
1 Nov   Hajduk Split (2/2)   H   W   1-0
Jennings, Rice, Nelson, Price, O'Leary, Young 1, Brady, Gatting, Stapleton, Heeley, Rix, Kosmina/Vaessen for Heeley/Kosmina
22 Nov   Red Star B'grade (3)   A   L   0-1
Jennings, Rice, Nelson, Price, O'Leary, Young, Heeley, Sunderland, Stapleton, Walford, Rix
6 Dec   Red Star B'grade (3)   H   D   1-1
Jennings, Rice, Nelson, Price, O'Leary, Young, Heeley, Sunderland, Stapleton 1, Gatting, , Rix, Kosmina for Heeley, Macdonald for Rix

APPEARANCES (Goals) Barron 3; Brady 37(13); Brignall 1; Devine 7; Gatting 21(1); Harvey 2; Heeley 10(1); Jennings 39; Kosmina 1; McDermott 2; Macdonald 4(2); Nelson 33(2); O'Leary 37(2); Price 39(8); Rice 39(1); Rix 39(3); Stapleton 41(17); Stead 2; Sunderland 37(9); Talbot 20; Vaessen 1; Walford 33(2); Young 33; Total: 23 players (61)

POSITION IN LEAGUE TABLE
	Pld	W	D	L	F	A	Pts
1st Liverpool	42	30	8	4	85	16	68
7th Arsenal	42	17	14	11	61	48	48

SEASON 1979-1980

FOOTBALL LEAGUE (DIVISION 1)
18 Aug   Brighton & HA   A   W   4-0
Jennings, Rice, Nelson, Talbot, O'Leary, Young, Brady 1, Sunderland 2, Stapleton 1, Price, Rix, Hollins for Brady
21 Aug   Ipswich T   H   L   0-2
Jennings, Rice, Nelson, Talbot, O'Leary, Young, Brady, Sunderland, Stapleton, Price, Rix, Hollins for Price
25 Aug   Manchester U   H   D   0-0
Jennings, Rice, Nelson, Talbot, O'Leary, Young, Gatting, Sunderland, Stapleton, Hollins, Rix, Walford for Gatting
1 Sep   Leeds U   A   D   1-1
Jennings, Rice, Nelson 1, Talbot, O'Leary, Young, Gatting, Sunderland, Stapleton, Hollins, Rix
8 Sep   Derby Co   A   L   2-3
Jennings, Rice, Nelson, Talbot, O'Leary, Young, Brady, Sunderland 1, Stapleton 1, Hollins, Rix
15 Sep   Middlesbrough   H   W   2-0
Jennings, Rice, Nelson , Talbot, O'Leary, Young, Brady, Sunderland 1, Stapleton 1, Hollins, Rix
22 Sep   Aston Villa   A   D   0-0
Barron, Rice, Nelson , Talbot, O'Leary, Young, Brady, Sunderland, Stapleton, Hollins, Rix
29 Sep   Wolverhampton W   H   L   2-3
Jennings, Rice, Nelson , Talbot, Walford, Young, Brady, Sunderland, Stapleton 1, Hollins 1, Rix, Price for Talbot
6 Oct   Manchester C   H   D   0-0
Jennings, Rice, Nelson , Talbot, O'Leary, Young, Brady, Sunderland, Stapleton, Hollins, Rix

9 Oct   **Ipswich T**   **A W 2-1**
Jennings, Walford, Nelson , Talbot, O'Leary, Young, Brady, Sunderland 1, Stapleton, Hollins, Rix 1

13 Oct   **Bolton W**   **A D 0-0**
Jennings, Rice, Nelson , Talbot, O'Leary, Young, Brady, Sunderland , Stapleton, Hollins, Rix

20 Oct   **Stoke C**   **H D 0-0**
Jennings, Rice, Nelson , Talbot, O'Leary, Young, Brady, Sunderland 1, Stapleton, Hollins, Rix

27 Oct   **Bristol C**   **A W 1-0**
Jennings, Rice, Nelson , Talbot, O'Leary, Young, Brady, Sunderland 1, Stapleton, Hollins, Rix

3 Nov   **Brighton & HA**   **H W 3-0**
Jennings, Devine, Nelson, Talbot, O'Leary, Young, Brady 1, Sunderland 1, Stapleton, Hollins, Rix 1, Gatting for Sunderland

10 Nov **Crystal Pal**   **A L   0-1**
Jennings, Devine, Nelson , Talbot, O'Leary, Young, Brady, Gatting, Stapleton, Price, Rix, Walford for Devine

17 Nov **Everton**   **H W 2-0**
Jennings, Devine, Nelson , Talbot, O'Leary, Young, Brady, Vaessen, Stapleton 2, Price, Rix, Gatting for Brady

24 Nov **Liverpool**   **H D 0-0**
Jennings, Devine, Nelson , Talbot, O'Leary, Young, Gatting, Sunderland, Stapleton, Price, Rix

1 Dec   **Nottingham F**   **A D 1-1**
Jennings, Devine, Nelson , Talbot, O'Leary, Walford, Gatting, Sunderland, Stapleton 1, Price, Rix

8 Dec   **Coventry C**   **H W 3-1**
Jennings, Devine, Nelson , Talbot, O'Leary 1, Walford, Brady, Sunderland 1, Stapleton 1, Hollins, Rix, Gatting for Nelson

15 Dec **WBA**   **A D 2-2**
Jennings, Devine, Nelson 1, Talbot, O'Leary, Walford, Brady, Sunderland , Stapleton 1, Hollins, Rix

21 Dec **Norwich C**   **H D 1-1**
Jennings, Devine, Nelson, Talbot, O'Leary, Walford, Brady, Sunderland , Stapleton 1, Hollins, Rix, McDermott for Nelson

26 Dec **Tottenham H**   **H W 1-0**
Jennings, Devine, Rice, Talbot, O'Leary, Young, Brady, Sunderland 1, Stapleton, Hollins, Rix

29 Dec **Manchester U**   **A L   0-3**
Jennings, Devine, Rice, Talbot, O'Leary, Young, Brady, Sunderland, Stapleton, Hollins, Rix, Walford for O'Leary

1 Jan   **Southampton**   **A W 1-0**
Jennings, Devine, Rice, Talbot, Walford, Young 1, Gatting, Sunderland, Stapleton, Hollins, Rix

12 Jan **Leeds U**   **H L   0-1**
Jennings, Rice, Nelson, Talbot, Walford, Young, Brady, Sunderland, Stapleton, Hollins, Rix

19 Jan **Derby Co**   **H W 2-0**
Jennings, Rice, Nelson, Talbot, Walford, Young 1, Brady 1, Sunderland, Stapleton, Price, Rix

9 Feb   **Aston Villa**   **H W 3-1**
Jennings, Rice, Nelson, Talbot, O'Leary, Young, Brady , Sunderland 2, Stapleton, Price, Rix 1

23 Feb **Bolton W**   **H W 2-0**
Jennings, Rice, Nelson, Talbot, O'Leary, Young 1 , Brady , Sunderland, Stapleton 1, Price, Rix, Vaessen for Rice

1 Mar   **Stoke C**   **A W 3-2**
Jennings, Devine, Nelson, Talbot, O'Leary, Young , Brady 1, Sunderland 1, Stapleton, Price 1, Rix

11 Mar **Bristol C**   **H D 0-0**
Jennings, Devine, Nelson, Talbot, O'Leary, Young, Brady, Vaessen, Stapleton, Price, Rix

15 Mar **Manchester C**   **A W 3-0**
Jennings, Devine, Nelson, Talbot, O'Leary, Young, Brady 2, Vaessen, Stapleton 1, Price, Rix, Gatting for Stapleton

22 Mar **Crystal Pal**   **H L   1-1**
Jennings, Devine, Nelson, Talbot, O'Leary, Young, Brady 1, Sunderland, Stapleton, Price, Rix

28 Mar **Everton**   **A W 1-0**
Barron, Rice, Nelson, Talbot, O'Leary, Young, Gatting 1, Sunderland, Vaessen, Price , Rix

2 Apr   Norwich C   A   D   1-2
Jennings, Devine, Nelson, Talbot, O'Leary, Young, Brady, Sunderland, Stapleton, Price, Rix 1, Vaessen for Nelson
5 Apr   Southampton   H   D   1-1
Jennings, Devine, Nelson, Talbot, O'Leary, Young, Brady, Sunderland 1, Stapleton, Price, Rix, Vaessen for Price
7 Apr   Tottenham H   A   W   2-1
Barron, Rice, Nelson, Talbot, O'Leary, Young, Brady, Devine, Vaessen 1, Hollins, Davis, Sunderland 1 for Brady
19 Apr   Liverpool   A   D   1-1
Jennings, Rice, Nelson, Talbot 1, O'Leary, Young, Gatting, Sunderland, Stapleton, Price, Hollins, Vaessen for Stapleton
26 Apr   WBA   H   D   1-1
Barron, Rice, Devine, Talbot, Walford, Young, Brady, Sunderland, Stapleton1, Hollins, Vaessen, Gatting for Young
3 May   Coventry C   A   W   1-0
Barron, Rice, Nelson, Talbot, Walford, Young, Gatting, Sunderland, Vaessen 1, Price, Hollins, Davis for Price
5 May   Nottingham F   H   D   0-0
Jennings, Devine, Nelson, Talbot, O'Leary, Young, Brady, Vaessen, Stapleton, Price, Rix, Hollins for Stapleton
16 May   Wolverhampton W   A   W   2-1
Jennings, Rice, Nelson, Talbot, Walford 1, Young, Brady, Sunderland, Stapleton 1, Price, Rix, Vaessen for Price
19 May   Middlesbrough   A   L   0-5
Jennings, Rice, Nelson, Talbot, Walford, Young, Brady, Sunderland, Stapleton, Price, Rix, Vaessen for Walford

FA CUP
5 Jan   Cardiff C (3)   A   D   0-0
Jennings, Rice, Devine, Talbot, Walford, Young, Gatting, Sunderland, Stapleton, Hollins, Rix
8 Jan   Cardiff C (3R)   H   W   2-1
Jennings, Rice, Nelson, Talbot, Walford, Young, Gatting, Sunderland 2, Stapleton, Hollins, Rix
26 Jan   Brighton & HA (4)   H   W   2-0
Jennings, Rice, Nelson 1, Talbot 1, O'Leary, Young, Brady, Sunderland, Stapleton, Price, Rix
5 Feb   Bolton W (5)   A   D   1-1
Jennings, Rice, Nelson, Talbot, O'Leary, Young, Brady, Sunderland, Stapleton 1, Price, Rix
19 Feb   Bolton W (5R)   H   W   3-0   1
Jennings, Rice, Nelson, Talbot, O'Leary, Young, , Brady, Sunderland 2, Stapleton 1, Price, Rix
8 Mar   Watford (6)   A   W   2-1
Jennings, Devine, Nelson, Talbot, O'Leary, Young, , Brady, Sunderland, Stapleton 2, Price, Rix, Gatting for Sunderland
12 Apr   Liverpool (SF)   D   0-0
Jennings, Rice, Nelson, Talbot, O'Leary, Young, Brady, Sunderland, Stapleton, Price, Rix, Walford for Nelson (at Sheffield Wed)
16 Apr   Liverpool (SFR)   D   1-1
Jennings, Rice, Walford, Talbot, O'Leary, Young, Brady, Sunderland 1, Stapleton, Price, Rix (at Aston Villa)
28 Apr   Liverpool (SFR)   D   1-1
Jennings, Rice, Devine, Talbot, O'Leary, Young, Brady, Sunderland 1, Stapleton, Price, Rix (at Aston Villa)
1 May   Liverpool (SFR)   W   1-0
Jennings, Rice, Devine, Talbot, O'Leary, Young, Brady, Sunderland , Stapleton, Price, Rix (at Coventry)
10 May   West Ham U (F)   L   0-1
Jennings, Rice, Devine, Talbot, O'Leary, Young, Brady, Sunderland , Stapleton, Price, Rix, Nelson for Devine (at Wembley)

FOOTBALL LEAGUE CUP

29 Aug   Leeds U (2)   A   D   1-1
Jennings, Rice, Nelson, Talbot, O'Leary, Young, Brady, Sunderland, Stapleton 1, Hollins, Rix
4 Sep   Leeds U (2R)   H   W   7-0
Jennings, Rice, Nelson 1, Talbot, O'Leary, Young, Brady 2, Sunderland 3, Stapleton 1, Hollins, Rix
25 Sep   Southampton (3)   H   W   2-1
Jennings, Rice, Nelson, Talbot, Walford, Young, Brady 1, Sunderland, Stapleton 1, Hollins, Rix
30 Oct   Brighton & HA (4)   A   D   0-0
Jennings, Rice, Nelson, Talbot, Walford, Young, Brady, Sunderland, Stapleton, Hollins, Rix, Gatting for Rice
13 Nov   Brighton & HA (4R)   H   W   4-0
Jennings, Devine, Nelson, Talbot, Walford, Young, Vaessen 2, Sunderland 2, Price, Rix
4 Dec   Swindon T (5)   H   D   1-1
Jennings, Devine, Nelson, Talbot, O'Leary, Walford, Gatting, Sunderland 1, Stapleton, Price, Rix, Hollins for Price
11 Dec   Swindon T (5R)   A   L   3-4
Jennings, Devine, Walford, Talbot 1, Walford, Young, Brady 2, Stapleton, Hollins, Rix

FA CHARITY SHIELD

11 Aug   Liverpool   L   1-3
Jennings, Rice, Nelson, Talbot, O'Leary, Walford, Brady, Sunderland 1, Stapleton, Price, Rix, Young for Nelson, Hollins for Price (at Wembley)

EUROPEAN CUP WINNERS CUP

19 Sep   Fenerbahce (1/1)   H   W   2-0
Jennings, Rice, Nelson, Talbot, O'Leary, Young 1, Brady, Sunderland 1, Stapleton, Hollins, Rix
3 Oct   Fenerbahce (1/2)   A   D   0-0
Jennings, Rice, Nelson, Talbot, O'Leary, Young, Brady, Sunderland, Stapleton, Hollins, Rix
24 Oct   Magdeburg (2/1)   H   W   2-1
Jennings, Rice, Nelson, Talbot, O'Leary, Young 1, Brady, Sunderland 1, Stapleton, Hollins, Rix
7 Nov   Magdeburg (2/2)   A   D   2-2
Jennings, Devine, Nelson, Talbot, O'Leary, Young , Brady 1, Gatting, Stapleton, Hollins, Rix, Price 1 for Hollins, , Walford for Nelson
5 Mar   IFK Gothenburg (3/1)   H   W   5-1
Jennings, Devine, Nelson, Talbot, O'Leary, Young 1, Brady 1, Sunderland 2, Stapleton, Price 1, Rix, Hollins for Brady, , McDermott for , Sunderland
19 Mar   IFK Gothenburg (3/2)   A   D   0-0
Jennings, Devine, Nelson, Talbot, O'Leary, Young , Brady, Stapleton, Price, Rix
9 Apr   Juventus (SF/1)   H   D   1-1
Jennings, Devine, Walford, Talbot, O'Leary, Young, Brady, Sunderland, Stapleton, Price, Rix, Vaessen for Devine, Rice for O'Leary, o/g Bettega
23 Apr   Juventus (SF/2)   A   W   1-0
Jennings, Rice, Devine, Talbot, O'Leary, Young, Brady, Sunderland, Stapleton, Price, Rix, Vaessen 1 for Price, Hollins for Talbot
14 May   Valencia (F)   D   0-0
Jennings, Rice, Nelson, Talbot, O'Leary, Young, Brady, Sunderland, Stapleton, Price, Rix, Hollins for Price (in Brussels, lost 4-5 on penalties)

APPEARANCES (Goals) Barron 5; Brady 34(7); Davis 2; Devine 20; Gatting 14(1); Hollins 26(1); Jennings 37; McDermott 1; Nelson 35(2); O'Leary 34(1); Price 22(1); Rice 26; Rix 38(4); Stapleton 39(14); Sunderland 37(14); Talbot 42(1); Vaessen 14(2); Walford 19(1); Young 38(3); Total 19 players (52)

POSITION IN LEAGUE TABLE

	Pld	W	D	L	F	A	Pts
1st Liverpool	42	25	10	7	81	30	60
4th Arsenal	42	18	16	8	52	36	52

SEASON 1980-1981

FOOTBALL LEAGUE (DIVISION 1)

16 Aug WBA A W 1-0
Jennings, Devine, Sansom, Talbot, O'Leary, Young, Vaessen, Price, Stapleton 1, Hollins, Rix

19 Aug Southampton H D 1-1
Jennings, Devine, Sansom, Talbot, O'Leary, Young, Hollins, Vaessen, Price, Stapleton 1, Rix,
McDermott for Talbot

23 Aug Coventry C A L 1-3
Jennings, Devine, Sansom, Talbot, O'Leary, Young, Hollins, Sunderland, Stapleton 1, Price, Rix, Rice
for Price

30 Aug Tottenham H H W 2-0
Jennings, Devine, Sansom, Talbot, O'Leary, Young, Hollins, Sunderland, Stapleton 1, Price 1, Rix

6 Sep Manchester C A D 1-1
Jennings, Devine, Sansom, Talbot, O'Leary, Young 1, Hollins, Sunderland, Stapleton, Price, Rix

13 Sep Stoke C H W 2-0
Jennings, Devine, Sansom 1, Talbot, O'Leary, Young, Hollins 1, Sunderland, Stapleton, Price, Rix

20 Sep Middlesbrough A L 1-2
Wood, Devine, Sansom,Talbot, O'Leary, Young, Hollins, Sunderland, Stapleton, Price, Rix 1

27 Sep Nottingham F H W 1-0
Wood, Devine, Sansom, Talbot, O'Leary, Young, Hollins, Sunderland, Stapleton, Gatting, Rix 1

4 Oct Leicester C H W 1-0
Wood, Devine, Sansom, Talbot, Walford, Young, Hollins, Sunderland, Stapleton 1, Gatting, Rix

7 Oct Birmingham C A L 1-3
Wood, Devine, Sansom, Talbot, Walford, Young, Hollins, Sunderland 1, Stapleton, Gatting, Rix

11 Oct Manchester U A D 0-0
Wood, Devine, Sansom, Talbot, Walford, Young, Hollins, Sunderland, Stapleton, Gatting, Rix

18 Oct Sunderland H D 2-2
Wood, Devine, Sansom, Talbot, Walford, Young 1   Hollins, Sunderland, Stapleton, Gatting 1, Rix,
McDermott for Talbot

21 Oct Norwich C H W 3-1
Wood, Devine, Sansom 1, Talbot 1, Walford, Young, Hollins, Sunderland, Stapleton, Gatting, Rix,
McDermott 1 for Hollins

25 Oct Liverpool A D 1-1
Wood, Devine, Sansom, Talbot, Walford, Young, Hollins, Sunderland 1, Stapleton, Price, Rix, Rice
for Price

1 Nov Brighton & HA H W 2-0
Wood, Devine, Sansom, Talbot, Walford, Young, Hollins, Sunderland, Stapleton, McDermott 1, Rix 1

8 Nov Leeds U A W 5-0
Wood, Devine, Sansom, Talbot 1, Walford, Young, Hollins 2, Sunderland 1, Gatting 1, McDermott, Rix

11 Nov Southampton A L 1-3
Wood, Devine, Sansom, Talbot Walford, Young, Hollins, Sunderland, McDermott, Gatting, Rix 1,
Price for Gatting

15 Nov WBA H D 2-2
Jennings, Devine, Sansom, Talbot, O'Leary, Young, Hollins, Sunderland, Stapleton, Gatting, Rix 1,
o/g Batson

22 Nov Everton H W 2-1
Jennings, Devine, Sansom, Talbot, O'Leary, Walford, Hollins, Sunderland, Stapleton 1, McDermott
1, Rix, Gatting for Sansom

29 Nov Aston Villa A D 1-1
Jennings, Devine, Sansom, Talbot1, Walford, Young, Hollins, Sunderland, Stapleton, Gatting, Rix

6 Dec Wolverhampton W H D 1-1
Jennings, Devine, Sansom, Talbot, Walford, Young, Hollins, McDermott, Stapleton 1, Gatting, Rix,
Vaessen for Hollins

13 Dec Sunderland A L 0-2
Jennings, Devine, Sansom, Talbot, Walford, Young, Price, McDermott, Stapleton, Gatting, Davis,
Vaessen for Gatting

20 Dec   Manchester U   H   W   2-1
Jennings, Devine, Sansom, Talbot, Walford, Young, Vaessen 1, McDermott, Stapleton, Gatting, Rix 1
26 Dec   Crystal Pal   A   D   2-2
Jennings, Devine, Sansom, Talbot, Walford, Young, Hollins, Vaessen, Stapleton 1, McDermott 1, Rix
27 Dec   Ipswich T   H   D   1-1
Jennings, Devine, Sansom, Talbot, Walford, Young, Hollins, Sunderland 1, Stapleton, Gatting, Rix
10 Jan   Everton   A   W   2-1
Jennings, Devine, Sansom, Davis, Walford, Young, Hollins, Vaessen 1, Stapleton, Gatting 1,
McDermott, Price for Hollins
17 Jan   Tottenham H   A   L   0-2
Jennings, Devine, Sansom, McDermott, Walford, Young, Hollins, Sunderland, Stapleton, Gatting, Rix
31 Jan   Coventry C   H   D   2-2
Jennings, Hollins, Sansom, Talbot 1 Walford, Young, Sunderland, Stapleton 1, Gatting, Rix
7 Feb   Stoke C   A   D   1-1
Jennings, Hollins, Sansom, Talbot, O'Leary Young, Sunderland, Stapleton 1, Gatting, Rix
21 Feb   Nottingham F   A   L   1-3
Jennings, Hollins, Sansom, Talbot, O'Leary Young, Sunderland, Stapleton 1, Gatting, Rix, Devine for
Gatting
24 Feb   Manchester C   H   W   2-0
Jennings, Devine, Sansom, Talbot 1, O'Leary Young, Hollins, Sunderland 1, Stapleton, Gatting, Rix
28 Feb   Middlesbrough   H   D   2-2
Jennings, Devine, Sansom, Talbot, O'Leary, Walford, Hollins 1, Sunderland, Stapleton 1, Gatting,
Rix, McDermott for Sunderland
7 Mar   Leicester C   A   L   0-1
Jennings, Devine, Sansom, Talbot, O'Leary, Young, Hollins, Sunderland, Stapleton, Gatting, Rix,
Price for Hollins
21 Mar   Norwich C   A   D   1-1
Jennings, Devine, Sansom, Talbot 1, O'Leary, Young, Nicholas,Sunderland, Stapleton, McDermott, Rix
28 Mar   Liverpool   H   W   1-0
Jennings, Devine, Sansom, Talbot, O'Leary, Young, Hollins, Sunderland 1, Stapleton, Nicholas, Rix,
Davis for Hollins
31 Mar   Birmingham C   H   W   2-1
Jennings, Devine, Sansom, Talbot, O'Leary 1, Young, Davis, Sunderland, Stapleton 1, Nicholas, Rix,
McDermott for Devine
4 Apr   Brighton & HA   A   W   1-0
Jennings, Devine, Sansom, Talbot, O'Leary, Young, Davis, Sunderland, Stapleton, Hollins 1, Rix
11 Apr   Leeds U   H   D   0-0
Jennings, Devine, Sansom, Talbot, O'Leary, Young, Hollins, Sunderland, Stapleton, Nicholas, Davis,
McDermott for Hollins
18 Apr   Ipswich T   A   W   2-0
Jennings, Devine, Sansom 1, Talbot, O'Leary, Young, Hollins, Sunderland, Stapleton, Nicholas 1,
Davis
20 Apr   Crystal Pal   H   W   3-2
Jennings, Devine, Sansom, Talbot 1, O'Leary, Young 1, Hollins, Sunderland, Stapleton, Nicholas,
Davis 1, McDermott for Sunderland
25 Apr   Wolverhampton W   A   W   2-1
Jennings, Devine, Sansom, Talbot, O'Leary, Young, Hollins, McDermott, Stapleton 1, Nicholas,
Davis (o/g Berry)
2 May   Aston Villa   H   W   2-0
Jennings, Hollins, Sansom, Talbot, O'Leary, Young 1, McDermott 1, Sunderland, Stapleton,
Nicholas, Davis, Nelson for Talbot

FA CUP
3 Jan   Everton (3)   A   L   0-2
Jennings, Devine, Sansom, Talbot, O'Leary, Young, Hollins, Sunderland, Stapleton, Gatting, Rix,
McDermott for Talbot

FOOTBALL LEAGUE CUP

26 Aug   Swansea (2)   A   D   1-1
Jennings, Devine, Sansom, Talbot, O'Leary, Young, Hollins, Sunderland, Stapleton 1, Price, Rix
2 Sep   Swansea (2R)   H   W   3-1
Jennings, Devine, Sansom, Talbot, Walford 1, Young, Hollins 1, Sunderland 1, Stapleton, Price, Rix
22 Sep   Stockport Co (3)   A   W   3-1
Wood, Devine, Sansom, Talbot, O'Leary, Young, Hollins 1, Sunderland 1, Stapleton 1, Price, Rix
14 Nov   Tottenham H (4)   A   L   0-1
Wood, Devine, Sansom, Talbot, Walford, Young, Hollins, Sunderland, Stapleton, Price, Rix,
McDermott for Hollins

APPEARANCES (Goals) Davis 10(1); Devine 39; Gatting 23(3); Hollins 38(5); Jennings 31; McDermott 23(5); Nelson 1; Nicholas 8(1); O'Leary 24(1); Price 12(1); Rice 2; Rix 35(5); Sansom 42(3);, Stapleton 40(14); Sunderland 34(7); Talbot 40(7); Vaessen 7(2); Walford 20; Wood 11; Young 40(4); o/g 2; Total 20 players (61)

POSITION IN LEAGUE TABLE

	Pld	W	D	L	F	A	Pts
1st Aston Villa	42	26	8	8	72	40	60
3rd Arsenal	42	19	15	8	61	45	53

SEASON 1981-1982

FOOTBALL LEAGUE (DIVISION 1)

29 Aug   Stoke C   H   L   0-1
Jennings, Devine, Sansom, Talbot, O'Leary, Young, Davis, Sunderland, McDermott, Nicholas, Rix,
Vaessen for Devine
2 Sep   WBA   A   W   2-0
Jennings, Devine, Sansom, Talbot, O'Leary, Young, Davis, Sunderland, McDermott, Nicholas, Rix
5 Sep   Liverpool   A   L   0-2
Jennings, Devine, Sansom, Talbot, O'Leary, Young, Hollins, Sunderland, McDermott, Nicholas, Rix,
Davis for Nicholas
12 Sep   Sunderland   H   D   1-1
Jennings, Hollins, Sansom, Talbot, O'Leary, Young, Davis, Sunderland 1, McDermott, Nicholas, Rix
19 Sep   Leeds U   A   D   0-0   1
Jennings, Hollins, Sansom, Talbot, O'Leary, Young, Davis, Sunderland 1, McDermott, Nicholas, Rix,
Devine for Nicholas
22 Sep   Birmingham C   H   W   1-0
Jennings, Devine, Hollins, Sansom, Talbot 1, O'Leary, Young, Davis, Sunderland, McDermott,
Hollins, Rix
26 Sep   Manchester U   H   D   0-0
Jennings, Devine, Hollins, Sansom, Talbot, O'Leary, Young, Hollins, Sunderland, Hawley, Nicholas,
Davis
3 Oct   Notts Co   A   L   1-2
Jennings, Hollins, Sansom, Talbot, O'Leary, Young, Davis, Sunderland, Hawley 1, Nicholas, Rix
10 Oct   Swansea C   A   L   0-2
Jennings, Devine, Sansom, Talbot, O'Leary, Young, Davis, Sunderland, Hawley 1, Nicholas, Hollins
17 Oct   Manchester C   H   W   1-0
Jennings, Hollins Sansom, Talbot, O'Leary, Whyte, McDermott, Sunderland, Meade 1, Nicholas, Rix
24 Oct   Ipswich T   A   L   1-2
Jennings, Hollins Sansom, Talbot, O'Leary, Young, Davis, Sunderland 1, Meade 1, Nicholas, Rix
31 Oct   Coventry C   H   W   1-0
Jennings, Hollins Sansom, Talbot, O'Leary, Whyte, McDermott, Vaessen, Hawley, Nicholas, Rix, o/g
Thomas
7 Nov   Aston Villa   A   W   2-0
Jennings, Devine, Sansom, Talbot 1, O'Leary, Whyte, Hollins, Vaessen, Davis, Nicholas, Rix 1

21 Nov   Nottingham F   A   W   2-1
Jennings, Devine, Sansom, Talbot 1, O'Leary, Whyte, Hollins, Sunderland 1, Davis, Nicholas, Rix

28 Nov   Everton   H   W   1-0
Jennings, Devine, Sansom, Talbot, O'Leary, Whyte, Hollins, Sunderland, Davis, Nicholas, Rix,
McDermott 1 for Devine

5 Dec   West Ham U   A   W   2-1
Jennings, Robson, Sansom, Talbot, O'Leary, Whyte 1, Hollins 1, Sunderland, Davis, Nicholas, Rix

20 Jan   Stoke C   A   W   1-0
Wood, Robson, Sansom, Talbot, O'Leary, Whyte, Hollins, Sunderland 1, Davis, Nicholas, Rix

23 Jan   Southampton   A   L   1- 3
Wood, Robson, Sansom, Talbot, O'Leary 1, Whyte, Hollins, Sunderland, Davis, Nicholas, Rix,
McDermott for O'Leary

26 Jan   Brighton & HA   H   D   0-0
Wood, Robson, Sansom, Talbot, Hollins, Whyte, McDermott, Sunderland, Davis, Nicholas, Rix
Meade for Davis

30 Jan   Leeds U   H   W   1-0
Wood, Hollins, Sansom, Talbot, O'Leary, Whyte, Vaessen 1 Sunderland, Davis, Nicholas, Rix

2 Feb   Wolverhampton W   H   W   2-1
Wood, Hollins, Sansom, Talbot, O'Leary, Whyte, Vaessen 1, Sunderland, Davis, Nicholas, Rix1,
Hawley for Sunderland

6 Feb   Sunderland   A   D   0-0
Wood, Hollins, Sansom, Talbot, O'Leary, Whyte, Vaessen Sunderland, Davis, Nicholas, Rix

13 Feb   Notts Co   H   W   1-0
Wood, Hollins, Sansom, Talbot, O'Leary, Whyte, Vaessen Sunderland, Davis, Nicholas, Rix, Meade
1 for Nicholas

16 Feb   Middlesbrough   H   W   1-0
Wood, Hollins, Sansom, Talbot, O'Leary, Whyte, Vaessen Sunderland, Davis, Nicholas, Rix 1,
Meade for Nicholas

20 Feb   Manchester U   A   D   0-0
Wood, Hollins, Sansom, Talbot, O'Leary, Whyte, Vaessen Sunderland, Davis, Nicholas, Rix, Meade
for Vaessen

27 Feb   Swansea C   H   L   0-2
Wood, Hollins, Sansom, Talbot, O'Leary, Whyte, Vaessen Sunderland, Davis, Nicholas, Rix, Meade
for Vaessen

6 Mar   Manchester C   A   D   0-0
Wood, Hollins, Sansom, Talbot, O'Leary, Whyte, Gorman, Sunderland, Davis, Robson, Rix

13 Mar   Ipswich T   H   W   1-0
Wood, Hollins, Sansom, Talbot, O'Leary, Whyte, Gorman, Sunderland, Davis, Robson 1, Rix

16 Mar   WBA   H   D   2-2
Wood, Hollins, Sansom, Talbot, O'Leary, Whyte, Gorman, Sunderland 1, Davis, Robson, Rix, Meade
1 for Gorman

20 Mar   Coventry C   A   L   0-1
Wood, Hollins, Sansom, Talbot, Devine, Whyte, Gorman, Sunderland, Davis, Robson, Rix, Meade for
Gorman

27 Mar   Aston Villa   H   W   4-3
Wood, Hollins, Sansom, Talbot, O'Leary, Whyte, Meade1, Sunderland 1, Davis, Robson, Rix 2

29 Mar   Tottenham H   A   D   2-2
Wood, Hollins, Sansom, Talbot, O'Leary, Whyte, Meade, Sunderland 2, Davis, Robson, Rix, Nicholas
for Davis

3 Apr   Wolverhampton W   A   D   1-1
Wood, Hollins, Sansom, Talbot, O'Leary, Whyte, Meade,Sunderland, Davis 1, Robson, Rix Hawley
for Meade

10 Apr   Brighton & HA   A   L   1-2
Wood, Hollins, Sansom, Talbot 1, O'Leary, Whyte, Meade, Sunderland, Davis, Robson, Nicholas

12 Apr   Tottenham H   H   L   1-3
Wood, Hollins, Sansom, Talbot, O'Leary, Whyte, Meade, Hawley 1, Nicholas, Robson, Rix,
McDermott for Robson

17 Apr   Nottingham F   H   W   2-0
Wood, Hollins, Sansom, Talbot1, O'Leary, Whyte, Meade, Hawley, Davis, Robson, Rix 1
24 Apr   Everton   A   L   1-2
Wood, Hollins, Sansom, Talbot, O'Leary, Whyte, Hawley, Sunderland, Davis, Robson, Rix 1,
Nicholas for Hollins
1 May   West Ham U   H   W   2-0
Wood, Hollins, Sansom, Talbot, O'Leary, Whyte 1, Hawley, Sunderland, Davis, Robson, Rix 1
4 May   Birmingham C   A   W   1-0
Wood, Hollins, Sansom, Talbot, O'Leary, Whyte, Hawley, Sunderland, Davis, Robson, Rix 1
8 May   Middlesbrough   A   W   3-1 0
Wood, Hollins, Sansom, Talbot 1, O'Leary, Whyte, Hawley, Sunderland, Davis 1, Robson, Rix 1,
Nicholas for Davis
11 May   Liverpool   H   D   1-1
Wood, Hollins, Sansom, Talbot, O'Leary, Whyte, Nicholas, Sunderland 1, Hawley, Robson, Rix,
Meade for Hawley
15 May   Southampton   H   W   4-1
Wood, Hollins, Sansom, Talbot, O'Leary, Whyte, Davis2, Sunderland, Hawley 1, Robson 1, Rix

FA CUP
2 Jan   Tottenham H (3)   A   W   0-1
Jennings, Robson, Sansom, Talbot, O'Leary, Whyte, Hollins, Sunderland, Rix, Nicholas, Davis

LEAGUE CUP
6 Oct   Sheffield U (2)   A   L   0-1
Jennings, Devine, Sansom, Talbot, O'Leary, Young, Rix, Sunderland, Hawley, Nicholas, Davis
27 Oct   Sheffield U (2)   H   W   2-1
Jennings, Hollins, Sansom, Talbot, O'Leary, Young 1, McDermott, Sunderland 1, Meade, Nicholas,
Rix
10 Nov   Norwich C (3)   H   W   1-0
Jennings, Hollins, Sansom, Talbot, O'Leary, Whyte, McDermott, Sunderland, Davis, Nicholas, Rix
1 Dec   Liverpool (4)   H   D   0-0
Jennings, Hollins, Sansom, Talbot, O'Leary, Whyte, McDermott, Sunderland, Davis, Nicholas, Rix,
Hankin for McDermott
8 Dec   Liverpool (4)   A   L   0-3
Woods, Robson, Hollins, Sansom, Talbot, O'Leary, Whyte, Holllins, Sunderland, Davis, Nicholas, Rix,
Hankin for Nicholas

APPEARANCES (Goals) Davis 38(4); Devine 11; Gorman 4; Hawley 14(3); Hollins 40(1); Jennings 16;
McDermott 13(1); Meade 16(4); Nicholas 31; O'Leary 40(1); Rix 39(9); Robson 20(2); Sansom 42;
Sunderland 38(11;, Talbot 42(7); Vaessen 10(2); Whyte 32(2); Wood 26; Young 10; o/g 1; Total 19 play-
ers (48)

POSITION IN LEAGUE TABLE
	Pld	W	D	L	F	A	Pts
1st Liverpool	42	26	9	7	80	32	87
5th Arsenal	42	20	11	11	48	37	71

SEASON 1982-1983

FOOTBALL LEAGUE (DIVISION 1)
28 Aug   Stoke C   A   L   1-2
Wood, Hollins, Sansom, Talbot, O'Leary, Whyte, Robson, Sunderland 1, Chapman, Woodcock, Rix,
Davis for Sunderland
31 Aug   Norwich C   H   D   1-1
Wood, Hollins, Sansom, Talbot, Davis, Whyte, Robson, Sunderland, Chapman, Woodcock 1, Rix,
Devine for Sansom

4 Sep   Liverpool   H   L   0-2
Wood, Hollins, Devine, Talbot, O'Leary, Whyte, Robson, Davis, Sunderland, Chapman, Woodcock, Rix

7 Sep   Brighton & HA   A   L   0-1
Wood, Hollins, Devine, Talbot, O'Leary, Whyte, Robson, Davis, Sunderland, Chapman, Woodcock, Rix, Hawley for Talbot

11 Sep   Coventry C   A   W   2-0
Wood, Hollins, Sansom, Talbot, O'Leary, Whyte, Davis, Robson, Chapman 1, Woodcock 1, Rix

18 Sep   Notts Co   H   W   2-0
Wood, Hollins 1, Sansom, Talbot, O'Leary, Whyte, Davis, Robson, Chapman, Woodcock, Rix 1

25 Sep   Manchester U   A   D   0-0
Wood, Hollins, Sansom, Talbot, O'Leary, Whyte, Davis, Robson, Chapman, Woodcock, Rix

2 Oct   West Ham U   H   L   2-3
Wood, Hollins, Sansom, Talbot 1, O'Leary, Whyte, Davis 1, Sunderland, Chapman, Woodcock, Rix

9 Oct   Ipswich T   A   W   1-0
Wood, Hollins, Sansom, Talbot, O'Leary, Whyte, Davis, Sunderland, Robson, Woodcock 1, Rix, Hawley for Hollins

16 Oct   WBA   H   W   2-0
Wood, Devine, Sansom, Talbot, O'Leary, Whyte, Davis, Sunderland 1, Robson, Woodcock 1, Rix

23 Oct   Nottingham F   A   L   0-3
Wood, Hollins, Sansom, Talbot, O'Leary, Whyte, Davis, Sunderland, Robson, Woodcock, Rix, Chapman for Robson

30 Oct   Birmingham C   H   D   0-0
Wood, O'Shea, Sansom, Talbot, O'Leary, Whyte, Davis, Sunderland, Robson, Woodcock, Rix, Chapman for Woodcock

6 Nov   Luton T   A   D   2-2
Wood, O'Shea, Sansom, Talbot 1, O'Leary, Whyte, Davis, Sunderland, Robson, Woodcock, Rix 1

13 Nov   Everton   H   D   1-1
Jennings, O'Shea, Sansom, Talbot, O'Leary, Whyte, Davis, Chapman, Robson, Woodcock, Rix, McDermott 1 for O'Leary

20 Nov   Swansea C   A   W   2-1
Wood, O'Shea, Sansom, Talbot, O'Leary, Whyte, Davis, Sunderland, Robson, Woodcock 1, Rix, Chapman1 for Woodcock

27 Nov   Watford   H   L   2-4
Wood, O'Shea, Sansom, Talbot 1, O'Leary, Whyte, Davis, Sunderland, Robson 1, Woodcock, Rix

4 Dec   Manchester C   A   L   1-2
Wood, O'Shea, Sansom, Talbot, O'Leary, Whyte, Davis, Sunderland, Chapman, Robson, Rix, McDermott 1 for O'Shea

7 Dec   Aston Villa   H   W   2-1
Wood, Hollins, Sansom, Talbot, O'Leary, Whyte 1; Davis, Sunderland, Robson, Woodcock 1, Rix

18 Dec   Sunderland   A   L   0-3
Jennings, Hollins, Sansom, Talbot, O'Leary, Whyte, Davis, Sunderland, Robson, Woodcock, Rix, Chapman for Davis

27 Dec   Tottenham H   H   W   2-0
Jennings, Hollins, Sansom, Talbot, O'Leary, Robson, Davis, Sunderland 1, Nicholas, Woodcock 1, Rix

28 Dec   Southampton   A   D   2-2
Jennings, Hollins, Sansom, Talbot, O'Leary, Robson, Davis, Sunderland, Nicholas, Woodcock 1, Rix, Chapman 1 for Woodcock

1 Jan   Swansea C   H   W   2-1
Jennings, Hollins, Sansom, Talbot, O'Leary, Robson, Davis, Sunderland 1, Petrovic, Woodcock 1, Rix, Chapman for Sunderland

3 Jan   Liverpool   A   L   1-3
Jennings, Hollins, Sansom, Talbot 1, O'Leary, Robson, Nicholas, Chapman, Petrovic, Woodcock, Rix

15 Jan   Stoke C   H   W   3-0
Jennings, Hollins 1, Sansom, Whyte, O'Leary, Nicholas, Davis, Sunderland, Petrovic 1, Woodcock, Rix 1, Talbot for O'Leary

22 Jan   Notts Co   A   L   0-1
Jennings, Hollins, Sansom, Davis, O'Leary, Nicholas, Robson, Sunderland, Petrovic, Woodcock, Rix, Talbot for Davis

5 Feb   Brighton & HA   H   W   3-1
Jennings, Hollins, Sansom, Robson, O'Leary, Nicholas, Talbot, Meade 2, Petrovic, Davis, Rix 1
26 Feb   West Bromwich   A   D   0-0
Jennings, Kay, Sansom, Robson, Whyte, Nicholas, Devine, Davis, Meade, Woodcock, Rix, Talbot for Rix
5 Mar   Nottingham F   H   D   0-0
Jennings, Hollins, Sansom, Robson, Whyte, Nicholas, Talbot, Davis, Sunderland, Woodcock, Rix, Meade for Sunderland
15 Mar   Birmingham C   A   L   1-2
Jennings, Hollins, Sansom, Robson, Whyte, Nicholas, Petrovic, Davis, Sunderland 1, Woodcock, Rix, Talbot for Petrovic
19 Mar   Luton T   H   W   4-1
Jennings, O'Leary, Sansom, Robson, Whyte, Nicholas, Talbot, Davis 1, Sunderland, Woodcock 3, Rix, Meade for O'Leary
22 Mar   Ipswich T   H   D   2-2
Wood, Hollins, Sansom, Devine, Whyte 1, Nicholas, Talbot, Davis, Sunderland, Woodcock, Rix 1
26 Mar   Everton   A   W   3-2
Wood, Robson 1, Sansom, Whyte, O'Leary, Nicholas, Talbot, Davis, Sunderland 1, Woodcock 1, Rix
2 Apr   Southampton   H   D   0-0
Wood, Kay, Sansom, Whyte, O'Leary, Nicholas, Talbot, Davis, Sunderland, Woodcock, Rix
4 Apr   Tottenham H   A   L   0-5
Wood, Robson, Sansom, Whyte, O'Leary, Nicholas, Talbot, Davis, Sunderland, Woodcock, Rix, Petrovic for Whyte
9 Apr   Coventry C   H   W   2-1
Wood, Robson, Sansom, Whyte Kay, Nicholas, Talbot, Davis, Petrovic, Woodcock 1, Rix 1, Chapman for Nicholas
20 Apr   Norwich C   A   L   1-3
Wood, Kay, Sansom, Talbot, O'Leary, Whyte, McDermott, Hill, Davis 1, Chapman, Rix, Hollins for Rix
23 Apr   Manchester C   H   W   3-0
Jennings, Kay, Sansom, Whyte, O'Leary, Nicholas, Talbot 3, Davis, McDermott, Woodcock, Hill, Hawley for Woodcock
30 Apr   Watford   A   L   1-2
Jennings, Kay, Sansom, Whyte, O'Leary, Nicholas, Talbot, Davis, McDermott 1, Hawley, Hill, Petrovic for Hawley
2 May   Manchester U   H   W   3-0
Jennings, Devine, Sansom, Whyte, O'Leary 1, Nicholas, Talbot 2, Davis, McDermott, Hawley, Hill, Petrovic for Hawley
7 May   Sunderland   H   L   0-1   0
Jennings, Devine, Sansom, Whyte, O'Leary, Nicholas, Talbot, Davis, Petrovic, McDermott, Hill, Hawley for Devine
10 May   West Ham U   A   W   3-1
Jennings, Kay, Sansom, Whyte 1, O'Leary, Nicholas, Talbot, Davis, Petrovic 1, McDermott 1, Hill
14 May   Aston Villa   A   L   1-2
Jennings, Devine, Sansom, Whyte, O'Leary, Nicholas, Talbot, Davis 1, McDermott, Petrovic, Hill

FA CUP
8 Jan   Bolton W (3)   H   W   2-1
Jennings, Hollins, Sansom, Talbot, O'Leary, Robson, Davis 1, Sunderland, Nicholas, Woodcock, Rix 1
29 Jan   Leeds U (4)   H   D   1-1
Jennings, Hollins, Sansom, Robson, O'Leary, Nicholas, Talbot, Sunderland 1, Petrovic, Woodcock, Rix
2 Feb   Leeds U (4R)   A   D   1-1
Jennings, Hollins, Sansom, Robson, O'Leary, Nicholas, Talbot, Sunderland, Petrovic, Woodcock, Rix 1, Davis for Sunderland
9 Feb   Leeds U (4R)   H   W   2-1
Jennings, Hollins, Sansom, Robson, O'Leary, Nicholas, Talbot, Meade, Petrovic, Woodcock 1, Rix 1
19 Feb   Middlesbrough (5)   A   D   1-1
Jennings, Hollins, Sansom, Robson, Whyte, Nicholas, Talbot, Davis, Petrovic, Woodcock, Rix 1

28 Feb   Middlesbrough (5R)   H   W   3-2
Jennings, Hollins, Sansom, Robson, Whyte, Nicholas, Talbot 1, Davis 1, Sunderland, Woodcock 1, Rix
12 Mar   Aston Villa (6)   H   W   2-0
Jennings, Hollins, Sansom, Robson, Whyte, Nicholas, Petrovic 1, Davis, Sunderland, Woodcock 1, Rix
16 Apr   Manchester U (SF)   L   1-2
Wood, Robson, Sansom, Whyte, O'Leary, Hollins, Talbot, Davis, Petrovic, Woodcock 1, Rix, Chapman for Robson (at Aston Villa)

MILK CUP
5 Oct   Cardiff C (2/1)   H   W   2-1
Wood, Hollins 1, Sansom, Talbot, O'Leary, Whyte, Davis 1, Sunderland, Robson, Woodcock, Rix
26 Oct   Cardiff C (2/2)   A   W   3-1
Wood, Hollins, Sansom, Talbot, O'Leary, Whyte, Davis 1, Sunderland 1, Robson, Woodcock 1, Rix
9 Nov   Everton (3)   A   D   1-1
Jennings, O'Shea, Sansom, Talbot, O'Leary, Whyte, Davis, Sunderland, Robson, Woodcock 1, Rix, Chapman for Sunderland
23 Nov   Everton (3R)   H   W   3-0
Wood, O'Shea, Sansom, Talbot, O'Leary, Whyte, Davis, Sunderland 3, Robson, Woodcock, Rix, Chapman for Sunderland
30 Nov   Huddersfield T (4)   H   W   1-0
Wood, O'Shea, Sansom, Talbot, O'Leary, Whyte, Davis, Sunderland 1, Robson, Woodcock, Rix
18 Jan   Sheffield Wed (5)   H   W   1-0
Jennings, Hollins, Sansom, Nicholas, O'Leary, Robson, Davis, Sunderland, Petrovic, Woodcock 1, Rix
15 Feb   Manchester U (SF/1)   H   L   2-4
Jennings, Hollins, Sansom, Robson, O'Leary, Nicholas 1, Talbot, Meade, Petrovic, Woodcock 1, Rix, Davis for O'Leary
23 Feb   Manchester U (SF/2)   A   L   1-2
Jennings, Hollins, Sansom, Robson, Whyte, O'Leary, Nicholas, Talbot, Meade 1, Petrovic, Woodcock, Rix, Davis for Hollins

UEFA CUP
14 Sep   Spartak Moscow (1/1)   A   L   2-3
Wood, Hollins, Sansom, Talbot, O'Leary, Whyte, Davis, Robson 1, Chapman 1, Woodcock, Rix
29 Sep   Spartak Moscow (1/2)   H   L   2-5   3
Wood, Hollins, Sansom, Talbot, O'Leary, Whyte, Davis, Robson, Chapman 1, Woodcock, Rix, Sunderland for Hollins, McDermott for Davis (o/g Dasaev)

APPEARANCES (Goals) Chapman 19(3); Davis 41(4); Devine 9; Hawley 6; Hill 7; Hollins 23(2); Jennings 19; Kay 7; McDermott 9(4); Meade 4(2);, Nicholas 21; O'Leary 36(1); O'Shea 6; Petrovic 13(2); Rix 36(6); Robson 31(2); Sansom 40; Sunderland 25(6); Talbot 42(9); Whyte 36(3); Wood 23; Woodcock 34(14); Total 22 players (58)

POSITION IN LEAGUE TABLE

	Pld	W	D	L	F	A	Pts
1st Liverpool	42	24	10	8	87	37	82
10th Arsenal	42	16	10	16	58	56	58

SEASON 1983-1984

FOOTBALL LEAGUE (DIVISION 1)
27 Aug   Luton T   H   W   2-1
Jennings, Robson, Sansom, Talbot, O'Leary, Hill, McDermott 1, Davis, Woodcock 1, Nicholas, Rix
29 Aug   Wolverhampton W   A   W   2-1
Jennings, Robson, Sansom, Talbot, O'Leary, Hill, McDermott, Davis, Woodcock, Nicholas 2, Rix

3 Sep   Southampton   A   L   0-1
Jennings, Robson, Sansom, Talbot, O'Leary, Hill, McDermott, Davis, Woodcock, Nicholas, Rix,
Whyte for McDermott
6 Sep   Manchester U   H   L   2-3
Jennings, Robson, Sansom, Talbot 1, O'Leary, Hill, McDermott, Davis, Woodcock 1, Nicholas, Rix,
Sunderland for McDermott
10 Sep Liverpool   H   L   0-2
Jennings, Robson, Sansom, Talbot, O'Leary, Hill, Sunderland, Davis, Woodcock, Nicholas, Rix
17 Sep Notts Co   A   W   4-0
Jennings, Robson, Sansom, Whyte, O'Leary, Hill, Sunderland, Davis, Woodcock 1, Nicholas, Rix 1,
Talbot 1 for Nicholas`(o/g Hunt)
24 Sep Norwich C   H   W   3-0
Jennings, Robson, Sansom, Whyte, O'Leary, Hill, Sunderland 2, Davis, Chapman 1, Nicholas, Rix,
McDermott for Nicholas
1 Oct   WBA   A   L   0-2
Jennings, Robson, Sansom, Whyte, O'Leary, Hill, Sunderland, Davis, Chapman, Nicholas, Rix
15 Oct Coventry C   H   L   0-1
Jennings, Robson, Sansom, Whyte, O'Leary, Hill, Sunderland, Davis, Chapman, Nicholas, Rix,
McDermott for Whyte
22 Oct Nottingham F   H   W   4-1
Jennings, Robson, Sansom, Whyte, O'Leary, Hill 1, Sunderland 1, Davis, Woodcock 2, Nicholas, Rix,
McDermott for Nicholas
29 Oct Aston Villa   A   W   6-2
Jennings, Robson, Sansom, Whyte, O'Leary, Hill, Sunderland, Davis, Woodcock 5, Nicholas, Rix,
McDermott 1 for Robson
5 Nov   Sunderland   H   L   1-2
Jennings, Robson, Sansom, Whyte, Adams, Hill, Sunderland, Talbot, Woodcock 1, Nicholas, Rix
McDermott for Sunderland
12 Nov Ipswich T   A   L   0-1
Jennings, Robson, Sansom, Whyte, O'Leary, Hill, Sunderland, Davis, Woodcock, Nicholas, Rix,
Gorman for Sunderland
19 Nov Everton   H   W   2-1
Jennings, Robson 1, Sansom, Whyte, O'Leary, Hill, Sunderland, Gorman, McDermott 1, Nicholas,
Rix, Meade for Sunderland
26 Nov Leicester C   A   L   0-3
Jennings, Robson, Sansom, Whyte, O'Leary, Kay, Sunderland, Davis, Woodcock, Nicholas, Rix,
Chapman for Rix
3 Dec   WBA   H   L   0-1
Jennings, Robson, Sansom, Caton, Adams, Hill, Madden, Gorman, McDermott, Nicholas, Allinson,
Meade for Robson
10 Dec West Ham U   A   L   1-3
Jennings, Hill, Sansom, Kay, Whyte 1, Caton, Madden, Gorman, Woodcock, Nicholas, Allinson,
Meade for Hill
17 Dec Watford   H   W   3-1
Jennings, Hill, Sansom, Cork, Whyte, Caton, Meade 3, Gorman, Woodcock, Nicholas, Allinson
26 Dec Tottenham H   A   W   4-2
Jennings, Hill, Sansom, Robson, O'Leary, Caton, Meade 2, Gorman, Woodcock, Nicholas 2,
Allinson, Cork for Robson
27 Dec Birmingham C   H   D   1-1
Jennings, Hill, Sansom, Cork, Whyte, Caton, Meade ,Gorman, Woodcock, Nicholas 1, Allinson,
McDermott for Caton
31 Dec Southampton   H   D   2-2
Jennings, Hill, Sansom, Cork 1, O'Leary, Caton, Meade, Gorman, Woodcock, Nicholas 1, Allinson
2 Jan   Norwich C   A   D   1-1
Jennings, Hill, Sansom, Cork, O'Leary, Caton, Meade Gorman, Woodcock 1, Nicholas, Allinson
14 Jan Luton T   A   W   2-1
Jennings, Kay, Sansom 1, Talbot, O'Leary, Caton, Meade, Gorman, Woodcock 1, Nicholas, Rix

21 Jan   Notts Co   H   D   1-1
Jennings, Kay, Sansom, Talbot, Adams, Caton, Meade, Gorman, Woodcock, Nicholas 1, Rix, McDermott for Adams

28 Jan   Stoke C   A   L   0-1
Jennings, Kay, Sansom, Talbot, O'Leary, Caton, McDermott, Gorman, Woodcock, Nicholas, Rix

4 Feb   WBA   H   L   0-2
Jennings, Kay, Sansom, Talbot, O'Leary, Caton, Meade, Gorman, Woodcock, Nicholas, Rix, Cork for Meade

11 Feb   Liverpool   A   L   1-2
Jennings, Hill, Sansom, Talbot, O'Leary, Caton, Cork, Davis, Woodcock, Nicolas, Rix 1, Allinson for Cork

18 Feb   Aston Villa   H   D   1-1
Jennings, Hill, Sansom, Talbot, O'Leary, Caton, Davis, Nicholas, Mariner, Woodcock, Rix 1

25 Feb   Nottingham F   A   W   1-0
Jennings, Hill, Sansom, Talbot, O'Leary, Caton, Davis, Nicholas, Mariner 1, Woodcock, Rix

3 Mar   Sunderland   A   D   2-2
Jennings, Hill, Sansom, Talbot, O'Leary, Caton, Davis, Nicholas 1, Mariner, Woodcock 1, Rix

10 Mar   Ipswich T   H   W   4-1
Jennings, Hill, Sansom, Talbot 1, O'Leary, Caton, Davis, Nicholas, Mariner 2, Woodcock 1, Rix, Allinson for Rix

17 Mar   Manchester U   A   L   0-4
Jennings, Hill, Sansom, Talbot, O'Leary, Caton, Robson, Nicholas, Mariner, Woodcock, Rix

24 Mar   Wolverhampton W   H   W   4-1
Jennings, Hill, Sansom, Talbot, O'Leary, Caton, Robson 1, Nicholas 1, Mariner, Woodcock 1, Rix 1

31 Mar   Coventry C   A   W   4-1
Jennings, Hill, Sparrow, Talbot 1, O'Leary, Whyte 1, Robson 1, Nicholas, Mariner 1, Woodcock, Rix, Kay for Jennings (Robson went in goal)

7 Apr   Stoke C   H   W   3-1
Lukic, Hill, Sparrow, Talbot, O'Leary, Caton, Robson, Nicholas 1, Mariner 1, Woodcock 1, Rix, Meade for Nicholas

9 Apr   Everton   A   D   0-0
Lukic, Hill, Sansom, Talbot, O'Leary, Caton, Robson, Nicholas, Mariner, Woodcock, Rix

21 Apr   Tottenham H   H   W   3-2
Lukic, Hill, Sansom, Talbot, O'Leary, Caton, Robson 1, Nicholas 1, Mariner, Woodcock 1, Rix, Davis for Rix

23 Apr   Birmingham C   A   D   1-1
Lukic, Hill, Sansom, Talbot, O'Leary, Caton, Robson, Nicholas, Mariner, Woodcock 1, Davis

28 Apr   Leicester C   H   W   2-1
Jennings, Hill, Sansom, Talbot, O'Leary, Caton, Robson, Nicholas, Mariner, Woodcock 1, Rix, Davis 1 for Talbot

5 May   WBA   A   W   3-1
Jennings, Hill, Sansom, Talbot 1, O'Leary, Caton, Robson 1, Nicholas, Mariner 1, Woodcock, Rix, Davis for Robson

7 May   West Ham U   H   D   3-3
Jennings, Hill, Sansom, Talbot 1, O'Leary, Caton, Robson 1, Nicholas, Mariner 1, Woodcock 1, Rix, Davis for Rix

12 May   Watford   A   L   1-2
Jennings, Hill, Sansom, Talbot1, O'Leary, Caton, Robson 1, Davis, Mariner, Meade, Rix

FA CUP
7 Jan   Middlesbrough (3)   A   L   2-3
Jennings, Hill, Sansom, Cork, O'Leary, Caton, Meade, Davis, Woodcock 1, Nicholas 1, Rix, Talbot for Cork

MILK CUP
4 Oct   Plymouth Arg (2/1) A   D   1-1
Jennings, Robson, Sansom, Whyte, O'Leary, Hill, Sunderland, Davis, Woodcock, Nicholas, Rix 1, Talbot for Woodcock

25 Oct   Plymouth Arg (2/2)   H   W   1-0
Jennings, Robson, Sansom, Whyte, O'Leary, Hill, Sunderland 1, Davis, Woodcock, Nicholas, Rix
9 Nov   Tottenham H (3)   A   W   2-1
Jennings, Robson, Sansom, Whyte, O'Leary, Hill, Sunderland, Davis, Woodcock 1, Nicholas 1, Rix
29 Nov   Walsall (4)   H   L   1-2
Jennings, Robson 1, Sansom, Whyte, O'Leary, Hill, Sunderland, Davis, Woodcock, Nicholas, Allinson

APPEARANCES (Goals) Adams 3, Allinson 9, Caton 26, Chapman 4(1), Cork 7(1), Davis 35(1), Gorman 2, Hill 37(1), Jennings 38, Kay 7, Lukic 4, Madden 2, Mariner 15(7), Meade 13(5), McDermott 13(2), Nicholas 41(11), O'Leary 36, Rix 34(4), Robson 28(6), Sansom 40(1) Sparrow 2, Sunderland 12(4), Talbot 27(6), Whyte 15(2), Woodcock 37(21), o/g 1, Total 25 players (74)

POSITION IN LEAGUE TABLE

	Pld	W	D	L	F	A	Pts
1st Liverpool	42	22	14	6	73	32	80
6th Arsenal	42	18	9	15	74	60	63

SEASON 1984-1985

FOOTBALL LEAGUE (DIVISION 1)
25 Aug   Chelsea   H   D   1-1
Jennings, Anderson, Sansom, Talbot, O'Leary, Caton, Robson, Davis, Mariner 1, Woodcock, Allinson
29 Aug   Nottingham F   A   L   0-2
Jennings, Anderson, Sansom, Talbot, O'Leary, Caton, Robson, Nicholas, Mariner, Woodcock, Davis, Allinson for Talbot
1 Sep   Watford   A   W   4-3
Jennings, Anderson, Sansom, Talbot 1, O'Leary, Caton, Robson, Davis, Mariner, Woodcock 1, Nicholas 2
4 Sep   Newcastle U   H   W   2-0
Jennings, Anderson 1, Sansom, Talbot 1, O'Leary, Caton, Robson, Davis, Mariner, Woodcock, Nicholas
8 Sep   Liverpool   H   W   3-1
Jennings, Anderson, Sansom, Talbot 2, O'Leary, Caton, Robson, Davis, Mariner, Woodcock 1, Nicholas
15 Sep   Ipswich T   A   L   1-2
Jennings, Anderson, Sansom, Talbot, O'Leary, Caton, Robson, Rix, Mariner, Woodcock, Nicholas 1
22 Sep   Stoke C   H   W   4-0
Jennings, Anderson, Sansom 1, Talbot, O'Leary, Caton, Robson, Rix, Mariner 1, Woodcock 2, Nicholas
29 Sep   Coventry C   A   W   2-1
Jennings, Anderson, Sansom, Talbot, O'Leary, Caton, Robson, Rix, Mariner 1, Woodcock 1, Nicholas, Davis for Talbot
6 Oct   Everton   H   W   1-0
Jennings, Anderson, Sansom, Talbot, O'Leary, Caton, Robson, Rix, Mariner, Woodcock, Nicholas 1
13 Oct   Leicester C   A   W   4-1
Jennings, Anderson 1, Sansom, Talbot 2, O'Leary, Caton, Robson, Rix 1, Allinson, Woodcock, Nicholas
20 Oct   Sunderland   H   W   3-2
Jennings, Anderson, Sansom, Talbot 1, O'Leary, Caton 1, Robson, Rix, Allinson 1, Woodcock, Nicholas, Davis for Woodcock
27 Oct   West Ham U   A   L   1-3
Jennings, Anderson, Sansom, Talbot, O'Leary, Hill, Robson, Rix, Allinson 1, Davis, Nicholas
2 Nov   Manchester U   A   L   2-4
Lukic, Anderson, Sansom, Talbot, O'Leary, Coton, Davis, Rix, Allinson 1, Woodcock 1, Nicholas, Adams for Rix
10 Nov   Aston Villa   H   D   1-1
Jennings, Anderson, Sansom, Talbot, O'Leary, Caton, Robson, Davis, Mariner 1, Woodcock, Nicholas, Allinson for Caton

17 Nov   WBA   H   W   1-0
Jennings, Anderson, Sansom, Talbot, O'Leary, Adams, Robson, Davis, Allinson, Woodcock 1, Nicholas

25 Nov   Sheffield Wed   A   L   1-2
Jennings, Anderson, Sansom, Talbot, O'Leary, Adams, Robson, Davis, Mariner, Woodcock 1, Nicholas, Allinson for O'Leary

1 Dec   Luton T   H   W   3-1
Lukic, Anderson 1, Sansom, Talbot, Adams, Caton, Robson, Davis, Mariner, Woodcock 1, Allinson 1

8 Dec   Southampton   A   L   0-1
Lukic, Anderson, Sansom, Talbot, O'Leary, Adams, Robson, Davis, Mariner, Woodcock, Allinson, Meade for Allinson

15 Dec   WBA   H   W   4-0
Lukic, Anderson, Sansom, Talbot1, Adams, Caton, Robson, Davis1, Mariner, Woodcock, Allinson2

22 Dec   Watford   H   D   1-1
Lukic, O'Leary, Hill, Talbot, Adams, Caton, Robson, Nicholas, Mariner, Woodcock, Allinson 1

26 Dec   Norwich C   A   L   0-1
Lukic, Anderson, Sansom, Talbot, O'Leary, Adams, Robson, Caton, Mariner, Woodcock, Allinson, Nicholas for Allinson

29 Dec   Newcastle U   A   W   3-1
Lukic, Anderson, Caton, Talbot 1, O'Leary, Adams, Robson, Nicholas 2, Mariner, Woodcock, Allinson

1 Jan   Tottenham H   H   L   1-2
Lukic, Anderson, Caton, Talbot, O'Leary, Adams, Robson Allinson, Mariner, Woodcock 1, Nicholas, Willams for Nicholas

19 Jan   Chelsea   A   D   1-1
Lukic, Anderson, Sansom, Talbot, O'Leary, Caton, Robson, Williams, Mariner 1, Woodcock, Nicholas

2 Feb   Coventry C   H   W   2-1
Lukic, Anderson, Sansom, Talbot, O'Leary, Caton, Robson, Williams, Mariner, Meade 1, Allinson 1, Nicholas for Caton

12 Feb   Liverpool   A   L   0-3
Lukic, Anderson, Sansom, Talbot, O'Leary, Adams, Robson, Williams, Mariner, Meade, Allinson Nicholas for Alinson

23 Feb   Manchester U   H   L   0-1
Lukic, Anderson, Sansom, Williams, O'Leary, Caton, Robson, Davis, Mariner, Woodcock, Nicholas, Talbot for Davis

2 Mar   West Ham U   H   W   2-1
Lukic, Anderson, Sansom, Williams, O'Leary, Caton, Robson 1, Davis, Mariner 1, Woodcock, Nicholas

9 Mar   Sunderland   A   D   0-0
Lukic, Anderson, Sansom, Talbot, O'Leary, Caton, Robson , Davis, Mariner, Woodcock, Nicholas

13 Mar   Aston Villa   A   D   0-0
Lukic, Anderson, Sansom, Talbot, O'Leary, Caton, Robson , Davis, Mariner, Woodcock, Nicholas, Meade for Woodcock

16 Mar   Leicester C   H   W   2-0
Lukic, Anderson, Sansom, Williams 1, Adams, Caton, Robson, Davis, Mariner, Meade 1, Nicholas, Talbot for Nicholas

19 Mar   Ipswich T   H   D   1-1
Lukic, Anderson, Sansom, Williams, Adams, Caton, Robson , Davis, Mariner, Meade 1, Nicholas, Talbot for Davis

23 Mar   Everton   A   L   0-2
Lukic, Anderson, Sansom, Williams, O'Leary, Caton, Robson, Rix, Mariner, Meade, Nicholas, Talbot for Robson

30 Mar   Stoke C   A   L   0-2
Lukic, Anderson, Sansom, Williams, O'Leary, Caton, Talbot, Rix, Mariner, Meade, Nicholas, Allinson for Meade

6 Apr   Norwich C   H   W   2-0
Lukic, Anderson, Sansom, Williams, O'Leary, Caton, Robson 1, Rix, Mariner, Talbot, Nicholas 1, Allinson for Mariner

13 Apr   Nottingham F   H   D   1-1
Lukic, Anderson, Sansom, Williams, O'Leary, Caton, Robson, Rix, Allinson 1, Talbot, Nicholas
17 Apr   Tottenham H   A   W   2-0
Lukic, Anderson, Sansom, Williams, O'Leary, Caton, Robson, Rix, Allinson, Talbot 1, Nicholas 1,
Mariner for O'Leary
20 Apr   WBA   A   L   0-1
Lukic, Anderson, Sansom, Williams, Adams, Caton, Robson, Rix, Allinson, Talbot, Nicholas, Mariner
for Adams
27 Apr   Sheffield Wed   H   W   1-0
Lukic, Anderson, Sansom, Williams, O'Leary, Caton, Robson, Rix, Mariner 1, Talbot, Nicholas,
Allinson for Robson
4 May   Luton T   A   L   1-3
Lukic, Anderson, Sansom, Talbot, O'Leary, Caton, Robson, Rix, Mariner, Allinson, Nicholas 1, Davis
for Caton
6 May   Southampton   H   W   1-0
Lukic, Anderson, Sansom, Talbot, Adams, Davis, Robson, Rix 1, Mariner, Allinson, Nicholas
11 May   WBA   A   D   2-2
Lukic, Anderson, Sansom, Talbot, O'Leary, Adams, Robson, Rix 1, Mariner, Davis, Nicholas, Allinson
1 for Nicholas

FA CUP
5 Jan   Hereford (3)   A   D   1-1
Lukic, Anderson, Caton, Talbot, O'Leary, Adams, Robson, Williams, Mariner, Woodcock 1, Nicholas,
Allinson for Nicholas
22 Jan   Hereford (3R)   H   W   7-2
Lukic, Anderson 1, Sansom, Talbot 2, O'Leary, Caton, Robson, Williams, Mariner 2, Woodcock 1,
Nicholas 1
26 Jan   York C (4)   A   L   0-1
Lukic, Anderson, Sansom, Talbot, O'Leary, Caton, Robson, Willams, Mariner, Woodcock, Nicholas,
Allinson for Nicholas

MILK CUP
25 Sep   Bristol R (2/1)   H   W   4-0
Jennings, Anderson 1, Sansom, Talbot, O'Leary, Caton, Robson, Rix, Mariner, Woodcock 1,
Nicholas 2
9 Oct   Bristol R (2/2)   A   D   1-1
Jennings, Anderson, Sansom, Talbot, O'Leary, Caton 1, Robson, Rix, Mariner, Woodcock, Nicholas
31 Oct   Oxford U (3)   A   L   2-3
Jennings, Anderson, Sansom, Talbot, O'Leary, Caton, Robson, Rix 1, Allinson 1, Woodcock,
Nicholas, Adams for Robson

APPEARANCES (Goals) Adams 16; Allinson 27(10); Anderson 41(3); Caton 35(1); Davis 24(1); Hill 2;,
Jennings 15; Lukic 27; Mariner 36(7); Meade 8(3); Nicholas 38(9); O'Leary 36; Rix 18(2); Robson 40(2;
Sansom 39(1); Talbot 41(10); Williams 15(1); Woodcock 27(10); o/g 1; Total 18 players (61)

POSITION IN LEAGUE TABLE

	Pld	W	D	L	F	A	Pts
1st Everton	42	28	6	8	88	43	90
7th Arsenal	42	19	9	14	61	49	66

SEASON 1985-1986

FOOTBALL LEAGUE (DIVISION 1)
17 Aug   Liverpool   A   L   0-2
Lukic, Anderson, Sansom, Williams, O'Leary, Caton, Robson, Allinson, Nicholas, Woodcock, Rix
20 Aug   Southampton   H   W   3-2
Lukic, Anderson, Sansom, Williams, O'Leary, Caton 1, Robson 1, Allinson, Nicholas, Woodcock 1, Rix

24 Aug Manchester U   H   L   1-2
Lukic, Anderson, Sansom, Williams, O'Leary, Caton, Robson, Allinson 1, Nicholas, Woodcock, Rix, Davis for Williams

27 Aug Luton T   A   D   2-2
Lukic, Anderson, Sansom, Davis, O'Leary, Caton, Robson, Allinson, Nicholas, Woodcock 1, Rix, Mariner for O'Leary (o/g Donaghy)

31 Aug Leicester C   H   W   1-0
Lukic, Anderson, Sansom, Davis, Mariner, Caton, Robson, Allinson, Nicholas, Woodcock 1, Rix

3 Sep WBA   A   W   1-0
Lukic, Anderson, Sansom, Davis, O'Leary, Caton, Robson, Allinson1, Nicholas, Woodcock 1, Rix

7 Sep Coventry C   A   W   2-0
Lukic, Anderson, Sansom, Davis, O'Leary, Caton, Robson, Allinson, Nicholas 1, Woodcock 1, Rix,

14 Sep Sheffield Wed   H   W   1-0
Lukic, Anderson, Sansom, Davis, O'Leary, Caton, Robson, Allinson 1, Nicholas, Woodcock, Rix,

21 Sep Chelsea   A   L   1-2
Lukic, Anderson, Sansom, Davis, O'Leary, Caton, Robson, Allinson, Nicholas 1, Woodcock, Rix

28 Sep Newcastle U   H   D   0-0
Lukic, Anderson, Sansom, Davis, O'Leary, Caton, Rocastle, Allinson, Nicholas, Woodcock, Rix, Whyte for Allinson

5 Oct Aston Villa   H   W   3-2
Lukic, Anderson 1, Sansom, Davis, O'Leary, Caton, Whyte 1 Allinson, Nicholas, Woodcock 1, Rix

12 Oct West Ham U   A   D   0-0
Lukic, Anderson, Sansom, Davis, O'Leary, Caton, Whyt Allinson, Nicholas, Woodcock, Rix, Rocastle for O'Leary

19 Oct Ipswich T   H   W   1-0
Lukic, Anderson, Sansom, Davis 1, O'Leary, Caton, Whyte Allinson, Nicholas, Woodcock, Rix, Rocastle for Nicholas

26 Oct Nottingham F   A   L   2-3
Lukic, Anderson, Sansom, Davis 1, O'Leary, Caton, Whyte, Allinson, Nicholas, Woodcock, Rix 1, Rocastle for Allinson

2 Nov Manchester C   H   W   1-0
Lukic, Anderson, Sansom, Davis 1, O'Leary, Caton, Williams, Allinson, Nicholas, Woodcock, Rix, Whyte for Allinson

9 Nov Everton   A   L   1-6
Lukic, Anderson, Sansom, Davis, O'Leary, Caton, Williams, Allinson, Nicholas 1, Woodcock, Rix

16 Nov Oxford U   H   W   2-1
Lukic, Anderson, Sansom, Davis 1, O'Leary, Caton, Williams, Robson, Nicholas, Woodcock 1, Hayes, Allinson for Woodcock

23 Nov WBA   A   D   0-0
Lukic, Anderson, Sansom, Davis, Keown, Caton, Williams, Robson, Nicholas, Woodcock, Hayes, Whyte for Hayes

30 Nov Birmingham C   H   D   0-0
Lukic, Anderson, Sansom, Davis, O'Leary, Caton, Williams, Robson, Nicholas, Woodcock, Hayes, Allinson for Williams

7 Dec Southampton   A   L   0-3
Lukic, Anderson, Sansom, Davis, O'Leary, Caton, Williams, Robson, Nicholas, Woodcock, Hayes, Allinson for Hayes

14 Dec Liverpool   H   W   2-0
Lukic, Anderson, Sansom, Davis, O'Leary Keown, Allinson, Robson, Nicholas 1, Quinn 1, Rix

21 Dec Manchester U   A   W   1-0
Lukic, Caesar, Sansom, Davis, O'Leary Keown, Allinson, Robson, Nicholas 1, Quinn, Rix

28 Dec WBA   H   W   3-1
Lukic, Caesar, Sansom, Davis, O'Leary Keown, Allinson, Robson, Nicholas 1, Quinn, Rix 1, Woodcock 1 for Robson

1 Jan Tottenham H   H   D   0-0
Lukic, Anderson, Sansom, Davis, O'Leary Keown, Allinson, Rocastle, Nicholas, Quinn, Rix 1

18 Jan Leicester C   A   D   2-2
Lukic, Anderson, Sansom, Davis, O'Leary Keown, Allinson, Robson 1, Nicholas 1, Quinn, Rix

1 Feb   Luton T   H   W   2-1
Lukic, Anderson, Sansom, Rocastle, O'Leary Keown, Allinson 1, Mariner, Nicholas, Quinn, Rix
1 Mar   Newcastle U   A   L   0-1
Lukic, Anderson, Sansom, Williams, O'Leary, Keown, Allinson, Rocastle, Nicholas, Woodcock, Rix,
Mariner for Woodcock
8 Mar   Aston Villa   A   W   4-1
Wilmot, Anderson, Sansom, Williams, O'Leary, Keown, Hayes 1, Rocastle 1, Nicholas 1, Woodcock,
Rix (o/g Elliot)
11 Mar   Ipswich T   A   W   2-1
Wilmot, Anderson, Sansom, Williams, O'Leary, Keown, Hayes 1, Rocastle, Nicholas 1, Woodcock 1,
Rix, Mariner for O'Leary
15 Mar   West Ham U   H   W   1-0
Lukic, Anderson, Sansom, Williams, O'Leary, Keown, Hayes, Rocastle, Nicholas, Woodcock 1, Rix
22 Mar   Coventry C   H   W   3-0
Lukic, Adams, Anderson, Sansom, Williams, O'Leary, Keown, Hayes 1, Rocastle, Nicholas,
Woodcock 1, Rix (o/g McInally)
29 Mar   Tottenham H   A   L   0-1
Lukic, Anderson, Sansom, Williams, O'Leary, Keown, Hayes, Rocastle, Nicholas, Quinn, Rix,
Mariner for Quinn
31 Mar   Watford   H   L   0-2
Lukic, Anderson, Sansom, Williams, O'Leary, Keown, Hayes, Rocastle, Nicholas, Mariner, Rix,
Robson for Hayes
1 Apr   Watford   A   L   0-3
Lukic, Anderson, Sansom, Williams, Adams, Keown, Robson, Rocastle, Nicholas, Woodcock, Rix,
Allinson for Williams
5 Apr   Manchester C   A   W   1-0
Lukic, Anderson, Sansom, Allinson, Adams, Keown, Robson 1, Rocastle, Nicholas, Quinn, Rix,
Mariner for Quinn
8 Apr   Nottingham F   H   D   1-1
Lukic, Anderson, Sansom, Allinson 1, Adams, Keown, Robson, Rocastle, Nicholas, Quinn, Rix,
Mariner for Rocastle
12 Apr   Everton   H   L   0-1
Lukic, Anderson, Sansom, Allinson, Adams, Keown, Robson, Davis, Nicholas, Quinn, Rix
16 Apr   Sheffield Wed   A   L   0-2
Lukic, Anderson, Sansom, Allinson, Adams, Keown, Robson, Davis, Nicholas, Woodcock, Rix
26 Apr   WBA   H   D   2-2
Lukic, Anderson, Sansom, Allinson 1, O'Leary, Adams, Robson 1, Davis, Hayes, Woodcock, Rix,
Quinn for Woodcock
29 Apr   Chelsea   H   W   2-0
Lukic, Anderson 1, Sansom, Keown, O'Leary, Adams, Robson, Davis, Nicholas 1, Woodcock, Rix,
Quinn for Rix
3 May   Birmingham C   A   W   1-0
Lukic, Anderson, Sansom, Keown, O'Leary, Adams, Robson, Davis, Nicholas, Woodcock 1, Rix
5 May   Oxford U   A   L   0-3
Lukic, Anderson, Sansom, Keown, O'Leary, Adams, Robson, Davis, Nicholas, Woodcock, Rix,
Allinson for O'Leary

FA CUP
4 Jan   Grimsby T (3)   A   W   4-3
Lukic, Anderson, Sansom, Davis, O'Leary, Keown, Allinson, Rocastle, Nicholas 3, Quinn, Rix 1
25 Jan   Rotherham U (4)   H   W   5-1
Lukic, Anderson, Sansom, Rocastle, O'Leary, Keown, Allinson 2, Robson 1, Nicholas 1, Quinn, Rix 1,
Woodcock for Robson
15 Feb   Luton T (5)   A   D   2-2
Lukic, Anderson, Sansom, Williams, O'Leary, Keown, Allinson 1, Rocastle 1, Nicholas, Woodcock,
Rix, Mariner for Nicholas
3 Mar   Luton T (5R)   H   D   0-0
Lukic, Anderson, Sansom, Williams, O'Leary, Keown, Allinson, Rocastle, Nicholas, Mariner, Rix (aet)

5 Mar   Luton T (5R)   A   L   0-3
Lukic, Anderson, Sansom, Williams, O'Leary, Keown, Allinson, Rocastle, Nicholas, Mariner, Hayes, Quinn for Hayes

MILK CUP
25 Sep   Hereford U (2/1)   A   D   0-0
Lukic, Anderson, Sansom, Davis, O'Leary, Caton, Robson, Allinson, Nicholas, Woodcock, Rix, Mariner for Robson
8 Oct   Hereford U (2/2)   H   W   2-1
Lukic, Anderson 1, Sansom, Davis, O'Leary, Caton, Whyte, Allinson, Nicholas 1, Woodcock, Rix, Rocastle for Davis (aet)
30 Oct   Manchester C (3)   A   W   2-1
Lukic, Anderson, Sansom, Davis, O'Leary, Caton, Williams, Allinson 1, Nicholas 1, Woodcock, Rix
19 Nov   Southampton (4)   H   D   0-0
Lukic, Anderson, Sansom, Davis, O'Leary, Caton, Robson, Allinson, Nicholas, Woodcock, Hayes, Allinson for Hayes
26 Nov   Southampton (4R)   A   W   3-1
Lukic, Anderson, Sansom, Davis, O'Leary, Caton, Robson 1, Allinson, Nicholas 1, Woodcock, Hayes 1
22 Jan   Aston Villa (5)   A   D   1-1
Wilmot, Anderson, Sansom, Rocastle, O'Leary, Caton, Robson, Allinson, Nicholas 1, Quinn, Rix, Woodcock for Robson
4 Feb   Aston Villa (5R)   H   L   1-2
Lukic, Wilmot, Anderson, Sansom, Rocastle, O'Leary, Caton, Mariner 1, Nicholas, Quinn, Rix, Woodcock for Allinson

APPEARANCES (Goals)
Adams 10; Allinson 33(6); Anderson 39(2); Caesar 20(1); Caton 20(1); Davis 29(4); Hayes 11(2); Keown 22; Lukic 40; Mariner 9; Nicholas 41(10); O'Leary 35; Quinn 12(1); Rix 38(3); Robson 27(4); Rocastle 16(1); Sansom 42; Whyte 7(1); Williams 17; Wilmot 2; Woodcock 33(11); o/g 3; Total 21 players (49)

POSITION IN LEAGUE TABLE

	Pld	W	D	L	F	A	Pts
1st Liverpool	42	26	10	6	89	37	88
7th Arsenal	42	20	9	13	49	47	69

SEASON 1986-1987

FOOTBALL LEAGUE (DIVISION 1)
23 Aug   Manchester U   H   W   1-0
Lukic, Anderson, Sansom, Robson, O'Leary, Adams, Rocastle, Davis, Quinn, Nicholas 1, Rix, Hayes for Rocastle
26 Aug   Coventry C   A   L   1-2
Lukic, Anderson 1, Sansom, Robson, O'Leary, Adams, Rocastle, Davis, Quinn, Nicholas, Rix, Hayes for Rix
30 Aug   Liverpool   A   L   1-2
Lukic, Anderson, Sansom, Robson, O'Leary, Adams 1, Rocastle, Davis, Quinn, Nicholas, Rix, Williams for Robson
2 Sep   Sheffield Wed   H   W   2-0
Lukic, Anderson, Sansom, Robson, O'Leary, Adams 1, Rocastle, Davis, Quinn 1, Nicholas, Rix, Hayes for Rocastle
6 Sep   Tottenham H   H   D   0-0
Lukic, Anderson, Sansom, Robson, O'Leary, Adams, Rocastle, Davis, Quinn, Nicholas, Rix, Hayes for Rocastle
13 Sep   Luton T   A   D   0-0
Lukic, Anderson, Sansom, Williams, O'Leary, Adams, Rocastle, Davis, Quinn, Nicholas, Rix, Groves for Rix
20 Sep   Oxford U   H   D   0-0
Lukic, Anderson, Sansom, Williams, O'Leary, Adams, Rocastle, Davis, Quinn, Nicholas, Rix, Groves for Rix

27 Sep   Nottingham F   A   L   0-1
Lukic, Anderson, Sansom, Williams, O'Leary, Adams, Rocastle, Davis, Quinn, Nicholas, Groves,
Allinson for Nicholas

4 Oct   Everton   A   W   1-0
Lukic, Anderson, Sansom, Williams 1, O'Leary, Adams, Rocastle, Davis, Quinn, Allinson, Groves,
Caesar for Groves

11 Oct   Watford   H   W   3-1
Lukic, Anderson, Sansom, Williams, O'Leary, Adams, Rocastle, Davis, Quinn 1, Groves 1, Hayes 1,
Allinson for O'Leary

18 Oct   Newcastle U   A   W   2-1
Lukic, Anderson 1, Sansom, Williams 1, O'Leary, Adams, Rocastle, Davis, Quinn, Groves, Hayes,
Caesar for Quinn

25 Oct   Chelsea   H   W   3-1
Lukic, Anderson, Sansom, Williams, O'Leary, Adams, Rocastle 1, Davis, Quinn, Groves, Hayes 2,
Allinson for Quinn

1 Nov   Charlton Ath   A   W   2-0
Lukic, Anderson, Sansom, Williams, O'Leary, Adams 1, Rocastle, Davis, Quinn, Groves, Hayes 1,
Caesar for Groves

8 Nov   West Ham U   H   D   0-0
Lukic, Anderson, Sansom, Williams, O'Leary, Adams, Rocastle, Davis, Quinn, Groves, Hayes

15 Nov   Southampton   A   W   4-0
Lukic, Anderson 1, Sansom, Williams, O'Leary, Adams, Rocastle, Davis, Quinn 1, Groves 1, Hayes 1,
Caesar for Rocastle

22 Nov   Manchester C   H   W   3-0
Lukic, Anderson 1, Sansom, Williams, O'Leary, Adams 1, Rocastle, Davis, Quinn 1, Allinson, Hayes,
Merson for Hayes

29 Nov   Aston Villa   A   W   4-0
Lukic, Anderson, Sansom, Williams, O'Leary, Adams, Rocastle 1, Davis, Quinn, Groves 1, Hayes 1
(o/g Keown)

6 Dec   WBA   H   W   3-1
Lukic, Anderson, Sansom, Williams, O'Leary, Adams, Rocastle, Davis, Quinn 1, Groves, Hayes 2,
Nicholas for Groves

13 Dec   Norwich C   A   D   1-1
Lukic, Anderson, Sansom, Williams, O'Leary, Adams, Rocastle, Davis, Quinn, Groves, Hayes 1,
Caesar for Groves

20 Dec   Luton T   H   W   3-0
Lukic, Anderson, Sansom, Williams, O'Leary, Adams 1, Rocastle, Davis, Quinn 1, Groves, Hayes 1,
Nicholas for Groves

26 Dec   Leicester C   A   D   1-1
Lukic, Anderson, Sansom, Williams, O'Leary, Adams, Rocastle, Davis, Quinn, Groves, Hayes 1,
Caesar for Groves

27 Dec   Southampton   H   W   1-0
Lukic, Anderson, Sansom, Williams, O'Leary, Adams, Rocastle, Davis, Quinn 1, Nicholas, Hayes,
Allinson for Hayes

1 Jan   Wimbledon   H   W   3-1
Lukic, Anderson, Sansom, Williams, O'Leary, Adams, Rocastle, Davis, Quinn, Nicholas 2, Hayes 1,
Allinson for Rocastle

4 Jan   Tottenham H   A   W   2-1
Lukic, Anderson, Sansom, Williams, O'Leary, Adams 1, Rocastle, Davis 1, Quinn, Nicholas, Hayes,
Rix for Quinn

18 Jan   Coventry C   H   D   0-0
Lukic, Anderson, Sansom, Williams, O'Leary, Adams, Rocastle, Davis, Quinn, Nicholas, Hayes, Rix
for Hayes

24 Jan   Manchester U   A   L   0-2
Lukic, Anderson, Sansom, Williams, O'Leary, Adams, Rocastle, Davis, Quinn, Nicholas, Hayes,
Caesar for Nicholas

14 Feb   Sheffield Wed   A   D   1-1
Lukic, Thomas, Sansom, Williams, O'Leary, Adams, Groves, Davis, Quinn 1, Rix, Hayes, Allinson for
Williams

25 Feb   Oxford U   A   D   0-0
Lukic, Anderson, Sansom, Thomas, O'Leary, Adams, Rocastle, Davis, Quinn, Groves, Hayes,
Nicholas for Groves
7 Mar   Chelsea   A   L   0-1
Lukic, Anderson, Sansom, Thomas, O'Leary, Adams, Rocastle, Caesar, Quinn, Allinson, Hayes,
Merson for Hayes
10 Mar   Liverpool   H   L   0-1
Lukic, Anderson, Sansom, Thomas, O'Leary, Adams, Rocastle, Groves, Quinn, Allinson, Hayes,
Caesar for Hayes
17 Mar   Nottingham F   H   D   0-0
Lukic, Anderson, Sansom, Williams, Caesar, Adams, Rocastle, Groves, Quinn, Nicholas, Thomas,
Allinson for Groves
21 Mar   Watford   A   L   0-2
Lukic, Caesar, Sansom, Thomas, O'Leary, Adams, Allinson, Davis, Quinn, Nicholas, Hayes, Rix for
Quinn
28 Mar   Everton   H   L   0-1
Lukic, Anderson, Sansom, Williams, O'Leary, Adams, Rocastle, Davis, Quinn, Nicholas, Hayes,
Groves for Hayes
8 Apr   West Ham U   A   L   1-3
Wilmot, Anderson, Thomas, Williams, O'Leary, Adams, Rocastle, Davis, Groves, Nicholas, Hayes 1,
Rix for Hayes
11 Apr   Charlton Ath   H   W   2-1
Lukic, Anderson, Sansom, Thomas, Williams, O'Leary, Adams, Rocastle, Davis 1, Quinn, Nicholas,
Hayes 1, Groves for Quinn
14 Apr   Newcastle U   H   L   0-1
Lukic, Anderson, Thomas, Williams, O'Leary, Adams, Rocastle, Davis, Groves, Nicholas, Hayes, Rix
for Rocastle
18 Apr   Wimbledon   A   W   2-1
Lukic, Anderson, Caesar, Williams, O'Leary, Adams, Rocastle 1, Merson 1, Nicholas, Rix, Allinson
for Rocastle
20 Apr   Leicester C   H   W   4-1
Wilmot, Anderson, Sansom, Williams, O'Leary, Adams, Hayes 2, Davis 1, Merson, Nicholas 1, Rix,
Caesar for O'Leary
25 Apr   Manchester C   A   L   0-3
Wilmot, Anderson, Thomas, Williams, Caesar, Adams, Hayes, Davis, Merson, Nicholas, Rix,
Allinson for Merson
2 May   Aston Villa   H   W   2-1
Wilmot, Anderson, Thomas, Williams, O'Leary, Adams, Rocastle, Davis, Quinn, Nicholas, Hayes 2,
Groves for Quinn
4 May   WBA   A   W   4-1
Wilmot, Anderson, Thomas, Williams, Caesar, Adams, Rix 2, Davis, Merson 1, Nicholas, Hayes 1
9 May   Norwich C   H   L   1-2
Wilmot, Anderson, Thomas, Williams, O'Leary, Adams, Rix, Davis, Merson 1, Nicholas, Hayes,
Groves for Anderson

FA CUP
10 Jan   Reading (3)   A   W   3-1
Lukic, Anderson, Sansom, Williams, O'Leary, Adams, Rocastle, Davis, Quinn, Nicholas 2, Hayes 1
31 Jan   Plymouth Arg (4)   H   W   6-1
Lukic, Anderson 2, Sansom, Williams, O'Leary, Adams, Rocastle 1, Davis 1, Quinn 1, Nicholas 1,
Hayes, Groves/Caesar for Hayes/Groves
21 Feb   Barnsley (5)   H   W   2-0
Lukic, Anderson, Sansom, Allinson, O'Leary, Adams, Rocastle, Davis, Quinn, Groves, Hayes 1,
Nicholas 1/Thomas for Quinn/Hayes
14 Mar   Watford (QF)   H   L   1-3
Lukic, Anderson, Sansom, Williams, O'Leary, Adams, Rocastle, Groves, Quinn, Allinson 1, Hayes,
Nicholas/Thomas for Allinson/Hayes

FOOTBALL LEAGUE (LITTLEWOODS) CUP
23 Sep   Huddersfield T (2/1)   H   W   2-0
Lukic, Anderson, Sansom, Williams, O'Leary, Adams, Rocastle, Davis 1, Quinn 1, Nicholas, Rix,
Groves for Quinn
7 Oct   Huddersfield T (2/2)   A   D   1-1
Lukic, Anderson, Sansom, Williams, O'Leary, Adams, Rocastle, Davis, Quinn, Allinson, Groves,
Hayes 1 for Allinson
28 Oct   Manchester C (3)   H   W   3-1
Lukic, Anderson, Sansom, Williams, O'Leary, Adams, Rocastle 1, Davis 1, Quinn, Groves, Hayes 1,
Allinson for Quinn
18 Nov   Charlton Ath (4)   H   W   2-0
Lukic, Anderson, Sansom, Williams, O'Leary, Adams, Rocastle, Davis, Quinn 1, Groves, Hayes,
Allinson for Groves (o/g Curbishley)
21 Jan   Nottingham F (QF)   H   W   2-0
Lukic, Anderson, Sansom, Williams, O'Leary, Adams, Rocastle, Davis, Quinn, Nicholas 1, Hayes 1,
Rix for Quinn
8 Feb   Tottenham H (SF/1)   H   L   0-1
Lukic, Caesar, Sansom, Williams, O'Leary, Adams, Groves, Davis, Quinn, Nicholas, Hayes,
Thomas/Rix for Caesar/Nicholas
1 Mar   Tottenham H (SF/2)   A   W   2-1
Lukic, Anderson 1, Sansom, Thomas, O'Leary, Adams, Rocastle, Davis, Quinn 1, Nicholas, Hayes,
Allinson for Nicholas
4 Mar   Tottenham H (SFR)   A   W   2-1
Lukic, Anderson, Sansom, Thomas, O'Leary, Adams, Rocastle 1, Davis, Quinn, Nicholas, Hayes,
Allinson 1 for Thomas
5 Apr   Liverpool (F)   W   2-1
Lukic, Anderson, Sansom, Williams, O'Leary, Adams, Rocastle, Davis, Quinn, Nicholas 2, Hayes,
Groves for Quinn/Thomas for Hayes (at Wembley)

APPEARANCES (Goals) Adams 42(6); Allinson 14; Anderson 40(4); Caesar 15; Davis 39(4); Groves
25(3);, Hayes 35(19); Lukic 36; Merson 7(3); Nicholas 28(4); O'Leary 39; Quinn 35(8); Rix 18(2); Robson
5; Rocastle 36(2); Sansom 35; Thomas 12; Williams 34(2); Wilmot 6; o/g 1; Total 19 players (58)

POSITION IN LEAGUE TABLE
	Pld	W	D	L	F	A	Pts
1st Everton	42	26	8	8	76	31	86
4th Arsenal	42	20	10	12	58	35	70

SEASON 1987-1988

FOOTBALL LEAGUE (DIVISION 1)
15 Aug   Liverpool   H   L   1-2
Lukic, Thomas, Sansom, Williams, O'Leary, Adams, Rocastle, Davis 1, Smith, Nicholas, Hayes,
Groves for Rocastle
19 Aug   Manchester U   A   D   0-0
Lukic, Thomas, Sansom, Williams, O'Leary, Adams, Rocastle, Davis, Smith, Nicholas, Hayes,
Groves for Nicholas
22 Aug   WBA   A   L   0-2
Lukic, Thomas, Sansom, Williams, O'Leary, Adams, Rocastle, Davis, Smith, Nicholas, Hayes, Rix for
Rocastle
29 Aug   Portsmouth   H   W   6-0
Lukic, Thomas, Sansom, Williams, O'Leary, Adams 1, Rocastle 1, Davis 1, Smith 3, Groves, Rix,
Merson/Richardson for Groves/Rix
31 Aug   Luton T   A   D   1-1
Lukic, Thomas, Sansom, Williams, O'Leary, Adams, Rocastle, Davis 1, Smith, Groves, Rix,
12 Sep   Nottingham F   A   W   1-0
Lukic, Thomas, Sansom, Williams, O'Leary, Adams, Rocastle, Davis, Smith 1, Groves, Rix, Hayes for
Rocastle

19 Sep   Wimbledon   H   W   3-0
Lukic, Thomas 1, Sansom, Williams, O'Leary, Adams, Rocastle 1, Davis, Smith 1, Groves, Rix, Merson/Richardson for Groves/Williams

26 Sep   West Ham U   H   W   1-0
Lukic, Thomas 1, Sansom, Williams, O'Leary, Adams, Rocastle, Davis, Smith, Groves, Rix, Hayes for Rocastle

3 Oct   Charlton Ath   A   W   3-0
Lukic, Thomas 1, Sansom, Williams, O'Leary, Adams 1, Rocastle, Davis, Smith, Groves 1, Rix, Hayes for Rocastle

10 Oct   Oxford U   H   W   2-0
Lukic, Thomas, Sansom, Williams 1, O'Leary, Adams, Rocastle, Davis 1, Smith, Groves, Richardson, Hayes/Caesar for Rocastle/Smith

18 Oct   Tottenham H   A   W   2-1
Lukic, Thomas 1, Sansom, Williams, O'Leary, Adams, Rocastle 1, Davis, Smith, Groves, Richardson, Hayes for Groves

24 Oct   Derby C   H   W   2-1
Lukic, Thomas 1, Sansom, Williams, O'Leary, Adams, Rocastle, Davis, Smith, Groves, Richardson 1, Merson for Groves

31 Oct   Newcastle U   A   W   1-0
Lukic, Thomas, Sansom, Williams, O'Leary, Adams, Rocastle, Davis, Smith 1, Groves, Richardson, Caesar/Hayes for Williams/Adams

3 Nov   Chelsea   H   W   3-1
Lukic, Thomas, Sansom, Williams, O'Leary, Adams, Rocastle, Davis, Smith, Groves, Richardson 2 (o/g Wegerle)

14 Nov   Norwich C   A   W   4-2
Lukic, Thomas 1, Sansom, Williams, O'Leary, Adams, Rocastle 2, Davis, Smith, Groves 1, Richardson, Caesar for Adams

21 Nov   Southampton   H   L   0-1
Lukic, Thomas, Sansom, Williams, O'Leary, Adams, Rocastle, Davis, Smith, Groves, Richardson, Quinn/Winterburn for Groves/Quinn

28 Nov   Watford   A   L   0-2
Lukic, Thomas, Sansom, Williams, O'Leary, Adams, Rocastle, Davis, Smith, Groves, Richardson, Hayes for Richardson

5 Dec   Sheffield Wed   H   W   3-1
Lukic, Thomas, Sansom, Williams, O'Leary, Adams, Rocastle, Davis, Smith, Groves 1, Richardson 1, Merson 1 for Davis

13 Dec   Coventry C   A   D   0-0
Lukic, Thomas, Sansom, Williams, O'Leary, Adams, Rocastle, Hayes, Smith, Groves, Richardson, Merson for Hayes

19 Dec   Everton   H   D   1-1
Lukic, Thomas, Sansom, Williams, O'Leary, Adams, Rocastle 1, Davis, Smith, Groves, Richardson, Merson for Richardson

26 Dec   Nottingham F   H   L   0-2
Lukic, Thomas, Sansom, Williams, O'Leary, Adams, Rocastle, Merson, Quinn, Groves, Richardson, Smith and Caesar for Merson and O'Leary

28 Dec   Wimbledon   A   L   1-3
Lukic, Thomas, Sansom, Williams, Caesar, Adams, Rocastle, Hayes, Quinn 1, Groves, Richardson, Smith for Hayes

1 Jan   Portsmouth   A   D   1-1
Lukic, Thomas, Winterburn, Williams, Caesar, Adams, Rocastle, Hayes, Quinn, Groves, Richardson, Smith 1 and Merson for Quinn and Groves

2 Jan   WBA   H   D   0-0
Lukic, Winterburn, Sansom, Williams, Caesar, Adams, Rocastle, Hayes, Smith, Merson, Richardson, Groves for Merson

16 Jan   Liverpool   A   L   0-2
Lukic, Winterburn, Sansom, Williams, Caesar, Adams, Rocastle, Hayes, Smith, Quinn, Richardson, Thomas and Groves for Caesar and Rocastle

24 Jan   Manchester U   H   L   1-2
Lukic, Thomas, Winterburn, Williams, O'Leary, Adams, Rocastle, Rix, Smith, Quinn 1, Richardson, Groves for Rix
13 Feb   Luton T   H   W   2-1
Lukic, Dixon, Winterburn, Thomas 1, O'Leary, Adams, Rocastle 1, Hayes, Smith, Quinn, Richardson, Caesar for Adams
27 Feb   Charlton Ath   H   W   4-0
Lukic, Winterburn, Sansom, Thomas 1, Caesar, Adams, Rocastle, Hayes, Smith 1, Merson 2, Richardson, Davis/Quinn for Merson/Richardson
6 Mar   Tottenham H   H   W   2-1
Lukic, Winterburn, Sansom, Thomas, Caesar, Adams, Rocastle, Hayes, Smith 1, Groves 1, Richardson
19 Mar   Newcastle U   H   D   1-1
Lukic, Dixon, Winterburn, Thomas, Caesar, Adams, Rocastle, Davis, Smith, Groves 1, Hayes, Quinn for Smith
26 Mar   Derby Co   A   D   0-0
Lukic, Dixon, Winterburn, Thomas, Caesar, Adams, Rocastle, Davis, Smith, Groves, Hayes, Richards/Quinn for Rocastle/Smith
30 Mar   Oxford U   A   D   0-0
Lukic, Winterburn, Sansom, Thomas, Caesar, Adams, Rocastle, Davis, Smith, Groves, Marwood, Merson/Quinn for Rocastle/Marwood
2 Apr   Chelsea   A   D   1-1
Lukic, Dixon, Winterburn, Williams, Caesar, Adams, Rocastle, Davis, Quinn, Groves, Hayes (o/g McLaughlin)
4 Apr   Norwich C   H   W   2-0
Lukic, Winterburn, Sansom, Williams, Caesar, Adams, Rocastle, Davis, Smith 1, Groves 1, Hayes
9 Apr   Southampton   A   L   2-4
Lukic, Winterburn, Sansom, Williams, Caesar, Thomas, Rocastle, Davis1, Smith, Groves, Hayes, Merson for Groves (o/g Bond)
12 Apr   West Ham U   A   W   1-0
Lukic, Winterburn, Sansom, Thomas 1, Caesar, Adams, Rocastle, Davis, Smith, Merson, Richardson, Rix for Richardson
15 Apr   Watford   H   L   0-1
Lukic, Winterburn, Sansom, Thomas, Caesar, Adams, Rocastle, Davis, Smith, Merson, Richardson, Hayes for Richardson
30 Apr   Sheffield Wed   A   D   3-3
Lukic, Winterburn, Sansom, Thomas, Caesar, Adams, Rocastle, Davis, Smith 1, Merson 2, Marwood, Richardson/Hayes for Davis/Winterburn
2 May   Coventry C   H   D   1-1
Lukic, Dixon, Sansom, Thomas, Caesar, Adams, Rocastle, Davis, Smith, Merson, Marwood 1, Hayes/Groves for Merson/Richardson
7 May   Everton   A   W   2-1
Lukic, Dixon, Sansom, Thomas 1, Caesar, Adams, Rocastle, Davis, Smith, Hayes 1, Marwood, Rix/Campbell for Caesar/Hayes

FA CUP
9 Jan   Millwall (3)   H   W   2-0
Lukic, Winterburn, Sansom, Williams, O'Leary, Adams, Rocastle 1, Hayes 1, Smith, Merson, Richardson, Groves for Merson
30 Jan   Brighton & HA (4)   A   W   2-1
Lukic, Winterburn, Sansom, Williams, O'Leary, Adams, Rocastle, Rix, Groves 1, Quinn, Richardson 1, Hayes for Rix
20 Feb   Manchester U (5)   H   W   2-1
Lukic, Winterburn, Sansom, Thomas, O'Leary, Adams, Rocastle, Hayes, Smith 1, Groves, Richardson, Rix for O'Leary (o/g Duxbury)
12 Mar   Nottingham F (6)   H   L   1-2
Lukic, Winterburn, Sansom, Thomas, O'Leary, Adams, Rocastle 1, Hayes, Smith, Groves, Richardson, Davis/Quinn for O'Leary/Hayes

FOOTBALL LEAGUE (LITTLEWOODS) CUP

23 Sep   Doncaster Rov (2/1)   A   W   3-0
Lukic, Thomas, Sansom, Williams 1, O'Leary, Adams, Rocastle, Davis, Smith 1, Groves, Rix, Richardson/Quinn for Groves/Rix

6 Oct   Doncaster Rov (2/2)   H   W   1-0
Lukic, Thomas, Sansom, Williams, Caesar, Adams, Rocastle 1, Davis, Smith 1, Groves Hayes

27 Oct   Bournemouth (3)   H   W   3-0
Lukic, Thomas 1, Sansom, Williams, O'Leary, Adams, Rocastle, Davis, Smith, Groves, Richardson 1, Merson for Groves

17 Nov   Stoke C (4)   H   W   3-0
Lukic, Thomas, Sansom, Williams, O'Leary 1, Adams, Rocastle 1, Davis, Smith, Groves, Richardson 1, Hayes for Groves

20 Jan   Sheffield Wed (5)   A   W   1-0
Lukic, Winterburn 1, Sansom, Williams, O'Leary, Adams, Rocastle, Rix, Smith, Quinn, Richardson, Groves for Quinn

7 Feb   Everton (SF/1)   A   W   1-0
Lukic, Winterburn, Sansom, Thomas, O'Leary, Adams, Rocastle, Hayes, Groves 1, Richardson, Caesar and Quinn for Rocastle and Smith

24 Feb   Everton (SF/2)   H   W   3-1
Lukic, Winterburn, Sansom, Thomas 1, O'Leary, Adams, Rocastle 1, Hayes, Smith 1, Groves, Richardson, Davis for O'Leary

24 Apr   Luton T (F)   L   2-3
Lukic, Winterburn, Sansom, Thomas, Caesar, Adams, Rocastle, Davis, Smith 1, Groves, Richardson, Hayes 1 for Groves (at Wembley)

APPEARANCES, LEAGUE ONLY (Goals) Adams, 39(2); Caesar 22; Campbell 1; Davis 29(5); Dixon 6; Groves 34(6); Hayes 27(1); Lukic 40; Marwood 4(1); Merson 15(5); Nicholas 3; O'Leary 23; Quinn 11(2); Richardson 29(4); Rix 10; Rocastle 40(7); Sansom 34(1); Smith 39(11); Thomas 37(9); Williams 29(1); Winterburn 17; o/g 3; Total 21 players (58)

POSITION IN LEAGUE TABLE

	Pld	W	D	L	F	A	Pts
1st Liverpool	40	26	12	2	87	24	90
6th Arsenal	40	18	12	10	58	39	66

SEASON 1988-1989

FOOTBALL LEAGUE (DIVISION 1)

27 Aug   Wimbledon   A   W   5-1
Lukic, Dixon, Winterburn, Thomas, Bould, Adams, Rocastle, Davis, Smith 3, Merson 1, Marwood 1

3 Sep   Aston Villa   H   L   2-3
Lukic, Dixon, Winterburn, Thomas, O'Leary, Adams, Rocastle, Davis, Smith 1, Merson, Marwood 1, Groves for Rocastle

10 Sep   Tottenham H   A   W   3-2
Lukic, Dixon, Winterburn 1, Thomas, O'Leary, Adams, Rocastle, Davis, Smith 1, Merson, Marwood 1, Groves/Richardson for Rocastle/Marwood

17 Sep   Southampton   H   D   2-2
Lukic, Dixon, Winterburn, Thomas, O'Leary, Adams, Rocastle, Davis, Smith 1, Merson, Marwood 1, Hayes/Richardson for Davis/Merson

24 Sep   Sheffield Wed   A   L   1-2
Lukic, Dixon, Winterburn, Thomas, O'Leary, Adams, Rocastle, Davis, Smith 1, Merson, Marwood, Groves for Merson

1 Oct   West Ham U   A   W   4-1
Lukic, Dixon, Winterburn, Thomas 1, Bould, Adams, Rocastle 1, Davis, Smith 2, Groves, Marwood, Hayes for Groves

22 Oct   WBA   H   W   2-1
Lukic, Dixon, Winterburn, Thomas, Bould, Adams 1, Rocastle, Richardson, Smith 1, Merson, Marwood, Groves for Merson

25 Oct   Luton T   A   D   1-1
Lukic, Dixon, Winterburn, Thomas, Bould, Adams, Rocastle, Richardson, Smith 1, Merson, Marwood

29 Oct   Coventry C   H   W   2-0
Lukic, Dixon, Winterburn, Thomas 1, Bould, Adams 1, Rocastle, Richardson, Smith, Merson,
Marwood, Groves/Hayes for Rocastle/Merson

6 Nov   Nottingham F   A   W   4-1
Lukic, Dixon, Winterburn, Thomas, Bould 1, Adams 1, Rocastle, Richardson, Smith 1, Merson,
Marwood 1, Hayes for Merson

12 Nov   Newcastle U   A   W   1-0
Lukic, Dixon, Winterburn, Thomas, Bould 1, Adams, Rocastle, Richardson, Smith, Hayes, Marwood,
Merson for Rocastle

19 Nov   Middlesbrough   H   W   3-0
Lukic, Dixon, Winterburn, Thomas, Bould, Adams, Rocastle 1, Richardson, Smith, Merson 2,
Marwod, Hayes for Marwood

26 Nov   Derby Co   A   L   1-2
Lukic, Dixon, Winterburn, Thomas 1, Bould, Adams, Rocastle, Richardson, Smith, Merson, Hayes,
Groves for Richardson

4 Dec   Liverpool   H   D   1-1
Lukic, Dixon, Winterburn, Thomas, Bould, Adams, Rocastle, Richardson, Smith 1, Merson,
Marwood, Hayes for Marwood

10 Dec   Norwich C   A   D   0-0
Lukic, Dixon, Winterburn, Thomas, Bould, Adams, Rocastle, Richardson, Smith, Merson, Marwood,
Hayes for Marwood

17 Dec   Manchester U   H   W   2-1
Lukic, Dixon, Winterburn, Thomas 1, Bould, Adams, Rocastle, Richardson, Smith, Merson 1, Marwood

26 Dec   Charlton Ath   A   W   3-2
Lukic, O'Leary, Winterburn, Thomas, Bould, Adams, Rocastle, Richardson, Smith, Merson 1,
Marwood 2

31 Dec   Aston Villa   A   W   3-0
Lukic, O'Leary, Winterburn, Thomas, Bould, Adams, Rocastle 1, Richardson, Smith 1, Merson,
Marwood, Groves 1 for Merson

2 Jan   Tottenham H   H   W   2-0
Lukic, O'Leary, Winterburn, Thomas 1, Bould, Adams, Rocastle, Richardson, Smith, Merson 1,
Marwood, Davis/Groves for Richardson/Marwood

14 Jan   Everton   A   W   3-1
Lukic, Dixon, Winterburn, Davis, O'Leary, Caesar, Rocastle, Richardson 1, Smith 1, Merson 1,
Marwood, Groves/Thomas for Merson/Marwood

21 Jan   Sheffield Wed   H   D   1-1
Lukic, Dixon, Winterburn, Davis, O'Leary, Caesar, Rocastle, Richardson, Smith, Merson 1,
Marwood, Groves/Thomas for Caesar/Rocastle

4 Feb   West Ham U   H   W   2-1
Lukic, Dixon, Winterburn, Thomas, O'Leary, Adams, Rocastle, Richardson, Smith 1, Merson, Groves
1, Bould/Hayes for O'Leary/Merson

11 Feb   Millwall   A   W   2-1
Lukic, Dixon, Winterburn, Thomas, O'Leary, Adams, Rocastle, Richardson, Smith 1, Merson,
Marwood 1, Bould for O'Leary

18 Feb   WBA   A   D   0-0
Lukic, Dixon, Winterburn, Thomas, O'Leary, Adams, Rocastle, Richardson, Smith, Merson,
Marwood, Bould/Hayes for Dixon/Merson

21 Feb   Coventry C   A   L   0-1
Lukic, Bould, Winterburn, Thomas, O'Leary, Adams, Rocastle, Richardson, Smith, Merson,
Marwood, Hayes for Marwood

25 Feb   Luton T   H   W   2-0
Lukic, Bould, Winterburn, Thomas, O'Leary, Adams, Rocastle, Richardson, Smith 1, Groves 1,
Marwood, Merson for Rocastle

28 Feb   Millwall   H   D   0-0
Lukic, Bould, Winterburn, Thomas, O'Leary, Adams, Rocastle, Richardson, Smith, Groves,
Marwood, Merson/Dixon for Rocastle/Richardson

11 Mar   Nottingham F   H   L   1-3
Lukic, Bould, Winterburn, Thomas, O'Leary, Adams, Rocastle, Richardson, Smith 1, Groves,
Marwood, Merson/Dixon for Bould/Groves

21 Mar   Charlton Ath   H   D   2-2
Lukic, Dixon, Winterburn, Davis 1, O'Leary, Adams, Rocastle 1, Richardson, Smith, Merson,
Marwood, Groves/Thomas for Richardson/Merson

25 Mar   Southampton   A   W   3-1
Lukic, Dixon, Winterburn, Davis, O'Leary, Adams, Rocastle 1, Richardson, Smith, Groves 1,
Marwood, Merson 1 for Groves

2 Apr   Manchester U   A   D   1-1
Lukic, Dixon, Winterburn, Davis, O'Leary, Adams, Rocastle, Richardson, Smith, Bould, Marwood,
Thomas/Merson for Davis/Marwood

8 Apr   Everton   H   W   2-0
Lukic, Dixon 1, Winterburn, Thomas, O'Leary, Adams, Rocastle, Richardson, Quinn 1, Bould,
Marwood, Merson for Marwood

15 Apr   Newcastle U   H   W   1-0
Lukic, Dixon, Winterburn, Thomas, O'Leary, Adams, Rocastle, Richardson, Quinn, Bould, Marwood
1, Merson/Groves for O'Leary/Rocastle

1 May   Norwich C   H   W   5-0
Lukic, Dixon, Winterburn 1, Thomas 1, O'Leary, Adams, Rocastle 1, Richardson, Smith 2, Bould,
Merson, Quinn/Hayes for Bould/Merson

6 May   Middlesbrough   A   W   1-0
Lukic, Dixon, Winterburn, Thomas, O'Leary, Adams, Rocastle, Richardson, Smith, Bould, Merson,
Hayes 1 for Merson

13 May   Derby Co   A   L   1-2
Lukic, Dixon, Winterburn, Thomas, O'Leary, Adams, Rocastle, Richardson, Smith 1, Bould, Merson,
Hayes/Groves for Bould/Merson

17 May   Wimbledon   H   D   2-2
Lukic, Dixon, Winterburn 1, Thomas, O'Leary, Adams, Rocastle, Richardson, Smith, Bould, Merson
1, Groves/Hayes for Bould/Merson

26 May   Liverpool   A   W   2-0
Lukic, Dixon, Winterburn, Thomas 1, O'Leary, Adams, Rocastle, Richardson, Smith 1, Bould,
Merson, Groves/Hayes for Bould/Merson

FA CUP
8 Jan   West Ham U (3)   A   D   2-2
Lukic, O'Leary, Winterburn, Thomas, Bould, Adams, Rocastle, Richardson, Smith, Merson 2,
Marwood, Davis/Groves for Bould/Marwood

11 Jan   West Ham U (3R)   H   L   0-1
Lukic, Dixon, Winterburn, Thomas, O'Leary, Adams, Rocastle, Richardson, Smith, Merson,
Marwood, Davis/Groves for Rocastle/Marwood

FOOTBALL LEAGUE (LITTLEWOODS) CUP
28 Sep   Hull C (2/1)   A   W   2-1
Lukic, Dixon, Marwood 1, Thomas, Bould, Adams, Rocastle, Davis, Smith, Groves, Marwood 1,
Hayes and Richardson for Groves and Rocastle

12 Oct   Hull C (2/2)   H   W   3-0
Lukic, Dixon, Winterburn, Thomas, Bould, Adams, Rocastle, Davis, Smith 2, Merson 1, Marwood,
Hayes and Richardson for Davis and Marwood

2 Nov   Liverpool (3)   A   D   1-1
Lukic, Dixon, Winterburn, Thomas, Bould, Adams, Rocastle 1, Richardson, Smith, Merson,
Marwood, Groves for Merson

9 Nov   Liverpool (3R)   H   D   0-0
Lukic, Dixon, Winterburn, Thomas, Bould, Adams, Rocastle, Richardson, Smith, Merson, Marwood,
Hayes for Merson

23 Nov   Liverpool (3R)   A   L   1-2
Lukic, Dixon, Winterburn, Thomas, Bould, Adams, Rocastle, Richardson, Smith, Merson 1, Marwood

APPEARANCES, LEAGUE ONLY (Goals) Adams 36(4); Bould 30(2); Caesar 2; Davis 12(1); Dixon 33(1); Groves 21(4); Hayes 17(1); Lukic 38; Marwood 31(9); Merson 37(10); O'Leary 26; Quinn 3(1); Richardson 34(1); Rocastle 38(6); Smith 36(23); Thomas 37(7); Winterburn 38(3); Total 17 players (73)

POSITION IN LEAGUE TABLE

	Pld	W	D	L	F	A	Pts
1st Arsenal	38	22	10	6	73	36	76

SEASON 1989-1990

FOOTBALL LEAGUE (DIVISION 1)

19 Aug   Manchester U   A   L   1-4
Lukic, Dixon, Winterburn, Thomas, O'Leary, Adams, Rocastle 1, Richardson, Smith, Merson, Marwood, Caesar/Groves for Adams/Merson

22 Aug   Coventry C   H   W   2-0
Lukic, Dixon, Winterburn, Thomas 1, O'Leary, Adams, Rocastle, Richardson, Smith, Merson, Marwood 1, Groves for Rocastle

26 Aug   Wimbledon   H   D   0-0
Lukic, Dixon, Winterburn, Thomas, O'Leary, Adams, Rocastle, Richardson, Smith, Merson, Marwood, Groves for Merson

9 Sep   Sheffield Wed   H   W   5-0
Lukic, Dixon, Winterburn, Thomas 1, O'Leary, Adams 1, Rocastle, Richardson, Smith 1, Merson 1, Marwood 1

16 Sep   Nottingham F   A   W   2-1
Lukic, Dixon, Winterburn, Thomas, O'Leary, Adams, Rocastle, Richardson, Smith, Merson 1, Marwood 1, Groves for Merson

23 Sep   Charlton Ath   H   W   1-0
Lukic, Dixon, Winterburn, Thomas, O'Leary, Adams, Rocastle, Richardson, Smith, Merson, Marwood 1p, Groves for Rocastle

30 Sep   Chelsea   A   D   0-0
Lukic, Dixon, Winterburn, Thomas, O'Leary, Adams, Rocastle, Richardson, Smith, Groves, Hayes, Merson for Rocastle

14 Oct   Manchester C   H   W   4-0
Lukic, Dixon, Winterburn, Thomas, O'Leary, Adams, Rocastle 1, Richardson, Smith, Groves 2, Marwood, Jonsson/Merson 1 for Richardson/Marwood

18 Oct   Tottenham H   A   L   1-2
Lukic, Dixon, Winterburn, Thomas 1, O'Leary, Adams, Rocastle, Richardson, Smith, Groves, Hayes, Jonsson/Merson for Richardson/Smith

21 Oct   Everton   A   L   0-3
Lukic, Dixon, Winterburn, Thomas, O'Leary, Adams, Rocastle, Richardson, Quinn, Merson, Hayes, Smith for Hayes

28 Oct   Derby Co   H   D   1-1
Lukic, Dixon, Winterburn, Thomas, O'Leary, Adams, Rocastle, Richardson, Smith 1, Quinn, Merson, Jonsson/Campbell for Winterburn/Quinn

4 Nov   Norwich C   H   W   4-3
Lukic, Dixon 2(1p), Winterburn, Thomas, O'Leary 1, Adams, Rocastle, Richardson, Smith, Quinn 1, Merson, Groves for Merson

11 Nov   Millwall   A   W   2-1
Lukic, Dixon, Winterburn, Thomas 1, O'Leary, Adams, Rocastle, Richardson, Smith, Quinn 1, Marwood, Groves for Quinn

18 Nov   WBA   H   W   3-0
Lukic, Dixon 1, Winterburn, Thomas, O'Leary, Adams, Rocastle, Richardson, Smith 1, Quinn, Marwood, Groves/Jonsson 1 for Rocastle/Marwood

26 Nov   Liverpool   A   L   1-2
Lukic, Dixon, Winterburn, Thomas, O'Leary, Adams, Rocastle, Richardson, Smith 1, Quinn, Groves, Hayes/Jonsson for Quinn/O'Leary

3 Dec   Manchester U   H   W   1-0
Lukic, Dixon, Winterburn, Thomas, O'Leary, Adams, Rocastle, Richardson, Smith, Groves 1, Marwood, Merson for Marwood

9 Dec   Coventry C   A   W   1-0
Lukic, Dixon, Winterburn, Thomas, O'Leary, Adams, Rocastle, Richardson, Smith, Groves, Marwood, Merson 1 for Marwood

16 Dec   Luton T   H   W   3-2
Lukic, Dixon, Winterburn, Thomas, O'Leary, Adams, Rocastle, Richardson, Smith 1, Groves, Marwood 1, Merson 1/Jonsson for Smith/Groves

26 Dec   Southampton   A   L   0-1
Lukic, Dixon, Winterburn, Thomas, O'Leary, Adams, Rocastle, Richardson, Smith, Merson, Marwood, Davis/Groves for Marwood/Merson

30 Dec   Aston Villa   A   L   1-2
Lukic, Dixon, Winterburn, Thomas, O'Leary, Adams 1, Groves, Richardson, Smith, Bould, Merson, Rocastle for Bould

1 Jan   Crystal Pal   H   W   4-1
Lukic, Dixon 1, Winterburn, Thomas, O'Leary, Adams 1, Groves, Richardson, Smith 2, Bould, Merson, Rocastle/Davis for Smith/Winterburn

13 Jan   Wimbledon   A   L   0-1
Lukic, Dixon, Winterburn, Davis, O'Leary, Adams, Groves, Richardson, Smith 2, Bould, Merson, Caesar/Rocastle for O'Leary/Smith

20 Jan   Tottenham H   H   W   1-0
Lukic, Dixon, Davis, Thomas, O'Leary, Adams 1, Rocastle, Richardson, Smith, Bould Groves

17 Feb   Sheffield Wed   A   L   0-1
Lukic, Dixon, Pates, Davis, O'Leary, Adams, Rocastle, Richardson, Smith, Bould, Merson, Caesar/Campbell for Pates/Richardson

27 Feb   Charlton Ath   A   D   0-0
Lukic, Dixon, Winterburn, Thomas, Bould, Adams, Rocastle, Richardson, Smith, Merson, Marwood, Campbell for Marwood

3 Mar   WBA   A   L   0-2
Lukic, Dixon, Winterburn, Thomas, Bould, Adams, Rocastle, Richardson, Smith, Merson, Groves, O'Leary/Campbell for Thomas/Smith

7 Mar   Nottingham F   H   W   3-0
Lukic, Dixon, Winterburn, Thomas, Bould, Adams 1, Rocastle, Richardson, Smith, Merson, Groves 1, Campbell 1/O'Leary for Merson/Groves

10 Mar   Manchester C   A   D   1-1
Lukic, Dixon, Winterburn, Thomas, Bould, Adams, Rocastle, Richardson, Smith, Campbell, Marwood 1, Hayes for Rocastle

17 Mar   Chelsea   H   L   0-1
Lukic, Dixon, Winterburn, Thomas, Bould, Adams, Rocastle, Richardson, Smith, Campbell, Groves, Hayes/O'Leary for Rocastle/Campbell

24 Mar   Derby Co   A   W   3-1
Lukic, Dixon, Winterburn, Thomas, Bould, Adams, Hayes 2, Richardson, Smith, Campbell 1, Groves, O'Leary/Ampadu for Bould/Campbell

31 Mar   Everton   H   W   1-0
Lukic, Dixon, Winterburn, Thomas, Bould, Adams, Hayes, Richardson, Smith 1, Campbell, Groves, O'Leary/Ampadu for Richardson/Campbell

11 Apr   Aston Villa   H   L   0-1
Lukic, Dixon, Winterburn, Thomas, Bould, Adams, Hayes, O'Leary, Smith, Campbell, Groves, Merson for Hayes

14 Apr   Crystal Pal   A   D   1-1
Lukic, Dixon, Winterburn, Thomas, Bould, Adams, Hayes 1, O'Leary, Smith, Campbell, Groves, Davis/Merson for Bould/Campbell

18 Apr   Liverpool   H   D   1-1
Lukic, Dixon, Winterburn, Thomas, Bould, Adams, Davis, O'Leary, Smith, Merson 1, Groves, Campbell/Pates for Groves/Bould

21 Apr   Luton T   A   L   0-2
Lukic, Dixon, Winterburn, Thomas, Bould, Adams, Davis, O'Leary, Smith, Merson, Campbell,

Figures shown as 2 etc. refer to goals scored by individual players

Hayes/Rocastle for O'Leary/Merson
28 Apr   Millwall   H   W   2-0
Lukic, Dixon, Winterburn, Thomas, Bould, Adams, Rocastle, Davis 1, Smith, Merson 1, Marwood, Campbell/Richardson for Marwood/Thomas
2 May   Southampton   H   W   2-1
Lukic, Dixon 1p, Thomas, Bould, Adams, Richardson, Davis, Smith, Merson, Marwood, Rocastle 1/Groves for Richardson/Marwood
5 May   Norwich C   A   D   2-2
Lukic, Dixon, Thomas, Hayes, Bould, Adams, Rocastle, Davis, Smith 2, Campbell, Groves, O'Leary/Thomas for Bould/Davis

FA CUP
6 Jan   Stoke C (3)   A   W   1-0
Lukic, Dixon, Davis, Thomas, O'Leary, Adams, Quinn 1, Richardson, Groves, Bould, Merson, Jonsson/Rocastle for Thomas/Merson
27 Jan   WBA (4)   H   D   0-0
Lukic, Dixon, Winterburn, Davis, O'Leary, Adams, Rocastle, O'Leary, Adams, Smith, Bould, Groves, Thomas/Merson for Davis/Bould
31 Jan   WBA (4R)   A   L   0-2
Lukic, Dixon, Winterburn, Thomas, O'Leary, Adams, Rocastle, O'Leary, Adams, Smith, Bould, Groves, Merson for Groves

FOOTBALL LEAGUE (LITTLEWOODS) CUP
19 Sep   Plymouth Arg (2/1)   H   W   2-0
Lukic, Dixon, Winterburn, Thomas, O'Leary, Adams, Rocastle, Richardson, Smith 1, Bould, Groves, Merson for Groves (o/g Brimacombe)
3 Oct   Plymouth Arg (2/2)   A   W   6-1
Lukic, Dixon, Winterburn, Thomas 3, O'Leary, Adams, Rocastle, Richardson, Smith 1, Groves 1, Hayes, Caesar/Merson for Dixon/Groves (o/g Byrne)
25 Oct   Liverpool (3)   H   W   1-0
Lukic, Dixon, Winterburn, Thomas, O'Leary, Adams, Rocastle, Richardson, Quinn, Merson, Hayes, Smith 1 for Hayes
22 Nov   Oldham Ath (4)   A   L   1-3
Lukic, Dixon, Winterburn, Thomas, O'Leary, Adams, Rocastle, Richardson, Smith, Quinn 1, Jonsson, Groves for Jonsson

FA CHARITY SHIELD
12 Aug   Liverpool   L   0-1
Lukic, Dixon, Winterburn, Thomas, O'Leary, Adams, Rocastle, Richardson, Smith, Caesar, Merson, Marwood/Quinn for Caesar/Smith (at Wembley)

APPEARANCES (Goals) Lukic 38; Adams 38(5); Ampadu 2; Bould 19; Caesar 3; Campbell 15(2); Davis 11(1); Dixon 38(5); Groves 30(4); Hayes 12(3); Jonsson 6(1); Merson 29(7); Marwood 17(6); O'Leary 34(1); Pates 2; Quinn 6(2); Richardson 33; Rocastle 33(2); Smith 38(10); Thomas 36(5); Winterburn 36; Total 19 players (54)

POSITION IN LEAGUE TABLE

	Pld	W	D	L	F	A	Pts
1st Liverpool	38	23	10	5	78	37	79
4th Arsenal	38	18	8	12	54	38	62

SEASON 1990-1991

FOOTBALL LEAGUE (DIVISION 1)
25 Aug   Wimbledon   A   W   3-0
Seaman, Dixon, Winterburn, Thomas, Bould, Adams, Rocastle, Davis, Smith 1, Merson 1, Limpar, Groves 1 for Limpar

29 Aug   Luton T   H   W   2-1
Seaman, Dixon, Winterburn, Thomas 1, Bould, Adams, Rocastle, Davis, Smith, Merson 1, Limpar,
Groves for Limpar

1 Sep   Tottenham H   H   D   0-0
Seaman, Dixon, Winterburn, Thomas, Bould, Adams, Rocastle, Davis, Smith, Merson, Limpar,
Groves for Merson

8 Sep   Everton   A   D   1-1
Seaman, Dixon, Winterburn, Thomas, Bould, Adams, Rocastle, Davis, Smith, Merson, Limpar,
Groves 1 for Smith

15 Sep   Chelsea   H   W   4-1
Seaman, Dixon 1p, Winterburn, Thomas, Bould, Adams, Rocastle 1, Davis, Groves, Merson 1,
Limpar 1, Campbell/Linighan for Groves/Bould

22 Sep   Nottingham F   A   W   2-0
Seaman, Dixon, Winterburn, Thomas, Bould, Adams, Rocastle 1, Davis, Groves, Merson, Limpar 1,
Smith for Rocastle

29 Sep   Leeds U   A   D   2-2
Seaman, Dixon, Winterburn, Jonsson, Bould, Adams, Rocastle, Davis, Smith, Merson, Limpar 2,
Hillier/Groves for Winterburn/Merson

6 Oct   Norwich C   H   W   2-0
Seaman, Dixon, Winterburn, Jonsson, Bould, Adams, Rocastle, Davis 2, Smith, Merson, Limpar,
Hillier/Groves for Limpar/Merson

20 Oct   Manchester U   A   W   1-0
Seaman, Dixon, Winterburn, Thomas, Bould, Adams, Rocastle, Davis, Smith, Merson, Limpar 1,
Groves for Rocastle

27 Oct   Sunderland   H   W   1-0
Seaman, Dixon 1p, Winterburn, Thomas, Bould, Adams, Rocastle, Davis, Smith, Merson, Limpar,
Groves for Rocastle

3 Nov   Coventry C   A   W   2-0
Seaman, Dixon, Winterburn, Thomas, Bould, Adams, Groves, Davis, Smith, Merson, Limpar 2,
Campbell/O'Leary for Smith/Groves

10 Nov   Crystal Pal   A   D   0-0
Seaman, Dixon, Winterburn, Thomas, Bould, Adams, O'Leary, Davis, Campbell, Merson, Limpar,
Groves/Smith for Merson/Limpar

17 Nov   Southampton   H   W   4-0
Seaman, Dixon, Winterburn, Thomas, Bould, Adams, Groves, Davis, Smith 2, Mersonl 1, Limpar 1,
O'Leary/Campbell for Dixon/Groves

24 Nov   WBA   A   W   3-1
Seaman, Dixon, Winterburn, Thomas, Bould, Adams, Groves, Davis, Smith 1, Merson 1, Limpar,
Campbell 1/O'Leary for Groves/Adams

2 Dec   Liverpool   H   W   3-0
Seaman, Dixon 1p, Winterburn, Thomas, Bould, Adams, O'Leary, Davis, Smith 1, Merson 1,
Limpar

8 Dec   Luton T   A   D   1-1
Seaman, Dixon, Winterburn, Thomas, Bould, Adams, O'Leary, Davis, Smith 1, Merson, Limpar,
Groves for Limpar

15 Dec   Wimbledon   H   D   2-2
Seaman, Dixon, Winterburn, Thomas, Bould, Adams 1, Groves, Davis, Smith, Merson 1, Limpar,
O'Leary for Winterburn

23 Dec   Aston Villa   A   D   0-0
Seaman, Dixon, Winterburn, Thomas, Bould, Linighan, Groves, Davis, Smith, Merson, Limpar,
Rocastle for Limpar

26 Dec   Derby Co   H   W   3-0
Seaman, Dixon, Winterburn, Thomas, Bould, Linighan, Rocastle, Davis, Smith 2, Merson 1, Limpar,
Campbell/O'Leary for Rocastle/Limpar

29 Dec   Sheffield U   H   W   4-1
Seaman, Dixon 1p, Winterburn, Thomas 1, Bould, Linighan, Groves, Davis, Smith 2, Merson, Limpar,
Cole/O'Leary for Groves/Winterburn

1 Jan   Manchester C   A   W   1-0
Seaman, Dixon, Winterburn, Thomas, Bould, Linighan, O'Leary, Davis, Smith 1, Merson, Limpar,
Hillier/Groves for O'Leary/Limpar
12 Jan   Tottenham H   A   D   0-0
Seaman, Dixon, Winterburn, Thomas, Bould, Linighan, O'Leary, Davis, Smith, Merson, Limpar,
Hillier/Groves for Davis/Merson
19 Jan   Everton   H   W   1-0
Seaman, Dixon, Winterburn, Thomas, Bould, Groves, O'Leary, Davis, Smith, Merson 1, Limpar,
Campbell/Hillier for Limpar/Bould
2 Feb   Chelsea   A   L   1-2
Seaman, Dixon, Winterburn, Thomas, Bould, Linighan, Groves, Davis, Smith 1, Merson, Limpar,
Hillier/Campbell for Bould/Limpar
23 Feb   Crystal Pal   H   W   4-0
Seaman, Dixon, Winterburn, Thomas, Bould, Linighan, O'Leary 1, Davis, Smith 1, Merson 1,
Campbell 1, Pates/Rocastle for Linighan/Merson
3 Mar   Liverpool   A   W   1-0
Seaman, Dixon, Winterburn, Thomas, Bould, Adams, O'Leary, Hillier, Smith, Merson 1, Campbell,
Rocastle/Davis for Campbell/Adams
17 Mar   Leeds U   H   W   2-0
Seaman, Dixon, Winterburn, Thomas, Bould, Adams, O'Leary, Hillier, Smith, Merson, Campbell 2
20 Mar   Nottingham F   H   D   1-1
Seaman, Dixon, Winterburn, Thomas, Bould, Adams, O'Leary, Davis, Smith, Merson, Campbell 1,
Groves/Limpar for Davis/Merson
23 Mar   Norwich C   A   D   0-0
Seaman, Dixon, Winterburn, Rocastle, Bould, Adams, O'Leary, Davis, Smith, Campbell, Limpar,
Groves/Linighan for Limpar/Rocastle
30 Mar   Derby Co   A   W   2-0
Seaman, Dixon, Winterburn, Campbell, Bould, Adams, Rocastle, Davis, Smith 2, Merson, Limpar,
Groves/Hillier for Limpar/Rocastle
3 Apr   Aston Villa   H   W   5-0
Seaman, Dixon, Winterburn, Hillier, Bould, Adams, Campbell 2, Davis 1, Smith 2, Merson, Limpar,
Thomas/Groves for Hillier/Merson
6 Apr   Sheffield U   A   W   2-0
Seaman, Dixon, Winterburn, Hillier, Bould, Adams, Campbell 1, Davis, Smith 1, Merson, Limpar,
Groves/Thomas for Merson/Limpar
9 Apr   Southampton   A   D   1-1
Seaman, Dixon, Winterburn, Hillier, Bould, Adams, Campbell, Davis, Smith, Groves, Limpar,
Thomas/Merson for Hillier/Limpar (o/g M. Adams)
17 Apr   Manchester C   H   D   2-2
Seaman, Dixon, Winterburn, Thomas, Bould, Adams, Campbell 1, Davis, Smith, Merson 1, Groves,
Limpar/O'Leary for Merson/Dixon
23 Apr   WBA   H   W   2-0
Seaman, Dixon 1p, Winterburn, Hillier, Bould, Adams, Campbell, Davis, Smith, Merson 1, Limpar,
O'Leary/Groves for Merson/Limpar
4 May   Sunderland   A   D   0-0
Seaman, Dixon, Winterburn, Hillier, Bould, Adams, Campbell, Davis, Smith, Merson, Groves,
O'Leary for Groves
6 May   Manchester U   H   W   3-1
Seaman, Dixon, Winterburn, Hillier, Bould, Adams, Campbell, Davis, Smith 3(1p), Merson, Limpar,
Thomas/O'Leary for Hillier/Limpar
11 May   Coventry C   H   W   6-1
Seaman, Dixon, Winterburn, Hillier, Bould, Adams, Campbell, Davis, Smith 1, Merson, Limpar 3,
Linighan/Groves 1 for Merson/Campbell (o/g Peake)

FA CUP
5 Jan   Sunderland (3)   H   W   2-1
Seaman, Dixon, Winterburn, Thomas, Bould, Linighan, Groves, Davis, Smith 1, Merson, Limpar 1,
O'Leary for Limpar

27 Jan   Leeds U (4)   H   D   0-0
Seaman, Dixon, Winterburn, Thomas, Bould, Groves, O'Leary, Davis, Smith, Merson, Limpar,
Hillier/Campbell for O'Leary/Limpar
30 Jan   Leeds U (4R)   A   D   1-1
Seaman, Dixon, Winterburn, Thomas, Bould, Linighan, Hillier, Davis, Smith, Merson, Limpar 1 (aet)
13 Feb   Leeds U (4R)   H   D   0-0
Seaman, Dixon, Winterburn, Thomas, Bould, Groves, O'Leary, Davis, Smith, Merson, Limpar,
Campbell/Linighan for Groves/Limpar (aet)
16 Feb   Leeds U (4R)   A   W   2-1
Seaman, Dixon 1, Winterburn, Thomas, Bould, Linighan, O'Leary, Davis, Smith, Merson 1, Campbell
27 Feb   Shrewsbury T (5)   A   W   1-0
Seaman, Dixon, Winterburn, Thomas 1, Bould, Adams, O'Leary, Hillier, Smith, Merson, Campbell,
Rocastle for Merson
9 Mar   Cambridge U (6)   H   W   2-1
Seaman, Dixon, Winterburn, Thomas, Bould, Adams 1, O'Leary, Hillier, Smith, Merson, Campbell 1,
Davis for Hillier
14 Apr   Tottenham H (SF)   L   1-3
Seaman, Dixon, Winterburn, Thomas, Bould, Adams, Campbell, Davis, Smith 1, Merson, Limpar,
Groves for Limpar (at Wembley)

FOOTBALL LEAGUE (RUMBLELOWS) CUP
25 Sep   Chester C (2/1)   A   W   1-0
Seaman, Dixon, Winterburn, Hillier, Bould, Adams, Rocastle, Davis, Smith, Merson 1, Groves,
Cambell for Rocastle
9 Oct   Chester C (2/2)   H   W   5-0
Seaman, Dixon, Winterburn, Hillier, Bould, Adams 1, Rocastle, Davis, Smith 1, Merson 1, Groves 2,
Campbell/O'Leary for Rocastle/Bould
30 Oct   Manchester C (3)   A   W   2-1
Seaman, Dixon, Winterburn, Thomas, Bould, Adams 1, Groves 1, Davis, Smith, Merson, Limpar,
Campbell for Limpar
28 Nov   Manchester U (4)   H   L   2-6
Seaman, Dixon, Winterburn, Thomas, Bould, Adams, Groves, Davis, Smith 2 Merson, Limpar,
Campbell for Limpar

APPEARANCES (Goals) Adams 30(1); Bould 38; Campbell 22(9); Cole 1; Davis 37(3); Dixon 38(5);
Groves 22(3); Hillier 16; Jonsson 2; Limpar 34(11); Linighan 10; Merson 37(13); O'Leary 21(1); Pates 1;
Rocastle 16(2); Seaman 38; Smith 37(22); Thomas 31(2); Winterburn 38; o/g 2; Total 19 players (72)

POSITION IN LEAGUE TABLE

	Pld	W	D	L	F	A	Pts
1st Arsenal	38	24	13	1	74	18	83*

*2 points deducted

SEASON 1991-1992

FOOTBALL LEAGUE (DIVISION 1)
17 Aug   WBA   H   D   1-1
Seaman, Dixon, Winterburn, Hillier, O'Leary, Adams, Campbell, Davis, Smith, Merson 1, Limpar,
Rocastle/Groves for O'Leary/Campbell
20 Aug   Everton   A   L   1-3
Seaman, Dixon, Winterburn 1,Hillier, O'Leary, Adams, Rocastle, Davis, Smith, Merson, Limpar,
Groves/Linighan for Limpar/Hillier
24 Aug   Aston Villa   A   L   1-3
Seaman, Dixon, Winterburn, Linighan, O'Leary, Adams, Rocastle, Davis, Smith 1, Merson, Limpar,
Groves/Thomas for O'Leary/Rocastle
27 Aug   Luton T   H   W   2-0
Seaman, Dixon, Winterburn, Thomas, Linighan, Adams, Rocastle, Davis, Smith 1, Merson 1, Limpar

31 Aug   Manchester C   H   W   2-1
Seaman, Dixon, Winterburn, Thomas, Linighan, Adams, Rocastle, Davis, Smith 1, Merson, Limpar 1,
Campbell/Pates for Rocastle/Limpar

3 Sep   Leeds U   A   D   2-2
Seaman, Dixon, Winterburn, Thomas, Linighan, Adams, O'Leary, Davis, Smith 2, Merson, Campbell,
Rocastle for Thomas

7 Sep   Coventry C   H   L   1-2
Seaman, Dixon, Winterburn, Campbell, Linighan, Adams 1, Rocastle, Davis, Smith, Merson, Limpar,
O'Leary/Thomas for Limpar/Davis

14 Sep   Crystal Pal   A   W   4-1
Seaman, Dixon, Winterburn, Hillier, Linighan, Adams, Rocastle, Groves, Smith 1, Merson, Campbell
2, Thomas 1/O'Leary for Groves/Hillier

21 Sep   Sheffield U   H   W   5-2
Seaman, Dixon 1p, Winterburn, Campbell 1, Linighan, Adams, Rocastle 1, Davis, Smith 1, Merson,
Groves 1, O'Leary/Thomas for Winterburn/Groves

28 Sep   Southampton   A   W   4-0
Seaman, Dixon, Winterburn, Thomas, Linighan, Adams, Rocastle 1, Wright 3, Smith, Merson,
Limpar, Campbell for Merson

5 Oct   Chelsea   H   W   3-2
Seaman, Dixon 1p, Winterburn, Thomas, Linighan, Pates, Rocastle, Wright 1, Smith, Campbell 1,
Limpar, Merson/O'Leary for Limpar/Wright

19 Oct   Manchester U   A   D   1-1
Seaman, Dixon, Winterburn, Davis, Pates, Adams, Rocastle, Wright, Smith 1, Merson, Campbell

26 Oct   Notts Co   H   W   2-0
Seaman, Dixon, Winterburn, Davis, Pates, Adams, Rocastle, Wright 1, Smith 1, Merson, Campbell,
Limpar for Campbell

2 Nov   West Ham U   H   L   0-1
Seaman, Dixon, Winterburn, Thomas, Pates, Linighan, Rocastle, Wright, Smith, Merson, Limpar,
Groves for Thomas

16 Nov   Oldham Ath   A   D   1-1
Seaman, Dixon, Winterburn, Hillier, Bould, Linighan, Rocastle, Wright 1, Smith, Merson, Pates,
O'Leary/Groves for Bould/Pates

23 Nov   Sheffield Wed   A   D   1-1
Seaman, Dixon, Winterburn, Hillier, Bould1, Linighan, Rocastle, Wright 1, Smith, Merson, Pates,
O'Leary for Hillier

1 Dec   Tottenham H   H   W   2-0
Seaman, Dixon, Winterburn, Hillier, Bould, Linighan, Rocastle, Wright 1, Smith, Merson, Campbell 1,
Limpar/O'Leary for Wright/Rocastle

8 Dec   Nottingham F   A   L   2-3
Seaman, Dixon, Winterburn, Hillier, Bould, Linighan, Rocastle, Campbell, Smith 1, Merson 1, Limpar,
Carter/O'Leary for Limpar/Bould

21 Dec   Everton   H   W   4-2
Seaman, Dixon, Winterburn, Hillier, Bould, Adams, Rocastle, Wright 4, Smith, Merson, Limpar,
O'Leary/Campbell for Rocastle/Merson

26 Dec   Luton T   A   L   0-1
Seaman, Dixon, Winterburn, O'Leary, Bould, Adams, Rocastle, Wright, Smith, Merson, Limpar,
Campbell for Limpar

28 Dec   Manchester C   A   L   0-1
Seaman, Dixon, Winterburn, O'Leary, Bould, Adams, Rocastle, Wright, Smith, Merson, Davis,
Linighan/Groves for Bould/O'Leary

1 Jan   Wimbledon   H   D   1-1
Seaman, Dixon, Winterburn, Hillier, Linighan, O'Leary, Adams, Rocastle, Wright, Smith, Merson 1,
Carter, Campbell for Wright

11 Jan   Aston Villa   H   D   0-0
Seaman, Dixon, Winterburn, Hillier, O'Leary, Adams, Rocastle, Campbell, Smith, Merson, Carter,
Groves for Merson

18 Jan   WBA   A   D   0-0
Seaman, Dixon, Winterburn, Davis, O'Leary, Adams, Rocastle, Wright, Smith, Merson, Carter

29 Jan Liverpool   A   L   0-2
Seaman, Dixon, Winterburn, Parlour, O'Leary, Adams, Rocastle, Wright, Smith, Merson, Carter, Bould/Groves for O'Leary/Parlour

1 Feb   Manchester U   H   D   1-1
Seaman, Dixon, Winterburn, Hillier, Bould, Adams, Rocastle 1, Wright, Smith, Merson, Carter, Pates/Limpar for Rocastle/Carter

8 Feb   Notts Co   A   W   1-0
Seaman, Dixon, Winterburn, Hillier, Bould, Adams, Pates, Wright, Smith 1, Merson, Groves, Parlour/Campbell for Winterburn/Groves

11 Feb Norwich C   H   D   1-1
Seaman, Dixon, Winterburn, Hillier, Bould, Adams, Pates, Wright, Smith, Merson 1, Limpar, Campbell/Parlour for Limpar/Winterburn

15 Feb Sheffield Wed   H   W   7-1
Seaman, Dixon, Winterburn, Hillier, Bould, Adams, Rocastle, Wright 1, Smith 1, Merson 1, Limpar 2, Campbell 2 for Smith

22 Feb Tottenham H   A   D   1-1
Seaman, Dixon, Winterburn, Hillier, Bould, Pates, Rocastle, Wright 1, Smith, Merson, Campbell, O'Leary/Limpar for Hillier/Rocastle

10 Mar Oldham Ath   H   W   2-1
Seaman, Dixon, Winterburn, Hillier, Bould, Adams, Rocastle, Wright 1, Smith, Merson 1, Limpar, O'Leary for Limpar

14 Mar West Ham U   A   W   2-0
Seaman, Dixon, Winterburn, Hillier, Bould, Adams, Rocastle, Wright 2, Smith, Merson, Groves, Campbell/O'Leary for Smith/Groves

22 Mar Leeds U   H   D   1-1
Seaman, Dixon, Winterburn, Hillier, Bould, Adams, Rocastle, Wright, O'Leary, Merson 1, Campbell, Parlour/Limpar for Hillier/Rocastle

28 Mar Wimbledon   A   W   3-1
Seaman, Dixon, Winterburn, Hillier, Bould, Adams, Parlour 1, Wright 1, Campbell 1, Merson, Groves, Limpar/Lydersen for Groves/Merson

31 Mar Nottingham F   H   D   3-3
Seaman, Dixon 1p, Winterburn, Hillier, Bould, Adams 1, Rocastle, Wright, Campbell, Merson 1, Limpar, Lydersen/Smith for Rocastle/Wright

4 Apr   Coventry C   A   W   1-0
Seaman, Dixon, Winterburn, Hillier, Bould, Adams, Lydersen, Wright, Campbell 1, Merson, Limpar, Rocastle/Smith for Winterburn/Limpar

8 Apr   Norwich C   A   W   3-1
Seaman, O'Leary, Lydersen, Hillier, Bould, Adams, Rocastle, Wright 2(1p), Campbell 1, Merson, Limpar, Morrow/Smith for O'Leary/Limpar

11 Apr Crystal Pal   H   W   4-1
Seaman, Lydersen, Winterburn, Hillier, Bould, Adams, Rocastle, Wright, Campbell 1, Merson 3, Limpar, Smith/Morrow for Limpar/Winterburn

18 Apr Sheffield U   A   D   1-1
Seaman, Lydersen, Winterburn, Hillier, Bould, Adams, Rocastle, Campbell 1, Smith, Merson, Limpar, Heaney for Limpar

20 Apr Liverpool   H   W   4-0
Seaman, Lydersen, Winterburn, Hillier 1, Bould, Adams, Rocastle, Wright 2, Campbell, Merson, Limpar 1, O'Leary for Lydersen

25 Apr Chelsea   A   D   1-1
Seaman, Dixon 1, Winterburn, Hillier, Bould, Adams, Rocastle, Wright, Campbell, Merson, Limpar, Smith/Merson for Limpar/O'Leary

2 May   Southampton   H   W   5-1
Seaman, Dixon, Winterburn, Hillier, Bould, Adams, Rocastle, Wright 3(1p), Campbell 1, Merson, Limpar, Smith 1/Parlour for Limpar/Merson

FA CUP

4 Jan   Wrexham (3)   A   L   1-2
Seaman, Dixon, Winterburn, Hillier, O'Leary, Adams, Rocastle, Campbell, Smith 1, Merson, Carter,

Groves for Campbell

FOOTBALL LEAGUE (RUMBELOWS) CUP
25 Sep   Leicester C (2/1)   A   D   1-1
Seaman, Dixon, Thomas, Campbell, Linighan, Adams, Rocastle, Davis, Wright 1, Merson, Groves,
O'Leary for Linighan
8 Oct   Leicester C (2/2)   H   W   2-0
Seaman, Dixon, Winterburn, Thomas, Pates, Adams, Rocastle, Wright 1, Smith, Merson 1,
Campbell, Groves for Wright
30 Oct   Coventry C (3)   A   L   0-1
Seaman, Dixon, Winterburn, Davis, Pates, Adams, Rocastle, Wright, Smith, Merson, Limpar,
Groves/Linighan for Limpar/Pates

FA CHARITY SHIELD
18 Aug   Tottenham H   D   0-0
Seaman, Dixon, Winterburn, Hillier, O'Leary, Adams, Rocastle, Davis, Smith, Merson, Campbell,
Thomas/Cole for Rocastle/Campbell (at Wembley)

EUROPEAN CUP
18 Sept FK Austria (1/1)   H   W   6-1
Seaman, Dixon, Winterburn, Campbell, Linighan 1, Adams, Rocastle, Davis, Smith 4, Merson,
Limpar 1, Groves for Limpar
2 Oct   FK Austria (1/2)   A   L   0-1
Seaman, Dixon, Winterburn, Thomas, Linighan, Adams, Rocastle, Campbell, Smith, Merson,
O'Leary, Groves for Merson
23 Oct   Benfica (2/2)   A   D   1-1
Seaman, Dixon, Winterburn, Davis, Pates, Adams, Rocastle, Campbell1, Smith, Merson, Limpar,
Groves/Thomas for Campbell/Limpar
6 Nov   Benfica (2/2)   H   L   1-3
Seaman, Dixon, Winterburn, Davis, Pates, Adams, Rocastle, Campbell 1, Smith, Merson, Limpar,
Bould /Grovesfor Pates/Limpar (aet)

APPEARANCES (Goals) Adams 35(2); Bould 25(1); Campbell 31(13); Carter 6; Davis 12; Dixon 38(4);
Groves 13(1); Heaney 1; Hillier 27(1); Limpar 29(4); Linighan 17; Lydersen 7; Merson 42(12); Morrow
2; O'Leary 25;, Parlour 6(1); Pates 11; Rocastle 39(4); Seaman 42; Smith 39(12); Thomas 10(1);
Winterburn 41(1); Wright 30(24); Total 23 players (81)

POSITION IN LEAGUE TABLE
	Pld	W	D	L	F	A	Pts
1st Leeds U	42	22	16	4	74	37	82
4th Arsenal	42	19	15	8	81	46	72

SEASON 1992-1993

FOOTBALL LEAGUE (DIVISION 1)
15 Aug   Norwich C   H   L   2-4
Seaman, Dixon, Winterburn, Hillier, Bould 1, Adams, Jensen, Smith, Campbell 1, Merson, Limpar,
Wright for Merson
18 Aug   Blackburn Rov   A   L   0-1
Seaman, Dixon, Winterburn, Hillier, Bould, Adams, Jensen, Smith, Campbell, Carter, Limpar,
Pates/Groves for Jensen/Limpar
23 Aug   Liverpool   A   W   2-0
Seaman, Dixon, Winterburn, Hillier, Pates, Adams, Jensen, Wright 1, Smith, Parlour, Limpar 1,
Merson for Limpar
26 Aug   Oldham Ath   A   W   2-0
Seaman, Dixon, Winterburn 1, Hillier, Bould, Adams, Parlour, Wright 1, Smith, Merson, Morrow,
Pates/Smith for Merson/Wright

29 Aug   Sheffield Wed   H   W   2-1
Seaman, Dixon, Winterburn, Hillier, Bould, Adams, Jensen, Wright, Smith, Merson 1, Parlour 1,
Smith for Merson

2 Sep   WBA   A   D   0-0
Seaman, Dixon, Winterburn, Hillier, Bould, Adams, Jensen, Wright, Smith, Merson, Parlour,
Pates/Smith for Hillier/Merson

5 Sep   Wimbledon   A   L   2-3
Seaman, Dixon, Winterburn, Pates, Bould, Adams, Jensen, Wright 2, Smith, Merson, Parlour,
O'Leary/Smith for Jensen/Adams

12 Sep   Blackburn Rov   H   L   0-1
Seaman, Dixon, Winterburn, Selley, Bould, Adams, Jensen, Wright, Smith, Merson, Parlour,
Campbell/Morrow for Parlour/Jensen

19 Sep   Sheffield U   A   D   1-1
Seaman, Dixon, Winterburn, Parlour, Bould, Adams, Jensen, Wright 1, Smith, Merson, Limpar,
Linighan/Flatts for Merson/Limpar

28 Sep   Manchester C   H   W   1-0
Seaman, Dixon, Winterburn, Hillier, Bould, Adams, Jensen, Wright 1, Smith, Merson, Campbell,
Limpar for Smith

3 Oct   Chelsea   H   W   2-1
Seaman, Dixon, Winterburn, Hillier, Bould, Adams, Jensen, Wright 1, Smith, Merson 1, Campbell,
Limpar for Merson

17 Oct   Nottingham F   A   W   1-0
Seaman, Dixon, Winterburn, Hillier, Bould, Adams, Jensen, Wright, Smith 1, Merson, Campbell,
Limpar/Pates for Wright/Jensen

24 Oct   Everton   H   W   2-0
Seaman, Dixon, Winterburn, Hillier, Bould, Adams, Jensen, Wright 1, Smith, Merson, Campbell,
Pates/Limpar 1 for Dixon/Wright

2 Nov   Crystal P   A   W   2-1
Seaman, Dixon, Morrow, Hillier, Bould, Adams, Jensen, Wright 1, Smith, Merson 1, Campbell,
Limpar for Wright

7 Nov   Coventry C   H   W   3-0
Seaman, Dixon, Morrow, Hillier, Bould, Adams, Jensen, Wright 1, Smith 1, Merson, Campbell 1,
Limpar for Campbell

21 Nov   Leeds U   A   L   0-3
Seaman, Dixon, Morrow, Hillier, Bould, Adams, Jensen, Wright, Campbell, Merson, Limpar,
Parlour/Miller for Hillier/Seaman

28 Nov   Manchester U   H   L   0-1
Seaman, Dixon, Morrow, Hillier, Bould, Adams, Jensen, Wright, Campbell, Merson, Limpar,
Parlour/Flatts for Jensen/Limpar

5 Dec   Southampton   A   L   0-2
Seaman, Dixon, Morrow, Hillier, Bould, Adams, Parlour Wright, Campbell, Merson, Flatts,
Jensen/Limpar for Dixon/Flatts

12 Dec   Tottenham H   A   L   0-1
Seaman, Lydersen, Winterburn, Hillier, Bould, Adams, Jensen, Wright, Campbell, Merson, Parlour,
Limpar for Jensen

19 Dec   Middlesbrough   H   D   1-1
Seaman, Lydersen, Winterburn, Hillier, Linighan, Adams, Flatts, Wright 1, Smith, Merson, Parlour,
Jensen/Campbell for Merson/Parlour

26 Dec   Ipswich T   H   D   0-0
Seaman, Lydersen, Winterburn, Hillier, Bould, Linighan, Jensen, Wright, Smith, Campbell, Flatts,
O'Leary Limpar for Jensen/Campbell

28 Dec   Aston Villa   A   L   0-1
Seaman, Lydersen, Winterburn, Hillier, Bould, Linighan, O'Leary, Wright, Smith, Campbell, Parlour,
Flatts/Limpar for Parlour/Hillier

9 Jan   Sheffield U   H   D   1-1
Seaman, Dixon, Winterburn, Hillier 1, Linighan, Adams, Jensen, Wright, Smith, Merson, Limpar,
O'Leary for Merson

16 Jan Manchester C   A   W   1-0
Seaman, Dixon, Winterburn, Hillier, Bould, Adams, Jensen, Campbell, Smith, Merson 1, Flatts

31 Jan Liverpool   H   L   0-1
Seaman, Dixon, Winterburn, Hillier, Linighan, Jensen, Carter, Campbell, Smith, Merson, Parlour,
O'Leary/Heaney for Hillier/O'Leary

10 Feb Wimbledon   H   L   0-1
Seaman, Keown, Winterburn, Hillier, Linighan, Jensen, Selley, Wright, Smith, Merson, Campbell,
Carter/Morrow for Merson/Smith

20 Feb Oldham Ath   A   W   1-0
Seaman, Keown, Morrow, Hillier, Linighan 1, Jensen, Selley, Campbell, Merson, Limpar, Carter for
Limpar

24 Feb Leeds U   H   D   0-0
Seaman, Keown, Winterburn, Hillier, Linighan, Jensen, Selley, Wright, Smith, Merson, Limpar,
Campbell for Limpar

1 Mar   Chelsea   A   L   0-1
Seaman, Dixon, Morrow, Hillier, Linighan, Keown, Jensen, Campbell, Smith, Merson, Flatts,
Lydersen/Carter for Hillier/Campbell

3 Mar   Norwich C   A   D   1-1
Seaman, Dixon, Winterburn, Davis, Linighan, Keown, Jensen, Wright 1, Parlour, Carter, Limpar,
Campbell for Limpar

13 Mar Coventry C   A   W   2-0
Seaman, Dixon, Keown, Davis, Linighan, Adams, Parlour, Wright 1, Campbell 1, Merson, Morrow,
Limpar/Hillier for Wright/Merson

20 Mar Southampton   H   W   4-3
Seaman, Keown, Winterburn, Davis, Linighan 1, Adams, Carter 2, Morrow, Campbell, Merson 1,
Limpar, Hillier/Dickov for Davis/Limpar

24 Mar Manchester U   A   D   0-0
Seaman, Dixon, Keown, Morrow, Linighan, Adams, Jensen, Wright, Campbell, Merson, Carter,
Parlour/Hillier for Carter/Adams

6 Apr   Middlesbrough   A   L   0-1
Seaman, O'Leary, Winterburn, Hillier, Linighan, Adams, Jensen, Wright, Smith, Carter, Limpar,
Morrow/Keown for Hillier/O'Leary

10 Apr Ipswich T   A   W   2-1
Seaman, O'Leary, Winterburn, Morrow, Linighan, Keown, Jensen, Campbell, Smith 1, Merson 1,
Carter, Adams/Parlour for O'Leary/Jensen

12 Apr Aston Villa   H   L   0-1
Seaman, Dixon, Winterburn, Selley, Keown, Adams, Morrow, Wright, Smith, Merson, Campbell,
Parlour/Linighan for Wright/Campbell

21 Apr Nottingham F   H   D   1-1
Seaman, Dixon, Winterburn, Selley, Linighan, Keown, Jensen, Wright 1, Campbell, Parlour, Carter,
Adams/Campbell for Winterburn/Parlour

1 May   Everton   A   D   0-0
Seaman, O'Leary, Lydersen, Davis, Linighan, Bould, Keown, Selley, Smith, Campbell, Carter,
Jensen/Heaney for Lydersen/Carter

4 May   WBA   H   D   0-0
Miller, Dixon, Keown, Davis, Linighan, Adams, Jensen, Campbell, Smith, Merson, Heaney, Carter
for Merson

6 May   Sheffield Wed   A   L   0-1
Miller, Lydersen, Keown, Marshall, O'Leary, Bould, Jensen, Selley, Smith, Heaney, Carter,
McGowan/Flatts for Jensen/Lydersen

8 May   Crystal Pal   H   W   3-0
Seaman, Dixon, Winterburn, Davis, Linighan, Adams, Carter, Wright 1, Campbell 1, Merson, Parlour,
Dickov 1/O'Leary for Carter/Wright

11 May Tottenham H   H   L   1-3
Miller, Lydersen, Keown, Marshall, O'Leary, Bould, Flatts, Selley, Smith, Dickov 1, Heaney,
McGowan/Carter for Lydersen/Flatts

FA CUP

2 Jan   Yeovil T (3)   A   W   3-1
Seaman, Dixon, Winterburn, Hillier, Bould, Adams, O'Leary, Wright 3, Smith, Merson, Limpar

25 Jan   Leeds U (4)   H   D   2-2
Seaman, Dixon, Winterburn, Hillier, Linighan, Adams, Jensen, Campbell, Smith, Merson 1, Parlour
1, Carter for Jensen

3 Feb   Leeds U (4R)   A   W   3-2
Seaman, Dixon, Winterburn, Selley, Linighan, Adams, Morrow, Wright 2, Smith 1, Merson, Parlour,
Campbell/O'Leary for Parlour/Winterburn (aet)

13 Feb   Nottingham F (5)   H   W   2-0
Seaman, Dixon, Winterburn, Hillier, Linighan, Adams, Jensen, Wright 2, Selley, Merson, Limpar,
Campbell/Morrow for Wright/Limpar

6 Mar   Ipswich T (6)   A   W   4-2
Seaman, Dixon, Winterburn, Davis, Linighan, Adams 1, Carter, Wright 1p, Smith, Merson, Morrow,
Hillier/Campbell 1 for Carter/Smith (o/g Whelan)

4 Apr   Tottenham H (SF)   W   1-0
Seaman, Dixon, Winterburn, Hillier, Linighan, Adams 1, Parlour, Wright, Campbell, Merson, Selley,
Smith/Morrow for Wright/Campbell (at Wembley)

15 May   Sheffield Wed (F)   D   1-1
Seaman, Dixon, Winterburn, Davis, Linighan, Adams, Jensen, Wright 1, Campbell, Merson, Parlour,
Smith/O'Leary for Parlour/Wright (at Wembley, aet)

20 May   Sheffield Wed (FR)   W   2-1
Seaman, Dixon, Winterburn, Davis, Linighan 1, Adams, Jensen, Wright 1, Smith, Merson, Campbell,
O'Leary for Wright (at Wembley, aet)

FOOTBALL LEAGUE (COCA-COLA) CUP

22 Sep   Millwall (2/1)   H   D   1-1
Seaman, Dixon, Winterburn, Hillier, Bould, Adams, Parlour, Wright, Smith, Merson, Limpar,
Campbell 1 for Limpar

7 Oct   Millwall (2/2)   A   D   1-1
Seaman, Dixon, Winterburn, Hillier, Bould, Adams, Jensen, Wright, Smith, Merson, Limpar,
Campbell 1, Parlour for Merson (won 3-1 on penalties)

28 Oct   Derby Co (3)   A   D   1-1
Seaman, Lydersen, Morrow, Hillier, Bould, Adams, Jensen, Campbell 1, Smith, Merson, Limpar

1 Dec   Derby Co (3R)   H   W   2-1
Seaman, Dixon, Morrow, Hillier, Bould, Adams, Parlour, Wright 1, Campbell 1, Merson, Flatts

6 Jan   Scarborough (4)   A   W   1-0
Seaman, Dixon, Winterburn 1, Hillier, Bould, Adams, O'Leary, Wright, Smith, Merson, Limpar,
Campbell for Merson

12 Jan   Nottingham F (5)   H   W   2-0
Seaman, Dixon, Winterburn, Hillier, Linighan, Adams, Jensen, Wright 2, Smith, Merson, Limpar,
Campbell for Limpar

7 Feb   Crystal Pal (SF/1)   A   W   3-1
Seaman, Dixon, Winterburn, Hillier, Linighan, Adams, Selley, Wright 1p, Smith 2, Merson, Campbell,
Morrow for Wright

10 Mar   Crystal Pal (SF/2)   H   W   2-0
Seaman, Dixon, Winterburn, Davis, Linighan 1, Adams, Carter, Wright 1, Smith, Merson, Morrow,
Hillier/Campbell for Winterburn/Smith

18 Apr   Sheffield Wed (F)   W   2-1
Seaman, O'Leary, Winterburn, Parlour, Linighan, Adams, Morrow1 , Campbell, Wright, Merson 1,
Davis (at Wembley)

APPEARANCES (Goals) Adams 35, Bould 24(1), Campbell 37(4), Carter 16(2), Davis 6, Dickov 3(2),
Dixon 29, Flatts 10, Groves 1, Heaney 5, Hillier 30(1), Jensen 32, Keown 16, Limpar 23(2), Linighan
21(2), Lydersen 8, Marshall 2, McGowan 2, Merson 33(6), Miller 4, Morrow 16, O'Leary 11, Parlour
21(1), Pates 7, Seaman 39, Selley 9, Smith 31(3), Winterburn 29(1), Wright 31(15), Total 29 players (40)

POSITION IN LEAGUE TABLE

	Pld	W	D	L	F	A	Pts
1st Manchester U	42	24	12	6	67	31	84
10th Arsenal	42	15	11	16	40	38	56

SEASON 1993-1994

FA CARLING PREMIERSHIP

14 Aug   Coventry C   H   L   0-3
Seaman, Dixon, Winterburn, Davis, Linighan, Adams, Jensen, Wright, Campbell, Merson, Limpar, McGoldrick/Keown for Jensen/Merson

16 Aug   Tottenham H   A   W   1-0
Seaman, Keown, Winterburn, Davis, Linighan, Adams, Jensen, Wright 1, Campbell, McGoldrick, Parlour

21 Aug   Sheffield Wed   A   W   1-0
Seaman, Keown, Winterburn, Davis, Linighan, Adams, Jensen, Wright 1, Campbell, McGoldrick, Parlour, Merson for Parlour

24 Aug   Leeds U   H   W   2-1
Seaman, Keown, Winterburn, Davis, Linighan, Selley, Merson 1, Wright, Campbell, McGoldrick, Parlour, Hillier for Davis, o/g Newsome

28 Aug   Everton   H   W   2-0
Seaman, Keown, Winterburn, Hillier, Linighan, Adams, Jensen, Wright 2, Campbell, McGoldrick, Parlour, Merson for Hillier

1 Sept   Blackburn Rov   A   D   1-1
Seaman, Keown, Winterburn, Davis, Linighan, Adams, Jensen, Wright, Campbell 1, McGoldrick, Parlour, Selley for Merson

11 Sept   Ipswich T   H   W   4-0
Seaman, Keown, Winterburn, Davis, Linighan, Adams, Jensen, Wright 1, Campbell 3, Merson, McGoldrick, Hillier/Limpar for Jensen/Merson

19 Sept   Manchester U   A   L   0-1
Seaman, Keown, Winterburn, Hillier, Linighan, Adams, Jensen, Wright, Campbell, Merson, McGoldrick, Davis/Smith for Hillier/Merson

25 Sept   Southampton   H   W   1-0
Seaman, Keown, Winterburn, Davis, Linighan, Adams, Jensen, Wright, Campbell, Merson 1, McGoldrick, Hillier for Davis

2 Oct   Liverpool   A   D   0-0
Seaman, Dixon, Winterburn, Davis, Linighan, Adams, Jensen, Wright, Campbell, Merson, McGoldrick

16 Oct   Manchester C   H   D   0-0
Seaman, Dixon, Winterburn, Davis, Linighan, Adams, Heaney, Wright, Smith, Parlour, McGoldrick, Campbell for Heaney

23 Oct   Oldham Ath   A   D   0-0
Seaman, Dixon, Winterburn, Davis, Linighan, Adams, Hillier, Wright, Smith, Merson, McGoldrick, Campbell for Hillier

Oct 30   Norwich C   H   D   0-0
Seaman, Dixon, Winterburn, Davis, Bould, Adams, Jensen, Wright, Smith, Merson, Limpar, Keown/Campbell for Winterburn/Smith

6 Nov   Aston Villa   H   L   1-2
Seaman, Dixon, Winterburn, Selley, Keown, Adams, Jensen, Wright 1, Campbell, Merson, Limpar

20 Nov   Chelsea   A   W   2-0
Seaman, Dixon, Winterburn, Davis, Linighan, Bould, Keown, Wright 1p, Smith 1, Merson, Selley, Morrow for Winterburn

24 Nov   West Ham U   A   D   0-0
Seaman, Dixon, Winterburn, Keown, Linighan, Bould, Morow, Wright, Smith, Merson, Limpar, Campbell/Miller for Limpar/Wright

27 Nov   Newcastle U   H   W   2-1
Seaman, Dixon, Winterburn, Morrow, Keown, Bould, Jensen, Wright 1, Smith 1, Merson, McGoldrick

4 Dec   **Coventry C**   **A**   **L**   **0-1**
Seaman, Dixon, Winterburn, Davis, Keown, Adams, Selley, Wright, Smith, Merson, McGoldrick, Bould/Campbell for Adams/McGoldrick

6 Dec   **Tottenham H**   **H**   **D**   **1-1**
Seaman, Dixon, Keown, Selley, Bould, Adams, Jensen, Wright 1, Smith, Merson, Limpar, Campbell for Smith

12 Dec   **Sheffield Wed**   **H**   **W**   **1-0**
Miller, Dixon, Morrow, Selley, Keown, Adams, Jensen, Wright 1, Smith, Merson, Limpar, Bould/Campbell for Keown/Merson

18 Dec   **Leeds U**   **A**   **L**   **1-2**
Seaman, Dixon, Winterburn, Selley, Bould, Adams, Jensen, Wright, Smith, Campbell 1, Limpar, Parlour/Morrow for Smith/Dixon

27 Dec   **Swindon T**   **A**   **W**   **4-0**
Seaman, Dixon, Winterburn, Parlour, Bould, Adams, Jensen, Wright 1, Campbell 3, Hillier, McGoldrick, Merson/Keown for Parlour/Adams

29 Dec   **Sheffield U**   **H**   **W**   **3-0**
Seaman, Dixon, Winterburn, Parlour, Bould, Adams, Jensen, Wright 1, Campbell 2, Hillier, McGoldrick, Merson/Keown for Parlour/Wright

1 Jan   **Wimbledon**   **A**   **W**   **3-0**
Seaman, Dixon, Winterburn, Parlour 1, Bould, Adams, Jensen, Wright 1, Campbell 1, Hillier, McGoldrick, Keown/Merson for Dixon/Jensen

3 Jan   **QPR**   **H**   **D**   **0-0**
Seaman, Dixon, Winterburn, Parlour, Bould, Adams, Jensen, Wright, Campbell, Hillier, McGoldrick, Keown for Jensen

15 Jan   **Manchester C**   **A**   **D**   **0-0**
Seaman, Dixon, Winterburn, Parlour, Bould, Adams, Jensen, Wright, Campbell, Hillier, McGoldrick, Merson/Keown for McGoldrick/Jensen

22 Jan   **Oldham Ath**   **H**   **D**   **1-1**
Seaman, Dixon, Winterburn, Parlour, Bould, Adams, Jensen, Wright 1p, Campbell, Hillier, McGoldrick, Keown/Meron for Jensen/McGoldrick

13 Feb   **Norwich C**   **A**   **D**   **1-1**
Seaman, Dixon, Winterburn, Davis, Bould, Adams, Jensen, Campbell 1, Smith, Merson, Parlour

19 Feb   **Everton**   **A**   **D**   **1-1**
Seaman, Dixon, Winterburn, Davis, Bould, Adams, Jensen, Campbell, Smith, Merson 1, Parlour, Keown/Hillier for Adams/Jensen

26 Feb   **Blackburn Rov**   **H**   **W**   **1-0**
Seaman, Dixon, Winterburn, Davis, Bould, Adams, Jensen, Campbell, Smith, Merson 1, Parlour

5 Mar   **Ipswich T**   **A**   **W**   **5-1**
Seaman, Dixon, Winterburn, Selley, Bould, Adams, Parlour 1, Wright 3, Smith, Limpar, Hillier, Merson/Keown for Limpar/Hillier, o/g Youds

19 Mar   **Southampton**   **A**   **W**   **4-0**
Seaman, Dixon, Winterburn, Keown, Linighan, Adams, Parlour, Wright 3, Campbell 1, Selley, Limpar, Smith for Limpar

22 Mar   **Manchester U**   **H**   **D**   **2-2**
Seaman, Dixon, Winterburn, Davis, Bould, Adams, Jensen, Wright, Smith, Merson 1, Selley, Campbell for Davis, o/g Pallister

26 Mar   **Liverpool**   **H**   **W**   **1-0**
Seaman, Dixon, Keown, Parlour, Bould, Linighan, Jensen, Wright, Campbell, Merson 1, Selley, Morrow/Smith for Jensen/Wright

2 Apr   **Swindon T**   **H**   **W**   **1-1**
Seaman, Dixon, Keown, Davis, Adams, Linighan, Jensen, Wright, Smith 1, Merson, Parlour, McGoldrick/Campbell for Jensen/Merson

4 Apr   **Sheffield U**   **A**   **D**   **1-1**
Seaman, Keown, Winterburn, Parlour, Bould, Adams, Campbell 1, Wright, Smith, Selley, McGoldrick, Dixon/Merson for Keown/McGoldrick

16 Apr   **Chelsea**   **H**   **W**   **1-0**
Seaman, Dixon, Morrow, Hillier, Keown, Adams, Selley, Wright 1, Campbell, Parlour, McGoldrick, Smith for Hillier

19 Apr   Wimbledon   H   D   1-1

Seaman, Dixon, Keown, Davis, Bould 1, Adams, Campbell, Wright, Smith, Parlour, Selley, Flatts for Davis

23 Apr   Aston Villa   A   W   2-1

Seaman, Dixon, Keown, Davis, Bould, Linighan, Campbell, Wright 2(1p), Smith, Morrow, Flatts, Parlour for Davis

27 Apr   QPR   A   D   1-1

Seaman, Dixon, Keown, Morrow, Linighan, Adams, Flatts, Wright, Smith, Merson 1, Parlour, Selley/McGoldrick for Keown/Flatts

30 Apr   West Ham U   H   L   0-2

Miller, McGoldrick, Winterburn, Davis, Bould, Linighan, Parlour, Wright, Campbell, Merson, Selley, Morrow/Dickov for McGoldrick/Merson

7 May   Newcastle U   A   L   0-2

Miller, Dixon, Winterburn, Davis, Bould, Adams, McGoldrick, Wright, Smith, Morrow, Selley, Parlour/Linighan for Davis/Dixon

POSITION IN LEAGUE TABLE

	Pld	W	D	L	F	A	Pts
1st Manchester U	42	27	11	4	80	38	92
4th Arsenal	42	18	17	7	53	28	71

APPEARANCES (Goals) Adams 35; Bould 25(1); Campbell 37(14); Davis 22; Dickov 1; Dixon 33; Flatts 3; Heaney 1; Hillier 15; Jensen 27; Keown 33; Limpar 10; Linighan 21; McGoldrick 26; Merson 33(7); Miller 4; Morrow 11; Parlour 27(2); Seaman 39; Selley 18; Smith 25(3); Winterburn 34; Wright 39 (23(5p)); o/g 3; 23 players 53

FA CUP

10 Jan   Millwall (3)   A   W   1-0

Seaman, Dixon, Winterburn, Parlour, Bould, Adams 1, Keown, Wright, Campbell, Hillier, McGoldrick, Merson/Jensen for Wright/Hillier

31 Jan   Bolton W (4)   A   D   2-2

Seaman, Dixon, Winterburn, Parlour, Bould, Adams 1, Keown, Wright 1, Campbell, Hillier, Merson, Smith for Parlour

9 Feb   Bolton W (4R)   H   L   1-3

Seaman, Dixon, Winterburn, Hillier, Bould, Adams, Campbell, Wright, Smith 1, Merson, Parlour, Keown/McGoldrick for Hillier/Wright

LEAGUE CUP

21 Sept   Huddersfield T (2/1)   A   W   5-0

Seaman, Keown, Winterburn, Davis, Linighan, Adams, Jensen, Wright 3, Campbell 1, Merson 1, McGoldrick, Hillier/Smith for Jensen/Merson

5 Oct   Huddersfield T (2/2)   H   D   1-1

Seaman, Dixon, Winterburn, Parlour, Linighan, Bould, Jensen, Smith 1, Campbell, Limpar, McGoldrick, Selley/Heaney for Jensen/McGoldrick

26 Oct   Norwich C (3)   H   D   1-1

Seaman, Dixon, Winterburn, Parlour, Linighan, Adams, Jensen, Wright 1, Smith, Merson, McGoldrick, Campbell/Davis for Merson/McGoldrick

10 Nov   Norwich C (3R)   A   W   3-0

Seaman, Dixon, Keown, Selley, Linighan, Bould, Jensen, Wright 2, Smith, Merson 1, Limpar

30 Nov   Aston Villa (4)   H   L   0-1

Seaman, Dixon, Winterburn, Morrow, Keown, Bould, Jensen, Wright, Smith, Merson, McGoldrick, Campbell/Davis for Dixon/Jensen

FA CHARITY SHIELD

7 Aug   Manchester U   D   1-1

Seaman, Dixon, Winterburn, Davis, Linighan, Adams, Jensen, Wright 1, Campbell, Merson, Limpar, Keown/McGoldrick for Dixon/Limpar (at Wembley, lost on penalties)

EUROPEAN CUP WINNERS' CUP

15 Sept   Odense (1/1)   A   W   2-1
Seaman, Selley, Winterburn, Davis, Linighan, Keown, Jensen, Wright 1, Campbell, Merson 1, McGoldrick, Smith for Wright

29 Sept   Odense (1/2)   H   D   1-1
Seaman, Dixon, Winterburn, Davis, Keown, Adams, Jensen, Wright, Campbell 1, Merson, McGoldrick, Smith for Wright

20 Oct   Standard Liege (2/1)   H   W   3-0
Seaman, Dixon, Winterburn, Davis, Keown, Adams, Jensen, Wright 2, Smith, Merson 1, McGoldrick, Linighan/Campbell for Keown/Wright

3 Nov   Standard Liege (2/2)   A   W   7-0
Seaman, Dixon, Winterburn, Davis, Keown, Adams 1, Jensen, Selley 1, Smith 1, Merson 1, Campbell 2, McGoldrick 1/Bould for Smith/Keown

2 Mar   Torino (3/1)   A   D   0-0
Seaman, Dixon, Winterburn, Davis, Bould, Adams, Jensen, Campbell, Smith, Merson, Hillier, Selley for Davis

15 Mar   Torino (3/2)   H   W   1-0
Seaman, Dixon, Winterburn, Davis, Bould, Adams 1, Jensen, Wright, Smith, Merson, Hillier, Selley/Keown for Hillier/Jensen

29 Mar   Paris St-Germain (SF/1) A   D   1-1
Seaman, Dixon, Winterburn, Davis, Bould, Adams, Jensen, Wright 1, Smith, Merson, Selley, Keown/Campbell for Davis/Smith

12 Apr   Paris St-Germain(SF/2) H   W   1-0
Seaman, Dixon, Winterburn, Davis, Bould, Adams, Jensen, Wright, Smith, Campbell 1, Selley, Hillier/Keown for Davis/Winterburn

4 May   Parma (F)   W   1-0
Seaman, Dixon, Winterburn, Davis, Bould, Adams, Campbell, Morrow, Smith 1, Merson, Selley, McGoldrick for Merson (in Copenhagen)

SEASON 1994-1995

FA CARLING PREMIERSHIP

20 Aug   Manchester C   H   W   3-0
Seaman, Dixon, Winterburn, Jensen, Bould, Adams, Campbell 1, Wright 1, Smith, Merson, Schwarz, Keown/Dickov for Adams/Merson, o/g Curle

23 Aug   Leeds U   A   L   0-1
Seaman, Dixon, Winterburn, Jensen, Bould, Adams, Campbell, Wright, Smith, Merson, Schwarz, Keown for Bould

28 Aug   Liverpool   A   L   0-3
Seaman, Dixon, Winterburn, Jensen, Keown, Adams, Campbell, Wright, Smith, Merson, Schwarz, Linighan/Davis for Jensen/Merson

31 Aug   Blackburn Rov   H   D   0-0
Seaman, Dixon, Winterburn, Jensen, Keown, Adams, Campbell, Wright, Smith, Merson, Schwarz, Dickov/Linighan for Merson/Adams

10 Sep   Norwich C   A   D   0-0
Seaman, Dixon, Winterburn, Selley, Keown, Adams, Parlour, Wright, Smith, Campbell, McGoldrick, Smith for McGoldrick

18 Sep   Newcastle U   H   L   2-3
Seaman, Dixon, Winterburn, Jensen, Keown, Adams 1, Parlour, Wright 1, Smith, Merson, McGoldrick, Selley/Campbell for Jensen/Parlour

25 Sep   West Ham U   A   W   2-0
Seaman, Dixon, Winterburn, Davis, Bould, Adams 1, Selley, Wright 1, Smith, Merson, McGoldrick, Linighan for Keown

1 Oct   Crystal P   H   L   1-2
Seaman, Dixon, Winterburn, Davis, Linighan, Adams, Selley, Wright 1, Smith, Merson, McGoldrick, Campbell for Davis

8 Oct   Wimbledon   A   W   3-1
Seaman, Dixon, Winterburn, Jensen, Bould, Adams, Parlour, Wright 1, Smith 1, Campbell 1, McGoldrick, Hillier for Schwarz

15 Oct   Chelsea   H   W   3-1
Seaman, Dixon, Winterburn, Jensen, Bould, Adams, Parlour, Wright 2, Smith, Campbell 1,
McGoldrick, Selley/Keown for Jensen/Adams
23 Oct   Coventry C   H   W   2-1
Seaman, Dixon, Adams, Selley, Bould, Keown, Campbell, Wright 2, Smith, Schwarz, Parlour,
McGoldrick for Wright
29 Oct   Everton   A   D   1-1
Seaman, McGoldrick, Winterburn, Jensen, Keown, Adams, Parlour, Campbell, Smith, Merson,
Schwarz 1, Selley/Linighan for Winterburn/Merson
6 Nov   Sheffield Wed   H   D   0-0
Seaman, Keown, Winterburn, Selley, Bould, Adams, Parlour, Dickov, Smith, Schwarz, McGoldrick,
Campbell for Smith
19 Nov   Southampton   A   L   0-1
Seaman, Dixon, Winterburn, Selley, Bould, Adams, Keown, Dickov, Campbell, McGoldrick,
Schwarz, Carter for McGoldrick
23 Nov   Leicester C   A   L   1-2
Seaman, Dixon, Winterburn, Selley, Bould, Linighan, Keown, Wright 1p, Dickov, Carter, Schwarz,
Campbell/Morrow for Linighan/Selley
25 Nov   Manchester U   H   D   0-0
Seaman, Dixon, Winterburn, Jensen, Bould, Adams, morrow, Wright, Smith, McGoldrick, Carter,
Dickov/Keown for Carter/Jensen
3 Dec   Nottingham F   A   D   2-2
Bartram, Dixon, Winterburn, Davis 1, Bould, Keown 1, Parlour, Hillier, Campbell, Flatts, Schwarz,
Shaw for Flatts
12 Dec   Manchester C   A   W   2-1
Bartram, Dixon, Winterburn, Morrow, Bould, Keown, Jensen, Campbell, Smith 1, Parlour, Schwarz 1
17 Dec   Leeds U   H   L   1-3
Bartram, Dixon, Winterburn, Morrow, Bould, Keown, Jensen, Campbell, Smith, Parlour, Schwarz,
Flatts/Linighan 1 for Smith/Jensen
26 Dec   Aston Villa   H   D   0-0
Bartram, Dixon, Winterburn, Morrow, Bould, Keown, Hughes, Dickov, Campbell, Parlour, Schwarz,
Flatts for Hughes
28 Dec   Ipswich T   A   W   2-0
Bartram, Dixon, Winterburn, Jensen, Bould, Keown, Campbell 1, Wright 1, Smith, Parlour, Schwarz,
Linighan/Dickov for Smith/Wright
31 Dec   QPR   H   L   1-3
Bartram, Dixon, Winterburn 1, Jensen, Bould, Keown, Campbell, Wright, Smith, Parlour, Schwarz,
Clarke for Smith
2 Jan   Tottenham H   A   L   0-1
Seaman, Dixon, Winterburn, Jensen, Bould, Linighan, Selley, Wright, Campbell, Parlour, Schwarz,
Smith for Selley
14 Jan   Everton   H   D   1-1
Seaman, Dixon, Winterburn, Jensen, Keown, Linighan, Hillier, Wright 1, Hartson, Parlour, Schwarz,
Kiwomya/Morrow for Hillier/Wright
21 Jan   Coventry C   A   W   1-0
Seaman, Dixon, Morrow, Keown, Bould, Linighan, Campbell, Wright, Hartson 1, Hillier, Schwarz,
Parlour/Kwomya for Hillier/Wright
24 Jan   Southampton   H   D   1-1
Seaman, Dixon, Morrow, Keown, Bould, Linighan, Jensen, Wright, Hartson 1, Parlour, Schwarz,
Hillier/Kiwomya for Keown/Parlour
4 Feb   Sheffield Wed   A   L   1-3
Seaman, Dixon, Winterburn, Jensen, Linighan 1, Adams, Selley, Campbell, Hartson, Merson,
Kiwomya, Keown/Parlour for Jensen/Selley
11 Feb   Leicester C   H   D   1-1
Seaman, Dixon, Winterburn, Jensen, Linighan, Adams, McGoldrick, Selley, Hartson, Merson 1,
Kiwomya, Keown/Parlour, for Selley/Jensen
21 Feb   Nottingham F   H   W   1-0
Seaman, Dixon, Winterubrn, Jensen, Bould, Linighan, McGoldrick, Merson, Kiwomya 1, Schwarz,
Helder

25 Feb Crystal Pal   A W 3-0
Seaman, Dixon, Winterburn, Jensen, Bould, Linighan, McGoldrick, Merson 1, Kiwomya 2, Schwarz, Helder, Morrow/Parlour for Winterburn/Morrow

5 Mar West Ham U   H L 0-1
Bartram, Dixon, Winterburn, Jensen, Bould, Linighan, Parlour, Wright, Helder, Merson, Schwarz, Morrow/Kiwomya for Jensen/Helder

8 Mar Blackburn Rov   A L 1-3
Bartram, Dixon, Winterburn, Morrow 1, Linighan, Adams, Parlour, Helder, Hartson, Merson, Schwarz, Wright/Bould for Hartson/Linighan

19 Mar Newcastle U   A L 0-1
Bartram, Dixon, Winterburn, Jensen, Bould, Adams, Morrow, Wright, Hartson, Merson, Helder, Parlour/McGoldrick for Helder/Hartson

22 Mar Manchester U   A L 0-3
Bartram, Dixon, Winterburn, Morrow, Bould, Adams, Keown, Wright, Kiwomya, Merson, Parlour, Helder for Parlour

1 Apr Norwich C   H W 5-1
Bartram, Dixon 1, Winterburn, Morrow, Bould, Adams, Hillier, Wright, Hartson 2, Merson 1, Helder, Keown/Kiwomya for Morrow/Hartson, o/g Newman

8 Apr QPR   A L 1-3
Seaman, Dixon, Winterburn, Schwarz, Bould, Adams 1, Morrow, Wright, Hartson, Merson, Helder, Hillier/Kiwomya for Morrow/Hartson

12 Apr Liverpool   H L 0-1
Seaman, Keown, Winterburn, Schwarz, Bould, Adams, Hillier, Wright, McGoldrick, Merson, Helder, Parlour/Hartson for Merson/Helder

15 Apr Ipswich T   H W 4-1
Seaman, Dixon, Winterburn, Schwarz, Bould, Adams, Keown, Wright 3, Hartson, Merson 1, Helder, Parlour/Kiwomya for Winterburn/Wright

17 April Aston Villa   A W 4-0
Seaman, Dixon, Winterburn, Schwarz, Bould, Adams, Keown, Wright 2(1p), Hartson 2, Merson, Parlour, Hillier/Kiwomya for Winterburn/Wright

29 Apr Tottenham H   H D 1-1
Seaman, Dixon, Winterburn, Schwarz, Bould, Adams, Keown, Wright 1p, Hartson, Merson, Helder, Parlour for Helder

4 May Wimbledon   H D 0-0
Seaman, Dixon, Winterburn, Jensen, Linighan, Adams, Parlour, Wright, Hartson, Merson, Helder, Kiwomya for Hartson

14 May Chelsea   A L 1-2
Seaman, Dixon, McGowan, Jensen, Bould, Adams, Parlour, Wright, Hartson 1, Merson, Helder, Linighan/Dickov for McGowan/Helder

FA CUP

7 Jan Millwall (3)   A D 0-0
Seaman, Dixon, Winterburn, Jensen, Bould, Linighan, Hillier, Wright, Smith, Parlour, Schwarz, Keown/Campbell for Jensen/Smith

18 Jan Millwall (3R)   H L 0-2
Seaman, Dixon, Winterburn, Jensen, Keown, Linighan, Hilier, Wright, Campbell, Parlour, Morrow, Adams, Flatts for Keown/Jensen

FOOTBALL LEAGUE (COCA-COLA) CUP

21 Sep Hartlepool U (2/1) A W 5-0
Seaman, Dixon, Keown, Davis, Linighan, Adams 1, Parlour, Wright 2, Smith 1, Merson 1, Selley, McGoldrick for Smith

5 Oct Hartlepool U (2/2) H W 2-0
Seaman, Dixon, Winterburn, Davis, Bould, Keown, Parlour, Dickov 1, Campbell 1, Hillier, McGoldrick

26 Oct Oldham Ath (3)   A D 0-0
Seaman, Dixon, Winterburn, Selley, Bould, Adams, Parlour, Campbell, Smith, Merson, Schwarz, Keown/McGoldrick for Dixon/Campbell

9 Nov   Oldham Ath (3R)   H   W   2-0
Seaman, Keown, Winterburn, Selley, Bould, Adams, Parlour, Dickov 2, Campbell, McGoldrick, Schwarz, Morrow/Dickov for Bould/Parlour
30 Nov   Sheffield Wed (4)   H   W   2-0
Seaman, Dixon, Winterburn, Morrow 1, Bould, Adams, Campbell, Wright 1, Smith, McGoldrick, Schwarz, Bartram/Dickov/Keown for Seaman, Morrow/McGoldrick
11 Jan   Liverpool (QF)   A   L   0-1
Seaman, Dixon, Winterburn, Jensen, Bould, Linighan, Hillier, Wright, Campbell, Parlour, Schwarz, Morrow/Dickov for Bould/Parlour

EUROPEAN CUP WINNERS CUP
15 Sep   Ormonia Nicosia (1/1) A   W   3-1
Seaman, Dixon, Winterburn, Schwarz, Linighan, Keown, Jensen, Wright 1, Smith, Merson 2, Parlour, Morrow for Schwarz
29 Sep   Ormonia Nicosia (1/2) H   W   3-0
Seaman, Dixon, Winterburn, Schwarz 1, Linighan, Adams, Jensen, Wright 2, Smith, Merson, Parlour, Hillier/Campbell for Jensen/Merson
20 Oct   Brondby (2/1)   A   W   2-1
Seaman, Dixon, Winterburn, Schwarz, Bould, Adams, Jensen, Wright 1, Smith 1, Campbell, Parlour
3 Nov   Brondby (2/2)   H   D   2-2
Seaman, Dixon, Winterburn, Selley 1, Keown, Adams, Jensen, Wright 1p, Smith, Merson, Parlour, Campbell/Bould for Wright/Dixon
2 Mar   Auxerre (3/1)   H   D   1-1
Seaman, Dixon, Winterburn, Schwarz, Bould, Adams, Jensen, Wright 1p, Kiwomya, Merson, McGoldrick, Hartson/Parlour for McGoldrick/Kiwomya
16 Mar   Auxerre (3/2)   A   W   1-0
Seaman, Dixon, Winterburn, Schwarz, Bould, Adams, Keown, Wright 1, Hartson, Merson, Parlour, Morrow for Hartson
6 Apr   Sampdoria (SF/1)   H   W   3-2
Seaman, Dixon, Winterburn, Schwarz, Bould 2, Adams, Hillier, Wright 1, Hartson, Merson, Parlour, Kiwomya/Morrow for Wright /Merson
20 Apr   Sampdoria (SF/2)   A   L   2-3
Seaman, Dixon, Winterburn, Schwarz1, Bould, Adams, Keown, Wright1, Hartson, Merson, Hillier, McGoldrick/Kiwomya for Hillier/Wright (won 3-2 on penalties, aet)
10 May   Real Zaragoza (F)   L   1-2
Seaman, Dixon, Winterburn, Schwarz, Linighan, Adams, Keown, Wright, Hartson1, Merson, Parlour, Morrow/Hillier for Winterburn/Keown (in Paris, aet)

APPEARANCES (Goals) Adams 27(3); Bartram 11; Bould 31; Campbell 23(4); Carter 3; Clarke 1; Davis 4(1); Dickov 9; Dixon 39(1); Flatts 3; Hartson 15(7); Helder 13; Hillier 9; Hughes 1; Jensen 24(1); Keown 31(1); Kiwomya 14(3); Linighan 20(2); McGoldrick 11; McGowan 1; Merson 24(4); Morrow 15(1); Parlour 30; Schwarz 34(2); Seaman 31; Selley 13; Shaw 1; Smith 19(2); Winterburn 39; Wright 31(18); o/g 2; Total 30 players (50)

POSITION IN LEAGUE TABLE
	Pld	W	D	L	F	A	Pts
1st Blackburn Rov	42	27	8	7	80	39	89
12th Arsenal	42	13	12	17	52	49	51

SEASON 1995-1996

FA CARLING PREMIERSHIP
20 Aug   Middlesbrough   H   D   1-1
Seaman, Dixon, Winterburn, Keown, Bould, Adams, Platt, Wright 1, Merson, Bergkamp, Parlour, Helder for Parlour
23 Aug   Everton   A   W   2-0
Seaman, Dixon, Winterburn, Keown, Bould, Adams, Platt 1, Wright 1, Merson, Bergkamp, Parlour, Jensen for Keown

26 Aug Coventry C   A   D   0-0
Seaman, Dixon, Winterburn, Keown, Bould, Adams, Platt, Wright, Merson, Bergkamp, Parlour, Jensen/Helder for Dixon/Parlour

29 Aug Nottingham F   H   D   1-1
Seaman, Dixon, Winterburn, Keown, Bould, Adams, Platt 1, Wright, Merson, Bergkamp, Parlour, Helder for Parlour

10 Sept Manchester C   A   W   1-0
Seaman, Dixon, Winterburn, Keown, Bould, Adams, Jensen, Wright, Merson, Bergkamp, Parlour, McGoldrick for Parlour

16 Sept West Ham U   H   W   1-0
Seaman, Dixon, Winterburn, Jensen, Bould, Adams, Parlour, Wright 1p, Merson, Bergkamp, Helder

23 Sept Southampton   H   W   4-2
Seaman, Dixon, Winterburn, Keown, Bould, Adams 1, Parlour, Wright 1, Merson, Bergkamp 2, Helder

30 Sept Chelsea   A   L   0-1
Seaman, Dixon, Winterburn, Keown, Bould, Adams, Parlour, Wright, Merson, Bergkamp, Jensen, Helder/Linighan for Jensen/Keown

14 Oct Leeds U   A   W   3-0
Seaman, Dixon, Winterburn, Keown, Bould, Adams, Parlour, Wright 1, Merson 1, Bergkamp 1, Helder

21 Oct Aston Villa   H   W   2-0
Seaman, Dixon, Winterburn, Keown, Bould, Adams, Parlour, Wright 1, Merson 1, Bergkamp, Helder

30 Oct Bolton W   A   L   0-1
Seaman, Dixon, Winterburn, Keown, Bould, Adams, Parlour, Wright, Merson, Bergkamp, Helder, Platt for Keown

4 Nov Manchester U   H   W   1-0
Seaman, Dixon, Winterburn, Keown, Bould, Adams, Platt, Wright, Merson, Bergkamp 1, Helder, Hartson for Wright

18 Nov Tottenham H   A   L   1-2
Seaman, Dixon, Winterburn, Keown, Bould, AdamsPlatt, Hartson, Merson, Bergkamp 1, Helder, Hillier for Helder

21 Nov Sheffield Wed   H   W   4-2
Seaman, Dixon, Winterburn 1, Keown, Bould, Adams, Platt, Hartson 1, Merson, Bergkamp 1, Helder, Dickov 1 for Helder

26 Nov Blackburn Rov   H   D   0-0
Seaman, Dixon, Winterburn, Keown, Bould, Adams, Platt, Hartson, Merson, Bergkamp, Hillier, Helder/Dickov for Keown/Hartson

2 Dec Aston Villa   A   D   1-1
Seaman, Dixon, Winterburn, Jensen, Bould, Adams, Platt 1, Wright, Merson, Hartson, Helder, Morrow/Dickov for Helder/Hartson

9 Dec Southampton   A   D   0-0
Seaman, Dixon, Winterburn, Keown, Bould, Adams, Platt, Wright, Merson, Hartson, Jensen, Clarke for Hartson

16 Dec Chelsea   H   D   1-1
Seaman, Dixon 1, Winterburn, Keown, Bould, Adams, Platt, Wright, Merson, Hartson, Jensen, Helder for Jensen

23 Dec Liverpool   A   L   1-3
Seaman, Dixon, Winterburn, Jensen, Keown, Linighan, Platt, Wright 1p, Merson, Parlour, Helder, Marshall/Hartson for Parlour/Helder

26 Dec QPR   H   W   3-0
Seaman, Dixon, Winterburn, Jensen, Keown, Adams, Platt, Wright 1, Merson 2, Dickov, Clarke

30 Dec Wimbledon   H   L   1-3
Seaman, Dixon, Winterburn, Jensen, Keown, Linighan, Platt, Wright 1, Merson, Bergkamp, Clarke, Dickov/Parlour for Clarke/Jensen

2 Jan Newcastle U   A   L   0-2
Seaman, Dixon, Winterburn, Keown, Bould, Adams, Platt, Wright, Merson, Bergkamp, Parlour, Clarke/Dickov for Bould/Parlour

13 Jan   Middlesbrough   A   W   3-2
Seaman, Dixon, McGowan, Jensen, Keown, Adams, Platt 1, Wright, Merson 1, Bergkamp, Helder 1

20 Jan   Everton   H   L   1-2
Seaman, Dixon, Winterburn, Jensen, Linighan, Marshall, Clarke, Wright 1, Merson, Bergkamp, Helder, Dickov for Clarke

3 Feb   Coventry C   H   D   1-1
Seaman, Dixon, Winterburn, Jensen, Linighan, Marshall, Clarke, Wright, Merson, Bergkamp 1, Helder, Hughes for Jensen

10 Feb   Nottingham F   A   W   1-0
Seaman, Dixon, Winterburn, Jensen, Linighan, Keown, Hillier, Wright, Merson, Bergkamp 1, Helder

24 Feb   West Ham U   A   W   1-0
Seaman, Dixon, Winterburn, Morrow, Linighan, Keown, Hillier, Hartson 1, Merson, Bergkamp, Parlour, Platt for Hillier

2 Mar   QPR   A   D   1-1
Seaman, Dixon, Winterburn, Morrow, Linighan, Keown, Platt, Hartson, Merson, Bergkamp 1, Parlour, Rose for Morrow

5 Mar   Manchester C   H   W   3-1
Seaman, Dixon 1, Winterburn, Rose Linighan, Keown, Platt, Hartson 2, Merson, Bergkamp, Parlour

16 Mar   Wimbledon   A   W   3-0
Seaman, Dixon, Winterburn 1, Marshall, Linighan, Keown, Platt 1, Wright, Merson, Bergkamp 1, Hartson

20 Mar   Manchester U   A   L   0-1
Seaman, Dixon, Winterburn, Marshall, Linighan, Keown, Platt, Wright, Merson, Bergkamp, Hartson, Hillier/Helder for Bergkamp/Merson

23 Mar   Newcastle U   H   W   2-0
Seaman, Dixon, Winterburn, Marshall 1, Linighan, Keown, Platt, Wright 1, Merson, Bergkamp, Hartson, Parlour/Helder for Wright/Winterburn

6 Apr   Leeds U   H   W   2-1
Seaman, Dixon, Winterburn, Marshall, Linighan, Keown, Platt, Wright 2, Merson, Bergkamp, Hartson

8 Apr   Sheffield Wed   A   L   0-1
Seaman, Dixon, Helder, Marshall, Linighan, Keown, Platt, Wright, Merson, Bergkamp, Hartson, Rose/Shaw for Helder/Hartson

15 Apr   Tottenham H   H   D   0-0
Seaman, Dixon, Winterburn, Marshall, Linighan, Keown, Platt, Wright, Merson, Bergkamp, Parlour, Helder for Merson

27 Apr   Blackburn Rov   A   D   1-1
Seaman, Dixon, Winterburn, Morrow, Linighan, Keown, Platt, Wright 1p, Merson, Bergkamp, Parlour, Rose/Shaw/Hartson for Morrow/Linighan/Wright

1 May   Liverpool   H   D   0-0
Seaman, Dixon, Winterburn, Marshall, Linighan, Keown, Platt, Hartson, Merson, Bergkamp, Parlour

5 May   Bolton W   H   W   2-1
Seaman, Dixon, Winterburn, Marshall, Linighan, Keown, Platt 1, Wright, Merson, Bergkamp 1, Parlour, Shaw/Hartson for Marshall/Wright

POSITION IN LEAGUE TABLE

	Pld	W	D	L	F	A	Pts
1st Manchester U	38	25	7	6	73	35	82
5th Arsenal	38	17	12	9	49	32	63

APPEARANCES (Goals) Adams 21(1), Bergkamp 33(11), Bould 19, Clarke 6, Dickov 7(1), Dixon 38(2), Hartson 19(4), Helder 24(1), Hillier 5, Hughes 1Jensen 15, Keown 34, Linighan 17, Marshall 11(1), McGoldrick 1, McGowan 1, Merson 38 (5), Morrow 4, Parlour 22, Platt 29(6), Rose 4, Seaman 38, Shaw 3, Winterburn 36(2), Wright 31(15(3p)), Total 25 players (48)

FA CUP

6 Jan   Sheffield U (3)   H   D   1-1
Seaman, Dixon, Winterburn, Jensen, Keown, Adams, Clarke, Wright 1, Merson, Hartson, Helder
17 Jan   Sheffield U (3R)   A   L   0-1
Seaman, Dixon, Winterburn, Jensen, Keown, Adams, Platt, Wright, Merson, Bergkamp, Helder,
Linighan/Clarke for Dixon/Jensen

LEAGUE CUP

19 Sept   Hartlepool U (2/1)   A   W   3-0
Seaman, Dixon, Winterburn, Jensen, Bould, Adams 2, Parlour, Wright 1, Merson, Bergkamp, Helder
3 Oct   Hartlepool U (2/2)   H   W   5-0
Seaman, Dixon, Winterburn, Keown, Bould, Adams, Parlour, Wright 3, Merson, Bergkamp 2,
Jensen, Helder/Hartson for Merson/Bergkamp
24 Oct   Barnsley (3)   A   W   3-0
Seaman, Dixon, Winterburn, Keown 1, Bould 1, Adams, Jensen, Wright, Merson, Bergkamp 1,
Helder, Hughes/Hartson for Jensen/Wright
29 Nov   Sheffield Wed (4)   H   W   2-1
Seaman, Dixon, Winterburn, Jensen, Bould, Adams, Platt, Wright 1p, Merson, Bergkamp, Hartson
1, Helder for Bergkamp
10 Jan   Newcastle U (5)   H   W   2-0
Seaman, Dixon, Winterburn, Keown, Bould, Adams, Platt, Wright 2, Merson, Bergkamp, Helder,
Jensen for Bould
14 Feb   Aston Villa (SF/1)   H   D   2-2
Seaman, Dixon, Winterburn, Jensen, Linighan, Keown, Hillier, Wright, Merson, Bergkamp 2, Helder,
Parlour for Helder
21 Feb   Aston Villa (SF/2)   A   D   0-0
Seaman, Dixon, Winterburn, Morrow, Linighan, Keown, Hillier, Wright, Merson, Bergkamp, Parlour,
Platt for Winterburn (lost on away goals)

SEASON 1996-1997

FA CARLING PREMIERSHIP

17 Aug   West Ham U   H   W   2-0
Seaman, Dixon, Winterburn, Keown, Bould, Linighan, Parlour, Morrow, Merson, Bergkamp 1p,
Hartson 1, Wright/Dickov for Hartson/Bergkamp
19 Aug   Liverpool   A   L   0-2
Seaman, Dixon, Winterburn, Keown, Bould, Linighan, Parlour, Morrow, Merson, Bergkamp,
Hartson, Wright/Hillier/Helder for Bergkamp/Hartson/Morrow
24 Aug   Leicester C   A   W   2-0
Seaman, Dixon, Winterburn, Keown, Bould, Linighan, Parlour, Morrow, Merson, Bergkamp 1p,
Hartson, Wright 1/Hillier for Bergkamp/Hartson
4 Sept   Chelsea   H   D   3-3
Lukic, Dixon, Winterburn, Keown 1, Bould, Linighan, Parlour, Morrow, Merson 1, Bergkamp,
Hartson, Platt/Wright 1 for Bould/Hartson
7 Sept   Aston Villa   A   D   2-2
Lukic, Dixon, Winterburn, Keown, Morrow, Linighan 1, Platt, Wright, Merson 1, Bergkamp, Parlour,
Hartson/Helder for Morrow/Bergkamp
16 Sept   Sheffield Wed   H   W   4-1
Seaman, Dixon, Winterburn, Keown, Bould, Linighan, Platt 1, Wright 3(1p), Merson, Parlour,
Hartson, Vieira for Parlour
21 Sept   Middlesbrough   A   W   2-0
Seaman, Dixon, Winterburn, Keown, Bould, Linighan, Platt, Wright 1, Merson, Vieira, Hartson 1,
Adams for Dixon
28 Sept   Sunderland   H   W   2-0
Seaman, Dixon, Winterburn, Keown, Bould, Adams, Platt, Wright, Merson, Vieira, Hartson 1,
Shaw/Parlour 1 for Winterburn/Merson
12 Oct   Blackburn Rov   A   W   2-0
Seaman, Dixon, Winterburn, Keown, Bould, Adams, Platt, Wright 2, Merson, Vieira, Hartson,
Parlour for Hartson

19 Oct   Coventry C   H   D   0-0
Seaman, Dixon, Winterburn, Keown, Bould, Adams, Platt, Wright, Merson, Vieira, Hartson,
Bergkamp for Hartson

26 Oct   Leeds U   H   W   3-0
Seaman, Dixon 1, Winterburn, Keown, Bould, Adams, Platt, Wright 1, Merson, Bergkamp 1, Vieira,
Morrow/Garde for Winterburn/Wright

2 Nov   Wimbledon   A   D   2-2
Seaman, Dixon, Winterburn, Keown, Bould, Adams, Platt, Wright 1, Merson 1, Bergkamp, Vieira,
Garde for Bergkamp

16 Nov   Manchester U   A   L   0-1
Seaman, Dixon, Winterburn, Keown, Bould, Adams, Platt, Wright, Merson, Bergkamp, Vieira

24 Nov   Tottenham H   H   W   3-1
Lukic, Dixon, Winterburn, Keown, Bould, Adams 1, Platt, Wright 1p, Merson, Bergkamp 1, Vieira,
Hartson/Parlour for Platt/Bergkamp

30 Nov   Newcastle U   A   W   2-1
Lukic, Dixon 1, Winterburn, Keown, Bould, Adams, Platt, Wright 1, Merson, Hartson, Vieira,
Linighan/Morrow/Parlour for Keown/Hartson/Merson

4 Dec   Southampton   H   W   3-1
Lukic, Dixon, Winterburn, Linighan, Bould, Adams, Platt, Wright 1p, Merson 1, Hartson, Vieira,
Shaw 1/Parlour for Platt/Hartson

7 Dec   Derby Co   H   D   2-2
Lukic, Dixon, Winterburn, Linighan, Bould, Adams 1, Platt, Wright, Merson, Hartson, Vieira 1, Shaw
for Linighan

21 Dec   Nottingham F   A   L   1-2
Lukic, McGowan, Winterburn, Keown, Bould, Linighan, Platt, Wright 1, Merson, Bergkamp, Garde,
Parlour/Hartson/Morrow for McGowan/Garde/Bergkamp

26 Dec   Sheffield Wed   A   D   0-0
Lukic, Parlour, Winterburn, Keown, Bould, Adams, Platt, Wright, Merson, Bergkamp, Garde,
Shaw/Marshall for Keown/Platt

28 Dec   Aston Villa   H   D   2-2
Lukic, Parlour, Winterburn, Keown, Bould, Adams, Garde, Wright 1, Merson 1, Bergkamp, Vieira,
Morrow for Garde

1 Jan   Middlesbrough   H   W   2-0
Lukic, Parlour, Winterburn, Keown, Bould, Adams, Garde, Wright 1, Merson, Bergkamp 1, Vieira,
Hartson/Morrow/Shaw for Garde/Merson/Bergkamp

11 Jan   Sunderland   A   L   0-1
Seaman, Parlour, Winterburn, Keown, Bould, Adams, Platt, Hartson, Merson, Bergkamp, Vieira,
Hughes for Winterburn

19 Jan   Everton   H   W   3-1
Seaman, Parlour, Winterburn, Keown, Bould, Adams, Platt, Wright, Merson 1, Bergkamp 1, Vieira 1,
Dixon/Hughes for Platt/Wright

29 Jan   West Ham U   A   W   2-1
Seaman, Dixon, Winterburn, Rose   Bould, Adams, Parlour 1, Wright 1, Merson, Hughes, Vieira,
Hartson/Marshall for Wright/Rose

1 Feb   Leeds U   A   D   0-0
Seaman, Dixon, Winterburn, Marshall, Bould, Adams, Parlour, Hartson, Merson, Hughes, Vieira,
Wright for Hartson

15 Feb   Tottenham H   A   D   0-0
Lukic, Dixon, Winterburn, Keown, Bould, Adams, Parlour, Wright, Merson, Bergkamp, Vieira,
Hughes for Merson

19 Feb   Manchester U   H   L   1-2
Lukic, Dixon, Winterburn, Keown, Bould, Adams, Parlour, Wright, Merson, Bergkamp 1, Vieira,
Hughes for Adams

23 Feb   Wimbledon   H   L   0-1
Lukic, Dixon, Winterburn, Garde, Bould, Marshall, Parlour, Wright, Merson, Bergkamp, Vieira,
Hughes/Morrow/Shaw for Garde/Bould/Parlour

1 Mar   Everton   A   W   2-0
Lukic, Dixon, Winterburn, Keown, Garde, Marshall, Platt, Wright 1, Hughes, Bergkamp 1, Vieira,
Morrow for Garde

8 Mar   Nottingham F   H   W   2-0
Lukic, Dixon, Winterburn, Keown, Marshall, Adams, Platt, Hughes, Merson, Bergkamp 2(1p), Vieira,
Morrow for Hughes
15 Mar   Southampton   A   W   2-0
Harper, Parlour, Winterburn, Keown, Marshall, Adams, Platt, Shaw 1, Hughes 1, Bergkamp, Vieira,
Garde for Shaw
24 Mar   Liverpool   H   L   1-2
Seaman, Dixon, Winterburn, Keown, Marshall, Adams, Platt, Wright 1, Hughes, Bergkamp, Vieira,
Parlour/Garde/Shaw for Dixon/Marshall/Hughes
5 Apr   Chelsea   A   W   3-0
Seaman, Dixon, Winterburn, Keown, Bould, Garde, Platt 1, Wright 1, Hughes, Bergkamp 1, Vieira,
Parlour/Anelka/Selley for Wright/Hughes/Vieira
12 Apr   Leicester C   H   W   2-0
Seaman, Dixon, Winterburn, Keown, Bould, Adams 1, Platt 1, Wright, Hughes, Bergkamp, Vieira,
Parlour for Hughes
19 Apr   Blackburn Rov   H   D   1-1
Seaman, Dixon, Winterburn, Keown, Bould, Adams, Platt 1, Wright, Hughes, Bergkamp, Vieira,
Parlour for Hughes
21 Apr   Coventry C   A   D   1-1
Seaman, Dixon, Winterburn, Keown, Bould, Adams, Platt, Wright1p, Merson, Bergkamp, Vieira,
Anelka/Parlour for Dixon/Merson
3 May   Newcastle U   H   L   0-1
Seaman, Dixon, Winterburn, Keown, Bould, Adams, Platt, Wright, Merson, Bergkamp, Vieira,
Parlour/Anelka for Adams/Platt
11 May   Derby Co   A   W   3-1
Seaman, Dixon, Winterburn, Keown, Bould, Platt, Wright 2, Merson, Bergkamp 1, Vieira,
Anelka/Parlour for Merson/Vieira

POSITION IN LEAGUE TABLE

	Pld	W	D	L	F	A	Pts
1st Manchester U	38	21	12	5	76	44	75
3rd Arsenal	38	19	11	8	62	32	68

APPEARANCES (Goals) Adams 28(3), Anelka 4, Bergkamp 29(12), Bould 33, Dickov 1, Dixon 32(2),
Garde 11, Harper 1, Hartson 19(3), Helder 2, Hillier 2, Hughes 14(1), Keown 33(1), Linighan 11(1),
Lukic 15, Marshall 8, McGowan 1, Merson 32(6), Morrow 14, Parlour 30(2), Platt 28(4), Rose 1,
Seaman 22, Selley 1, Shaw 8(2), Vieira 31(2), Winterburn 38, Wright 35(23), Total 28 players (62)

FA CUP
4 Jan   Sunderland (3)   H   D   1-1
Lukic, Parlour, Winterburn, Keown, Bould, Adams, Morrow, Hartson 1, Merson, Bergkamp, Vieira,
Shaw for Morrow
15 Jan   Sunderland (3R)   A   W   2-0
Seaman, Parlour, Winterburn, Keown, Bould, Adams, Platt, Hughes 1, Merson, Bergkamp 1, Vieira
4 Feb   Leeds U (4)   H   L   0-1
Seaman, Dixon, Morrow, Keown, Bould, Adams, Parlour, Wright, Merson, Hughes, Vieira, Hartson
for Hughes

LEAGUE CUP
23 Oct   Stoke C (3)   A   D   1-1
Seaman, Dixon, Winterburn, Keown, Bould, Adams, Platt, Wright 1, Merson, Bergkamp, Vieira,
Hartson for Bergkamp
13 Nov   Stoke C (3R)   H   W   5-2
Seaman, Dixon, Winterburn, Keown, Bould, Adams, Platt 1, Wright 2(1p), Merson 1, Bergkamp 1,
Vieira, Hartson/Morrow for Vieira/Bergkamp
27 Nov   Liverpool (4)   A   L   2-4
Lukic, Dixon, Winterburn, Keown, Bould, Adams, Platt, Wright 2p, Merson, Hartson, Vieira,
Parlour/Morrow for Merson/Winterburn

UEFA CUP
10 Sept Borussia M'bach (1/1) H L 2-3
Seaman, Dixon, Winterburn, Keown, Linighan, Parlour, Platt, Wright 1, Merson 1, Bergkamp, Hartson, Helder/Bould for Parlour/Bergkamp
25 Sept Borussia M'bach (1/2) A L 2-3
Seaman, Linighan, Winterburn, Keown, Bould, Adams, Platt, Wright 1, Merson 1, Vieira, Hartson, Parlour/Helder for Linighan/Adams

SEASON 1997-1998

FA CARLING PREMIERSHIP
9 Aug Leeds U A D 1-1
Seaman, Garde, Bould, Grimandi, Winterburn, Parlour, Vieira, Petit, Overmars, Wright 1, Bergkamp, Platt/Hughes for Vieira/Overmars
11 Aug Coventry C H W 2-0
Seaman, Garde, Marshall, Grimandi, Winterburn, Parlour, Vieira, Petit, Overmars, Wright 2, Bergkamp, Platt/Hughes for Petit/Overmars
23 Aug Southampton A W 3-1
Seaman, Garde, Bould, Grimandi, Winterburn, Parlour, Vieira, Petit, Overmars 1, Wright, Bergkamp 2, Platt/Marshall/Boa Morte for Grimandi/Petit/Overmars
27 Aug Leicester C A D 3-3
Seaman, Dixon, Bould, Grimandi, Winterburn, Parlour, Vieira, Petit, Overmars, Wright, Bergkamp 3, Anelka/Platt/Hughes for Parlour/Overmars/Wright
30 Aug Tottenham H H D 0-0
Seaman, Dixon, Bould, Grimandi, Winterburn, Parlour, Vieira, Petit, Overmars, Wright, Bergkamp, Platt/Anelka for Parlour/Petit
13 Sep Bolton W H W 4-1
Seaman, Dixon, Bould, Grimandi, Winterburn, Parlour 1, Vieira, Petit, Overmars, Wright 3, Bergkamp, Platt/Boa Morte/Anelka for Parlour/Overmars/Wright
21 Sep Chelsea A W 3-2
Seaman, Dixon, Bould, Adams 1, Winterburn, Parlour, Vieira, Petit, Overmars, Wright, Bergkamp 2, Boa Morte/Grimandi for Parlour/Overmars
24 Sep West Ham U H W 4-0
Seaman, Dixon, Bould, Adams, Winterburn, Parlour, Vieira, Petit, Overmars 2, Wright 1p, Bergkamp1, Grimandi/Platt/Anelka for Dixon/Winterburn/Wright
27 Sep Everton A D 2-2
Seaman, Grimandi, Bould, Adams, Winterburn, Parlour, Vieira, Petit, Overmars 1, Wright 1, Bergkamp, Boa Morte/Platt/Garde for Parlour/Vieira/Wright
4 Oct Barnsley H W 5-0
Seaman, Dixon, Bould, Adams, Winterburn, Parlour 1, Vieira, Petit, Overmars, Wright 1, Bergkamp 2, Platt 1/Anelka/Boa Morte for Parlour/Overmars/Wright
18 Oct Crystal Pal A D 0-0
Seaman, Grimandi, Bould, Adams, Winterburn, Parlour, Vieira, Petit, Boa Morte, Wright, Bergkamp, Platt/Mendez for Parlour/Boa Morte
26 Oct Aston Villa H D 0-0
Seaman, Dixon, Bould, Adams, Winterburn, Parlour, Vieira, Petit, Boa Morte, Wright, Bergkamp, Platt/Anelka for Parlour/Boa Morte
1 Nov Derby Co A L 0-3
Seaman, Dixon, Bould, Adams, Winterburn, Parlour, Vieira, Petit, Platt, Wright, Anelka, Boa Morte/Wreh for Winterburn/Anelka
9 Nov Manchester U H W 3-2
Seaman, Dixon, Grimandi, Adams, Winterburn, Parlour, Vieira 1, Platt 1, Overmars, Wright, Anelka 1, Bould/Wreh for Vieira/Anelka
22 Nov Sheffield Wed A L 0-2
Seaman, Dixon, Keown, Adams, Winterburn, Parlour, Platt, Grimandi, Overmars, Wright, Mendez, Hughes/Marshall/Wreh for Parlour/Grimandi/Mendez

30 Nov   Liverpool   H   L   0-1
Seaman, Dixon, Keown, Adams, Winterburn, Hughes, Platt, Petit, Overmars, Wright, Bergkamp, Wreh/Grimandi for Hughes/Petit

6 Dec   Newcastle U   A   W   1-0
Seaman, Dixon, Keown, Adams, Winterburn, Parlour, Platt, Petit, Overmars, Wright 1, Bergkamp

13 Dec   Blackburn Rov   H   L   1-3
Seaman, Dixon, Keown, Adams, Winterburn, Parlour, Platt, Petit, Overmars 1, Wright, Bergkamp, Vieira/Boa Morte for Parlour/Platt

26 Dec   Leicester C   H   W   2-1
Seaman, Dixon, Bould, Keown, Winterburn, Parlour, Vieira, Platt 1, Overmars, Wright, Bergkamp, Hughes/Anelka for Platt/Wright, o/g Walsh

28 Dec   Tottenham H   A   D   1-1
Seaman, Dixon, Bould, Keown, Winterburn, Parlour 1, Vieira, Petit, Overmars, Anelka, Bergkamp, Grimandi/Hughes/Rankin for Dixon/Anelka/Bergkamp

10 Jan   Leeds U   H   W   2-1
Seaman, Dixon, Bould, Keown, Winterburn, Parlour, Vieira, Petit, Overmars 2, Wright, Bergkamp

17 Jan   Coventry C   A   D   2-2
Seaman, Dixon, Bould, Keown, Winterburn, Parlour, Vieira, Petit, Upson, Anelka 1, Bergkamp 1, Grimandi/Boa Morte for Keown/Anelka

31 Jan   Southampton   H   W   3-0
Manninger, Grimandi, Bould, Adams 1, Winterburn, Parlour, Hughes, Petit, Overmars, Anelka 1, Bergkamp 1, Platt/Wreh for Hughes/Anelka

8 Feb   Chelsea   H   W   2-0
Manninger, Grimandi, Bould, Adams, Winterburn, Parlour, Hughes 2, Petit, Overmars, Anelka, Bergkamp, Dixon/Wright/Platt for Grimandi/Overmars/Anelka

21 Feb   Crystal Pal   H   W   1-0
Manninger, Dixon, Keown, Grimandi 1, Upson, Venazza, Vieira, Hughes, Boa Morte, Platt, Anelka, McGowan for Vernazza

2 Mar   West Ham U   A   D   0-0
Manninger, Dixon, Keown, Adams, Upson, Hughes, Vieira, Petit, Overmars, Platt, Anelka, Winterburn/Boa Morte for Upson/Platt

11 Mar   Wimbledon   A   W   1-0
Manninger, Dixon, Keown, Adams, Winterburn, Parlour, Vieira, Petit, Overmars, Wreh 1, Bergkamp, Garde/Hughes/Boa Morte for Parlour/Overmars/Wreh

14 Mar   Manchester U   A   W   1-0
Manninger, Dixon, Keown, Adams, Winterburn, Petit, Vieira, Petit, Overmars 1, Wreh, Bergkamp, Anelka/Garde for Wreh/Parlour

28 Mar   Sheffield Wed   H   W   1-0
Seaman, Dixon, Keown, Adams, Winterburn, Parlour, Vieira, Hughes, Overmars, Wreh, Bergkamp 1, Garde/Anelka/Grimandi for Dixon/Parlour/Wreh

31 Mar   Bolton W   A   W   1-0
Seaman, Grimandi, Keown, Adams, Winterburn, Parlour, Vieira, Petit, Overmars, Anelka, Wreh 1, Hughes/Bould/Platt for Overmars/Wreh/Anelka

11 Apr   Newcastle U   H   W   3-1
Seaman, Garde, Bould, Adams, Winterburn, Parlour, Vieira, Petit 1, Overmars, Anelka 2, Wreh, Platt/Hughes/Boa Morte for Overmars/Anelka/Wreh

13 Apr   Blackburn Rov   A   W   4-1
Seaman, Garde, Bould, Adams, Winterburn, Parlour 2, Vieira, Petit, Overmars, Anelka 1, Bergkamp 1, Platt/Hughes for Overmars/Anelka

18 Apr   Wimbledon   H   W   5-0
Seaman, Garde, Upson, Adams 1, Winterburn, Parlour, Vieira, Petit 1, Overmars 1, Anelka, Bergkamp 1, Dixon/Wreh 1/Platt for Garde/Vieira/Anelka

25 Apr   Barnsley   A   W   2-0
Seaman, Dixon, Keown, Adams, Winterburn, Platt, Vieira, Petit, Overmars 1, Anelka, Bergkamp 1, Wreh for Anelka

29 Apr   Derby Co   H   W   1-0
Seaman, Dixon, Keown, Adams, Winterburn, Parlour, Vieira, Petit 1, Overmars, Anelka, Bergkamp, Wreh/Platt for Bergkamp/Anelka

3 May   Everton   H   W   4-0
Seaman, Dixon, Keown, Adams 1, Winterburn, Parlour, Vieira, Petit, Overmars 2, Anelka, Wreh, Wright/Bould for Anelka/Wreh, o/g Bilic
6 May   Liverpool   A   L   0-4
Manninger, Dixon, Bould, Upson, Grimandi, Parlour, Platt, Hughes, Boa Morte, Wright, Wreh, Vieira/Mendez/Anelka for Parlour/Wreh/Wright
10 May Aston Villa   A   L   0-1
Seaman, Grimandi, Keown, Adams, Winterburn, Parlour, Vieira, Petit, Overmars, Wright, Anelka, Platt/Wreh for Parlour/Wright

FA CUP
3 Jan   Port Vale (3)   H   D   0-0
Seaman, Grimandi, Keown, Bould, Winterburn, Parlour, Vieira, Petit, Overmars, Anelka, Bergkamp, Hughes/Boa Morte/Wreh for Parlour/Petit/Anelka
14 Jan Port Vale (3R)   A   D   1-1
Dixon, Bould, Keown, Winterburn, Parlour, Vieira, Hughes, Overmars, Wright, Berkamp1, Grimandi/Anelka/Boa Morte for Vieira/Overmars/Wright (won on penalties aet)
24 Jan Middlesbrough (4) A   W   2-1
Manninger, Dixon, Bould, Adams, Winterburn, Parlour 1, Vieira, Petit, Overmars 1, Anelka, Bergkamp, Grimandi for Dixon
15 Feb Crystal Pal (5)   H   D   0-0
Manninger, Dixon, Bould, Grimandi, Winterburn, Parlour, Hughes, Petit, Overmars, Anelka, Bergkamp, Vieira/Platt/Wreh for Bould/Hughes/Anelka
25 Feb Crystal Pal (5R) A   W   2-1
Manninger, Dixon, Keown, Adams, Upson, Boa Morte, Vieira, Platt, Hughes, Anelka 1, Bergkamp 1, Overmars/Crowe for Upson/Bergkamp
8 Mar   West Ham U (6)   H   D   1-1
Manninger, Dixon, Keown, Adams, Winterburn, Parlour, Vieira, Petit, Overmars, Anelka 1, Bergkamp1, Wreh for Anelka
17 Mar West Ham U (6R)   A   D   1-1
Manninger, Dixon, Keown, Adams, Winterburn, Garde, Vieira, Petit, Overmars, Anelka, Bergkamp1p, Hughes/Wreh/Boa Morte for Petit/Overmars/Anelka/Petit (won 4-3 on penalties aet)
5 Apr   Wolverhampton W (SF)   W   1-0
Seaman, Grimandi, Keown, Adams, Winterburn, Petit, Vieira, Petit, Overmars, Anelka, Wreh 1 Bould/Hughes/Platt for Keown/Wreh/Anelka (at Aston Villa)
16 May Newcastle U (F)   W   2-0
Seaman, Dixon, Keown, Adams, Winterburn, Petit, Vieira, Petit, Overmars 1, Anelka 1, Wreh, Platt/Grimandi for Wreh (at Wembley)

FOOTBALL LEAGUE (COCA-COLA) CUP
14 Oct Birmingham C (3) H   W   4-1
Manninger, Dixon, Marshall, Grimandi, Upson, Mendez 1, Platt 1, Vernazza, Hughes, Wreh, Boa Morte 2, Crowe/Muntasser for Dixon/Boa Morte (aet)
18 Nov Coventry C (4)   H   W   1-0
Manninger, Dixon, Bould, Keown, Upson, Petit, Platt, Mendez, Hughes, Anelka, Bergkamp 1, Wreh/Marshall for Mendez/Anelka (aet)
6 Jan   West Ham U (QF)   A   W   2-1
Seaman, Grimandi, Keown, Bould, Winterburn, Petit, Vieira, Petit, Overmars 1, Wright 1, Bergkamp, Wreh/Hughes for Overmars/Wright
28 Jan Chelsea (SF/1)   H   W   2-1
Manninger, Grimandi, Bould, Adams, Winterburn, Petit, Hughes 1, Petit, Overmars 1, Anelka, Bergkamp, Platt for Grimandi
18 Feb Chelsea (SF/2)   A   L   1-3
Manninger, Dixon, Grimandi, Adams, Winterburn, Petit, Vieira, Petit, Overmars, Anelka, Bergkamp 1p, Platt/Hughes for Winterburn/Parlour

UEFA CUP

16 Sep   PAOK Salonika (1/1)   A   L   0-1
Seaman, Dixon, Bould, Adams, Winterburn, Parlour, Vieira, Petit, Overmars, Wright, Anelka,
Platt/Boa Morte/Wreh for Parlour/Overmars/Anelka

30 Sep   PAOK Salonika (1/2)   H   W   1-1
Seaman, Dixon, Bould, Adams, Winterburn, Parlour, Vieira, Petit, Overmars, Wright, Bergkamp 1,
Platt/Anelka for Parlour/Overmars

POSITION IN LEAGUE TABLE

	Pld	W	D	L	F	A	Pts
1st Arsenal	38	23	9	6	68	33	78

APPEARANCES (Goals) Adams 26(3); Anelka 26(6); Bergkamp 28(16); Boa Morte 15; Bould 24; Dixon
28; Garde 10; Grimandi 22(1); Hughes 17(2); Keown 18; Manninger 7; Marshall 3; McGowan 1;
Mendez 3; Overmars 32(12); Parlour 34(3); Petit 32(3); Platt 31(3); Rankin 1; Seaman 31; Upson 5;
Vernazza 1; Vieira 33(2); Winterburn 36(1); Wreh 16(3); Wright 24(10); o/g 1; Total 26 players (67)

SEASON 1998-1999

FA CARLING PREMIERSHIP

17 Aug   Nottingham F   H   W   2-1
Seaman, Dixon, Keown, Adams, Winterburn, Parlour, Vieira, Petit 1, Overmars 1, Anelka, Bergkamp

22 Aug   Liverpool   A   D   0-0
Seaman, Dixon, Keown, Bould, Winterburn, Parlour, Vieira, Petit, Overmars, Anelka, Bergkamp,
Vivas for Vieira

29 Aug   Charlton Ath   H   D   0-0
Seaman, Dixon, Keown, Adams, Winterburn, Parlour, Veira, Petit, Overmars, Anelka, Bergkamp,
Vivas/Wreh/Hughes for Dixon/Anelka/Vieira

9 Sep   Chelsea   A   D   0-0
Seaman, Dixon, Keown, Adams, Winterburn, Parlour, Vieira, Overmars, Anelka, Bergkamp,
Garde/Hughes/Wreh for Overmars/Anelka/Bergkamp

12 Sep   Leicester C   A   D   1-1
Seaman, Dixon, Keown, Bould, Winterburn, Parlour, Vieira, Hughes 1, Overmars, Wreh, Bergkamp,
Anelka/Garde/Vivas for Wreh, Vieira and Dixon

20 Sep   Manchester U   H   W   3-0
Seaman, Dixon, Keown, Adams 1, Winterburn, Parlour, Vieira, Hughes, Overmars, Anelka 1,
Bergkamp, Ljungberg 1 for Anelka

26 Sep   Sheffield Wed   A   L   0-1
Manninger, Vivas, Keown, Adams, Winterburn, Parlour, Vieira, Petit, Overmars, Anelka, Bergkamp,
Bould/Hughes/Ljungberg for Parlour/Petit/Overmars

4 Oct   Newcastle U   H   W   3-0
Seaman, Dixon, Keown, Adams, Winterburn, Ljungberg, Vieira, Petit, Overmars, Anelka 1,
Bergkamp 2(1p), Bould/Hughes/Mendez for Keown/Petit/Ljungberg

17 Oct   Southampton   H   D   1-1
Seaman, Dixon, Keown, Adams, Winterburn, Parlour, Vieira, Hughes, Overmars, Anelka 1,
Bergkamp, Wreh for Parlour

25 Oct   Blackburn Rov   A   W   2-1
Seaman, Dixon, Keown, Bould, Winterburn, Ljungberg, Vieira, Petit 1, Overmars, Anelka 1,
Bergkamp

31 Oct   Coventry C   A   W   1-0
Seaman, Dixon, Keown, Bould, Winterburn, Parlour, Vieira, Petit, Overmars, Anelka 1, Ljungberg,
Boa Morte/Hughes for Ljungberg/Overmars

8 Nov   Everton   H   W   1-0
Seaman, Dixon, Keown, Grimandi, Winterburn, Parlour, Vieira, Petit, Overmars, Anelka 1, Ljungberg

14 Nov   Tottenham H   H   D   0-0
Seaman, Dixon, Keown, Adams, Winterburn, Parlour, Vieira, Petit, Overmars, Anelka, Ljungberg,
Wreh/Boa Morte for Anelka/Ljungberg

21 Nov   Wimbledon   A   L   0-1
Seaman, Dixon, Keown, Adams, Winterburn, Parlour, Vieira, Petit, Overmars, Anelka, Bergkamp,
Hughes/Wreh/Ljungberg for Overmars/Bergkamp/Vieira
29 Nov   Middlesbrough   H   D   1-1
Seaman, Dixon, Keown, Bould, Winterburn, Parlour, Garde, Ljungberg, Overmars, Anelka 1, Wreh,
Vivas/Boa Morte/Caballero for Winterburn/Ljungberg/Wreh
5 Dec   Derby Co   A   D   0-0
Seaman, Dixon, Keown, Bould, Vivas, Parlour, Garde, Grimandi, Overmars, Anelka, Wreh,
Ljungberg/Boa, Morte for Garde/Wreh
13 Dec   Aston Villa   A   L   2-3
Seaman, Dixon, Keown, Bould, Vivas, Parlour, Vieira, Ljungberg, Overmars, Anelka, Bergkamp 2,
Grimandi/Boa, Morte for Parlour/Ljungberg
20 Dec   Leeds U   H   W   3-1
Manninger, Dixon, Keown, Bould, Vivas, Ljungberg, Vieira 1, Petit1, Overmars, Anelka, Bergkamp,
Grimandi/Wreh for Ljungberg 1/Overmars
26 Dec   West Ham U   H   W   1-0
Manninger, Dixon, Keown, Bould, Vivas, Parlour, Vieira, Petit, Overmars 1, Anelka, Bergkamp,
Wreh/Grimandi for Anelka/Vivas
28 Dec   Charlton Ath   A   W   1-0
Manninger, Dixon, Keown, Bould, Winterburn, Parlour, Vieira, Petit, Overmars 1p, Boa Morte,
Bergkamp, Vivas/Wreh/Grimandi for Winterburn/Boa, Morte/Bergkamp
9 Jan   Liverpool   H   D   0-0
Manninger, Dixon, Keown, Bould, Grondin, Parlour, Vieira, Petit, Overmars, Anelka, Boa, Morte,
Upson/Garde/Wreh for Bould/Overmars/Anelka
16 Jan   Nottingham F   A   W   1-0
Manninger, Dixon, Keown 1, Adams, Winterburn, Parlour, Garde, Petit, Overmars, Anelka,
Bergkamp, Vivas/Upson for Overmars/Anelka
31 Jan   Chelsea   H   W   1-0
Seaman, Dixon, Keown, Adams, Winterburn, Parlour, Garde, Petit, Overmars, Anelka, Bergkamp1,
Upson/Vivas/Diawara for Anelka/Overmars/Bergkamp
6 Feb   West Ham U   A   W   4-0
Seaman, Dixon, Keown, Adams, Winterburn, Parlour 1, Vieira, Petit, Overmars 1, Anelka 1,
Bergkamp 1
17 Feb   Manchester U   A   D   1-1
Seaman, Dixon, Bould, Adams, Winterburn, Parlour, Vieira, Hughes, Overmars, Anelka 1, Kanu,
Garde/Vivas/Diawara for Overmars/Winterburn/Kanu
20 Feb   Leicester C   H   W   5-0
Seaman, Dixon, Grimandi, Adams, Vivas, Parlour 2, Vieira, Garde, Overmars, Anelka 3, Bergkamp,
Diawara/Kanu/Hughes for Overmars/Anelka/Vieira
28 Feb   Newcastle U   A   D   1-1
Seaman, Dixon, Keown, Adams, Winterburn, Parlour, Vieira, Garde, Overmars, Anelka 1, Bergkamp,
Hughes/Upson for Garde/Overmars
9 Mar   Sheffield Wed   H   W   3-0
Seaman, Dixon, Keown, Adams, Vivas, Parlour, Vieira, Ljungberg, Overmars, Anelka, Bergkamp 2,
Diawara/Kanu 1/Petit for Anelka/Parlour/Ljungberg
13 Mar   Everton   A   W   2-0
Seaman, Dixon, Keown, Adams, Winterburn, Parlour 1, Vieira, Petit, Overmars, Anelka, Bergkamp
1p, Vivas/Upson for Overmars/Anelka
20 Mar   Coventry C   H   W   2-0
Seaman, Dixon, Keown, Adams, Winterburn, Parlour 1, Vieira, Petit, Overmars 1, Anelka,
Bergkamp, Ljungberg/Diawara/Kanu for Dixon/Anelka/Overmars
3 Apr   Southampton   A   D   0-0
Seaman, Dixon, Keown, Adams, Winterburn, Parlour, Vieira, Ljungberg, Diawara, Anelka, Kanu,
Boa, Morte/Vivas/Bould for Ljungberg/Diawara/Keown
6 Apr   Blackburn Rov   H   W   1-0
Seaman, Dixon, Keown, Adams, Winterburn, Parlour, Vieira, Vivas, Overmars, Diawara, Bergkamp
1, Kanu/Bould for Diawara/Overmars

19 Apr   Wimbledon   H   W   5-1
Seaman, Vivas, Keown, Adams, Winterburn, Parlour 1, Vieira 1, Petit, Overmars, Kanu 1, Bergkamp 1, Diawara/Bould for Bergkamp/Keown, o/g Thatcher

24 Apr   Middlesbrough   A   W   6-1
Seaman, Dixon, Bould, Adams, Winterburn, Parlour, Vieira 1, Petit, Overmars 1, Anelka 2, Kanu 2, Diawara/Vivas/Hughes for Kanu/Overmars/Petit

2 May   Derby Co   H   W   1-0
Seaman, Dixon, Bould, Adams, Winterburn, Parlour, Vieira, Petit, Overmars, Anelka 1, Kanu, Bergkamp/Hughes/Diawara for Anelka/Overmars/Kanu

5 May   Tottenham H   A   W   3-1
Seaman, Dixon, Keown, Adams, Winterburn, Parlour, Vieira, Petit 1, Overmars, Anelka 1, Bergkamp, Vivas/Kanu 1/Grimandi for Parlour/Bergkamp/Overmars

11 May   Leeds U   A   L   0-1
Seaman, Dixon, Keown, Adams, Winterburn, Parlour, Vieira, Peti, Overmars, Anelka, Bergkamp, Kanu/Diawara/Vivas for Overmars/Parlour/Winterburn

16 May   Aston Villa   H   W   1-0
Seaman, Dixon, Keown, Adams, Vivas, Parlour, Vieira, Petit, Overmars, Anelka, Bergkamp, Ljungberg/Kanu 1/Diawara for Vivas/Anelka/Overmars

APPEARANCES, LEAGUE ONLY (Goals) Adams 26(1), Anelka 35(17), Bergkamp 29(12), Boa Morte 8, Bould 19, Caballero 1, Diawara 12, Dixon 36, Garde 10, Grimandi 8, Grondin 1, Hughes 14(1), Kanu 12(6), Keown 34(1), Ljungberg 16(1), Manninger 6, Mendez 1, Overmars 37(6), Parlour 35(6), Petit 27(4), Seaman 32, Upson 5, Vieira 34(3), Vivas 23, Winterburn 30, Wreh 12, o/g 1, Total 29 players (59)

POSITION IN LEAGUE TABLE

	Pld	W	D	L	F	A	Pts
1st Manchester U	38	22	13	3	80	37	79
2nd Arsenal	38	22	12	4	59	17	78

CHARITY SHIELD
9 Aug   Manchester U   W   3-0
Seaman, Dixon, Keown, Adams, Winterburn, Parlour, Vieira, Petit, Overmars 1, Bergkamp, Anelka 1, Wreh 1/Hughes/Boa Morte/Bould/Grimandi for Bergkamp/Overmars/Petit/Adams/Vieira (at Wembley)

FA CUP
4 Jan   Preston NE (3)   A   W   4-2
Manninger, Dixon, Keown, Bould, Vivas, Parlour, Vieira, Petit 2, Overmars 1, Mendez, Boa Morte 1, Caballero/Garde for Mendez/Overmars

24 Jan   Wolverhampton W (4) A   W   2-1
Manninger, Dixon, Upson, Adams, Winterburn, Parlour, Garde, Petit, Overmars 1, Anelka, Bergkamp 1, Vivas/Grimandi/Hughes for Garde/Anelka/Overmars

13 Feb   Sheffield U (5)   H   W   2-1
Seaman, Vivas, Grimandi, Bould, Winterburn, Parlour, Vieira 1, Garde, Overmars 1, Diawara, Bergkamp, Hughes/Kanu for Garde/Diawara (declared void, but still included in club statistics)

23 Feb   Sheffield U (5)   H   W   2-1
Seaman, Vivas, Bould, Adams, Winterburn, Parlour, Vieira, Hughes, Overmars 1, Anelka, Bergkamp 1, Kanu/Garde/Diawara for Anelka/Bergkamp/Overmars

6 Mar   Derby Co (6)   H   W   1-0
Seaman, Dixon, Keown, Adams, Winterburn, Parlour, Hughes, Ljungberg, Overmars, Anelka, Bergkamp, Vivas/Kanu 1/Diawara for Ljungberg/Hughes/Overmars

11 Apr   Manchester U (SF)   D   0-0
Seaman, Dixon, Keown, Adams, Winterburn, Parlour, Vieira, Vivas, Overmars, Anelka, Bergkamp, Ljungberg/Kanu for Overmars/Anelka (at Aston Villa)

14 Apr   Manchester U (SFR)   L   1-2
Seaman, Dixon, Keown, Adams, Winterburn, Parlour, Vieira, Petit, Ljungberg, Anelka, Bergkamp 1, Overmars/Kanu/Bould for Ljungberg/Parlour/Petit (at Aston Villa)

LEAGUE (WORTHINGTON) CUP
28 Oct   Derby Co (3)   A   W   2-1
Manninger, Vivas 1, Grimandi, Upson, Grondin, Ljungberg, Garde, Mendez, Hughes, Wreh, Boa
Morte, Crowe/Riza for Upson/Wreh, o/g Carse;u
11 Nov   Chelsea (4)   H   L   0-5
Manninger, Vivas, Grimandi, Upson, Grondin, Ljungberg, Garde, Hughes, Boa Morte, Wreh,
Bergkamp, Mendez/Caballero for Garde/Bergkamp

CHAMPIONS LEAGUE
Group matches
16 Sep   Lens   A   D   1-1
Seaman, Dixon, Keown, Adams, Winterburn, Parlour, Vieira, Petit, Overmars 1, Anelka, Bergkamp,
Hughes/Garde for Petit/Bergkamp
30 Sep   Panathinaikos   H   W   2-1
Seaman, Dixon, Keown 1, Adams 1, Winterburn, Garde, Vieira, Petit, Overmars, Anelka, Bergkamp,
Vivas for Garde (at Wembley)
21 Oct   Dynamo Kiev   H   D   1-1
Seaman, Dixon, Keown, Adams, Winterburn, Parlour, Garde, Hughes, Overmars, Anelka, Bergkamp
1, Vivas for Anelka (at Wembley)
4 Nov   Dynamo Kiev   A   L   1-3
Seaman, Dixon, Keown, Bould, Winterburn, Parlour, Vieira, Petit, Vivas, Wreh, Boa, Morte,
Grimandi/Hughes 1/Garde for Bould/Vivas/Boa Morte
25 Nov   Lens   H   L   0-1
Seaman, Dixon, Keown, Adams, Winterburn, Parlour, Garde, Hughes, Overmars, Anelka, Wreh,
Bould/Vivas/Boa Morte for Adams/Garde/Wreh (at Wembley)
9 Dec   Panathinaikos   A   W   3-1
Seaman, Vivas, Upson, Bould, Grondin, Grimandi, Vernazza, Mendez 1, Boa Morte 1, Anelka 1,
Wreh, M.Black for Mendez

SEASON 1999-2000

FA CARLING PREMIERSHIP
7 Aug   Leicester C   H   W   2-1
Manninger, Dixon, Keown, Grimandi, Winterburn, Parlour, Vieira, Petit, Ljungberg, Kanu,
Bergkamp1, Henry/Overmars/Silvinho for Ljungberg/Parlour/Bergkamp (o/g F.Sinclair)
10 Aug   Derby Co   A   W   2-1
Manninger, Dixon, Keown, Upson, Winterburn, Parlour, Vieira, Petit 1, Henry, Kanu, Bergkamp 1,
Silvinho/Luzhny/Boa Morte for Parlour/Kanu/Henry
14 Aug   Sunderland   A   D   0-0
Manninger, Dixon, Keown, Upson, Silvinho, Parlour, Vieira, Petit, Henry, Kanu, Bergkamp,
Ljungberg/Boa, Morte for Petit/Bergkamp
22 Aug   Manchester U   H   L   1-2
Manninger, Dixon, Keown, Upson, Silvinho, Parlour, Vieira, Ljungberg 1, Henry, Kanu, Bergkamp,
Overmars/Suker for Kanu/Henry
25 Aug   Bradford C   H   W   2-0
Manninger, Vivas, Keown, Grimandi, Silvinho, Parlour, Vieira 1, Ljungberg, Henry, Kanu 1p,
Bergkamp, Overmars/Suker/Upson for Henry/Bergkamp/Kanu
28 Aug   Liverpool   A   L   0-2
Manninger, Dixon, Keown, Adams, Winterburn, Parlour, Vieira, Ljungberg, Overmars, Henry,
Bergkamp, Suker/Silvinho for Overmars/Parlour
11 Sept   Aston Villa   H   W   3-1
Manninger, Dixon, Keown, Adams, Winterburn, Parlour, Vieira, Grimandi, Overmars, Suker2,
Bergkamp, Silvinho/Kanu1/Henry for Suker/Bergkamp/Overmars
18 Sept   Southampton   A   W   1-0
Manninger, Dixon, Keown, Adams, Winterburn, Ljungberg, Vieira, Grimandi, Overmars, Kanu,
Bergkamp, Parlour/Henry1/Luzhny for Ljungberg/Kanu/Overmars
25 Sept   Watford   H   W   1-0
Manninger, Luzhny, Keown, Adams, Silvinho, Parlour, Vieira, Ljungberg, Overmars, Kanu 1, Henry,
Suker/Bergkamp/Vivas for Ljungberg/Henry/Kanu

3 Oct   West Ham U   A L   1-2
Seaman, Luzhny, Keown, Adams, Silvinho, Ljungberg, Vieira, Grimandi, Henry, Suker 1, Bergkamp, Overmars/Kanu for Luzhny/Henry

16 Oct   Everton   H W   4-1
Seaman, Dixon 1, Keown, Adams, Winterburn, Parlour, Vieira, Grimandi, Overmars, Suker 2, Bergkamp, Silvinho/Kanu 1/Ljungberg for Overmars/Bergkamp/Parlour

23 Oct   Chelsea   H W   3-2
Seaman, Dixon, Keown, Adams, Silvinho, Parlour, Ljungberg, Petit, Overmars, Kanu 3, Suker, Henry/Vivas/Vernazza for Ljungberg/Petit/Overmars

30 Oct   Newcastle U   H D   0-0
Seaman, Luzhny, Keown, Adams, Winterburn, Ljungberg, Vieira, Grimandi, Silvinho, Henry, Suker, Bergkamp/Overmars/Upson for Henry/Silvinho/Keown

7 Nov   Tottenham H   A L   1-2
Seaman, Dixon, Keown, Adams, Winterburn, Ljungberg, Vieira 1, Petit, Overmars, Kanu, Bergkamp, Suker/Grimandi for Kanu/Petit

20 Nov   Middlesbrough   H W   5-1
Seaman, Dixon, Grimandi, Adams, Winterburn, Parlour, Ljungberg, Petit, Overmars 3, Kanu, Bergkamp 2, Upson/Vivas/Suker for Grimandi/Dixon/Bergkamp

28 Nov   Derby Co   H W   2-1
Manninger, Luzhny, Upson, Adams, Winterburn, Parlour, Grimandi, Petit, Overmars, Henry2, Bergkamp, Kanu/Suker/Malz for Bergkamp/Henry/Overmars

4 Dec   Leicester C   A W   3-0
Manninger, Dixon1, Upson, Adams, Winterburn, Silvinho, Grimandi 1, Petit, Overmars 1, Henry, Kanu, Vivas/Hughes/Barrett for Upson/Silvinho/Henry

18 Dec   Wimbledon   H D   1-1
Manninger, Dixon, Luzhny, Grimandi, Winterburn, Silvinho, Ljungberg, Petit, Overmars, Henry 1, Kanu, Suker for Winterburn

26 Dec   Coventry C   A L   2-3
Seaman, Dixon, Keown, Adams, Winterburn, Ljungberg 1, Grimandi, Petit, Overmars, Henry, Kanu, Suker 1 for Grimandi

28 Dec   Leeds U   H W   2-0
Seaman, Luzhny, Grimandi, Adams, Silvinho, Ljungberg 1, Vieira, Petit, Overmars, Henry 1, Kanu, Suker/Winterburn for Henry/Petit

3 Jan   Sheffield Wed   A D   1-1
Seaman, Luzhny, Grimandi, Adams, Silvinho, Ljungberg, Vieira, Petit 1, Overmars, Henry, Kanu, Winterburn/Suker for Overmars/Kanu

15 Jan   Sunderland   H W   4-1
Seaman, Dixon, Keown, Luzhny, Silvinho, Parlour, Vieira, Petit, Ljungberg, Henry 2, Suker 2, Malz/Barrett for Ljungberg/Henry

24 Jan   Manchester U   A D   1-1
Seaman, Dixon, Keown, Grimandi, Silvinho, Parlour, Vieira, Petit, Ljungberg 1, Hughes, Henry, Winterburn/Malz for Silvinho/Hughes

5 Feb   Bradford C   A L   1-2
Seaman, Dixon, Keown, Grimandi, Winterburn, Parlour, Ljungberg, Petit, Malz, Henry 1, Suker, Bergkamp for Malz

13 Feb   Liverpool   H L   0-1
Seaman, Dixon, Keown, Grimandi, Silvinho, Parlour, Vieira, Petit, Ljungberg, Henry, Bergkamp, Overmars/Suker/Luzhny for Petit/Bergkamp/Ljungberg

26 Feb   Southampton   H W   3-1
Seaman, Dixon, Keown, Adams, Silvinho, Parlour, Vieira, Petit, Ljungberg 2, Bergkamp 1, Overmars for Bergkamp

5 Mar   Aston Villa   A D   1-1
Seaman, Dixon 1, Keown, Grimandi, Silvinho, Parlour, Vieira, Petit, Henry, Kanu, Bergkamp, Overmars/Luzhny/Winterburn for Bergkamp/Grimandi/Petit

12 Mar   Middlesbrough   A L   1-2
Seaman, Luzhny, Winterburn, Grimandi, Silvinho, Parlour, Vieira, Petit, Ljungberg, Henry, Kanu, Manninger/Bergkamp 1/Suker for Seaman/Ljungberg/Parlour

19 Mar   Tottenham H   H   W   2-1
Manninger, Dixon, Luzhny, Adams, Silvinho, Parlour, Vieira, Grimandi, Overmars, Henry 1, Kanu,
Ljungberg/Winterburn for Henry/Overmars [Chris Armstrong own goal]
26 Mar   Coventry C   H   W   3-0
Seaman, Dixon, Luzhny, Grimandi 1, Winterburn, Parlour, Vieira, Petit, Overmars, Henry 1,
Bergkamp, Kanu 1/Ljungberg/Suker for Bergkamp/Henry/Overmars
1 Apr   Wimbledon   A   W   3-1
Seaman, Dixon, Keown, Luzhny, Silvinho, Parlour, Vieira, Grimandi, Overmars, Kanu 2, Bergkamp,
Petit/Henry 1/Winterburn for Overmars/Kanu/Bergkamp
16 Apr   Leeds U   A   W   4-0
Seaman, Dixon, Keown 1, Adams, Silvinho, Parlour, Vieira, Petit, Ljungberg, Henry 1, Bergkamp,
Kanu 1/Overmars 1/Winterburn for Bergkamp/Henry/Petit
23 Apr   Watford   A   W   3-2
Seaman, Luzhny, Keown, Grimandi, Winterburn, Parlour 1, Vieira, Petit, Overmars, Henry 2,
Bergkamp, Silvinho for Overmars
29 Apr   Everton   A   W   1-0
Seaman, Dixon, Keown, Adams, Silvinho, Parlour, Grimandi, Petit, Overmars 1, Kanu, Bergkamp,
Vieira/Winterburn/Black for Bergkamp/Overmars/Petit
2 May   West Ham U   H   W   2-1
Seaman, Dixon, Luzhny, Adams, Silvinho, Parlour, Vieira, Grimandi, Overmars 1, Kanu, Bergkamp,
Petit 1 for Dixon
6 May   Chelsea   H   W   2-1
Seaman, Dixon, Grimandi, Adams, Silvinho, Parlour, Vieira, Petit, Overmars, Henry2, Bergkamp,
Winterburn/Kanu/Luzhny for Overmars/Bergkamp/Petit
9 May   Sheffield Wed   H   D   3-3
Seaman, Dixon 1, Keown, Luzhny, Winterburn, Parlour, Grimandi, Vieira, Overmars, Kanu, Henry 1,
Bergkamp/Silvinho 1 for Parlour/Winterburn
17 May   Newcastle U   A   L   2-4
Manninger, Luzhny, Keown, Weston, Cole, Parlour, Vernazza, Malz 1, Winterburn, Kanu 1, Suker,
Silvinho/McGovern/Gray for Parlour/Weston/Kanu

APPEARANCES (Goals) Adams 21; Barrett 2; Bergkamp 28(6); Black 1; Boa Morte 2; Cole 1; Dixon
28(4); Gray 1; Grimandi 28(2); Henry 31(17); Hughes 2; Kanu 31(12); Keown 27(1); Ljungberg 26(6);
Luzhny 21; Malz 5(1); Manninger 15; McGovern 1; Overmars 31(7); Parlour 30(1); Petit 26(3); Seaman
24; Silvinho 31(1); Suker 22(8); Upson 8; Vernazza 2; Vieira 30(2); Vivas 5; Weston 1; Winterburn 28;
own goals 2; Total 30 players (73)

POSITION IN LEAGUE TABLE

	Pld	W	D	L	F	A	Pts
1st Manchester Utd	38	28	7	3	97	45	91
2nd Arsenal	38	22	7	9	73	43	73

FA CUP
13 Dec   Blackpool (3)   H   W   3-1
Manninger, Dixon, Luzhny, Adams 1, Silvinho, Ljungberg, Grimandi 1, Petit, Overmars 1, Suker,
Henry, Kanu/Hughes for Suker/Ljungberg
9 Jan   Leicester C (4)   H   D   0-0
Seaman, Dixon, Keown, Grimandi, Silvinho, Ljungberg, Vieira, Petit, Malz, Suker, Henry, Kanu for
Malz
19 Jan   Leicester C (4R)   A   D   0-0
Seaman, Dixon, Keown, Grimandi, Silvinho, Parlour, Vieira, Petit, Malz, Suker, Henry, Hughes for
Malz (lost 6-5 on penalties aet)

WORTHINGTON CUP
12 Oct   Preston NE (3)   H   W   2-1
Seaman, Luzhny, Grimandi, Upson, Winterburn, Parlour, Vernazza, Malz 1, Silvinho, Kanu 1, Henry,
Overmars/Wreh for Vernazza/Kanu

30 Nov   Middlesbrough (4)   A   D   2-2
Manninger, Vivas, Luzhny, Upson, Silvinho, Parlour, Vernazza, Malz, Black, Suker1, Henry1,
Weston/Pennant/Cole for Luzhny/Black/Parlour (lost 3-1 on penalties aet)

CHAMPIONS LEAGUE
14 Sept   Fiorentina   A   D   0-0
Manninger, Luzhny, Keown, Adams, Winterburn, Ljungberg, Vieira, Grimandi, Overmars, Suker,
Bergkamp, Kanu/Henry for Suker/Bergkamp
22 Sept   AIK Solna   H   W   3-1
Manninger, Dixon, Keown, Adams, Winterburn, Ljungberg 1, Vieira, Grimandi, Overmars, Suker 1,
Bergkamp, Silvinho/Kanu/Henry 1 for Grimandi/Overmars/Ljungberg (at Wembley)
29 Sept   Barcelona   A   D   1-1
Mannigner, Dixon, Keown, Adams, Winterburn, Parlour, Vieira, Grimandi, Overmars, Kanu 1,
Bergkamp, Suker/Henry/Ljungberg for Bergkamp/Parlour/Overmars
19 Oct   Barcelona   H   L   2-4
Seaman, Dixon, Keown, Adams, Winterburn, Ljungberg, Vieira, Parlour, Overmars 1, Kanu,
Bergkamp 1, Upson/Suker/Henry for Keown/Kanu/Ljungberg (at Wembley)
27 Oct   Fiorentina   H   L   0-1
Seaman, Dixon, Keown, Adams, Winterburn, Parlour, Vieira, Petit, Overmars, Kanu, Bergkamp,
Ljungberg/Vivas/Suker for Parlour/Petit/Dixon
2 Nov   AIK Solna   A   W   3-2
Manninger, Dixon, Luzhny, Upson, Winterburn, Ljungberg, Vieira, Petit, Overmars 2, Kanu, Suker 1,
Vivas/Malz/Hughes for Luzhny/Petit/Suker (at Wembley)

UEFA CUP
25 Nov   Nantes (1/1)   H   W   3-0
Seaman, Vivas, Grimandi, Adams, Winterburn 1, Ljungberg, Vieira, Petit, Overmars 1, Kanu,
Bergkamp 1, Parlour/Suker/Henry for Petit/Ljungberg/Kanu
9 Dec   Nantes (1/2)   A   D   3-3
Manninger, Dixon, Grimandi 1, Adams, Winterburn, Ljungberg, Vieira, Petit, Overmars 1, Kanu,
Henry 1, Silvinho/Vivas/Suker for Overmars/Ljungberg/Henry
2 Mar   Dep'vo La Coruna (2/1) H   W   5-1
Seaman, Dixon 1, Keown, Luzhny, Silvinho, Ljungberg, Grimandi, Overmars, Henry 2, Bergkamp 1,
Kanu 1/Suker/Parlour for Overmars/Henry/Bergkamp
9 Mar   Dep'vo La Coruna (2/2) A   L   1-2
Seaman, Dixon, Luzhny, Winterburn, Silvinho, Parlour, Vieira, Petit, Ljungberg, Henry 1, Kanu,
Suker/Malz/Vernazza for Henry/Kanu/Winterburn
16 Mar   Werder Bremen (3/1)   H   W   2-0
Seaman, Dixon, Luzhny, Adams, Silvinho, Parlour, Vieira, Grimandi, Ljungberg 1, Henry 1,
Bergkamp, Kanu/Overmars/Suker for Parlour/Bergkamp/Henry
23 Mar   Werder Bremen (3/2)   A   W   4-2
Manninger, Dixon, Adams, Silvinho, Parlour 3, Vieira, Grimandi, Ljungberg, Henry 1, Kanu,
Petit/Overmars/Winterburn for Adams/Kanu/Vieira
6 Apr   Lens (SF/1)   H   W   1-0
Seaman, Dixon, Keown, Grimandi, Silvinho, Parlour, Vieira, Petit, Overmars, Kanu, Bergkamp 1,
Ljungberg/Suker for Overmars/Bergkamp
20 Apr   Lens (SF/2)   A   W   2-1
Seaman, Dixon, Keown, Adams, Silvinho, Parlour, Vieira, Petit, Ljungberg, Henry 1, Bergkamp,
Kanu1/Overmars/Grimandi for Bergkamp/Ljungberg/Henry
17 May   Galatasaray (F)   0-0
Seaman, Dixon, Keown, Adams, Silvinho, Parlour, Vieira, Petit, Overmars, Henry, Bergkamp,
Kanu/Suker for Bergkamp/Overmars (in Copenhagen, lost 4-1 on penalties aet)

SEASON 2000-2001

FA CARLING PREMIERSHIP
19 Aug   Sunderland   A   L   0-1
Seaman, Dixon, Keown, Adams, Silvinho, Parlour, Grimandi, Vieira, Ljungberg, Henry, Kanu,
Pires/Bergkamp/Lauren for Ljungberg/Grimandi/Dixon

21 Aug   Liverpool   H   W   2-0
Seaman, Luzhny, Keown, Adams, Silvinho, Lauren 1, Grimandi, Vieira, Pires, Henry 1, Bergkamp, Kanu for Bergkamp

26 Aug   Charlton Ath   H   W   5-3
Seaman, Dixon, Keown, Adams, Silvinho 1, Lauren, Grimandi, Vieira 2, Pires, Henry 2, Kanu, Bergkamp for Lauren

6 Sept   Chelsea   A   D   2-2
Seaman, Dixon, Keown, Luzhny, Silvinho 1, Lauren, Grimandi, Parlour, Pires, Henry 1, Kanu, Bergkamp/Wiltord/Ljungberg for Dixon/Parlour/Pires

9 Sept   Bradford C   A   D   1-1
Seaman, Dixon, Keown, Luzhny, Cole 1, Parlour, Grimandi, Ljungberg, Pires, Henry, Wiltord, Kanu for Wiltord

16 Sept   Coventry C   H   W   2-1
Seaman, Luzhny, Keown, Adams, Silvinho, Parlour, Grimandi, Ljungberg, Pires, Bergkamp, Wiltord 1, Henry/Vernazza 1/Kanu for Wiltord/Parlour/Bergkamp

23 Sept   Ipswich T   A   D   1-1
Seaman, Vivas, Keown, Luzhny, Silvinho, Parlour, Grimandi, Ljungberg, Bergkamp 1, Henry, Wiltord, Kanu/Vernazza for Wiltord/Grimandi

1 Oct   Manchester U   H   W   1-0
Seaman, Luzhny, Keown, Adams, Silvinho, Parlour, Grimandi, Ljungberg, Bergkamp, Henry 1, Kanu, Vivas/Wiltord for Kanu/Bergkamp

14 Oct   Aston Villa   H   W   1-0
Seaman, Dixon, Grimandi, Adams, Silvinho, Lauren, Parlour, Vieira, Bergkamp, Henry 1, Pires, Wiltord/Kanu/Luzhny for Henry/Pires/Bergkamp

21 Oct   West Ham U   A   W   2-1
Seaman, Lauren, Keown, Luzhny, Silvinho, Ljungberg, Grimandi, Vieira, Bergkamp, Wiltord, Pires 1, Parlour/Henry/Kanu for Ljungberg/Wiltord/Bergkamp, o/g Ferdinand

28 Oct   Manchester C   H   5-0
Lukic, Luzhny, Keown, Adams, Cole 1, Parlour, Grimandi, Vieira, Bergkamp 1, Henry 2, Pires, Ljungberg/Wiltord 1 for Pires/Parlour

4 Nov   Middlesbrough   A   W   1-0
Lukic, Dixon, Keown, Adams, Silvinho, Parlour, Grimandi, Vieira, Ljungberg, Henry 1p, Bergkamp, Lauren for Bergkamp

11 Nov   Derby Co   H   D   0-0
Lukic, Luzhny, Keown, Grimandi1, Silvinho, Ljungberg, Parlour, Vieira, Bergkamp, Henry, Wiltord, Dixon/Kanu for Grimandi/Ljungberg

18 Nov   Everton   A   L   0-2
Manninger, Dixon, Keown, Luzhny, Cole, Ljungberg, Pires, Parlour, Bergkamp, Kanu, Wiltord, Upson for Dixon

26 Nov   Leeds U   A   L   0-1
Manninger, Luzhny, Keown, Adams, Silvinho, Lauren, Parlour, Vieira, Pires, Henry, Wiltord, Kanu for Silvinho

2 Dec   Southampton   H   W   1-0
Manninger, Luzhny, Keown, Adams, Silvinho, Ljungberg, Grimandi, Vieira, Bergkamp, Wiltord, Pires, Dixon/Henry/Kanu for Silvinho/Wiltord/Pires, o/g Lunderkvam

9 Dec   Newcastle U   H   W   5-0
Manninger, Dixon, Keown, Adams, Vivas, Ljungberg, Grimandi, Parlour 3, Pires, Henry 1, Kanu 1, Lauren/Bergkamp/Luzhny for Grimand/Kanu/Ljungberg

18 Dec   Tottenham H   A   D   1-1
Manninger, Dixon, Keown, Adams, Silvinho, Ljungberg, Grimandi, Parlour, Pires, Henry, Kanu, Vieira 1/Bergkamp/Wiltord for Grimandi/Pires/Kanu

23 Dec   Liverpool   A   L   0-4
Manninger, Dixon, Keown, Luzhny, Silvinho, Parlour, Grimandi, Vieira, Ljungberg, Henry, Bergkamp, Pires,/Wiltord/Kanu for Luzhny/Ljungberg/Bergkamp

26 Dec   Leicester C   H   W   6-1
Manninger, Dixon, Stepanovs, Adams 1, Silvinho, Parlour, Grimandi, Vieira 1, Pires, Henry 3, Kanu, Ljungberg 1/Vivas/Cole for Kanu/Grimandi/Pires

30 Dec   Sunderland   H   D   2-2

Manninger, Dixon 1, Stepanovs, Adams, Silvinho, Grimandi, Vieira 1, Ljungberg, Pires, Henry, Kanu, Parlour/Danilievicius for Kanu/Henry

1 Jan   Charlton Ath   A   L   0-1
Manninger, Dixon, Stepanovs, Grimandi, Silvinho, Parlour, Vivas, Vieira, Pires, Ljumgberg, Kanu, Danilievicius/Cole/Malz for Pires/Silvinho/Grimandi

13 Jan   Chelsea   H   D   1-1
Seaman, Dixon, Stepanovs, Keown, Silvinho, Ljungberg, Parlour, Vieira, Pires 1, Henry, Wiltord, Vivas for Ljungberg

20 Jan   Leicester C   A   D   0-0
Seaman, Dixon, Keown, Adams, Silvinho, Ljungberg, Parlour, Vieira, Pires, Henry, Wiltord, Edu for Ljungberg/Bergkamp for Edu

30 Jan   Bradford C   H   W   2-0
Seaman, Dixon, Stepanovs, Adams, Cole, Lauren 1, Parlour 1, Vieira, Pires, Henry, Bergkamp, Grimandi/Kanu for Lauren/Bergkamp

3 Feb   Coventry C   A   W   1-0
Seaman, Dixon, Stepanovs, Adams, Cole, Lauren, Parlour, Vieira, Pires, Wiltord, Bergkamp 1, Grimandi/Vivas for Lauren/Pires

10 Feb   Ipswich T   H   W   1-0
Seaman, Dixon, Stepanovs, Adams, Cole, Lauren, Parlour, Grimandi, Pires, Wiltord, Bergkamp, Henry 1/Ljungberg for Lauren/Wiltord

25 Feb   Manchester U   A   L   1-6
Seaman, Luzhny, Stepanovs, Grimandi, Cole, Silvinho, Parlour, Viiera, Pires, Henry 1, Wiltord, Ljungberg/Vivas for Cole/Parlour

3 Mar   West Ham U   H   W   3-0
Seaman, Dixon, Grimandi, Adams, Cole, Ljungberg, Lauren, Vieira, Pires, Wiltord 3, Bergkamp, Vivas/Henry/Edu for Cole/Wiltord/Pires

18 Mar   Aston Villa   A   D   0-0
Manninger, Dixon, Grimandi, Luzhny, Silvinho, Ljungberg, Lauren, Vieira, Parlour, Wiltord, Bergkamp, Pires/Henry/Vivas for Ljungberg/Wiltord/Parlour

31 Mar   Tottenham H   H   W   2-0
Seaman, Dixon, Keown, Adams, Cole, Lauren, Parlour, Vieira, Pires1, Henry1, Wiltord, Kanu/Luzhny for Lauren/Dixon

11 Apr   Manchester C   A   W   4-0
Seaman, Luzhny, Stepanovs, Keown, Cole, Lauren, Parlour, Edu, Ljungberg 2, Wiltord 1, Kanu 1, Vieira/Henry/Vivas for Edu/Wiltord/Parlour

14 Apr   Middlesbrough   H   L   0-3
Seaman, Dixon, Keown, Adams, Silvinho, Ljungberg, Vieira, Edu, Pires, Henry, Kanu, Wiltord/Parlour for Edu/Ljungberg

21 Apr   Everton   H   W   4-1
Seaman, Dixon, Keown, Adams, Cole, Ljungberg1, Grimandi1, Vieira, Pires, Henry1, Wiltord1, Vivas/Silvinho for Grimandi/Pires

28 Apr   Derby `Co   A   W   2-1
Seaman, Dixon, Keown, Adams, Cole, Lauren, Grimandi, Vieira, Ljungberg, Wiltord, Kanu 1, Henry/Pires 1/Parlour for Lauren/Ljungberg and Kanu

5 May   Leeds U   H   W   2-1
Seaman, Dixon, Keown, Adams, Cole, Ljungberg 1, Grimandi, Vieira, Pires, Henry, Wiltord 1, Parlour for Wiltord

15 May   Newcastle U   A   D   0-0
Seaman, Dixon, Keown, Adams, Cole, Lauren, Parlour, Vieira, Pires, Henry, Bergkamp, Kanu for Bergkamp

18 May   Southampton   A   L   2-3
Manninger, Grimandi, Keown, Adams, Cole 1, Ljungberg 1, Parlour, Vieira, Pires, Henry, Bergkamp, Kanu/Edu/Upson for Bergkamp/Ljungberg/Pires

POSITION IN LEAGUE TABLE

	Pld	W	D	L	F	A	Pts
1st Manchester U	38	24	8	6	79	31	80
2nd Arsenal	38	20	10	8	63	38	70

APPEARANCES (Goals) Adams 26(1); Bergkamp 25(3); Cole 17(3); Danilievicius 2; Dixon 29(1); Edu 5; Grimandi 30(1); Henry 35(17); Kanu 27(3); Keown 28; Lauren 18(2); Ljungberg 31(6); Lukic 3; Luzhny 19; Malz 1; Manninger 11; Parlour 33(4); Pires 33(4); Seaman 24; Silvinho 24(2); Stepanovs 9; Upson 2; Vernazza 2(1); Vieira 30(5); Vivas 12; Wiltord 27(8); o/g 2; Total 26 players (63)

WORTHINGTON LEAGUE CUP
1 Nov   Ipswich T (3)   H   L   1-2
Taylor, Weston, Stepanovs 1, Upson, Cole, Vivas, Pennant, Vernazza, Barrett, Wiltord, Volz, Mendez,/Wreh/Canoville for Pennant/Volz/Weston

FA CUP
6 Jan   Carlisle U (3)   A   W   1-0
Manninger, Dixon, Stepanovs, Vivas, Cole, Ljungberg, Vieira, Parlour, Pires, Bergkamp, Wiltord1, Silvinho/Danilievicius/Malz for Ljungberg/Wiltord/Cole
27 Jan   QPR (4)   A   W   6-0
Seaman, Dixon, Stepanovs, Adams, Cole, Lauren, Vieira, Parlour, Pires 1, Bergkamp 1, Wiltord 2, Grimandi/Malz/Vivas for Lauren/Pires/Vieira (o/gs Plummer, Rose)
18 Feb   Chelsea (5)   H   W   3-1
Seaman, Dixon, Stepanovs, Luzhny, Cole, Lauren, Vieira, Ljungberg, Pires, Henry 1p, Bergkamp, Wiltord 2/Vivas for Pires/Bergkamp
10 Mar   Blackburn Rov (6)   H   W   3-0
Seaman, Dixon, Luzhny, Adams 1, Cole, Lauren, Grimandi, Ljungberg, Pires 1, Bergkamp, Wiltord 1, Silvinho/Vieira/Henry for Ljungberg/Pires/Bergkamp
8 Apr   Tottenham H (SF)   W   2-1
Seaman, Dixon, Keown, Adams, Silvinho, Lauren, Vieira 1, Parlour, Pires 1, Henry, Wiltord, Ljungberg/Cole for Pires/Wiltord (at Manchester U)
12 May   Liverpool (F)   L   1-2
Seaman, Dixon, Keown, Adams, Cole, Ljungberg 1, Vieira, Grimandi, Pires, Henry, Wiltord, Parlour/Kanu/Bergkamp for Wiltord/Ljungberg/Dixon (in Cardiff)

CHAMPIONS LEAGUE
First Group Phase
12 Sept Sparta Prague   A   W   1-0
Seaman, Dixon, Keown, Luzhny, Silvinho 1, Ljungberg, Vieira, Grimandi, Pires, Henry, Kanu, Wiltord/Vivas for Henry/Ljungberg
20 Sept Shakhtar Donetsk   H   W   3-2
Seaman, Dixon, Keown 2, Luzhny, Silvinho, Ljungberg, Vieira, Grimandi, Pires, Henry, Kanu, Wiltord 1/Bergkamp for Pires/Ljungberg
27 Sept Lazio   H   W   2-0
Seaman, Luzhny, Keown, Adams, Silvinho, Ljungberg 2, Vieira, Parlour, Bergkamp, Henry, Kanu, Vivas/Wiltord for Bergkamp/Henry
17 Oct   Lazio   A   D   1-1
Lukic, Dixon, Keown, Luzhny, Silvinho, Ljungberg, Vieira, Grimandi, Parlour, Henry, Kanu, Pires 1/Lauren/Wiltord for Parlour/Grimandi/Ljungberg
25 Oct   Sparta Prague   H   W   4-2
Seaman, Dixon 1, Vivas, Luzhny, Silvinho, Lauren 1, Vieira, Parlour 1, Pires, Henry, Kanu 1, Cole/Bergkamp/Wiltord for Silvinho/Pires/Henry
7 Nov   Shakhtar Donetsk   A   L   0-3
Taylor, Dixon, Keown, Upson, Cole, Lauren, Parlour, Vivas, Wiltord, Henry, Kanu, Ljungberg/Vernazza for Henry/Parlour

SECOND GROUP PHASE
22 Nov   Spartak Moscow   A   L   1-4
Manninger, Luzhny, Keown, Adams, Silvinho 1, Ljungberg, Vivas, Parlour, Pires, Henry, Kanu, Wiltord/Lauren for Kanu/Pires
5 Dec   Bayern Munich   H   D   2-2
Manninger, Luzhny, Keown, Adams, Cole, Ljungberg, Vieira, Grimandi, Pires, Henry 1, Kanu 1, Wiltord/Lauren for Pires/Luzhny

13 Feb   Lyons   A   W   1-0
Seaman, Dixon, Grimandi, Adams, Cole, Lauren, Vieira, Parlour, Pires, Henry 1, Kanu, Ljungberg/Vivas for Pires/Kanu

21 Feb   Lyons   H   D   1-1
Seaman, Dixon, Grimandi, Luzhny, Cole, Ljungberg, Vieira, Parlour, Pires, Henry, Bergkamp 1, Wiltord/Lauren/Kanu for Bergkamp/Pires/Henry

6 Mar   Spartak Moscow   H   W   1-0
Seaman, Dixon, Grimandi, Adams, Cole, Ljungberg, Lauren, Vieira, Pires, Henry 1, Bergkamp, Wiltord/Kanu/Vivas for Pires/Bergkamp/Henry

14 Mar   Bayern Munich   A   L   0-1
Seaman, Dixon, Grimandi, Adams, Cole, Ljungberg, Lauren, Vieira, Pires, Henry, Kanu, Wiltord/Parlour/Silvinho for Kanu/Ljungberg/Pires

4 Apr   Valencia (QF/1)   H   W   2-1
Seaman, Dixon, Keown, Adams, Cole, Ljungberg, Vieira, Parlour 1, Pires, Henry 1, Kanu, Wiltord/Lauren for Ljungberg/Kanu

17 Apr   Valencia (QF/2)   A   L   0-1
Seaman, Dixon, Keown, Adams, Cole, Lauren, Vieira, Parlour, Pires, Henry, Wiltord, Ljungberg/Kanu for Parlour/Pires

SEASON 2001-2002

FA BARCLAYCARD PREMIERSHIP

18 Aug   Middlesbrough   A   W   4-0
Seaman, Lauren, Campbell, Adams, Cole, Parlour, Pires 1p, Vieira, Ljungberg, Henry 1, Wiltord, Bergkamp 2/Grimandi/Van Bronckhorst for Henry/Ljungberg/Wiltord

21 Aug   Leeds U   H   L   1-2
Seaman, Lauren, Campbell, Adams, Cole, Parlour, Pires, Vieira, Ljungberg, Henry, Wiltord 1, Bergkamp/Jeffers/Van Bronckhorst for Parlour/Wiltord/Ljungberg

25 Aug   Leicester C   H   W   4-0
Seaman, Lauren, Campbell, Adams, Cole, Ljungberg 1, Vieira, Van Bronckhorst, Pires, Bergkamp, Wiltord 1, Grimandi/Henry 1/Kanu 1 for Ljungberg/Wiltord/Bergkamp

8 Sept   Chelsea   A   D   1-1
Seaman, Lauren, Keown, Adams, Cole, Wiltord, Grimandi, Van Bronckhorst, Pires, Bergkamp, Henry 1, Kanu/Ljungberg/Campbell for Bergkamp/Wiltord/Adams

15 Sept   Fulham   A   W   3-1
Seaman, Lauren, Campbell, Keown, Cole, Parlour, Pires, Vieira, Ljungberg 1, Henry 1, Jeffers, Bergkamp 1/Wiltord/Grimandi for Jeffers/Pires/Henry

22 Sept   Bolton W   H   D   1-1
Seaman, Luzhny, Grimandi, Adams, Cole, Parlour, Vieira, Van Bronckhorst, Bergkamp, Henry, Wiltord, Upson/Jeffers 1/Piros for Grimandi/Van Bronckhorst/Parlour

29 Sept   Derby Co   A   W   2-0
Wright, Lauren, Upson, Keown, Cole, Ljungberg, Vieira, Van Bronckhorst, Pires, Henry 2 (1p), Jeffers, Kanu/Luzhny/Grimandi for Jeffers/Ljungberg/Henry

13 Oct   Southampton   A   W   2-0
Wright, Lauren, Campbell, Upson, Cole, Ljungberg, Vieira, Van Bronckhorst, Pires 1, Henry 1, Wiltord, Bergkamp/Parlour/Grimandi for Wiltord/Ljungberg/Van Bronckhorst

20 Oct   Blackburn Rov   H   D   3-3
Wright, Lauren, Keown, Upson, Van Bronckhorst, Parlour, Vieira, Grimandi, Pires 1, Henry 1, Bergkamp 1, Wiltord/Kanu for Pires/Parlour

27 Oct   Sunderland   A   D   1-1
Wright, Lauren, Campebll, Keown, Upson, Parlour, Vieira, Van Bronckhorst, Ljungberg, Kanu 1, Wiltord, Henry/Bergkamp for Wiltord/Kanu

4 Nov   Charlton Ath   H   L   2-4
Wright, Lauren, Keown, Grimandi, Cole, Ljungberg, Vieira, Van Bronckhorst, Pires, Henry 2(1p), Bergkamp, Wiltord for Cole

17 Nov   Tottenham H   A   D   1-1
Wright, Lauren, Campbell, Keown, Cole, Parlour, Vieira, Grimandi, Pires 1, Bergkamp, Wiltord, Kanu for Bergkamp

25 Nov Manchester U   H   W   3-1
Taylor, Lauren, Campbell, Upson, Cole, Parlour, Vieira, Pires, Ljungberg 1, Henry 2, Kanu,
Bergkamp/Grimandi for Kanu/Pires
1 Dec Ipswich T   A   W   2-0
Taylor, Lauren, Campbell, Upson, Cole, Parlour, Vieira, Pires, Ljungberg 1, Henry 1p, Kanu,
Bergkamp/Van Bronckhorst/Edu for Kanu/Pires/Ljungberg
9 Dec Aston Villa   H   W   3-2
Taylor, Lauren, Campbell, Upson, Cole, Parlour, Vieira, Pires, Ljungberg, Henry 2, Bergkamp,
Keown/Wiltord 1/Kanu for Upson/Ljungberg/Bergkamp
15 Dec West Ham U   A   D   1-1
Taylor, Lauren, Campbell, Keown, Cole 1, Grimandi, Vieira, Pires, Bergkamp, Henry, Wiltord,
Edu/Kanu for Wiltord/Pires
18 Dec Newcastle U   H   L   1-3
Taylor, Lauren, Campell, Keown, Cole, Parlour, Vieira, Pires 1, Kanu, Henry, Wiltord, Van
Bronckhorst/Bergkamp for Kanu/Wiltord
23 Dec Liverpool   A   W   2-1
Taylor, Lauren, Campbell, Keown, Cole, Parlour, Pires, Van Bronckhorst, Ljungberg 1, Henry 1p,
Kanu, Upson/Luzhny/Wiltord for Pires/Kanu/Henry
26 Dec Chelsea   H   W   2-1
Taylor, Lauren, Campbell 1, Keown, Cole, Parlour, Vieira, Pires, Ljungberg, Henry, Kanu, Van
Bronckhorst/Wiltord 1/Bergkamp for Parlour/Ljungberg/Kanu
29 Dec Middlesbrough   H   W   2-1
Taylor, Luzhny, Campbell, Keown, Cole 1, Ljungberg, Vieira, Van Bronckhorst, Pires 1, Henry, Kanu,
Bergkamp/Wiltord/Grimandi for Kanu/Ljungberg/Henry
13 Jan Liverpool   H   D   1-1
Taylor, Luzhny, Campbell, Keown, Upson, Ljungberg 1, Vieira, Grimandi, Pires, Henry, Kanu,
Bergkamp/Wiltord/Dixon for Kanu/Pires/Luzhny
20 Jan Leeds U   A   D   1-1
Wright, Luzhny, Campbell, Keown, Cole, Parlour, Vieira, Pires 1, Ljungberg, Henry, Bergkamp, Van
Bronckhorst/Wiltord/Dixon for Ljungberg/Bergkamp/Luzhny
23 Jan Leicester C   A   W   3-1
Wright, Luzhny, Campbell, Keown, Cole, Parlour, Vieira, Van Bronckhorst 1, Pires, Henry 1,
Bergkamp, Grimandi/Wiltord 1/Upson for Parlour/Bergkamp/Van Bronckhorst
30 Jan Blackburn Rov   A   W   3-2
Wright, Luzhny, Campbell, Keown, Cole, Parlour, Vieira, Pires, Wiltord, Henry 1, Bergkamp 2, Van
Bronckhorst/Upson/Grimandi for Wiltord/Keown/Pires
2 Feb Southampton   H   D   1-1
Wright, Luzhny, Campbell, Upson, Cole, Parlour, Vieira, Pires, Wiltord 1, Henry, Bergkamp, Van
Bronckhorst/Grimandi/Edu for Vieira/Cole/Bergkamp
10 Feb Everton   A   W   1-0
Wright, Luzhny, Campbell, Stepanovs, Upson, Parlour, Vieira, Grimandi, Van Bronckhorst, Henry,
Wiltord 1, Dixon for Upson
23 Feb Fulham   H   W   4-1
Seaman, Luzhny, Campbell, Stepanovs, Van Bronckhorst, Parlour, Vieira 1, Pires, Lauren 1, Henry 2,
Wiltord, Dixon/Grimandi/Aladiere for Van Bronckhorst/Pires/Henry
2 Mar Newcastle U   A   W   2-0
Seaman, Dixon, Campbell 1, Stepanovs, Luzhny, Lauren, Vieira, Grimandi, Pires, Bergkamp 1,
Wiltord, Kanu/Edu for Bergkamp/Wiltord
5 Mar Derby Co   H   W   1-0
Seaman, Lauren, Campbell, Stepanovs, Luzhny, Parlour, Vieira, Pires 1, Wiltord, Henry, Bergkamp,
Dixon/Edu for Luzhny/Wiltord
17 Mar Aston Villa   A   W   2-1
Seaman, Lauren, Campbell, Stepanovs, Luzhny, Ljungberg, Vieira, Edu 1, Pires 1, Bergkamp,
Wiltord, Dixon/Grimandi/Kanu for Stepanovs/Ljungberg/Bergkamp
30 Mar Sunderland   H   W   3-0
Seaman, Luzhny, Campbell, Adams, Cole, Wiltord 1, Vieira 1, Edu, Ljungberg, Bergkamp 1, Henry,
Grimandi/Jeffers/Kanu for Wiltord/Ljungberg/Bergkamp

1 Apr   Charlton Ath   A   W   3-0
Seaman, Dixon, Campbell, Keown, Cole, Wiltord, Vieira, Grimandi, Ljungberg 1, Bergkamp, Henry 2, Luzhny/Edu for Cole/Bergkamp

6 Apr   Tottenham H   H   W   2-1
Seaman, Lauren 1p, Campbell, Adams, Luzhny, Wiltord, Vieira, Edu, Ljungberg 1, Bergkamp, Henry, Dixon/Parlour/Kanu/Dixon for Bergkamp/Edu/Wiltord

21 Apr   Ipswich T   H   W   2-0
Seaman, Lauren, Keown, Adams, Cole, Parlour, Vieira, Edu, Ljungberg 2, Bergkamp, Henry, Kanu/Grimandi for Edu/Bergkamp

24 Apr   West Ham U   H   W   2-0
Seaman, Lauren, Keown, Adams, Cole, Parlour, Vieira, Edu, Ljungberg 1, Bergkamp, Henry, Kanu 1/Grimandi/Dixon for Edu/Bergkamp/Lungberg

29 Apr   Bolton W   A   W   2-0
Seaman, Lauren, Keown, Adams, Cole, Parlour, Vieira, Edu, Ljungberg 1, Bergkamp, Wiltord 1, Dixon/Kanu/Campbell for Edu/BergkampWiltord

8 May   Manchester U   A   W   1-0
Seaman, Lauren, Campbell, Keown, Cole, Parlour, Vieira, Edu, Ljungberg, Kanu, Wiltord 1, Dixon for Kanu

11 May   Everton   H   W   4-3
Wright, Dixon, Stepanovs, Luzhny, Cole, Parlour, Grimandi, Edu, Wiltord, Bergkamp 1, Henry 2, Jeffers 1/Vieira/Taylor for Wiltord/Parlour/Wright

POSITION IN LEAGUE TABLE

	Pld	W	D	L	F	A	Pts
1st Arsenal	38	26	9	3	79	36	87

APPEARANCES (Goals) Adams 10; Aladiere 1; Bergkamp 33(9); Campbell 31(2); Cole 29(2); Dixon 13; Edu 14(1); Grimandi 26; Henry 33(24); Jeffers 6(2); Kanu 23(3); Keown 22; Lauren 27(2); Ljungberg 25(12); Luzhny 18; Parlour 27; Pires 28(9); Seaman 17; Stepanovs 6; Taylor 10; Upson 14; Van Bronckhorst 21(1); Vieira 36(2); Wiltord 33(10); Wright 12; Total 25 players (79)

FA CUP

5 Jan   Watford (3)   A   W   4-2
Taylor, Luzhny, Campbell, Keown, Cole, Ljungberg 1, Vieira, Van Bronckhorst, Pires, Henry 1, Kanu 1, Wiltord/Bergkamp 1 for Henry/Kanu

27 Jan   Liverpool (4)   H   W   1-0
Wright, Luzhny, Campbell, Keown, Cole, Wiltord, Vieira, Van Bronckhorst, Pires, Henry, Bergkamp 1, Parlour/Upson/Grimandi for Pires/Wiltord/Van Bronckhorst

16 Feb   Gillingham (5)   H   W   5-2
Wright, Dixon, Campbell, Adams 1, Juan, Parlour 1, Vieira, Edu, Wiltord 2, Jeffers, Kanu 1, Henry/Pires/Grimandi for Jeffers/Edu/Kanu

9 Mar   Newcastle U (6)   A   D   1-1
Wright, Dixon, Campbell, Stepanovs, Lauren, Ljungberg, Vieira, Grimandi, Edu 1, Wiltord, Kanu, Pires/Bergkamp for Ljungberg/Edu

23 Mar   Newcastle U (6R)   H   W   3-0
Wright, Luzhny, Campbell 1, Adams, Cole, Ljungberg, Vieira, Edu, Pires 1, Bergkamp 1, Wiltord, Grimandi/Jeffers/Dixon for Pires/Edu/Wiltord

14 Apr   Middlesbrough (SF)   W   1-0
Wright, Lauren, Campbell, Keown, Luzhny, Wiltord, Vieira, Edu, Ljungberg, Bergkamp, Henry, Dixon/Parlour/Kanu for Luzhny/Campbell/Bergkamp, o/g Festa (at Manchester U)

4 May   Chelsea (F)   W   2-0
Seaman, Lauren, Campebll, Adams, Cole, Wiltord, Parlour 1, Vieira, Ljungberg 1, Bergkamp, Henry, Edu/Kanu/Keown for Bergkamp/Henry/Wiltord (in Cardiff)

LEAGUE CUP

5 Nov   Manchester U (3)   H   W   4-0
Wright, Luzhny, Tavlaridis, Stepanovs, Van Bronckhorst, Parlour, Grimandi, Edu, Pennant, Kanu 1p, Wiltord 3(1p), Halls/Ricketts/Itonga for Van Bronckhorst/Pennant/Grimandi

27 Nov   Grimsby T (4)   H   W   2-0

Taylor, Tavlaridis, Keown, Stepanovs, Juan, Inamoto, Van Bronckhorst, Edu 1, Pennant, Bergkamp, Wiltord 1, Svart/Aladiere/Halls for Pennant/Van Bronckhorst/Inamoto

11 Dec   Blackburn Rov (5)   A   L   0-4

Taylor, Tavlaridis, Keown, Upson, Van Bronckhorst, Inamoto, Grimandi, Edu, Pennant, Kanu, Wiltord, Stepanovs/Aladiere/Halls for Inamoto/Pennant/Tavlaridis

CHAMPIONS LEAGUE
First Group Phase

11 Sept   Mallorca   A   L   0-1

Seaman, Lauren, Campbell, Keown, Cole, Ljungberg, Vieira, Van Bronckhorst, Pires, Henry, Wiltord, Kanu/Jeffers/Parlour for Ljungberg/Wiltord/Pires

19 Sept   Schalke   H   W   3-2

Seaman, Lauren, Grimandi, Keown, Van Bronckhorst, Parlour, Vieira, Pires, Ljungberg 1, Henry 2(1p), Wiltord, Bergkamp/Inamoto/Upson for Wiltord/Pires/Henry

26 Sept   Panathinaikos   A   L   0-1

Seaman, Lauren, Keown, Upson, Cole, Parlour, Vieira, Pires, Ljungberg, Henry, Wiltord, Van Bronckhorst/Jeffers/Kanu for Parlour/Wiltord/Ljungberg

16 Oct   Panathinaikos   H   W   2-1

Wright, Lauren, Campbell, Upson, Cole, Ljungberg, Vieira, Van Bronckhorst, Pires, Henry 2(1p), Wiltord, Parlour/Bergkamp/Grimandi for Pires/Wiltord/Henry

24 Oct   Mallorca   H   W   3-1

Wright, Lauren, Campbell, Keown, Van Bronckhorst, Ljungberg, Vieira, Grimandi, Pires 1, Henry 1, Bergkamp 1, Wiltord/Kanu/Parlour for Bergkamp/Grimandi/Ljungberg

30 Oct   Schalke   A   L   1-3

Wright, Luzhny, Campbell, Upson, Cole, Parlour, Edu, Grimandi Pires, Kanu, Wiltord 1, Stepanovs/Keown/Pennant for Upson/Campbell/Kanu

SECOND GROUP PHASE

21 Nov   Dep'vo La Coruna   A   L   0-2

Wright, Lauren, Campbell, Upson, Cole, Vieira, Pires, Ljungberg, Henry, Wiltord, Taylor/Kanu/Edu for Wright/Wiltord/Van Bronckhorst

4 Dec   Juventus   H   W   3-1

Taylor, Lauren, Campbell, Upson, Cole, Parlour, Vieira, Pires, Ljungberg 2, Henry 1, Kanu, Bergkamp/Grimandi/Keown for Kanu/Henry/Cole

19 Feb   Bayer Leverkusen   A   D   1-1

Seaman, Lauren, Campbell, Stepanovs, Van Bronckhorst, Parlour, Vieira, Pires 1, Kanu, Henry, Wiltord, Grimandi/Edu for Wiltord/Kanu

27 Feb   Bayer Leverkusen   H   W   4-1

Seaman, Dixon, Campbell, Stepanovs, Lauren, Grimandi, Vieira 1, Pires 1, Wiltord, Henry 1, Bergkamp 1, Edu/Inamoto/Pennant forGrimandi/Lauren/Wiltord

12 Mar   Dep'vo La Coruna   H   L   0-2

Seaman, Lauren, Campbell, Stepanovs, Luzhny, Wiltord, Vieira, Grimandi, Pires, Bergkamp, Henry, Kanu/Ljungberg for Wiltord/Grimandi

20 Mar   Juventus   A   L   0-1

Seaman, Dixon, Campbell, Luzhny, Lauren, Ljungberg, Vieira, Edu, Pires, Kanu, Henry, Wiltord/Cole for Lauren/Kanu

FA CHARITY SHIELD

8 Oct, 1930   **Sheffield Wed**   **2-1**
Keizer, Parker, Hapgood, Seddon, Roberts, John, Hulme 1, Brain, Lambert, Jack 1, Bastin
(at Chelsea, attendance: 25,000)

7 Oct, 1931   **WBA**   **1-0**
Preedy, Parker, Hapgood, C.Jones, Roberts, Haynes, Hulme, Jack, Lambert, James, Bastin
1 (at Aston Villa, attendance: 21,276)

18 Oct, 1933   **Everton (A)**   **3-0**
Moss, Male, Hapgood, C.Jones, Sidey, John, Birkett 2, Bowden 1, Coleman, James, Hill
(attendance: 30,000)

28 Nov, 1934   **Manchester C (H)**   **4-0**
Moss, Male, Hapgood, Hill, Sidey, Copping, Birkett 1, Marshall 1, Drake 1, John, Bastin 1
(attendance: 10,888)

23 Oct, 1935   **Sheffield Wed (H)**   **0-1**
Wilson, Male , Hapgood, Hill, Joy, Copping, Milne, Crayston, Dunne, Davidson, Bastin
(attendance: 30,000)

28 Oct, 1936   **Sunderland (A)**   **1-2**
Swindin, L.Compton, Hapgood, Crayston, Joy, Copping, Milne, Bowden, Kirchen 1,
Davidson, D.Compton (attendance: 30,000)

26 Sept, 1938   **Preston NE (H)**   **2-1**
Swindin, Male, L.Compton, Crayston, Joy, Copping, Kirchen, L.Jones, Drake 2, B.Jones,
Cumner (attendance: 35,000)

6 Oct, 1948   **Manchester U (H)**   **4-3**
Swindin, Barnes, Smith, Macaulay, L.Compton, Mercer, Roper, Logie, Lewis 2, Rooke 1,
B.Jones 1 (attendance: 31,000)

12 Oct, 1953   **Blackpool (H)**   **3-1**
Kelsey, Wills, Barnes, Forbes, Dodgin, Mercer, Holton, Logie, Lawton 1, Lishman 2, Roper
(attendance: 39,853)

11 Aug, 1979   **Liverpool**   **1-3**
Jennings, Rice, Nelson, Talbot, O'Leary, Walford, Brady, Sunderland 1, Stapleton, Price,
Rix Young/Hollins for Nelson/Price (at Wembley, attendance: 92,000)

12 Aug, 1989   **Liverpool**   **0-1**
Lukic, Dixon, Winterburn, Thomas, O'Leary, Adams, Rocastle, Richardson, Smith, Caesar,
Merson, Quinn/Marwood for Smith/Caesar (at Wembley, attendance: 63,149)

10 Aug, 1991   **Tottenham H**   **0-0**
Seaman, Dixon, Winterburn, Hillier, O'Leary, Adams, Rocastle, Davis, Smith, Merson,
Campbell, Thomas/Cole for Rocastle/Campbell (at Wembley, attendance: 65,483)

7 Aug, 1993   **Manchester U**   **1-1**
Seaman, Dixon, Winterburn, Davis, Linighan, Adams, Jensen, Wright 1, Campbell, Merson,
Limpar, Keown, McGoldrick for Dixon/Limpar (at Wembley, attendance: 66,519, lost 4-5 on
penalties)

9 Aug, 1998   **Manchester U**   **3-0**
Seaman, Dixon, Keown, Adams (Bould), Winterburn, Parlour, Vieira, Petit, Overmars 1,
Anelka 1, Bergkamp, Grimandi/Boa Morte/Hughes/Wreh 1 for
Vieira/Petit/Overmars/Bergkamp) (at Wembley, attendance: 67,342)

1 Aug, 1999 **Manchester U** **2-1**
Manninger, Dixon, Keown, Grimandi, Winterburn, Parlour 1, Vieira, Petit, Silvinho, Ljungberg,
Kanu 1p, Luzhny/Boa Morte for Parlour/Silvinho (at Wembley, attendance: 70,185)

NORTH LONDON DERBIES

Arsenal moved to London in the summer of 1913. The first north London derby took place
at Tottenham Hotspur on January 15, 1921.

LEAGUE DIVISION ONE (home team given first)

Date	Result	Attendance
15 Jan, 1921	Tottenham H 2, Arsenal 1	39,221
	(Arsenal scorer: Rutherford)	
22 Jan, 1921	Arsenal 3 (Rutherford 2, White), Tottenham H 2	60,600
15 Apr, 1922	Tottenham H 2, Arsenal 0	40,394
22 Apr, 1922	Arsenal 1 (Graham (pen)), Tottenham H 0	42,000
23 Sept, 1922	Tottenham H 1, Arsenal 2 (Boreham 2)	40,582
30 Sept, 1922	Arsenal 0, Tottenham H 2	55,000
17 Nov, 1923	Arsenal 1 (Townrow), Tottenham H 1	50,000
24 Nov, 1923	Tottenham H 3, Arsenal 0	31,624
25 Oct, 1924	Arsenal 1 (Brain), Tottenham H 0	51,000
28 Feb, 1925	Tottenham H 2, Arsenal 0	29,457
29 Aug, 1925	Arsenal 0, Tottenham H 1	53,183
2 Jan, 1926	Tottenham H 1, Arsenal 1 (Baker)	43,221
18 Dec, 1926	Arsenal 2 (Butler, Brain), Tottenham H 4	49,429
7 May, 1927	Tottenham H 0, Arsenal 4 (Brain 2, Tricker 2)	29,555
2 Jan, 1928	Arsenal 1 (Hoar), Tottenham H 1	13,518
7 Apr, 1928	Tottenham H 2, Arsenal 0	39,193
16 Sept, 1933	Tottenham H 1, Arsenal 1 (Bowden)	56,612
31 Jan, 1934	Arsenal 1 (Bastin), Tottenham H 3	68,674
20 Oct, 1934	Arsenal 5 (Drake 3, Beasley, o/g Evans),	70,544
	Tottenham H 1	
6 Mar, 1935	Tottenham H 0, Arsenal 6 (Kirchen 2, Drake 2,	47,714
	Dougall, Bastin (pen))	
26 Aug, 1950	Arsenal 2 (Roper, Barnes (pen)), Tottenham H 2	64,638
23 Dec, 1950	Tottenham H 1, Arsenal 0	54,898
29 Sept, 1951	Arsenal 1 (Holton), Tottenham H 1	68,164
9 Feb, 1952	Tottenham H 1, Arsenal 2 (Roper, Forbes)	66,438
20 Sept, 1952	Tottenham H 1, Arsenal 3 (Goring, Milton, Logie)	69,247
7 Feb, 1953	Arsenal 4 (Holton 2, Lishman, Logie), Tottenham H 0	69,051
10 Oct, 1953	Tottenham H 1, Arsenal 4 (Logie 2, Milton,	69,821
	Forbes (pen))	
27 Feb, 1954	Arsenal 0, Tottenham H 3	64,311
4 Sept, 1954	Arsenal 2 (Logie, Lishman), Tottenham H 0	53,971
15 Jan, 1955	Tottenham H 0, Arsenal 1 (Lawton)	36,263
10 Sept, 1955	Tottenham H 3, Arsenal 1 (Roper)	51,029
14 Jan, 1956	Arsenal 0, Tottenham H 1	60,606
20 Oct, 1956	Arsenal 3 (Herd 2, Haverty), Tottenham H 1	60,588
13 Mar, 1957	Tottenham H 1, Arsenal 3 (Bowen 2, Tapscott)	64,555
12 Oct, 1957	Tottenham H 3, Arsenal 1 (Holton)	60,671
22 Feb, 1958	Arsenal 4 (o/g Henry, Clapton, Nutt, Herd),	59,116
	Tottenham H 4	
13 Sept, 1958	Arsenal 3 (Nutt, Herd 2), Tottenham H 1	63,565
31 Jan, 1959	Tottenham H 1, Arsenal 4 (Groves, Herd,	60,241
	Henderson 2)	
5 Sept, 1959	Arsenal 1 (Barnwell), Tottenham H 1	60,791
16 Jan, 1960	Tottenham H 3, Arsenal 0	58,962

10 Sept, 1960	Arsenal 2 (Herd, Ward), Tottenham H 3	59,868
21 Jan, 1961	Tottenham H 4, Arsenal 2 (Henderson, Haverty)	65,251
26 Aug, 1961	Tottenham H 4, Arsenal 3 (Skirton, Charles 2)	59,371
23 Dec, 1961	Arsenal 2 (Charles, Skirton), Tottenham H 1	63,440
6 Oct, 1962	Tottenham H 4, Arsenal 4 (Court 2, MacLeod, Strong)	61,749
23 Feb, 1963	Arsenal 2 (Strong, Baker), Tottenham H 3	59,980
15 Oct, 1963	Arsenal 4 (Eastham 2, (1p),Baker, Strong), Tottenham H 4	67,857
22 Feb, 1964	Tottenham H 3, Arsenal 1 (Strong)	57,261
10 Oct, 1964	Tottenham H 3, Arsenal 1 (Baker)	55,959
23 Feb, 1965	Arsenal 3 (Radford, Baker 2), Tottenham H 1	48,367
11 Sept, 1965	Tottenham H 2, Arsenal 2 (Brown own goal, Baker)	53,962
8 Mar, 1966	Arsenal 1 (Court), Tottenham H 1	51,805
3 Sept, 1966	Tottenham H 3, Arsenal 1 (Sammels)	56,271
7 Jan, 1967	Arsenal 0, Tottenham H 2	49,851
16 Sept, 1967	Arsenal 4 (Radford, Neill (p), Graham, Addison), Tottenham H 0	62,936
20 Jan, 1968	Tottenham H 1, Arsenal 0	57,885
10 Aug, 1968	Tottenham H 1, Arsenal 2 (Beal own goal, Radford)	56,280
24 Mar, 1969	Arsenal 1 (Sammels), Tottenham H 0	43,972
16 Sept, 1969	Arsenal 2 (Robertson, Radford), Tottenham H 3	55,280
2 May, 1970	Tottenham H 1, Arsenal 0	46,969
5 Sept, 1970	Arsenal 2 (Armstrong 2), Tottenham H 0	48,931
3 May, 1971	Tottenham H 0, Arsenal 1 (Kennedy)	51,992
24 Nov, 1971	Tottenham H 1, Arsenal 1 (Kennedy)	52,884
11 May, 1972	Arsenal 0, Tottenham H 2	42,038
9 Dec, 1972	Tottenham H 1, Arsenal 2 (Storey, Radford)	47,515
14 Apr, 1973	Arsenal 1 (Storey), Tottenham H 1	50,863
13 Oct, 1973	Tottenham H 2, Arsenal 0	41,856
16 Feb, 1974	Arsenal 0, Tottenham H 1	38,892
19 Oct, 1974	Tottenham H 2, Arsenal 0	36,294
26 Apr, 1975	Arsenal 1 (Kidd), Tottenham H 0	43,762
27 Sept, 1975	TottenhamH 0, Arsenal 0	37,064
3 Apr, 1976	Arsenal 0, Tottenham H 2	42,031
27 Dec, 1976	Tottenham H 2, Arsenal 2 (Macdonald 2)	47,751
11 Apr, 1977	Arsenal 1 (Macdonald), Tottenham H 0	47,432
23 Dec, 1978	Tottenham H 0, Arsenal 5 (Sunderland 3, Stapleton, Brady)	42,273
10 Apr, 1979	Arsenal 1 (Stapleton), Tottenham H 0	53,896
26 Dec, 1979	Arsenal 1 (Sunderland), Tottenham H 0	44,560
7 Apr, 1980	Tottenham H 1, Arsenal 2 (Vaessen, Sunderland)	41,365
30 Aug, 1980	Arsenal 2 (Price, Stapleton), Tottenham H 0	54,045
17 Jan, 1981	Tottenham H 2, Arsenal 0	32,994
29 Mar, 1982	Tottenham H 2, Arsenal 2 (Sunderland 2)	40,940
12 Apr, 1982	Arsenal 1 (Hawley), Tottenham H 3	48,897
27 Dec, 1982	Arsenal 2 (Sunderland, Woodcock), Tottenham H 0	51,497
4 Apr, 1983	Tottenham H 5, Arsenal 0	43,642
26 Dec, 1983	Tottenham H 2, Arsenal 4 (Nicholas 2, Meade 2)	38,756
21 Apr, 1984	Arsenal 3 (Robson, Nicholas, Woodcock), Tottenham H 2	48,831
1 Jan, 1985	Arsenal 1 (Woodcock), Tottenham H 2	48,714
17 Apr, 1985	Tottenham H 0, Arsenal 2	40,399
1 Jan, 1986	Arsenal 0, Tottenham H 0	45,109
29 Mar, 1986	Tottenham H 1, Arsenal 0	33,247
6 Sept, 1986	Arsenal 0, Tottenham H 0	44,707
4 Jan, 1987	Tottenham H 1, Arsenal 2 (Adams, Davis)	37,723
18 Oct, 1987	Tottenham H 1, Arsenal 2 9Rocastle, Thomas)	36,680
6 Mar, 1988	Arsenal 2 (Smith, Groves), Tottenham H 1	37,143

10 Sept, 1988	Tottenham H 2, Arsenal 3 (Winterburn, Marwood, Smith)	32,621
2 Jan, 1989	Arsenal 2 (Merson, Thomas), Tottenham H 0	45,129
18 Oct, 1989	Tottenham H 2, Arsenal 1 (Thomas)	33,944
20 Jan, 1990	Arsenal 1 (Adams), Tottenham H 0	46,132
1 Sept, 1990	Arsenal 0, Tottenham H 0	40,009
12 Jan, 1991	Tottenham H 0, Arsenal 0	34,753
1 Dec, 1991	Arsenal 2 (Wright, Campbell), Tottenham H 0	38,892
22 Feb, 1992	Tottenham H 1, Arsenal 1 (Wright)	33,124
12 Dec, 1992	Tottenham H 1, Arsenal 0	33,707
11 May, 1993	Arsenal 1 (Dickov), Tottenham H 3	26,393
16 Aug, 1993	Tottenham H 0, Arsenal 1 (Wright)	28,355
6 Dec, 1993	Arsenal 1 (Wright), Tottenham H 1	35,669
2 Jan, 1995	Tottenham H 1, Arsenal 0	28,747
29 Apr, 1995	Arsenal 1 (Wright (pen)), Tottenham H 1	38,377
18, Nov 1995	Tottenham H 2, Arsenal 1 (Bergkamp)	32,894
15 Apr, 1996	Arsenal 0, Tottenham H 0	38,273
24 Nov, 1996	Arsenal 3 (Wright (pen), Adams, Bergkamp), Tottenham H 1	38,264
15 Feb, 1997	Tottenham H 0, Arsenal 0	33,039
30 Aug, 1997	Arsenal 0, Tottenham H 0	38,102
28 Dec, 1997	Tottenham H 1, Arsenal 1(Parlour)	29,610
14 Nov, 1998	Arsenal 0, Tottenham H 0	38,278
5 May, 1999	Tottenham H 1, Arsenal 3 (Bergkamp 2, Kanu)	36,019
7 Nov, 1999	Tottenham H 2, Arsenal 1 (Vieira)	36,085
19 Mar, 2000	Arsenal 2 (Henry, o/g Armstrong), Tottenham H 1	38,131
18 Dec, 2000	Tottenham H 1, Arsenal 1 (Vieira)	36,062
31 Mar, 2001	Arsenal 2 (Henry, Pires), Tottenham H 0	38,121
19 Nov, 2001	Tottenham H 1, Arsenal 1 (Pires)	36,049
6 Apr, 2002	Arsenal 2 (Ljungberg, Lauren (pen)) Tottenham H 1	38,186

FA CUP

Jan 8, 1949 3rd round	Arsenal 3 (McPherson, Roper, Lishman), Tottenham H 0	47,314
2 Jan, 1982 3rd round R	Tottenham H 1, Arsenal 0	38,421
14 Apr, 1991 SF (at Wembley)	Arsenal 1 (Smith), Tottenham H 3	77,893
4 Apr, 1993 SF (at Wembley)	Arsenal 1 (Adams), Tottenham H 0	76,263
8 Apr, 2001 SF (at Old Trafford)	Arsenal 2 (Vieira, Pires), Tottenham H 1	63,541

LEAGUE CUP

20 Nov, 1968 SF/1	Arsenal 1 (Radford), Tottenham H 0	55,237
4 Dec, 1968 SF/2	Tottenham H 1, Arsenal 1 (Radford)	55,923
4 Nov, 1980 4th round	Tottenham H 1, Arsenal 0	42,511
9 Nov, 1983 3rd round	Tottenham 1, Arsenal 2 (Nicholas, Woodcock)	48,200
8 Feb, 1987 SF/1	Arsenal 0, Tottenham H 1	41,256
1 Mar, 1987 SF/2	Tottenham H 1, Arsenal 2 (Anderson, Quinn)	37,099

4 Mar, 1987   Tottenham H 1, Arsenal 2 (Allinson, Rocastle)   41,005
SF/R

CHARITY SHIELD
10 Aug,1991   Arsenal 0, Tottenham H 0   65,483
(at Wembley)

ARSENAL RESERVES

LONDON COMBINATION

Season	Pld	W	D	L	F	A	Pts	Position
1919-20	36	18	10	8	81	41	46	2nd
1920-1	36	12	4	20	57	63	28	9th
1921-2	40	21	13	6	67	47	55	2nd
1922-3	40	20	9	11	80	49	49	1st
1923-4	44	16	11	17	69	66	43	6th
1924-5	44	17	12	15	62	54	46	6th
1925-6	44	20	6	18	83	68	46	5th
1926-7	42	30	4	8	124	45	64	1st
1927-8	42	27	7	8	105	46	61	1st
1928-9	42	26	7	9	108	42	59	1st
1929-30	42	30	5	7	132	55	65	1st
1930-1	42	28	6	8	120	48	62	1st
1931-2	42	27	8	7	111	43	62	2nd
1932-3	46	31	5	10	145	57	67	3rd
1933-4	46	32	5	9	129	44	69	1st
1934-5	46	33	5	8	131	50	71	1st
1935-6	46	29	5	12	117	55	63	3rd
1936-7	46	30	8	8	139	39	68	1st
1937-8	46	28	15	3	116	42	71	1st
1938-9	46	30	7	9	139	57	67	1st

FOOTBALL COMBINATION

Season	Pld	W	D	L	F	A	Pts	Position
1946-7	30	23	3	4	83	29	49	1st
(Arsenal beat Portsmouth 3-0 in the play-off final)								
1947-8	30	20	6	4	55	26	46	1st
(Arsenal lost the play-off final 2-0 to West Ham U)								
1948-9	30	20	5	5	62	31	45	1st
(Arsenal lost play-off final 3-1 to Chelsea)								
1949-50	30	15	4	11	59	33	34	3rd
1950-1	30	21	5	4	73	25	47	1st
(Arsenal beat Chelsea 5-0 in the play-off final)								
1951-2	30	18	7	5	70	32	43	2nd
1952-3	30	12	4	14	47	46	28	9th
1953-4	30	13	8	9	56	36	34	6th
1954-5	30	15	6	9	73	43	36	4th
1955-6	42	19	8	15	96	76	46	9th
1956-7	42	22	9	11	105	65	53	7th
1957-8	42	22	7	13	103	64	51	6th
1958-9	34	15	10	9	86	60	40	4th
1959-60	34	15	6	13	62	45	36	7th
1960-1	34	12	11	11	76	62	35	6th
1961-2	34	21	5	8	97	46	47	2nd
1962-3	34	25	5	4	105	40	55	1st
1963-4	34	19	3	12	87	48	41	6th
1964-5	34	17	5	12	73	54	39	6th
1965-6	34	21	7	6	90	37	49	2nd

1966-7	32	18	4	10	60	41	40	2nd
1967-8	28	11	6	11	33	28	28	7th
1968-9	25	20	4	1	71	18	44	1st
1969-70	25	18	5	2	66	23	41	1st
1970-1	42	23	12	7	83	32	58	2nd
1971-2	40	14	11	15	59	52	39	13th
1972-3	40	23	11	6	79	37	57	3rd
1973-4	41	16	13	13	51	38	45	9th
1974-5	40	21	8	11	50	32	50	5th
1975-6	42	16	14	12	54	42	46	8th
1976-7	43	19	10	13	54	41	48	6th
1977-8	42	15	14	13	60	45	44	10th
1978-9	42	13	18	11	55	44	44	10th
1979-80	42	26	7	9	96	48	59	2nd
1980-1	42	20	13	9	68	48	53	6th
1981-2	38	10	12	16	47	51	32	11th
1982-3	42	17	13	12	65	46	47	6th
1983-4	42	29	8	5	96	30	66	1st
1984-5	42	27	8	7	117	46	62	2nd
1985-6	41	26	10	5	124	41	62	2nd (one game not played)
1986-7	38	23	7	8	77	42	53	3rd
1987-8	38	19	5	14	77	48	43	8th
1998-9	38	20	12	6	83	44	52	2nd
1989-90	38	26	6	6	84	51	84	1st (3pts for a win)
1990-1	38	18	8	11	65	54	62	7th
1991-2	38	22	8	10	80	49	72	3rd
1992-3	3	12	15	11	57	46	51	11th
1993-4	38	13	6	19	67	76	45	15th
1994-5	38	11	14	13	61	69	47	14th
1995-6	38	22	10	6	82	37	76	3rd
1996-7	22	10	5	7	49	30	35	6th
1997-8	34	20	9	5	71	26	69	3rd
1998-9	28	13	6	9	47	32	45	9th

PREMIERSHIP RESERVE LEAGUE SOUTH

1999-2000	24	10	7	7	49	32	37	6th
2000-1	24	10	3	11	49	40	33	7th
2001-2	26	15	5	6	49	27	30	2nd

FA YOUTH CUP

1954-5

1st round	Leiston (H)	9-1
2nd round	Leyton Orient (H)	1-3

1955-6

2nd round	Gorleston (H)	3-0
3rd round	Fulham (A)	2-0
4th round	Luton T (H)	2-1
5th round	Bristol C (A)	3-4

1956-7

1st round	Aveley (H)	6-1
2nd round	Leyton Orient (H)	3-0
3rd round	Charlton Ath (H)	4-1
4th round	Chelsea (H)	3-0
5th round	West Ham U (A)	1-3

1957-8

1st round	Briggs Sports (A)	7-0
2nd round	Brentwood (A)	8-0
3rd round	Watford (A)	0-0
3rd round R	Watford (H)	1-0
4th round	Charlton Ath (A)	1-1
4th round R	Charlton Ath (H)	5-2
5th round	Icknield (H)	5-0
SF/1	Chelsea (A)	1-3
SF/2	Chelsea (H)	1-3

1958-9

1st round	Tottenham H (H)	2-0
2nd round	Dagenham (A)	3-1
3rd round	QPR (H)	5-0
4th round	Bristol C (H)	2-1
5th round	Reading (H)	5-0
SF/1	West Ham U (A)	1-1
SF/2	West Ham U (H)	0-1

1959-60

1st round	Leyton Orient (H)	1-1
1st round R	Leyton Orient (A)	4-2
2nd round	Norwich C (H)	4-0
3rd round	Brentford (A)	2-0
4th round	West Ham U (H)	0-3

1960-1

1st round	Chelmsford (A)	8-1
2nd round	Norwich C (H)	3-0
3rd round	Millwall (A)	8-0
4th round	Oxford U (A)	9-0
5th round	West Ham U (H)	3-0
SF/1	Chelsea (A)	0-2
SF/2	Chelsea (H)	0-2

1961-2

Preliminary round	Norwich C (H)	6-1
1st round	QPR (H)	4-1
2nd round	Ford U (H)	12-0
3rd round	Chelsea (H)	1-2

1962-3

2nd round	Leyton Orient (H)	4-1
3rd round	Fulham (H)	2-1
4th round	Exeter C (H)	3-0
5th round	Wolverhampton W (A)	1-1
5th round R	Wolverhampton W (H)	0-4

1963-4

2nd round	Bexley (A)	5-1
3rd round	Chelsea (H)	3-1
4th round	West Ham U (H)	2-1
5th round	Swindon T (A)	0-2

1964-5

2nd round	West Ham U (A)	7-0
3rd round	Tottenham H (H)	0-0
3rd round R	Tottenham H (A)	3-1 (aet)
4th round	Portsmouth (A)	2-0
5th round	Watford (H)	0-0
5th round R	Watford (A)	5-2
SF/1	Chelsea (H)	4-1
SF/2	Chelsea (A)	0-2
F/1	Everton (H)	1-0
F/2	Everton (A)	1-3 (aet)

1965-6

2nd round	Brentford	5-0
3rd round	Fulham (H)	8-3
4th round	Wolverhampton W (H)	1-0
5th round	Bristol C (H)	3-2
SF/1	QPR (A)	1-1
SF/2	QPR (H)	3-2
F/1	Sunderland (A)	1-2
F/2	Sunderland (H)	4-1

1966-7

2nd round	Watford (A)	5-0
3rd round	Charlton Ath (H)	4-0
4th round	Millwall (A)	3-1
5th round	Southampton (H)	0-0
5th round R	Southampton (A)	0-2

1967-8

2nd round	Leyton Orient (A)	3-0
3rd round	Chelsea (A)	1-3

1968-9

2nd round	Charlton Ath (H)	4-0
3rd round	Gillingham (A)	5-1
4th round	Chelsea (A)	1-2

1969-70

2nd round	Watford (A)	2-0
3rd round	Gillingham (A)	5-1
4th round	Chelsea (A)	1-2

1970-1

2nd round	QPR (A)	6-0
3rd round	Leicester C (A)	1-0
4th round	Coventry C (H)	1-0
5th round	Birmingham C (H)	2-1
SF/1	Wolverhampton W (H)	2-0
SF/2	Wolverhampton W (A)	1-0
F/1	Cardiff C (H)	0-0
F/2	Cardiff C (A)	2-0

1971-2

2nd round	Charlton Ath (H)	3-1
3rd round	Luton T (H)	4-0
4th round	QPR (H)	2-0
5th round	Bolton W (A)	1-0
SF/1	Aston Villa (H)	0-0
SF/2	Aston Villa (A)	0-1

1972-3

2nd round	Brighton & HA (H)	5-0
3rd round	Norwich C (H)	1-0
4th round	Manchester U (A)	2-2
4th round R	Manchester U (H)	2-0
5th round	Bristol C (A)	0-2

1973-4

2nd round	Crystal Pal (H)	3-0

3rd round	Bristol C (A)	4-1
4th round	Sheffield Wed (H)	3-1
5th round	Middlesbrough (A)	3-0
SF/1	Tottenham H (A)	0-1
SF/2	Tottenham H (H)	0-1

1974-5

2nd round	Soham T Ran (A)	5-1
3rd round	Oxford U(H)	3-0
4th round	WBA (H)	3-1
5th round	Ipswich T (A)	0-1

1975-6

2nd round	Luton T (H)	7-0
3rd round	Wigston Fields (H)	4-1
4th round	Crystal Pal (H)	0-2

1976-7

2nd round	Luton T (A)	0-0
2nd round R	Luton T (H)	1-0
3rd round	Crystal Pal (A)	2-2
3rd round R	Crystal Pal (H)	0-0
3rd round R	Crystal Pal (A)	0-4

1977-8

2nd round	West Ham U (A)	0-0
2nd round R	West Ham U (H)	1-0
3rd round	WBA (A)	0-2

1978-9

2nd round	Peterborough U (A)	0-0
2nd round R	Peterborough U (H)	4-2
3rd round	Luton T (A)	0-1

1979-80

2nd round	Charlton Ath (A)	3-0
3rd round	Tottenham H (H)	0-1

1980-1

2nd round	Wimbledon (H)	6-0
3rd round	QPR (H)	1-1
3rd round R	QPR (A)	2-2 (aet)
3rd round R	QPR (H)	0-1

1981-2

2nd round	Gillingham (H)	3-0
3rd round	Southampton (H)	0-1

1982-3

2nd round	Norwich C (H)	2-2
2nd round R	Norwich C (A)	2-4

1983-4

2nd round	Carshalton (A)	2-0
3rd round	Bristol Rov (A)	4-4
3rd round R	Bristol Rov (H)	3-1
4th round	Cambridge U (H)	1-0

5th round	Aston Villa (H)	2-1
SF/1	Stoke C (A)	2-3
SF/2	Stoke C (H)	0-3

1984-5

2nd round	Wimbledon (A)	0-2

1985-6

2nd round	Plymouth Arg (A)	5-0
3rd round	Luton T (A)	0-0
3rd round R	Luton T (H)	2-0
4th round	Wimbledon (H)	1-0
5th round	Millwall (A)	1-1
5th round R	Millwall (H)	4-1
SF/1	Manchester C (H)	1-0
SF/2	Manchester C (A)	1-2 (aet,
Arsenal lost on penalties)		

1986-7

2nd round	Southampton (H)	0-3

1987-8

2nd round	Millwall (A)	5-1
3rd round	Wimbledon (A)	2-0
4th round	Southampton (A)	2-1
5th round	Crewe Alex (A)	1-1
5th replay	Crewe Alex (H)	5-1
SF/1	Nottingham F (H)	1-1
SF/2	Nottingham F (H)	3-0
F/1	Doncaster Rov (A)	5-0
F/2	Doncaster Rov (H)	1-1

1988-9

2nd round	Epsom (A)	11-0
3rd round	Luton T (H)	3-2
4th round	WBA (H)	2-0
5th round	Newcastle U (A)	0-1

1989-90

2nd round	Luton T (H)	2-2
2nd round R	Luton T (A)	4-2
3rd round	Oxford U (A)	5-1
4th round	Portsmouth (H)	0-1

1990-1

2nd round	Notts Co (A)	0-0
2nd round R	Notts Co (H)	1-1
2nd round R	Notts Co (A)	1-2

1991-2

2nd round	Brighton & HA (A)	5-2
3rd round	Watford (H)	4-0
4th round	Everton (H)	1-2

1992-3

2nd round	Southend (A)	4-2
3rd round	Swindon T (A)	2-5

1993-4

2nd round	Colchester U (A)	3-2
3rd round	Brentford (A)	1-1
3rd round R	Brentford (H)	3-1
4th round	Burnley (A)	1-0
5th round	Stoke C (H)	2-1
SF/1	Bradford C (A)	1-0
SF/2	Bradford C (A)	1-0
F/1	Millwall (A)	2-3
F/2	Millwall (H)	3-0

1994-5

2nd round	Brighton & HA (H)	5-0
3rd round	QPR (A)	2-0
4th round	Manchester U (A)	1-2

1995-6

2nd round	Coventry C (A)	2-1
3rd Round	Wimbledon (H)	3-4

1996-7

2nd round	Ipswich T (A)	0-1

1997-8

2nd round	Exeter C (A)	1-1
2nd round R	Exeter C (H)	2-0
3rd round	Notts Co (A)	6-1
4th round	Bristol C (H)	3-1
Fifth round	Leeds U (A)	0-1

1998-9

3rd round	Grimsby (A)	5-1
4th round	Preston NE (A)	4-1
5th round	Crystal Pal (H)	0-0
5th round R	Crystal Pal (A)	1-0
6th round	West Ham U (A)	0-4

1999-2000

3rd round	Sheffield U (A)	2-0
4th round	Watford (H)	3-1
5th round	Nottingham F (H)	0-0
5th replay	Nottingham F(A)	1-0
6th round	Leeds U (H)	1-1
6th replay	Leeds U (A)	5-2
SF/1	Middlesbrough (H)	1-0
SF/2	Middlesbrough (A)	1-1
F/1	Coventry C (A)	3-1
F/2	Coventry C (H)	2-0

2000-1

3rd round	Sunderland (H)	1-0
4th round	Middlesbrough (H)	3-1
5th round	Oldham Ath (A)	3-1
6th round	Aston Villa (H)	2-0
SF/1	Ipswich T (H)	3-4
SF/2	Ipswich T (A)	4-2
F/1	Blackburn Rov (H)	5-0
F/2	Blackburn Rov (A)	1-3

2001-2

3rd round	Colchester U (H)	5-0
4th round	Crewe Alex (A)	1-0
5th round	Blackburn Rov (H)	0-2

From the season 1997-8, Arsenal also competed in the FA Premier Academy (under 19) League, with the following results

1997-8

Won Southern Conference League title
U19 playoffs

F/1	Tottenham H (A)	2-0
F/2	Tottenham H (H)	0-1

1988-9

U19 playoffs

QF	Everton (A)	1-2

U17 playoffs

3rd round	Blackburn Rov (H)	2-2

1998-9

U19 playoffs

QF	Everton (A)	1-2

U17 playoffs

3rd round	Blackburn Rov (H)	2-2*

*lost on penalties

1999-2000

U19 playoffs

F/1	West Ham U (A)	5-5
F/2	West Ham U (H)	1-1*

*lost on penalties

U17

F/1	Crewe Alex (A)	0-1
F/2	Crewe Alex (H)	4-2

2000-1

U19 playoffs

SF	QPR (A)	1-1*

*lost on penalties

2001-2
U19 playoffs

F/1	Liverpool (A)	5-1
F/2	Liverpool (H)	2-3

U17 playoffs

QF	Newcastle U (H)	1-2

ARSENAL LADIES

Formed: 1987
President: David Dein
Members: National Premier League
General manager: Vic Akers
Assistant coaches: Danny O'Shea, Fred Donnelly

Secretary/treasurer: Clare Wheatley
Club captain: Sian Williams
Academy director: Fed Donnelly
Assistant Academy director: Sian Williams
Centre of Excellence director: Richard Blair
Physios: Vic Akers, Dawn Compton, Gemma Davis
Commercial manager: Sylvia Gore

Honours
National Premier League
Champions 1992-3, 1994-5, 1996-7, 2000-1
Runners-up 1997-8, 1998-9
National League Cup
Winners 1991-2, 1992-3, 1993-4, 1997-8, 1998-9, 1999-2000, 2000-1
FA Cup
Winnerrs 1992-3, 1994-5, 1997-8, 1998-9, 2000-1
AXA Challenge Cup
Winners 1998-9
AXA Charity Shield
Winners 2001-2

National League South
Champions 1991-2
London Senior County Cup Winners 1994-5, 1995-6, 1996-7, 1999-2000
Middlesex Senior Cup
Runners-up 1994-5
Highfield Cup
Winners 1990-1
Reebok Cup
Winners 1991-2, 1995-6
Runners-up 1998-9

International Honours
England: Sian Williams, Faye White, Marieanne Spacey, Kirsty Pealling, Angela Banks, Clare Wheatley, Casey Stoney, Julie Fletcher, Kelley Few
Ireland: Ciara Grant, Emma Byrne, Yvonne Tracy
Scotland: Pauline MacDonald, Nikki Grant
Wales: Jayne Ludlow
Japan: Meg Ogawa

First published in Great Britain in 2002 by
Hamlyn, a division of Octopus Publishing Group Ltd
2–4 Heron Quays, London E14 4JP

ISBN 0 600 60633 3

A CIP catalogue record for this book is available from the British
Library

Page make up by Publish on Demand Ltd

Printed and bound in the United Kingdom by Mackays of Chatham

10 9 8 7 6 5 4 3 2 1

Executive Editor Trevor Davies
Project Editor Camilla James
Design Manager Tokiko Morishima
Designer Stephen Cary
Senior Production Controller Ian Paton